INTERVENTIONS
NEW STUDIES IN MEDIEVAL CULTURE
Ethan Knapp, Series Editor

THE ART
of VISION

*Ekphrasis in
Medieval
Literature and
Culture*

Edited by

ANDREW JAMES JOHNSTON,
ETHAN KNAPP, *and* MARGITTA ROUSE

THE OHIO STATE UNIVERSITY PRESS
COLUMBUS

Library of Congress Cataloging-in-Publication Data

The art of vision : ekphrasis in medieval literature and culture / edited by Andrew James Johnston, Ethan Knapp, and Margitta Rouse.

    pages cm — (Interventions: new studies in medieval culture)

 Includes bibliographical references and index.

 ISBN 978-0-8142-1294-3 (cloth : alk. paper)

 1. Ekphrasis. 2. Literature, Medieval--History and criticism. 3. Description (Rhetoric)—History—To 1500. I. Johnston, Andrew James, editor. II. Knapp, Ethan, 1966– editor. III. Rouse, Margitta, 1970– editor. IV. Series: Interventions (Columbus, Ohio)

 PN682.E46A78 2015

 809'.02—dc23

2015019905

Cover design by Mia Risberg

Type set in Adobe Minion Pro

Printed by Thomson-Shore, Inc.

9 8 7 6 5 4 3 2 1

Contents

Acknowledgments

First and foremost, the editors wish to thank the contributors, who have been a pleasure to work with and who have shown great patience as this collection has evolved. Further, we would like to thank the German Research Association, which funded the *Art of Vision* workshop at Freie Universität Berlin in March 2010. The workshop sparked off the idea for this book, bringing together an international cohort of medievalists currently working in the field of visuality. We would also like to thank our colleagues and friends who supported the project during various stages: Aranye Fradenburg, Elisabeth Kempf, David Matthews, Jenna Mead, Wolfram Keller, Jennifer Wawrzinek, Russell West-Pavlov, and Kai Wiegandt. Special thanks go to Martin Bleisteiner and Sven Durie, our graduate assistants, for offering invaluable help in putting the manuscript into a publishable form, and Malcolm Litchfield and Eugene O'Connor, our editors at The Ohio State University Press, for shepherding us through the publication process. Lastly, we would like to express our sorrow for the passing of one of the contributors, Darryl J. Gless. His presence was a highlight of the conference at which this collection began, both in the excellence of his scholarship and the pleasure of his company.

THE EDITORS

Introduction

THE DYNAMICS OF EKPHRASIS

Andrew James Johnston,
Ethan Knapp, and
Margitta Rouse

*E*kphrasis has long asserted itself as a durable provocation within the field of the literary. It is, to say the least, a very old issue. Indeed, one might even call it old-fashioned—not only because it goes back to Homer and the very beginnings of the Western canon as we know it, but also because the ekphrastic has been accused of possessing a suspect tendency to be enlisted in the service of aesthetic conservatism. Yet, at the same time, the increasing interest in the intermedial we have been witnessing for the last thirty years, and especially the growing fascination with visual culture that has been in evidence since about 1990, has placed ekphrasis at the center of a variety of contemporary debates, suggesting that, far from being old-fashioned, ekphrasis is lodged at the site of a radical nexus between the apparently incommensurable modes of visual and verbal representation. In medieval English studies in particular, ekphrasis and the relations between the visual and the literary in general have over the last decade and a half received a prominence that testifies to their continuing potential for generating passionate debate.[1]

---

1. To mention only some of the most important publications of the last fifteen years or so: Suzanne Conklin Akbari, *Seeing through the Veil: Optical Theory and Medieval Allegory* (Toronto: University of Toronto Press, 2004); Claire Barbetti,

1

The trope of ekphrasis has played a surprisingly significant role in recent considerations of late medieval cultural history. Take, for example, James Simpson's magisterial account of late medieval English literature, *Reform and Cultural Revolution*. In his historical analysis of literary writing in English during the transition from the medieval to the early modern period, Simpson pointedly excludes the Lollards from the realm of the literary and thus from the purview of his study. He argues that because their well-attested iconophobia prevented them from producing truly artistic texts, Lollard writers do not merit a place of their own in a literary history of England.[2] Taking their claims to iconophobia literally, he dismisses them from the literary field and implicitly banishes them to the ostensibly unattractive sphere of religious polemic. Consequently, there are comparatively few Lollards in what, at the beginning of the twenty-first century, has arguably become the definitive literary history of England's later Middle Ages.

As was to be expected, this did not exactly meet with general approval. Bruce Holsinger, especially, criticized this aspect of Simpson's account, maintaining that, for all their professed iconophobia, Lollard writings do actually possess a powerful visual streak and tend to be fully conversant with a time-honored ekphrastic rhetoric meant to render verbal descriptions vividly lifelike according to the classical concept of *enargeia*. Amongst other things, Holsinger argues that Lollard texts employ their highly developed capacity for a vivid rhetorical rendering of aesthetic and visual experience in the context of an effective critique of the late medieval Church's ever-increasing tendency toward splendid display. Due to their willingness and ability to incorporate visual experience into textual experience, Lollard texts betray, therefore, an impressive degree of aesthetic self-consciousness; that is, the type of aesthetic self-consciousness conventionally taken as one of the defining markers of the

Ekphrastic Medieval Visions: A New Discussion in Interarts Theory (New York: Palgrave Macmillan, 2011); Suzannah Biernoff, *Sight and Embodiment in the Middle Ages* (Houndmills: Palgrave Macmillan, 2002); Peter Brown, *Chaucer and the Making of Optical Space* (Oxford: Peter Lang, 2007); Emma Campbell and Robert Mills, eds., *Troubled Vision: Gender, Sexuality, and Sight in Medieval Text and Image* (New York: Palgrave Macmillan, 2004); Carolyn P. Collette, *Species, Phantasms and Images: Vision and Medieval Psychology in The* Canterbury Tales (Ann Arbor: University of Michigan Press, 2001); Dallas G. Denery II, *Seeing and Being Seen in the Later Medieval World: Optics, Theology and Religious Life* (Cambridge: Cambridge University Press, 2005); Jeremy Dimmick, James Simpson, and Nicolette Zeeman, *Images, Idolatry, and Iconoclasm in Late Medieval England: Textuality and the Visual Image* (Oxford: Oxford University Press, 2002); Shannon Gayk, *Image, Text, and Religious Reform in Fifteenth-Century England* (Cambridge: Cambridge University Press, 2010); Maidie Hilmo, *Medieval Images, Icons, and Illustrated English Texts: From the Ruthwell Cross to the Ellesmere Chaucer* (Farnham: Ashgate, 2004); Sarah Stanbury, *The Visual Object of Desire in Late Medieval England* (Philadelphia: University of Pennsylvania Press, 2008).

2. James Simpson, *Reform and Cultural Revolution, The Oxford English Literary History*, Vol. 2, *1350–1547* (Oxford: Oxford University Press, 2002), p. 392.

literary.[3] It is not our purpose here to take sides—each of these two views comes with its own advantages and limitations.[4]

What makes the differences between Simpson's and Holsinger's views so particularly interesting for our purposes is the way they highlight the continuing theoretical and political relevance of the various approaches to ekphrasis and the particular tensions that underlie them. When Simpson takes his cue from Lollard iconophobia and hence denies the heretics a role in literature with a capital L, then he is, to a certain extent, implicitly subscribing to what one might call a *narrow* version of ekphrasis. This narrow notion of ekphrasis adheres to the now classic definition provided by James A. W. Heffernan. In Heffernan's terms, ekphrasis is to be understood as "the verbal representation of visual representation."[5] To put it differently: the literary description of a work of visual art.

Heffernan's version of ekphrasis begins with Homer's description of the shield of Achilles in book XVIII of the *Iliad* and continues all through literary history. Ancient as his concept of ekphrasis is, it was not explicitly theorized as such until the 1950s. Instead, for more than two millennia the narrow notion of ekphrasis existed as a well-known literary commonplace and played a crucial, albeit indirect, role in discussions on the relationship between the visual and the verbal in literature.[6] But it was hardly ever consciously discussed in its specificity.[7]

---

3. Bruce Holsinger, "Lollard Ekphrasis: Situated Aesthetics and Literary History," *Journal of Medieval and Early Modern Studies* 35 (2005): 67–89.

4. Besides, there are certain shortcomings the two approaches actually share, such as a disregard of ekphrasis as a specifically narrative rather than a merely decorative or rhetorical feature. The "poems for paintings" tradition, which cuts itself off from those aspects of the ancient tradition that use ekphrasis for the purposes of narrative politics, is still very much alive. For a recent example, see Stephen Cheeke, *Writing for Art: The Aesthetics of Ekphrasis* (Manchester: Manchester University Press, 2008), p. 3.

5. James A. W. Heffernan, *Museum of Words: The Poetics of Ekphrasis from Homer to Ashbery* (Chicago: University of Chicago Press, 1993), p. 3.

6. For a recent discussion of the notion of ekphrasis that insists that works of art "have no special status at all" in classical theoretical discussions of the term, that they are "among the many 'things' (pragmata) that may be described," see Janice Hewlett Koelb, *The Poetics of Description: Imagined Places in European Literature* (New York: Palgrave Macmillan, 2006), p. 2. Similarly, Ruth Webb reminds us again that "at no point in antiquity (or Byzantium) was ekphrasis confined to a single category of subject matter, nor can every text about images be claimed as ekphrasis in the ancient sense. . . . [The] central function of ekphrasis [is] making the listener 'see' the subject in their mind's eye. An ekphrasis may itself constitute a commentary on the act of viewing, but this common feature is not central to the [classical] definition of ekphrasis" (*Ekphrasis, Imagination and Persuasion in Ancient Rhetorical Theory and Practice* [Farnham: Ashgate 2009], p. 2). See also her earlier discussion of the concept in "Ekphrasis Ancient and Modern: The Invention of a Genre," *Word and Image* 15 (1999): 7–18.

7. For a concise critical history of the debate on ekphrasis, see Haiko Wandhoff,

Holsinger's view of ekphrasis, on the other hand, is an example of what one might call the *broad* view of ekphrasis. Thus, his position succeeds in being two seemingly opposed things at the same time, namely radically modern and very traditional. His perspective is radically modern because it fits easily with some of the basic principles of the study of visual culture as theorized most prominently by W. J. T. Mitchell. According to Mitchell, the verbal is always suffused with the visual and vice versa: "All media are mixed media, and all representations are heterogeneous; there are no 'purely' visual or verbal arts, though the impulse to purify media is one of the central utopian gestures of modernity."[8] Western culture's vigorous attempts to keep the verbal and the visual apart always prove futile and testify to the West's particular ideological commitments rather than provide insight into the supposedly fundamental—and fundamentally different—nature of verbal and visual representation. Thus Mitchell's approach seeks to erase the powerful distinctions between the verbal and the visual that make Heffernan's definition possible in the first place. If the verbal and the visual are always already inextricably mixed, then the definition of "a verbal representation of a visual representation" begins to look problematic. This has recently been emphasized by Claire Barbetti, who contends that the "gaping hole in this definition should be considered shocking, because it is not the visual work of art, the visual representation being represented; it is the perception of the visual representation that is interpreted and translated into a verbal form."[9] And then of course, however emphatically the Lollards may have professed their iconophobia, there was simply no way their writings could have escaped the ever-present pull of the visual within the textual. In other words, if we accept Mitchell's (post)modern epistemological perspective, then the foundations of iconophobia are unmasked as an ideological illusion. And yet iconophobia was an important medieval concern, one that twice led the Byzantine Empire to the brink of civil war and that considerably exercised the minds

---

Ekphrasis. Kunstbeschreibungen und virtuelle Räume in der Literatur des Mittelalters, Trends in Medieval Philology 3 (Berlin: de Gruyter, 2003), pp. 2–15; see also Mario Klarer, *Ekphrasis: Bildbeschreibungen als Repräsentationstheorie bei Spenser, Sidney, Lyly und Shakespeare* (Tübingen: Niemeyer, 2001), pp. 2–22.

8. W. J. T. Mitchell, *Picture Theory: Essays on Verbal and Visual Representation* (Chicago: University of Chicago Press, 1994), p. 5.

9. Barbetti, *Ekphrastic Medieval Visions,* p. 11. Barbetti's own concept of ekphrasis remains unclear. She avoids a binary conception of word and image by expanding the notion of vision to denote composition in all art forms; thus the "verbal translation of composition is ekphrasis" (p. 2). But since she leaves the concept of translation unspecified, it seems that her opposition of seeing/composing and writing reinstates a binary opposition because it implies seeing to occur in a different medium from writing.

of Chaucer and his contemporaries as well as succeeding generations,[10] not to mention the iconoclasm of the Reformation.

If on the one hand, Holsinger's critique of Simpson expresses political commitments similar to those endorsed by scholars interested in questions of visual culture in general, then on the other, Holsinger's insistence on the visual quality, on the lifelikeness of the images in Lollard rhetoric, brings him back to the specific definition of ekphrasis originally found in the rhetorical handbooks of classical antiquity, the Middle Ages, and the early modern period. This concept of ekphrasis focuses on the issue of detailed description and the problem of the lifelikeness of verbal depiction. It does not—at least not at the level of rhetorical theory—single out the description of works of art as anything special, and hence, it is not concerned with visual representation *as representation*.[11]

Within the context sketched here, the distinction between the classical emphasis on lifelikeness, on the one hand, and the specific perspectives chosen by students of visual culture, on the other, is of crucial importance. Since a lifelike description may potentially be applied to any given object in reality, the idea of lifelikeness considerably expands the notion of ekphrasis if compared to Heffernan's definition with its exclusive focus on works of art. Yet at the same time, like Heffernan's definition, a notion of ekphrasis based on lifelikeness still clings to the issue of mimetic representation, to the idea of artistically imitating something that exists in real life. Even if the object represented in words may not in fact represent anything beyond itself, it must still be represented in some kind of recognizable fashion. In order to be lifelike, the verbal depiction must relate to something that does indeed possess some kind of clearly recognizable extratextual visual reality. But when it comes to medieval discourses of lifelikeness, we may actually be in for a surprise. As Michael Camille has pointed out, while many medieval theorists may appear to happily be endorsing the familiar rhetorical *ideal* of ekphrastic lifelikeness, their actual *idea* of lifelikeness often differs considerably from those conveyed by ancient rhetoricians; ideas expressed, amongst other things, in famous anecdotes about the illusionistic triumphs of painters such as Zeuxis or Apelles. When referring to the quality of lifelikeness, medieval writers were in fact often thinking not of the illusionistic quality of a painting but rather of images giving the impression either of being alive or of coming to life.[12] This is

---

10. For a discussion of Byzantine iconoclasm and its impact on Western Christianity, see Hilmo, *Medieval Images*, pp. 13–27.

11. Ruth Webb, "Ekphrasis Ancient and Modern," 10.

12. Michael Camille, *The Gothic Idol: Ideology and Image-Making in Medieval Art* (Cambridge: Cambridge University Press, 1989, pp. 44–47.

a lifelikeness that applies less to the question of aesthetic representation than to an artifact's ability to move beholders or even to magically or miraculously overcome its own nature as a mere material object. An apparently representational problem from classical antiquity thus turns into an epistemological or even a metaphysical one in the Middle Ages. Consequently, the medieval lifelikeness in question does not depend on the illusionistic quality of the artwork: it might just as well occur in a work of supreme hieratic stylization or schematic simplicity.

Besides, we must always remember that, as Margaret Bridges stresses, it is quite possible for what one might call an "ordinary" description in a literary text to be far more visual in quality than a passage fulfilling all the formal conditions of ekphrasis in the rigorous fashion demanded by Heffernan's definition.[13] Holsinger dismisses what we term the narrow view because of its supposed self-centeredness. He states that ekphrasis "has a strong claim to consideration as the most narcissistic mode of literary discourse" and that ekphrasis constitutes "a mode in and by which literary language gazes at the visual as a lens upon the beauty of its own performance."[14] For Holsinger, this supposedly narcissistic mode of representation refuses to address political issues and celebrates instead an aesthetic sophistication that attempts to deny the contextual pressures that always impinge on the literary, indeed, that give it shape in the first place. But even where ekphrasis seems to be assuming the insipidly aestheticizing character critiqued by Holsinger, where it resembles a mere "narcissistic exhibition of writerly prowess,"[15] or where it appears to rest content in the blissful isolation of aesthetic self-reflexivity, it may nevertheless play an important role in unravelling the different economies of the visual in literature. Self-reflexivity may well strain against the boundaries imposed by the cult of the aesthetic and in so doing highlight the ideological implications of the apparent aesthetic purity it is supposedly locked in. If some of us are willing to perceive iconophobia as an easily deconstructed ideological ploy, then we have even less reason to trust the veil of political indifference under which aesthetic self-reflexivity frequently strives to hide its objects. If anything then, ekphrasis in its many shapes and guises challenges us to seek the conflicted in the aesthetic, to see the alleged narcissism of self-reflexivity in art less as a straightforward given but rather as provoking us to unpack the manifold political, epistemological, or even theological issues present in any aesthetic statement.

---

13. Margaret Bridges, "The Picture in the Text: Ecphrasis as Self-Reflexivity in Chaucer's *Parliament of Fowles*, *Book of the Duchess* and *House of Fame*," *Word and Image* 5 (1989): 152 [151–58].

14. Holsinger, "Lollard Ekphrasis," p. 75.

15. Holsinger, "Lollard Ekphrasis," p. 76.

Moreover, since scholars have tended to posit a close link between the rise of Western modernity and the entrenchment of the verbal-visual binary, the issue of medieval ekphrasis ought to be particularly illuminating for scholars who refuse to accept the simplistic binaries of the medieval versus the (early) modern. Because the Middle Ages have consistently been cast in the role of the all-purpose Other of Western modernity,[16] medieval ekphrasis has not only been reviled for its supposed aesthetic narcissism, but it has also frequently been depicted as belonging to an epoch when the distinctions between word and image were far less rigidly drawn. Alternatively, medieval ekphrasis is conceived of as a point of origin playing an important role in erecting the barriers between the verbal and the visual that have become one of the defining characteristics of modernity. Unfortunately, all these perspectives subject medieval visual and poetic experience to a set of critical terms entirely dependent on modernity's self image.[17]

This is the point where this volume seeks to intervene. Rather than perceiving premodern experience of the visual and of visual art as a mere precursor of modernity's regimes of aesthetic power, or else as the straightforward Other of modern visuality, as a period of blissful intermedial innocence when the visual and verbal could still freely mix, the essays collected here explore the multilayered complexities of ekphrasis—in the broadest possible senses—in medieval texts. This volume seeks to situate ekphrasis in the contexts of contemporary medieval debates in order to demonstrate how, far from representing a single, monolithic phenomenon, ekphrasis responds to a plethora of challenges, ranging from Lollard iconophobia to the problem of the gaze in aristocratic culture, from the visionary experience of medieval mysticism to the issue of the materiality of the aesthetic object in ecclesiastical and secular cultures alike, or to the question of visual art as a form of signification that probes the very boundaries of the signifying process itself. Moreover, the editors of and contributors to this volume see ekphrasis in the Middle Ages not as a simple reflection of contemporary medieval debates on the verbal and the visual in all their shapes and guises, but instead as a privileged space where all manner of discourses are refracted through the complex lens of verbalized visuality. For this reason, and within our specific

16. Lee Patterson, *Chaucer and the Subject of History* (Madison: University of Wisconsin Press, 1991), p. 8.

17. For a discussion of how the Middle Ages are frequently trapped in an image of the exact opposite of modernity, see Andrew James Johnston, *Performing the Middle Ages from Beowulf to Othello* (Turnhout: Brepols, 2008), pp. 1–11; for a recent collection of essays approaching the issue of periodization from a variety of theoretical viewpoints, see Andrew Cole and D. Vance Smith, eds., *The Legitimacy of the Middle Ages: On the Unwritten History of Theory* (Durham & London: Duke University Press, 2010).

context, we refrain from offering our own definition of ekphrasis but regard it as a dynamic literary topos. Due to the different contextual pressures it responds to, this topos is realized in many different verbal manifestations, which are determined by the shifting and often contradictory notions of vision, seeing and verbalized visuality to be encountered in medieval texts. Indeed, as the German art historian Hans Belting stresses, the very notion of what constitutes an image may well differ from period to period and language to language. Latin *imago* and German *Bild* can refer to both pictures, that is, clearly circumscribed artistic works of visual representation, and images in the broader sense, including mental images or images conjured in visionary experience, both of which played important roles in medieval engagements with the visual.[18] Besides, as will become evident in the individual contributions to this volume, medieval notions of the ekphrastic are frequently inflected by epistemological concepts and concerns that have no discernible equivalent or counterpart in modern visual experience. Medieval notions of sight, for instance, differed considerably from modern ones, ranging from Platonic views of vision as a form of touch, through Alhazen's idea that objects emitted rays, to Roger Bacon's attempt to bring these theories together and conceive of sight and visual perception as a cooperative process between the eye and the object.[19] In a similar vein, the ventricular medieval model of the brain relied on mental images as fundamental for processing sense perception and turning its impressions into meaningful thought. The image was thus accorded an epistemological function completely lost to modern theorists.

Then there is allegory, one of the Middle Ages' dominant modes of intellectual exploration and textual interpretation. Medieval allegory relied heavily on visual metaphors, such as that of truth being hidden under a veil or visible only in some kind of refracted form, as St. Paul famously expressed it in 1 Corinthians 13:12, *per speculum in enigmate* [through a glass in a dark manner]. Medieval poetic allegories tend, moreover, to betray a considerable predilection for the descriptive, for an excess of detail that generates veritable cascades of ekphrastic moments in literature. Consequently, as L. O. Aranye Fradenburg has shown for Gavin Douglas's *Palice of Honour*—a text discussed in this volume, too—such a language of plenitude may well contribute to performatively constructing typically courtly medieval "arts of rule," (e.g., pageants and tournaments) through its "exhibitionism, theatricaliza-

---

18. Hans Belting, *The Anthropology of Images: Picture, Medium, Body*, trans. Thomas Dunlap (Princeton: Princeton University Press, 2011), p. 2.

19. For a lucid discussion of medieval scientific theories of sight, see Brown, *Chaucer and the Making of Optical Space*, pp. 41–86.

tion and phenomenalization."[20] And even where allegory did primarily serve the otherworldly purposes it was ostensibly shaped for, by no means did it preclude a fascination with the beauty and physicality of the visible, material world. On the contrary, as Umberto Eco explains, for a twelfth-century monastic theologian like Hugh of St. Victor the visible beauty of the world constituted an image of the invisible beauty of God.[21] The concept of image discussed here cannot be understood in terms of mimetic representation: due to humanity's ineluctably postlapsarian condition, God's beauty fundamentally exceeds the human capacity for perception and representation. Nor is this concept of image purely allegorical or symbolic since it does permit medieval Christians to experience an aspect of God's divinity aesthetically, a divinity itself defined as being fundamentally aesthetic in nature.

Hence, as Shannon Gayk and others have emphasized, we need to understand that the very concepts of representation available to the Middle Ages could be very different from what they have become in modernity. The already mentioned Lollard iconophobia, for instance, can be seen, amongst other things, as a radical reaction against the powerful *incarnational aesthetic* of the later Middle Ages, an aesthetic capable of legitimizing both expansive verbal and visual "ymaginaciouns" of things not, in fact, detailed in the Bible.[22] But the very term "incarnational aesthetic" already presupposes that in the Middle Ages the aesthetic was capable of participating in discourses—in this case theological ones—that modernity tends to see as categorically distinct from the sphere of art. If an aesthetic is capable of being "incarnational," then such an aesthetic must of necessity jar with any postromantic/modern attempt to create a space for the purely aesthetic. But at the same time, it would be dangerous to deny the Middle Ages any concept of the aesthetic at all or to argue that any given medieval aesthetic was always entirely enveloped or dominated by some other, ideally religious form of discourse. Indeed, there is evidence that medieval writers themselves could be very conscious of the contradictions between the different discourses of art and vision available to them and that they were actually willing to confront and possibly even exploit these contradictions. As Sarah Stanbury has perceptively observed, Chaucer "restricts ekphrasis, the description of a work of art, entirely to images that would have been classed as pagan idols—and hence safely outside the

---

20. L. O. Aranye Fradenburg, *City, Marriage, Tournament: Arts of Rule in Late Medieval Scotland* (Madison: University of Wisconsin Press, 1991), p. 185.

21. Umberto Eco, *Art and Beauty in the Middle Ages*, trans. Hugh Bredin (New Haven: Yale University Press, 1986), pp. 56–58 [originally published as *Sviluppo dell'estetica medievale* (Milan: Marzorati, 1959)].

22. Gayk, *Image, Text, and Religious Reform*, p. 22.

contested discourse."[23] Chaucer thus responded to contemporary reformist debates on religious image making (e.g., Lollard iconophobia) in a manner that carefully respected conflict-ridden cultural boundaries and yet used the world of classical antiquity as a stage on which to perform daring explorations into the world of ekphrasis.

In the Middle Ages, we argue, the poetic experience of the visual can indeed probe issues very similar to the ones modern visuality grapples with, but it usually does so in very different discursive circumstances and, consequently, with often surprisingly different results. Hence, amongst other things, we see our discussion of the visual experience in medieval literature as a contribution to the debates on those increasingly irksome discursive boundaries that have for centuries set the medieval apart from the modern. And one reason why we have chosen to occupy this particular discursive space is precisely because of modernity's predilection for defining itself, amongst other things, through specific forms of distinguishing between the verbal and the visual, as well as of dividing the realm of the aesthetic and from its Other.

The essays in this volume discuss ekphrasis from a broad number of different perspectives in a variety of vernacular literatures (Middle English, Middle Scots, Medieval Latin, Middle High German, Medieval French, Early Modern English) though with a strong emphasis on the British Isles. There are four clearly visible categories that help to structure the contributions.

In the first section of this volume, "Ekphrasis and the Object," there is a strong interest in the way ekphrasis intersects with the materiality of medieval culture, a perspective that displays strong links to the recent trend toward material culture in the humanities. Valerie Allen discusses Baudri of Bourgeuil's early-twelfth-century poem *Adelae Comitissae*, which describes an ornate tapestry depicting the successes of William the Conqueror. This poem offers an instance of medieval ekphrasis that at first glance seems to fulfill the strict definition of a poetic representation of visual art, yet at the same time it resists abstraction in ways that point to larger, systemic difficulties in categorizing the art of the Early and High Middle Ages under the sign of the aesthetic. Where the identification with form and the preoccupation with surfaces and textures keep ekphrasis in the material, the ekphrastic description "is on the way back toward becoming the object again,"[24] and in the end, we discover a mode of representation in which the artistic object borders on the amuletic.

---

23. Stanbury, *Visual Object of Desire in Late Medieval England*, p. 15.
24. Darrel Mansell, "Metaphor as Matter," *Language and Literature* 15 (1992): 116 [109–20].

Opening with a study of the lists in Chaucer's short lyric, "The Former Age," Sarah Stanbury investigates the relationship of ekphrasis and inventory. She argues that in the trilingual world of late medieval England, ekphrastic lists served as powerful tools for promoting linguistic and regional identity. Inventories, many of them lists of tools and household objects, regularly superimposed English words on a Latin or French base, marking classes of material objects as regional and specifically English. Texts designed for multilingual learning in England, among them Walter de Bibbesworth's *Tretiz* and Caxton's *Dialogues,* use lists for instruction in vocabulary as well as conduct and daily household management. These texts and others like them link words for things with worldly plenitude, as if to say that the sign of membership in the gentry is not only bilingualism but also one's storehouse of names for things.

John M. Bowers's contribution troubles our longstanding confidence that a medieval writer's first audiences can be presumed to understand his text's figural meanings. Attentive to the historical context of Lollard iconoclasm in England during the later fourteenth century, Bowers examines Chaucer's uses of ekphrasis as expressions of an increasingly anxious desire to allow literary images to speak for themselves, starting with the stained-glass images in *Book of the Duchess,* then the pagan statuary in the "Knight's Tale," and finally Book I of the *House of Fame*—where the poet's classic deployment of ekphrasis as "speaking images" dramatizes the urgency of having visual images identify themselves and disclose their own meanings.

A second group of essays, "The Desire of Ekphrasis," delves deeply into the issue of ekphrasis both as a goal and as a site of desire, a phenomenon that engenders emotions both in pleasurable but also in destabilizing and subversive ways. Claudia Olk addresses the enigmatic encounter between the resurrected Christ and Mary Magdalene, which has been at the center of pictorial narratives since early Christianity. The numerous paintings of the scene capture the very moment in which Christ forbids Mary to touch him since he has not yet returned to his father. His famous words, *noli me tangere,* mark a site of transition between desire and fulfillment. Presenting a visual and a verbal encounter of the religious and the secular sphere, this scene puts into dialogue word and image, as well as sight and touch. Focusing on *The Digby Play of Mary Magdalene* and Shakespeare's *The Winter's Tale,* Olk examines the discursive and pictorial traditions that have informed and accompanied these plays.

Anke Bernau examines the ways in which the poem *Pearl* mediates affect and cognition in memory primarily through the figure of ekphrasis. Exploring the trope's importance to medieval memory theory, Bernau argues that the poem itself constitutes a kind of extended and doubled example of ekphrasis—a meditation on a beautiful object (the pearl/ the maiden) that is at the same time the creation of a highly ornate artifact (the poem), which displays the centrality of the image to memory as well as other mental and creative processes, such as education, composition, meditation, and prayer. The chapter is concerned with the *Pearl*-poet's profound ambivalence toward the poetic and rhetorical uses of images, raising in turn fundamental ethical questions about the making of poetry.

Kathryn Starkey draws on three scenes in Gottfried von Strassburg's *Tristan,* to investigate Gottfried's use of ekphrasis as a didactic-psychological tool. One use of ekphrasis introduces the lovers into a public setting: the hunt in which Mark's men first encounter Tristan, and Isolde's appearance at the Irish court where she refutes the Steward's claims of bravery. Starkey argues that these scenes urge us to reflect on the effect of the protagonists' splendid appearance in order to warn us about the psychology of visualization and its manipulation of an audience. Another use of ekphrasis, the description of Petitcreiu demonstrates by contrast how beauty can both be appreciated and withstood. Gottfried ultimately emphasizes the ability of ekphrasis to enslave the discerning listener to the power and beauty of the visual.

The third section of this volume, "The Epistemology of Ekphrasis," turns to the late medieval and early modern epistemology of ekphrasis and traces how the trope tends to retain the medieval obsession with the didactic and the allegorical. Darryl J. Gless argues that Edmund Spenser's *Faerie Queene* often creates the illusion of visuality by inducing readers to recall familiar visual images like the Seven Deadly Sins and the Seven Corporal Works of Mercy but then supplying more nonvisual detail than visual. Such passages promise vision but provide ratiocination instead, as is most apparent in the progressively less visualizable House of Holiness and the "vision" of the Heavenly Jerusalem, which requires readers to supply most of what they "see." Gless concludes that Spenser's progressive replacement of the merely visual with casuistical ratiocination and recollections of the Word counterbalances the iconoclastic energies that critics have habitually discerned within the poem.

Andrew James Johnston and Margitta Rouse's essay is concerned with the political implications of ekphrasis in Gavin Douglas's early-sixteenth-century dream poem *The Palice of Honour*. In the Middle Scots poem, different view(ing)s of honor are contrasted as part of an allegorical journey to know honor: first, as a visual representation of tales of honorable deeds within a costly mirror that heals anyone who gazes into it, and second, as a lifelike representation of honor as an all-powerful, threatening monarch who almost destroys anyone who looks at him. Taken on its own, the mirror scene suggests that aesthetic representation is successful, even healing. When Honour strikes violently from within the inner sanctum of his palace, it becomes evident however that courtly culture suppresses the constant threat of violence through aesthetic deflection. It is through a multifaceted interplay of various manifestations of ekphrasis that the destructive aspects of the courtly concept of honor are literally made visible in this poem: ekphrasis here takes on the form of a complex argumentative structure.

Suzanne Conklin Akbari examines ekphrasis as a specifically temporal function in Christine de Pizan's *Livre de la Mutacion de Fortune.* Akbari argues that ekphrasis has the potential of freezing moments in time, which—as opposed to reconstructing a linear narrative of time—provide a contemplative, synoptic view of the past. For Christine, the stasis of ekphrasis serves not only as a means to investigate time but also as a template for self-improvement and spiritual reform. Akbari explores the crucial role of the "sale merveilleuse," or "marvellous chamber," in organizing the narrative conception of universal history and links this with Christine's integration of Boethian ideas concerning the nature of change.

Finally, the fourth section, "The Borders of Ekphrasis," is concerned with the ways in which medieval ekphrasis betrays a tendency to always problematize the borders and the limits of our understanding and of the processes through which human beings signify. Ethan Knapp's essay asks how ekphrasis functions in medieval poetry when the object of representation is the human face. Knapp draws on art historical investigations of the rise of portraiture as the very emblem of modern realism, as well as on the long poetical tradition of physiognomy, and relates these approaches to Walter Benjamin's work on allegory in order to examine the descriptions of faces in three of the principal poets of the period: Chaucer, Gower, and Hoccleve. He argues that these poets share a sense of the face as a hermeneutic mystery but that they also adapt faces in distinct ways: Chaucer tends to fix on facial descriptions at moments in which his narratives grind to a halt in a burst of ekphrastic pathos; for Gower, the face is more strictly anatomical, and it often stands for a dangerous boundary between external world and internal self; for Hoccleve, the face is a paradoxical image, one that should by its nature speak, but that most often stands mute.

The final two essays in this volume, by Hans Jürgen Scheuer and Larry Scanlon, respectively, explore the relation between ekphrasis and mimesis for the Middle Ages. Modern critics tend to understand ekphrastic passages in epic texts as instances of a representation of representation. They assume that the tension between language and visuality is solved by a narrative dynamic that continually unfolds the pregnant moment of description. Hans Jürgen Scheuer points out that in this perspective critics tend to miss one of the core aspects of the premodern understanding of mimesis. According to the ancient tradition (since Plato), mimesis aims at the animation and dynamization of mental images. Apart from these phantasms or *imagines agentes,* which are shaped by the movement of a pneuma within the psychic apparatus, there is no possible communication between soul and the outside world. The visual itself is thus only conceivable as a mental representation, formed by the physiological, rational, and magic schematisms of perception. As a consequence, Scheuer's essay is not interested in the question of how Chaucer's "Merchant's Tale" depicts its subject, the marriage between Januarius and May but focuses rather on the perceptional process that can be traced in the text. In this regard, the essay takes as its point of departure the failure of ekphrasis and follows the narrator's attempts to bypass his ineptitude via allusions to Martianus Capella's *Marriage of Philology to Mercury* and to the marriage of Amor and Psyche in Apuleius's *Metamorphoses,* in order to reconstruct the particular model of the soul that governs Chaucer's quintessentially ekphrastic art beyond mere description.

Larry Scanlon's essay uses as its primary example the ending vision of the late fourteenth-century Middle English poem *Pearl* read through "*L'effet de réel,*" or "The Reality Effect," of Roland Barthes. Scanlon argues that as a rhetorical structure the trope of ekphrasis literally inhabits the difference between signifier and signified. It thus provides all modes of literary and narrative mimesis with a rhetorical means for marking the plasticity of their own representational limits. Noting the prevalence of the trope of ekphrasis in twentieth-century fiction and poetry, he shows that this mimetic capacity subtends the ostensible distinction between modern realism and premodern forms of mimesis, and thus calls the validity of this distinction itself into question: realism as a category of analysis can apply as fruitfully to medieval literature as to modern literature, and modern realism, in its continual quest to transgress the limits of its own conventions, is driven by its own hidden, transcendent desires.

PART I

EKPHRASIS AND THE OBJECT

Chapter 1

EKPHRASIS AND THE OBJECT[1]

Valerie Allen

*W*ell known as an analogue of the Bayeux Tapestry, the description of the wall hanging in the bedchamber of Adela, dedicatee of a long Latin panegyric poem in elegiac distiches by the Benedictine monk Baudri, abbot of Bourgeuil, also provides a rich example of ekphrasis at the turn of the eleventh into the twelfth century. With Baudri's description as a case study, this essay points out ways in which definitions of ekphrasis since the nineteenth century do not well fit high medieval poetry and attempts an articulation of some assumptions that might fit better. Rarefied by literary theory into the distillate of poetic process, as poetry in the act of self-reflection, ekphrasis tracks the difference between medieval and modern poetics, a difference that rests on different understandings of form and of the category of the aesthetic, and on the relationship between materiality and textuality.

The following summary of the poem and its context is brief, as each

---

1. With thanks once more for helpful feedback from my reading group: Jen Brown, Glenn Burger, Matthew Goldie, Steve Kruger, Michael Sargent, and Silvia Tomasch; also to Kathryn Starkey for her references and to Sarah-Grace Heller for sharing her knowledge about textiles.

has been described elsewhere.[2] Baudri dedicates his poem to Adela, daughter of William the Conqueror, mother of the future King Stephen of England, and patroness of the arts. The poem comprises a dream vision of 1368 lines in which the poet dreams that he sees Adela's bedchamber, the description of which occupies almost the entire poem. It quickly appears that the chamber is a microcosm of human history and learning: a *mappa mundi* adorns the floor (ll. 719–947); on the ceiling, a map of the heavens (ll. 573–718); statues of maidens representing Philosophy and the seven liberal arts surround the bed, along with an image of Medicine, accompanied by Hippocrates and Galen (ll. 948–1254; 1255–1342); four tapestries sheathe the walls. The first, hanging on the smaller end of the chamber, the making of which Adela herself supervises and directs (ll. 103–4), portrays the creation of the world (ll. 101–40); the second, along one length of the wall, tells of biblical and ecclesiastical history (ll. 145–68); the third, along the other length, represents classical mythology and the history of Rome (ll. 169–206); the fourth, in pride of place around the countess's bed, recounts the exploits of William the Conqueror (ll. 207–572), this last arousing speculation about connections between Baudri's poem and the Bayeux Tapestry.[3] Although extant artifacts such as tapestries and floor mosaics attest to the historical possibility that such a chamber might have existed, the hyperbolic pitch of Baudri's lines suggests a narrative intent of eulogy rather than empirical observation. The poem steps even further away from verisimilitude toward what is perhaps its ultimate purpose: to repre-

---

2. Jean-Yves Tilliette, "La chambre de la comtesse Adèle: savoir scientifique et technique littéraire dans le C. CXCVI de Baudri de Bourgueil," *Romania: revue consacrée à l'étude des langues et des littératures romanes* 102.1 (1981): 145–71. Mary J. Carruthers, *The Craft of Thought: Meditation, Rhetoric, and the Making of Images, 400–1200*, Cambridge Studies in Medieval Literature (Cambridge: Cambridge University Press, 1998), pp. 213–20. Kimberly A. LoPrete, *Adela of Blois: Countess and Lord (c. 1067–1137)* (Dublin: Four Courts, 2007), pp. 191–204. For particular comparison with the Bayeux Tapestry, see also Shirley Ann Brown and Michael W. Herren, "The *Adelae Comitissae* of Baudri de Bourgeuil and the Bayeux Tapestry," *Anglo-Norman Studies* 16 (1993): 55–73; and the introductory notes in Martin K. Foys, ed., *The Bayeux Tapestry: Digital Edition* (Leicester: Scholarly Digital Editions, 2003).

3. All references to the poem are from Jean-Yves Tilliette, ed. and trans., "Adelae Comitissae," in *Baudri de Bourgueil, Poèmes: Tome 2* (Paris: Belles Lettres, 2002). See also the partial translation into English by Michael W. Herren, "Baudri de Bourgueil, *Adelae Comitissae*," in *The Bayeux Tapestry: History and Bibliography*, ed. Shirley Ann Brown, with contribution by Michael W. Herren (Woodbridge: Boydell and Brewer, 1988), pp. 167–77. Monika Otter has an English poetry translation of the full text: "Baudri of Bourgueil, 'To Countess Adela'," *Journal of Medieval Latin* 11 (2001): 61–142. For recent general discussion, see Bernard S. Bachrach, "The Norman Conquest, Countess Adela, and Abbot Baudri," *Anglo-Norman Studies XXXV: Proceedings of the Battle Conference 2012*, ed. David Bates (Woodbridge: Boydell and Brewer, 2013), pp. 65–78. All translations of Baudri's poem are mine, in consultation with the modern translations.

sent the chamber as a microcosm of thought, making it function mnemo-technologically as a place to recollect "in an orderly fashion the matter of a general education, the 'foundations' of what Adela's children will learn."[4]

Sumptuous as each *objet d'art* in the chamber is, the tapestry relating William the Conqueror's deeds steals the limelight, occupying over a quarter of the poem, and it is this particular ekphrastic episode that is explored here. Baudri introduces William as the rightful heir of Normandy, temporarily dispossessed, restored to his birthright as much by courage as heredity (ll. 235–42). Then comes Halley's comet, presage of momentous political change (ll. 243–58); William holds a council of war, declaring Harold as a perjurer and usurper and himself the proper pretender to the English throne (ll. 259–328); the Normans support his claim, prepare a battle fleet, and set sail (ll. 329–86); they land and defeat the English, who take William as their king (ll. 389–552); Baudri summarizes William's ascent from duke to king, and gives a concluding description of the tapestry and an address to his own poem (ll. 553–82).

BARE WORDS: EKPHRASIS

Before even mentioning William, the subject of this tapestry, Baudri comments on its textile composition for, as he notes earlier in the poem, the hangings are precious as much for their materials as for their workmanship (l. 96).

> Ambit enim lectum dominae mirabile uelum
> Quod tria materia iungat et arte noua.
> Nam manus artificis sic attenuauerat artem
> Vt uix esse putes quod tamen esse scias.
> Aurea precedunt, argentea fila sequuntur,
> Tercia fila quidem serica semper erant.
> Sic quoque cura sagax tenuauerat ambo metalla
> Tenuius ut nil hoc posse fuisse rear.
> Tam subtilis erat quam texit aranea tela
> Et tenuis plus, si tenuior esse potest.
> Quid subtile magis non Pallas nere doceret,
> Si praesens Pallas nentibus ipsa foret.
> Non meliore stilo formas perarasset Arachne,
> Si studio praesens ipsa magistra foret.
> Fama uetusta refert, nisi fama uetusta sit anceps,
> Has geminas artes exeruisse suas,

---

4. Carruthers, *Craft of Thought*, p. 214.

Vt studio celebri sibi uendicet utraque nomen—
Aggrediuntur opus, historias replicant.
Incumbit Pallas itidemque incumbit Arachne;
Propositae titulus laudis utramque ciet.
Sed neutram sperem praesens opus exuperasse,
Cum superet praesens et precio et studio.
Interlucebant rutilo discrimine gemmae
Et margaritae non modici precii.
Denique tantus erat uelo fulgorque decorque
Vt Phebi dicas exuperasse iubar.
(ll. 207–32)

For around the bed of my lady runs a marvelous curtain that conjoins three materials and is in the new style. For the hand of the artist had so refined his art that you could barely believe it to be what you nonetheless know it to be. First come the gold strands, those of silver following, and the third strands were always of silk. Keen attention had so also tempered the two metals that to my mind nothing could have been finer. It was more delicate than the web that a spider weaves, and finer still, if anything can be finer. Pallas could not have taught how to spin anything more fine had she herself been there in person to assist the spinners. Arachne could not have composed forms in better style had she herself been there in person to supervise the effort. An old story has it—if this old story be not in doubt—that they pitched their twinned skills so that each might defend her name with her renowned skill. They approach the work, unwind stories. Pallas leant forward, likewise Arachne leant forward; the title of honor desired spurs on one and the other. But neither I expect could surpass the present work, for the present work excels in worth and effort. Gems with their varying fire shone forth, as well as pearls of no moderate worth. In a word, such was the brilliance and adornment of the curtain that you might say that they outstripped the splendor of Phoebus.

The digression upon the spinning contest between Pallas and Arachne establishes the analogy between making cloth and making poems as the competitors "unwind stories." Pallas and Arachne are to spinning as needlework and poetry are to unraveling stories. Baudri plies his trade of story-unraveling through crafted words with as much skill as Pallas and Arachne can spin. Baudri offers Adela a work of art that comments upon a work of art. There is a problem here of categorization, for in ancient oratory, whence ekphrasis as a technical term originates, the term refers to vivid description "of any length, of any subject matter, composed in verse or prose, using any verbal techniques."[5] Ekphrasis was not understood as description exclusively of art, and—translated by the Romans as *descriptio*—came to associate in medieval rhetorical treatises with a wide network of terms, such as *effictio, notatio, explicatio,* and so on. In this way, medieval "ekphrasis" retains the breadth of the original device's rhetorical function. Ekphrases specifically of works of art nonetheless do inhabit the broad descriptive category as *pragmata,* descriptions of objects or actions—an elision that explains the story-like, nonstatic nature of the descriptions of artifacts.[6] It is then possible to speak of a medieval poetic trope of vividly described artifacts, crafted with skill and artistry: the necklace awarded to Beowulf, the marble sculptures carved into the side of the mountain of Dante's *Purgatorio,* Baudri's description of Adela's tapestry. Even living flesh in the form of young maidens is described in medieval romance as if artwork, with Dame Nature as the artist who sculpts and paints her handiwork. In this pragmatic aspect, premodern ekphrasis affirms its ethical force. The artistry that the poetry celebrates is banausic, the demonstrable skill learned in the muscle, practical rather than theoretical. Baudri has sweated over his *carmen* (ll. 1343–44). Like those of the poet, the deft movements of the weaver bespeak a strategic intelligence wholly focused on making and doing; simultaneously, perhaps paradoxically, this hymn to craft mystifies the mechanics of production, for it is unclear which part of the hanging is woven and which embroidered—an equivocation found in other such ekphrases that evokes an element of the marvelous.[7] In so describing this highly wrought tapestry, Baudri aligns himself with a descriptive tradition that celebrates form as shape—no surprise then that Ovid's *Metamorphoses* should be one source for this poem.[8] This kind of medieval ekphrasis, which delights in making and shape-shifting, belongs to a descriptive tradition essentially poetic rather than exegetical, which by contrast could be literal, even "scientific," as Beryl Smalley notes.[9]

---

5. Ruth Webb, *Ekphrasis, Imagination and Persuasion in Ancient Rhetorical Theory and Practice* (Farnham: Ashgate 2009), p. 8.

6. Janice Hewlett Koelb, *The Poetics of Description: Imagined Places in European Literature* (New York: Palgrave Macmillan, 2006), pp. 2 and 24.

7. Sarah-Grace Heller, "Obscure Lands and Obscured Hands: Fairy Embroidery and the Ambiguous Vocabulary of Medieval Textile Decoration," *Medieval Clothing and Textiles* 5 (2009): 15–35.

8. Tilliette, "La chambre de la comtesse Adèle," pp. 154–55.

9. Cited by Mary Carruthers in *Craft of Thought* (p. 184), where she discusses Richard of St. Victor, who in the later twelfth century attempts to "objectify and de-trope the ekphrasis" of Ezekiel's vision of the temple, "understanding it less as an instance of rhetorical *allegoria* and more as the linguistically 'transparent' description of an object."

The fascination with shapes, plasticity, counting, word lengths, and grammatical endings is particularly characteristic of Latin poetry and ultimately asserts that metrical form is a necessary if not a sufficient condition of poetry. Writing almost a century later than Baudri, Geoffrey of Vinsauf opens his *New Poetry* by worrying himself about how to address Pope Innocent, the dedicatee of the poem, because the name does not scan in hexameters:

> Papa stupor mundi, si dixero Papa Nocenti
> Acephatum nomen tribuam, sed si caput addam
> Hostis erit metri.[10]
> (ll. 1–3)

> Holy Father, wonder of the world, if I say Pope Nocent I shall give you a name without a head; but if I add the head, your name will be at odds with the metre.

His solution is to:

> Divide sic nomen, "In," praefer, et adde nocenti
> Efficiturque comes metri.
> (ll. 7–8)

> Divide the name thus: set down first "In," then add "nocent" and it will be in friendly accord with the metre.

The ingenuity of the wordsmith can bend language like soft metal into elegant new shapes. Art becomes art by inhabiting its own spatial dimensions. It is precisely this intimacy with what might tendentiously be called the *mechanics* of versification that gives rise to the perception of medieval poetics as untheoretical and preaesthetic. Essentially workmen, medieval artists "lacked a theory of the fine arts. They had no conception of art in the modern sense, as the construction of objects whose primary function is to be enjoyed aesthetically."[11]

It is not a new argument that the aesthetic was born in the eighteenth century and that art before that period—most notoriously, that of the High

---

10. Latin text in Edmond Faral, *Les arts poétiques du XIIe et du XIIIe siècle: recherches et documents sur la technique littéraire du moyen âge* (1924, repr. Paris: Champion, 1962), p. 197. Translation by Margaret F. Nims, Poetria Nova *of Geoffrey of Vinsauf,* Medieval Sources in Translation 6 (Toronto: Pontifical Institute of Medieval Studies, 1967), p. 15.

11. Umberto Eco, *Art and Beauty in the Middle Ages,* trans. Hugh Bredin (New Haven: Yale University Press, 1986), p. 97.

Middle Ages—is preaesthetic. Emerging out of epistemology, the aesthetic bridges the cognitive gap between the generalities of reason and the particularities of sense (*aesthetic* of course means *senses* as in *anaesthetic*). Its particularity negotiates between impracticable universality and untheorizable individuality, promising resolution to the struggle between the useful and the beautiful, between means and ends.[12] Where beauty used to exist in the service of something, of religion or of political power, where poems were dedicated to countesses or popes, now in this revolution of thought, it breaks free of ideological servitude and serves only its own ends, self-reflecting, disinterested even when occasional or celebratory. The hallmark of this new poetic doctrine is symbol, which fuses word and meaning and overcomes otherness, unlike its stiff, "unpoetic" (and by implication, medieval) predecessor allegory, in which the relation between words and meanings is arbitrary.[13] Metaphor, the building brick of poetry, augments from verbal flourish to a mode of thought.

One of the consequences of this symbolic turn is a loosened connection with external form, a certain reluctance to define poetry by such epiphenomena as verse length. When Wordsworth juxtaposes two sets of verses, metrically and stylistically alike, some from a ballad, the others doggerel, he asks wherein the difference lies: "Not from the metre, not from the language, not from the order of the words." The doggerel cannot "excite thought or feeling in the Reader."[14] Poetry, that is, reveals itself more in its aesthetic function than in outward appearance. Although metrical form never had been a sufficient condition of poetry—Aristotle himself asserts that Herodotus versified still amounts to history[15]—the rules of versification come increasingly to seem just that: rules.

In this context, ekphrasis rarefies into the act of poetry commenting on its own practice as an end in itself, the representation of representation. Webb observes how one can search "in vain for any unambiguous use of the term [ekphrasis] to mean 'description of a work of art' in any source before the late nineteenth century."[16] Leo Spitzer's 1955 essay on Keats's "Ode" is formative in

12. Terry Eagleton, *The Ideology of the Aesthetic* (Oxford: Blackwell, 1990), esp. ch. 1 [13–30].

13. Drawing from Goethe, Murray Krieger discusses the relationship between symbol and allegory in *Words about Words about Words: Theory, Criticism, and the Literary Text* (Baltimore: Johns Hopkins University Press, 1988), ch. 15 [271–88].

14. Michael Mason, ed., Preface to *Lyrical Ballads* (1802) (London: Longman, 1992), p. 85 (ll. 897–923).

15. Aristotle, *Poetics*, ed. and trans. Stephen Halliwell (Cambridge, MA: Harvard University Press, 1995), ch. 9, 1415a, l. 39–1415b, l. 3.

16. Webb, *Ekphrasis*, p. 5.

the evolution of the concept, in which he represents the poet sinning against the urn by historical curiosity, where hitherto it had stood "unmolested by antiquarians."[17] The poet eventually learns that the urn's message is not historical but "purely aesthetic,"[18] Spitzer's interpretation of the poem validating Webb's description of latter-day ekphrasis as "art meditating on itself."[19]

This aesthetic turn seems to leave medieval art not yet having attained the age of reason. Baudri's aesthetic delight lies in wonder at the luxury of the tapestry, in the object itself rather than in any abstract convulsion of self-reflection. Precisely because of the intimacy between medieval poetics and form, precisely because external form serves as the measure of the beautiful, ornament is all. Superabundance performs what contemporary Suger said of St. Denis's treasures: that the "wonderful and uninterrupted light of most luminous windows"[20] and "the loveliness of the many-coloured gems" transport one from an inferior mundane to a higher world.[21] Suger's golden, jeweled chalices and vases themselves perform beauty and enact devotion.[22] They magnify, in the older sense of beautification through amplification. Baudri's ekphrasis less offers penetrating insight into the nature of poetic representation than it describes surfaces, than it lists and names, indulging an impulse to catalogue a single act out of inventing and inventorying—an impulse entirely in keeping with the art of his age. Baudri's aesthetic sensibility is thoroughly superficial as well as sweatily workmanlike.

> La profusion de formes et de couleurs qui ne laissent pas un pouce carré de pierre nue est pour Baudri et pour ses contemporains un critère de beauté. C'est ce qu'Edgar De Bruyne appelle l'esthétique du "gold and glitter." Elle se caractérise par la précision du détail . . . et surtout le goût du brillant—la tapisserie "l'emporte sur l'éclat de Phébus," le pavement est "plus lumineux que le verre," les statues "resplendissent." Une telle description nous rappelle à propos que l'art roman était tout le contraire d'un art dépouillé.[23]

---

17. Leo Spitzer, "The 'Ode on a Grecian Urn,' or Content vs. Metagrammar," in *Comparative Literature* 7 (1955): 209 [203–25]. Webb notes the importance of Spitzer's essay (*Ekphrasis*, p. 34). See also Koelb, *Poetics of Description*, pp. 1–5.

18. Spitzer, "'Ode on a Grecian Urn,'" p. 219.

19. Webb, *Ekphrasis*, p. 35.

20. Erwin Panofsky, ed. and trans., *De Consecratione*, iv, in *Abbot Suger on the Abbey Church of St.-Denis and its Art Treasures*, 2nd ed. (Princeton: Princeton University Press, 1979), pp. 100–101 (ll. 21–22).

21. Erwin Panofsky, ed. and trans., *De Administratione*, xxxiii, in *Abbot Suger on the Abbey Church of St.-Denis and its Art Treasures*, 2nd ed. (Princeton: Princeton University Press, 1979), pp. 62–63 (ll. 27–28).

22. Panofsky, *De Administratione*, pp. 76–81.

23. Tilliette, "La chambre de la comtesse Adèle," pp. 152–53.

The profusion of forms and colors that leaves not one square inch of stone bare is for Baudri and his contemporaries a requirement of beauty. It is what Edgar De Bruyne calls the aesthetic of "gold and glitter," characterized by preciseness of detail . . . and most of all by a taste for radiance—the tapestry "surpasses the brightness of Phebus," the flooring is "more luminous than glass," the statues "gleam." Such description opportunely reminds us that Romanesque is the exact opposite of minimalist art.

Such is the vertiginous effect of this high ornamentation that Tilliette questions the objectivity of the description.[24] Yet as a general statement about the medieval rhetorical descriptive tradition, bias is a given, objectivity rarely if ever a desideratum. Medieval poetic ekphrasis does not aim to present its object clinically or comprehensively; it selects, omits, and trades in superlatives, for it does not simply describe, it describes vividly by speaking forth (*ek* + *phrasis*). With its roots in classical oratory, medieval ekphrasis is driven by the epideictic impulse, its business to praise or blame, to persuade rather than to predicate.[25] Its underlying premise is that vivid description must be partial in both senses of the word: committed (hence not objective) and selective (hence incomplete). If an object can be described without passion, hence partiality, then it is not worth describing.

At issue here is the extent to which ekphrasis mediates the object in such a way that certain properties of the object emerge only by its interconnection with words, only by the act of description. If the only purpose of ekphrasis were to offer to the mind's eye through vivid description what is absent from the physical eye, then any description of an object already visible or vividly recollected would be redundant. If however ekphrastic mediation colors the reality described, then it can never be redundant for it speaks for an object (present or not) by bringing to attention aspects of the object not immediately apparent, even if in doing so it partially blocks direct access to that object. By magnifying the object through description, ekphrasis ensures its place as a necessary supplement to the object. Although Baudri's tapestry will not have been familiar to his audience (because it is fictional) its narrative of William's exploits, occupying well over three hundred lines, is indeed well known, already visible to the mind's eye. His ekphrasis nonetheless sheds light on the already familiar "seen," speaking forth what may not have been heard clearly in all the noise of chronicle:

24. Tilliette, "La chambre de la comtesse Adèle," pp. 147–49.
25. Webb traces the connection between ekphrasis and enargeia, which is more general than a figure of speech, as it refers to the linguistic "capacity to visualize a scene" (*Ekphrasis*, p. 105). See also pp. 51, 85–86 and 128. Also for *enarg[e]ia*, Richard A. Lanham, *A Handlist of Rhetorical Terms*, 2nd ed. (Berkeley: University of California Press, 1991), p. 64.

Guillelmus consul rex est de consule factus.
Sanguinis effusi nuncia stella fuit.
Optinuit regnum rex optinuitque ducatum
Dux, et sic nomen Caesaris optinuit.
Solus et ipse duos, dum uixit, rexit honores,
Cunctis Caesaribus altior et ducibus
Nemo ducum melior, non regum fortior alter,
Rex diadema gerens, dux ducis arma tulit.
(ll. 553–60)

Count William, from consul, has been made king. The star was a presage
of blood spilled. The king occupied his kingdom and the duke his duchy:
thus he obtained the name of Caesar. Alone, while he lived, he exercised this
double office, greater than all other Caesars and dukes. No duke was better,
no king stronger. As king, bearing the crown, as duke, he bore the arms of
a duke.

Any attempt then to access the thing-in-itself by working backward through
ekphrastic description will founder in superlativeness and incompleteness,
in too much and too little detail. This assumption perhaps informs the opening of Murray Krieger's book on ekphrasis, in which he considers the hope-
less task of "reverse ekphrasis," that is, of reconstructing Achilles' shield from
Homer's description of it in the *Iliad;* or Aeneas's from Virgil's description in
the *Aeneid;* or the Grecian urn from Keats's "Ode."[26] Baudri's hyperboles, easily overlooked as just so much rhetorical furniture—"Pallas could not have
taught how to spin anything more fine had she herself had been there in
person to assist the spinners" (ll. 217–18)—acquire more weight in the realization that the poetic representation only works in one direction, from *res* to
verbum, that the rhetorically heightened description stands as both *terminus
a quo* and *terminus ad quem,* that it is not a recipe. Baudri openly admits the
artifice of his description:

Naues et proceres procerumque uocabula uelum
Illud habet, uelum si tamen illud erat.
(ll. 385–86)

This hanging represents the ships, the leaders, and the names of the leaders,
that is, if only that hanging really existed.

---

26. Murray Krieger, *Ekphrasis: The Illusion of the Natural Sign* (Baltimore: Johns Hopkins
University Press, 1992), pp. xiii–xiv.

What exist are the words of Baudri's description, the names by which he summons things to presence, for only in language does the thing remain as it originally was, bare names are all we have. "Stat rosa pristina nomine, nomina nuda tenemus."[27]

Thus far the argument has established that a special subclass of medieval ekphrases, even if not necessarily so called, describes artwork. In such instances, preoccupation with form predominates, with its artisanal "madeness," with a thing done. Its attention to surfaces and externals generates a characteristically medieval delight in excess, luminosity, richness, and hyperbole that, for all its luxury, seems by the standards of eighteenth-century poetics and later to fall short of a fully aesthetic, disinterested appreciation of art that delights in the existence of the work for its own beautiful sake rather than for its capacity to magnify anything else. Partial in every sense of the word, medieval ekphrasis inevitably distorts its object of description by the superlatives in which it trades. Stating this idea more strongly, ekphrasis can be said to transform its object by virtue of its poetic mediation. It ultimately constitutes the reality of the object whether or not that object exists as historical artifact.

Veras crediderim uiuasque fuisse figuras
Ni caro, ni sensus deesset imaginibus.
(ll. 563–64)

I would have believed the figures in the images to have been real and living had not (the hanging) lacked flesh and sensation.

Haec quoque, si credas haec uere uela fuisse,
In uelis uere, cartula nostra, legas.
(ll. 567–68)

Oh manuscript of ours, if you believe these hangings truly to have existed, you would read truly these things also on those hangings.

The subjunctive mood of Baudri's address to his script, the counterfactual conditionality of the statement, registers his nuanced understanding of truth.

---

27. Lines by twelfth-century Benedictine, Bernard of Cluny, which close Umberto Eco's novel, *The Name of the Rose,* trans. William Weaver (Orlando: Harcourt, Brace & Co., 1983), p. 502. See Herman Charles Hoskier, ed., *De Contemptu Mundi: A Bitter Satirical Poem of 3000 Lines upon the Morals of the XIIth Century by Bernard of Morval* (London: Bernard Quaritch, 1929), Liber I, l. 952 (p. 33). "Roma" not "rosa" is a variant reading.

Preaesthetic such art may be in a historically exact sense of the term, yet it is fully witting of the recursive nature of poetic representation, aware that poetry at some level always refers to its own craft even when its business is about something else.

Baudri's ekphrasis is less about a velum, as in some denotative assertion, than it is a text/ile of allusion, to invoke a familiar pun implied by the analogy between the woven threads of the hanging and his own spinning of the story. Ekphrasis incants rather than describes. By the conjury of his song (Latin *carmen* meaning both metrical verse and spell), bare words thicken into textile while textile subsists in text. What medieval ekphrasis lacks in aestheticism it makes up for in bewitchment.

ONE OBJECT STUCK ON TOP OF ANOTHER

As an act of verbal representation, ekphrasis stands in for—even replaces—its material object (whether it historically exists or not). Krieger writes: "Since we are dealing in either poem [viz., *Iliad* and *Aeneid*] with a verbal representation of a fictional visual representation, and thus representation at a second remove . . . the material dissipates into the airiness of words."[28] Ekphrasis is supposed even to bypass the materiality of writing, treating words as if they were transparent. Were one to step back to consider the letters with which the words are written, "we would have left the genre of ekphrasis," says J. W. T. Mitchell, "for concrete or shaped poetry, and the written signifiers would themselves take on iconic characteristics."[29] However sensuous the language, ekphrasis leaves behind the page and does not inhabit its letters or the spaces between them; in this it underwrites "an aesthetic that judged works apart from their material substrate."[30] It is questionable, however, whether such a characterization befits this poem, which Baudri refers to as his "carmine carta" (l. 1347) [parchment of my song]. Certainly, this ability to "imagine the 'text' as something detached from the physical reality of a page" does occur in the Middle Ages, for Ivan

28. Krieger, *Ekphrasis*, p. xv.

29. J. W. T. Mitchell, *Picture Theory: Essays on Verbal and Visual Representation* (Chicago: University of Chicago Press, 1994), p. 158.

30. Roger Chartier, *Inscription and Erasure: Literature and Written Culture from the Eleventh to the Eighteenth Century,* trans. Arthur Goldhammer (Philadelphia: University of Pennsylvania Press, 2007), p. viii. Chartier's work is apposite to the argument of this essay, both generally for "refusing to separate the analysis of symbolic meanings from that of the material forms by which they are transmitted" (p. vii), and specifically for his consideration of Baudri's poems (other than *Adelae Comitissae*) in the three materials used for composition: wax, parchment, and stone (pp. 1–12).

Illich locates a similar phenomenon in the twelfth century, in the shift from monastic to scholastic reading practice, where memorization of a specific page that incarnates words gives way to a more abstract reception of those words without consideration of their concrete inscription.[31] Yet in the medieval poetic context, the identification with form and the preoccupation with surfaces and textures keep ekphrasis in the material. Baudri's address to his own poem as "cartula" locates it as a dimensioned object in the hand rather than as an aesthetic judgment in the mind. Other poems of his witness a comparable materialization of language: Constance, a correspondent of Baudri's, has touched his songs with her bare hand ("Et tetigi nuda carmina uestra manu").[32]

> He [Baudri] trims his verses to fit the exquisite tablets that his friend the Abbot of Séez gave him . . . broad enough to hold an hexameter, long enough to take eight lines, and coated with green wax, not black, because green is more pleasing to the eye. . . . Baudri was very particular about the colouring of his capitals . . . because since the verses are very indifferent, he would like to make sure of readers by the beauty of the MS.[33]

The abstractness of representation gives way in Baudri's ekphrasis to something closer to the concreteness of collage, to the sticking of one kind of surface, dimension, or texture on top of another, by which process each layer of artwork partially frames, partially occludes, and all the time embellishes what lies beneath and within.

Strategically situated in the heart of the chamber, this commemorative tapestry of William frames Adela's bed (ll. 581–82), and then itself is framed by the two tapestries running down the length of the room, the starry ceiling, and T-map flooring. Baudri notes that he stops thunderstruck on the threshold of the chamber ("substans in limine primo," l. 93) as he takes in the scene before him, the liminal pause nudging readers to note that the frame of the *parergon* has been passed, that they are inside art's spell. The tapestry of William and Adela's bed are at the far end of the chamber from him, for he notes that the tapestry portraying the Creation is at the end nearest the

---

31. Ivan Illich, *In the Vineyard of the Text: A Commentary to Hugh's Didascalicon* (Chicago: University of Chicago Press, 1993), p. 4. For Hugh of St. Victor's directives for memorization of the manuscript page, see Mary Carruthers, *The Book of Memory: A Study of Memory in Medieval Culture* (Cambridge: Cambridge University Press, 1990), pp. 261–66.

32. Tilliette, Poem §200, in *Baudri de Bourgueil*, 2:130. See also Helen Waddell, *The Wandering Scholars*, 7th ed. (London: Fontana, 1968), p. 117.

33. Waddell, *Wandering Scholars*, pp. 115–16. Also Chartier, *Inscription and Erasure*, pp. 2–5.

entrance, where the room is at its narrowest (ll. 139–40), while the two tapestries portraying biblical history and classical mythology run the length of the bedroom (ll. 141–42). How Baudri was able to view the tapestry of the Creation from his standing position at the doorway is a question that chafes only if perspectival realism is expected to prevail. Oneiric license grants omnivision to the dreamer. So from this privileged position on the threshold of a microcosm, Baudri the dreamer sees recent events of Anglo-Norman politics set like a jewel into the heart of human history, held in balance by cosmic forces, wrapped around by providence. A sacred page, the hanging is inscribed with events guided by God's hand and foretold by the "hairy" star of Halley's Comet. The hanging can just as easily be thought of as a frame, setting off human actions into crafted art as historical event that, once placed inside the border of the wall hanging, turns into commemorative, epideictic work.

Baudri's *dispositio* of cosmic matter and occurrences includes careful internal arrangement by counterpoint. The images along two of the walls run as both two parallel lines and as a series arranged *punctus contra punctum*, Hebrew image matching Greek image.

> At domus in longum, uelis obtenta duobus,
> Temporibus eiusdem dissona signa dabat.
> Sensus imaginibus erat alter, et altera gens est:
> Hac genus Hebreum, hac fabula Greca fuit.
> (ll. 141–44)

> But the edifice along the length enveloped by two hangings showed different images from the same era. The direction of the images was twofold—it was also about two peoples: on one side the Hebrew race, on the other Greek mythology.

This arrangement of Old Testament and Greek stories emphasizes the methodical order of the chamber.[34] Laid out according to principles of internal symmetry between discordant opposites that together compose a concordant totality, the chamber invokes a geometrical idealization of space reminiscent of high medieval art, where divine order is expressed through

---

34. For the significance of the arrangement, see Carruthers, *Craft of Thought*, p. 217, and notes in Tilliette's edition, *Baudri de Bourgueil*, 2:168.

abstract structures.[35] This is matter methodized, banausic art made obedient to reason and number.[36]

Baudri describes the wall hanging as woven of gold and of silver thread of a fineness finer than gossamer. The third thread used is silk. Into this surface are sewn gems of "varying fire" that gleam intermittently through the samite along with pearls of high value—much more ornate than its analogue, the Bayeux Tapestry, which comprises wool embroidery on a linen base cloth. This imaginary hanging possesses sheen from silk, radiance from gold, silver, and gemstones and pearls, which combine luster in the form of light reflected from its surface with translucence, emanating from its outermost laminae.[37] It possesses texture and density from the stiffness of the noble metals and the convexity of the gems. Quite possibly, it also possesses pattern. Upon this rich base cloth is embroidered script.

> Porro recenseres titulorum scripta legendo
> In uelo veras historiasque nouas.
> (ll. 233–34)

Furthermore, by reading the script of the titles you could tell the stories, true and new, on the hanging.

> Regis diuitiae, sua gloria, bella, triumphi
> In uelo poterant singula uisa legi.
> Veras crediderim uiuasque fuisse figuras
> Ni caro, ni sensus deesset imaginibus.
> Littera signabat sic res et quasque figuras,
> Vt quisquis uideat, si sapit, ipsa legat.
> (ll. 561–66)

---

35. Madeline H. Caviness relates this artistic principle with two twelfth-century writers, Richard of St. Victor and Theophilus ("Images of Divine Order and the Third Mode of Seeing," *Gesta* 22.2 [1983]: 99–120).

36. Vincent Debiais also considers the idealization of matter, although his concern is more with how art completes actual recollections (for example, of Adèle's chamber or the Bayeux Tapestry) ("The Poem of Baudri for Countess Adèle: A Starting Point for a Reading of Medieval Latin Ekphrasis," *Viator* 44.1 [2013]: 95–106).

37. Max Bauer, *Precious Stones: A Popular Account of their Characters, Occurrence and Applications, with an Introduction to their Determination, for Mineralogists, Lapidaries, Jewellers, etc. with an Appendix on Pearls and Coral*, trans. L. J. Spencer (London: Charles Griffin, 1904), p. 589.

The riches of the king, his glory, battles, triumphs could be read in a single image on this hanging. I would have believed the figures in the images to have been real and living had not (the hanging) lacked flesh and sensation. Writing marked out both the events and figures in such a way that whoever sees it can read it, if he knows how to.

The embroidering of script onto the weaving far exceeds the Bayeux Tapestry's terse legends, for William's long speeches occupy over eighty lines of Baudri's poem.[38] Although he does not specify whether the pictorial images (as distinct from the lettering) are woven or embroidered, it seems more likely that they were embroidered, as he mentions them in the same breath as the script (ll. 385–86). Although no details relate how the gemstones and pearls were disposed through the hanging other than the observation that they "shone forth" ("interlucebant"), the radiance of the gems emphasizes the narrative just as vigorously as any verbal emphasis. Valued for their whiteness and brightness, pearls dramatically highlight in medieval art, especially Byzantine, where they limn holy figures, surrounding them with light and functioning much as a halo.[39] In the book cover of the later-ninth-century Lindau Gospels, probably of Frankish provenance, which is organized around an evident quaternity, pearls pick out the four angles of the cross.[40] Christ, the pearl beyond all price, sits at the center in quincunx arrangement. Compare the five gems that adorn the cross in the *Dream of the Rood* or the Anglo-Saxon Fuller brooch, where five gems depict the five senses, with sight occupying the central position as the most privileged faculty. The quincunx arrangement incorporates within it the tetradic arrangement and appears ubiquitously in medieval art: it is the shape of a crucifix—four points of a cross with Christ set in between them; the shape of a cloister—a quadrangle with a cross or fountain in its center; the shape of a page—a center surrounded by four corners; it might even be said to be Adela's chamber—four tapestried walls with the countess's bed as the centerpiece. From all this profusion rational order emerges.

---

38. Tilliette, "La chambre de la comtesse Adèle," p. 151. See also Debiais, "Poem of Baudri."

39. For example, the late-tenth-, early-eleventh-century Byzantine book cover, with Christ Pantokrator surrounded by saints, used as the jacket illustration of the exhibition catalogue, *The Glory of Byzantium: Art and Culture of the Middle Byzantine Era A.D. 843–1261*, eds. Helen C. Evans and William D. Wixom (New York: Metropolitan Museum of Art, 1997), p. 88. The silk, embroidered inscriptions, and stitching of gems and pearls onto the face of the textile suggest Byzantine influence. See R. Howard Bloch, *A Needle in the Right Hand of God: The Norman Conquest of 1066 and the Making and Meaning of the Bayeux Tapestry* (New York: Random House, 2006), pp. 152–54.

40. Paul Needham, *Twelve Centuries of Bookbindings 400–1600* (New York and London: The Pierpoint Morgan Library and Oxford University Press, 1979), pp. 27–29.

Baudri's hanging figures an inordinate amount of lettering along with images embroidered onto a base cloth of metallic thread decorated with gemstones. The effect would be hopelessly busy to present-day taste, although for Baudri it is an exercise in sumptuosity. It serves as a "pagina" or canvas upon which the story of the conquest is told in letters and images. The page represents the condition of textual possibility, ground of representation, and scene of language and thought; in theory blank like parchment, a neutral space to serve as means and bearer of record. Baudri's hanging however is lumpy, crusted with jewels, stiffened with metal filaments, and already tells a story in shapes, colors, materials, surfaces, and textures before the images of or words about William the Conqueror imposed upon it can tell their story. Already a text prior to lettering and picture prior to images, the hanging comprises objects piled on top of each other, collage-like, which achieve a visual effect similar to Romanesque relief sculpture. Constructed in the "new style" (l. 208), a phrase alluding to architectural design, the tapestry is at once a monument, textile, and manuscript, a *fabric* in every sense. So ornate is this "sacra pagina" that it is none too clear which is ground cloth and which embroidery. The distinction matters, for on it rests larger hermeneutic dyads, namely, means and end, form and content, vehicle and tenor, where the page always occupies the lesser term: the means *to* the end, the form *of* content, the vehicle *of* meaning. Background runs the danger of overshadowing foreground, what is represented is at risk of disappearing into how it is represented. Balance lost or at least under threat, on the edge of vertigo, the foreground of the page seems to turn into the frame of the background, which now assumes the place of foreground. As one beautiful object gets stuck on top of another, the dizziness only intensifies as page, script and border change places, the layers of textures densify, kernal and encrustation compact, materiality and textuality become coterminous. With weaving framed by gemstones, script and pictures, other tapestries, the room's threshold, and the poem itself, which is framed by parchment, different media pile up, creating an effect not dissimilar to that of the chiastic series between the *Dream of the Rood*'s poem with a cross in it (which speaks a poem, which speaks of a cross . . .) and the Ruthwell (and Brussels) cross with a poem on it (which speaks of a cross, which speaks a poem . . .).

Baudri's hanging places a frame or parergon around the *oeuvre* or *ergon* of the historical conquest.[41] But the distinction between the two has been

---

41. Kant uses the terms in his *Critique of Judgment* to distinguish between the *oeuvre* and its frame, which announces that what lies within its border belongs to a different, aesthetic order of reality. Jacques Derrida problematizes the distinction in *The Truth in Painting*, trans. Geoff Bennington and Ian McLeod (Chicago: University of Chicago Press, 1987), pp. 37–82.

called into question by the instances considered in this essay. The frames are not merely ornamental *hors d'oeuvres* but in this context become the form or spatial outline of the work, more aptly, the *scrinium* or shrine that augments and speaks forth its precious object, supplementing what is lost or hidden, functioning more as exoskeleton than receptacle. Ekphrases frame their objects, frames speak forth their pictures. In Baudri's ekphrasis, *descriptio* and material form converge, making function ever follow form. As Vincent Debiais notes, William's words "acquire a certain thickness and visual reality," making the "connection between *imago* and *poesis*" central to the meaning of the work.[42]

When Suger of St. Denis describes his abbey's store of ecclesiastical utensils—chalices ("calices") and vases ("vasa") all for Eucharistic purposes ("ad Dominicae mensae servicium")—he "frames" their consecrated beauty in the service of God by inscribing them with an elegiac distich, making them speak forth their reason for being:[43]

Dum libare Deo gemmis debemus et auro,
Hoc ego Suggerius offero vas Domino.

For as long as we ought to offer libations to God with gems and gold, I, Suger, offer this vase to the Lord.

Includi gemmis lapis iste meretur et auro.
Marmor erat, sed in his marmore carior est.

It is fitting that this stone (porphyry vase) be enframed with gems and gold. It was marble, but in these (gems and gold) it is more precious than marble.

Elegaic couplets were the metrical choice for giving voice to objects, used as they were in Greek art, where, as Spitzer notes with reference to Keats's Grecian Urn, "mute statues or tombstones" were made to speak.[44] Pithy enough to be carved into alabaster, the distichs animate objects. Baudri's elegiac distichs—all bound up into a "libellus" and personally delivered to Adela—make a mute tapestry speak in the same way that an inscription makes a book warn the reader against thieving it or an item of jewelry invokes the power of the saint whose name is written there. Such *tituli* approach the category that Don Skemer names "textual amulets," protective objects whose

42. Debiais, "Poem of Baudri," 104.
43. Panofsky, *De Administratione,* p. 78 (ll. 21–22 and 33–34).
44. Spitzer, "'Ode on a Grecian Urn,'" p. 220.

magical properties reside in the letters themselves, being thereby distinct from other kinds of enchantment such as incanted spells or stones with special virtues.[45] Just as the *Dream of the Rood*'s prosopopeia gives voice to a cross or a riddle speech to an undeclared object, so the lines of this poem frame a textile with ekphrastic words, announcing in that workmanlike act the design of the piece. Baudri's *descriptio* becomes thoroughly materialized through its stitched distichs, gesturing towards an ancient kind of *écriture* in which ekphrasis does not represent so much as it simply points to, adhering and accreting itself to its referent, animating it with crafty letters stuck onto the surface in a way similar to the picto-hieroglyphic labels of dreams and ancient paintings noted by Freud.[46]

In different ways, both high medieval and postmodern poetics rematerialize textuality. Where Baudri's ekphrasis conjures rather than describes through enchanting words, deconstruction, notes Jacques Derrida, "interferes with solid structures," and in that insistence on materializing representation, it remains "always distinct from an analysis or a 'critique.'"[47] Both exhibit language's brute refusal to lose the material presence of its lettering, to shed the page and become symbol. The symbolic can only occur when the material is left behind, and in this sense high medieval art—wall hangings, poems, the "barbarously splendid" book covers[48]—is preaesthetic and unsymbolic—figural yes, symbolic no. In late medieval ekphrastic description, there is perhaps a case to be made for the preciousness of poetry being already on the way to the symbolic, to the abstract kind of representation that enables the aesthetic turn of later centuries. Yet in the earlier art considered here of Baudri's *carmen*, ekphrasis borders on the amuletic.

---

45. Don C. Skemer, *Binding Words: Textual Amulets in the Middle Ages* (University Park: Pennsylvania State University Press, 2006).

46. An observation made in *Interpretation of Dreams* while discussing the means of representing speech in dreams. The passage is commented on by Jacques Derrida in *Writing and Difference,* trans. Alan Bass (Chicago: University of Chicago Press, 1978), p. 218.

47. Derrida, *Truth in Painting*, p. 19.

48. See Martin Conway, "Some Treasures of the Time of Charles the Bald," *Burlington Magazine for Connoisseurs* 26 (1915): 236–41.

Chapter 2

MULTILINGUAL LISTS AND CHAUCER'S "THE FORMER AGE"[1]

Sarah Stanbury

haucer's Boethian lyric "The Former Age" is a poem that catalogues an exceptional number of material and made things. In
the first age, when people led a sweet and peaceful life, they
ate nuts, hawthorn berries, pig food, apples, and grain and drank water
from the cold well. In that blissful time, they slept on grass and leaves,
not yet knowing feather-down or bleached sheets, and were free as
well from the knowledge of the handmill, spice grinder, plough, fire,
flint, coin, ships, sword, spear, hauberk, and plate armor. As insightful readings by John Norton-Smith, A. V. C. Schmidt, Andrew Galloway, and Nicola Masciandaro have shown, the lyric offers a critique of
modernity that is particularly targeted at technology, or craft. By naming the knowledge of manufacture that people in the first age lacked,
the poem indicts the mechanical skills of the present one. Schmidt
in particular comments on the peculiarities of Chaucer's lexicon in
creating this picture of amplitude and lack, knowledge and ignorance.
One example is the poem's liberal use of a relay of alliterating echoes:
"welde"/"wod" (l. 17); "fyr"/"flint" (l. 13); "flee"/"former"/ "flesh"

---

1. I would like to thank Robert Stein (in memoriam) and Mark Amsler for their
helpful comments on this essay.

(l. 18–19).[2] Another is the poem's novel vocabulary. Sixteen words in this poem of sixty-four lines appear nowhere else in Chaucer's poetry, and several terms may even be Chaucerian coinages.[3]

The poem's vocabulary also departs from Chaucerian practice in its stripped-down, bullet-like simplicity. Many lines are built almost entirely of monosyllabic words, especially those that amplify the technological lack of the first age: "No man the fyr out of the flint yit fond" (l. 13); "no ship yit karf the wawes grene and blewe" (l. 21); "No toures heye and walles rounde or square" (l. 24). While the poem's monosyllabic lexis is no doubt dictated in part by the demands of rhyme and alliteration, it also seems driven by mimetic representation: simple words for simple folks in simple times. What has not been noted, however, is the extent to which the poem's vocabulary seems determined by what today we would call etymological choice or what Chaucer may have understood as the choice between native and non-native words.[4] In this poem, many of the substantives derive from Old English: *quern, melle, hawes, welle, mader, welde, wood, flesh, egge, spere, ware, fetheres, shete.* Generalities or social conditions, on the other hand, are more likely to be enumerated in words of French origin: *cheryce, avarice, humblesse, emperice, taylage, tyrannye, doublenesse, tresoun, envye.*[5] Are these groupings merely a consequence of the peculiarity of English language history that derives monosyllabic nouns from English origins and polysyllabic words from French and Latin, or do they reflect choices on Chaucer's part to inflect terms by language register?

---

2. Citations from "The Former Age" are from Larry D. Benson, ed., *The Riverside Chaucer,* 3rd ed. (Boston: Houghton Mifflin, 1987), pp. 650–51.

3. A. V. C. Schmidt, "Chaucer and the Golden Age," *Essays in Criticism* 26 (1976): 102–3 [99–124]; John Norton-Smith, "Chaucer's *Etas Prima,*" *Medium Aevum* 32 (1963): 117–24; and Andrew Galloway, "Chaucer's Former Age and the Fourteenth-Century Anthropology of Craft: The Social Logic of a Premodernist Lyric," *ELH* 63 (1996): 535–54; and Nicola Masciandaro, *The Voice of the Hammer: The Meaning of Work in Middle English Literature* (Notre Dame: University of Notre Dame Press, 2007), pp. 94–116.

4. Etymology today refers to the diachronic history of word origins, a field that emerged from nineteenth-century comparative philology, though the practice and term have a long history. See Mark Amsler, *Etymology and Grammatical Discourse in Late Antiquity and the Early Middle Ages* (Amsterdam: John Benjamins, 1989), pp. 1–11 and 136–72. "Ethimologique" is the term for the series Deschamps uses to describe the derivation of "Angleterre" from "la terre Angelique," the land of Angles, in his lyric praising Chaucer, however tongue in cheek, as "Grant translateur, noble Gieffroy Chaucier;" as cited in Ardis Butterfield, *The Familiar Enemy: Chaucer, Language, and Nation in the Hundred Years War* (Oxford: Oxford University Press, 2009), p. 145.

5. Language derivations are based on Christopher Cannon, *The Making of Chaucer's English* (Cambridge: Cambridge University Press, 1998) and the Oxford English Dictionary (Oxford University Press, 2015, WEB, accessed March 19, 2015). *OED.*

This essay examines the lexicons of accumulation in "The Former Age," and proposes that the poem's words for things bespeak an engagement with historical change and linguistic translation. The lyric, itself a translation from Boethius with material drawn as well from Ovid, Jean de Meun, and Deschamps, levels a critique of the present age that is built, in part, on its adroit voicing of language registers that imagine the past through a native lexis. Recent work on multilingualism in late medieval England has increasingly pointed to the complex overlay of French and English, with French language and literature, as Ardis Butterfield puts it, everywhere an "insistent and conflicted presence."[6] Although it may be true, as Butterfield also notes, that "the deep structure of Anglo-French in Chaucer's English makes it hard to know when he felt he was using a 'French' word," *words,* clustered in groups such as lists, may more transparently overlay language with item and gesture toward native or continental lexical registers.[7] In the long *occupatio* describing Arcite's funeral in the "Knight's Tale," Chaucer changes his sources to add native species of trees. While elm, alder, ash, fir, yew, and hazel overlap with the catalogue in Boccaccio, Chaucer's list adds "ook," "birch," "aspe," "holm" [holm oak], "popler," "wylugh" [willow], "plane," box," "chasteyn" [chestnut], "lynde," "laurer" [laurel]," "mapul," "thorn," "bech," "ew," and "whippeltree" [dogwood] (ll. 2921–23), Brenda Deen Schildgen observes, and with the exception of the laurel and the poplar, all are words of Old English origin.[8] She further suggests that these anglicizings, followed by an account of the flight of the birds, animals, and old gods from their denuded forest, deepen the romance's critique of royal privilege—in this case, the right to cut down forests for aristocratic use. It is worth noting in this regard that the ironic nod to a lost golden age invoked in the opening of the "Wife of Bath's Tale" superimposes a catalogue of buildings, artifacts of a disparaged modernity, on the "grene mede" (l. 861) of "th'olde dayes" of King Arthur: "halles, chambres, kichenes, boures / Citees, burghes, castels, hye toures / Thropes, bernes, shipnes, dayeryes" (ll. 869–71), a catalogue that elides the expulsion of the fairies, brought about by the infestation of friars, with the transformation from rural to built landscape. In the developed world, the architecture is distinctively multilingual or at least polyglot. The three-line catalogue, which devotes one line for the home, one for the city,

---

6. Ardis Butterfield, "Chaucerian Vernaculars," *Studies in the Age of Chaucer* 31 (2009): 51 [25–51].

7. Butterfield, "Chaucerian Vernaculars," p. 38.

8. Brenda Deen Schildgen, "Reception, Elegy, and Eco-Awareness: Trees in Statius, Boccaccio, and Chaucer," *Comparative Literature* 65 (2013): 96 [85–100].

and the third for the farm, draws primarily on words of English origin for house and farm, and from French for the city.[9]

And of course word length itself also points to language origins. Chaucer's aureate style is built on a polysyllabic diction evocative of Romance privilege, as Christopher Cannon puts it—even if those were words he created himself out of English roots.[10] His low style, alternatively, is rich in monosyllabic words that gesture to England rather than the Continent.[11] In "The Former Age," I propose, Chaucer's uses of simple as well as aureate diction match language not just to level—low or high—but also to history and home.

This essay also explores the relationships between Chaucer's literary lists in "The Former Age" and nonliterary French/English word lists circulating in late medieval England. In French language primers, such as Walter de Bibbesworth's *Tretiz* and Caxton's *Dialogues,* word lists taxonomize the world and its things as they hold out the promise that language learning equates with mastery of objects in their plenitude. Lists serve as language aids, tools for naming the world and knowing its particulars. Business inventories, such as the mixed-language indentures Chaucer assumed when he took on the job as Clerk of the King's Works, overlay English, Latin, and French to group craft terms by language in ways that bespeak an everyday patois of language mixing for purposes of enumeration. The mixed language of Chaucer's business inventories might also be of value for understanding the sociolinguistic registers of words that he draws on to construct literary catalogues, at least as demonstrated in "The Former Age." Richly informative archival sources for information about late medieval building technology and the maintenance of the royal palaces, the indentures are also informative documents of Chaucer's worldliness. In far greater precision and detail than any other records from his life, the indentures give us information about things that Chaucer may actually have seen. What can the indentures tell us about the "social life of things" to borrow a phrase from Arjun Appadurai, when objects are classified not only by shape, use, or material but also language?[12] Origins or word derivations form an organizing principle of some of his literary lists, I will argue, in ways that tease out national or transnational place/word associa-

---

9. The exceptions are "burghes" (OE); "toures," which derives from both English and French; and "dayeryes," which derives from Anglo-French, according to Cannon, *Making,* p. 271.

10. Cannon, *Making,* pp. 151 and 81.

11. Ralph W. V. Elliott, *Chaucer's English* (London: Deutsch, 1974), p. 191; in Cannon, *Making,* p. 158n.

12. Arjun Appadurai, *The Social Life of Things: Commodities in Cultural Perspective* (Cambridge: Cambridge University Press, 1997).

tions. Chaucer, writing in trilingual, fourteenth-century England and accustomed to classifying tools and technologies by language, chooses words of English origin to give a specifically English inflexion to certain classes or groups of things.

Above all this essay reflects on the relationships among material things and the categories that classify them in multilingual England. Lists, which by definition are classificatory structures, often gesture to the very languages from which, in the absence of a syntactical grammatical matrix, their words derive; by offering up objects as unsubordinated accumulation, lists may put their items into a resonant relationship with place, however unspecified that surrounding may be. In their naked lexicality, objects in lists evoke or demand other housings, such as temporality and language. What is the place, the moment in time, and the language to which these objects, grouped together, *belong*?

1.

In its transformation of its sources, Chaucer's "The Former Age" seems notably intentional in its listing and materializing, using accumulation to evoke technology and its lack and also to regionalize or anglicize the first age and the present one. In relation to Boethius's *Consolation of Philosophy*, the lyric's most direct source, the material things that flesh out Chaucer's Golden Age seem notably impoverished and the technologies of the present time paradoxically productive of pleasure. "The Former Age" is a loose translation of the Fifth Metrum in Book II, voicing commonplaces about the Golden Age also familiar from Ovid and Jean de Meun.[13] Chaucer's poem supplies, in significant degree, concrete, material detail to Boethius and to his own translation, the *Boece*. The *Boece* names "accornes of ookes" as the single food with which people in the first age slaked their hunger.[14] In "The Former Age" acorns amplify to "mast, hawes, and swich pounage" [nuts, hawthorn berries, and pig food] (l. 7). In the *Boece*, people in this first age slept "holsome slepes upon the gras, and drunken of the rennynge waters, and layen undir the schadwes of the heye pyn-trees."[15] In contrast, "The Former Age" names the made things of the present that people in earlier times lacked: walls,

---

13. For the lyric as a gloss on both Boethius and on Chaucer's own translation of Boethius, see James M. Dean, *The World Grown Old in Later Medieval Literature* (Cambridge, MA: Medieval Academy of America, 1997), p. 274.

14. *Riverside Chaucer*, p. 415.

15. *Riverside Chaucer*, pp. 415–16.

"doun of fetheres," and "bleched shete" (l. 45). Similarly, the lyric's echoes of Ovid, Deschamps, and Jean de Meun also underscore the absence of those luxuries in Chaucer's rather crabbed "Golden Age." In *The Metamorphoses,* which describes the Golden Age, like the First Age of Chaucer's lyric, as innocent of technology, people gather "wild strawberries on mountainsides, small cherries, / and acorns fallen from Jove's spreading oak."[16] In the *Roman de la Rose,* the Golden Age was a time of even more luxurious simplicity where people gathered "pommes, poires, noiz et chastaignes / Boutons et meures et pruneles, / Framboises, freses et ceneles / Feves et pois"[17] [apples, pears, nuts, chestnuts, rose hips, mulberries, sloes, raspberries, strawberries, haws, broad beans, peas]—a brimming, bucolic French plenitude that contrasts markedly with Chaucer's pinched English woodland larder, which supplies only "mast, hawes, and swich pounage" (l. 8) [nuts, hawthorn berries, and pig food].

The passage on dyes is even more telling of an enumerative practice that not only adds substantives but also correlates objects with English origins and uses. In the *Boece,* Chaucer adds a substantial gloss to explain the extraction and Mediterranean origins of Tyrian purple, an important commercial pigment: "Ne they coude nat medle the bryghte fleezes of the contre of Seryens with the venym of Tyrie (*this to seyn, thei coude nat deyen white fleezes of Syrien contre with the blood of a maner schellefyssche that men fynden in Tirie, with whiche blood men deyen purpre*)."[18] In marked contrast, pigments named in "The Former Age" come not from shellfish in Lebanon but from "mader, welde, or wood," three widely used and locally grown English plants whose names all derive from Old English roots: "No mader, welde, or wood no litestere / Ne knew; the flees was of his former hewe" (ll. 17–18). "Mader" is *Rubia tinctorum,* a plant commonly cultivated for the red pigment derived from its root; "welde" is *Reseda luteola,* a plant used for yellow; "wood" is *Isatis tinctoria* or dyer's woad, whose leaves were widely used for blue. None of these dyes were used to color Syrian fleeces: "The flees was of his former hewe." L. O. Purdon notes that wool dying was an important English industry, with woad dyers, or woadmen, so much in demand that reckless

---

16. "fraga legebant/cornaque et in duris haerentia mora rubetis/ et quae deciderant patula Iovis arbore glandes" (*Metamorphoses,* Book 1, ll. 104–6, *The Latin Library,* http://www.thelatinlibrary.com/ovid/ovid.met1.shtml); English translation: Ovid, *Metamorphoses,* trans. and ed. Charles Martin (New York: Norton, 2010), ll. 145–46.

17. Guillaume de Lorris et Jean de Meun, *Le Roman de la Rose,* ed. Armand Strubel (Paris: Librairie Générale Française, 1992), p. 456 (ll. 8372–74); English translation: *The Romance of the Rose,* ed. Charles Dahlberg (Princeton, NJ: Princeton University Press, 1971), p. 154.

18. *Riverside Chaucer,* pp. 415–16.

techniques of dying led to legal regulation in the 1360s.[19] Whether or not the reference to "mader," "welde," and "woad" would conjure the controversies about woaders, the names localize the pigments as a list of native plants. If fleeces weren't dyed in the first age, it was fleeces from English sheep and pigments from English plants that weren't used.

Lists of negatives also contribute to amplitude, as if the absent technologies of the first age were a cipher for our own failures to know the past, with alliterating lists of things and technologies filling up both empty past and decadent present. Although dyers in the first age didn't know "mader, welde, or woad," nothing in the poem suggests the plants weren't there, and indeed, in naming them the poem suggests their presence. A notable feature of the lyric's list-making lies in the shifting locations of plenitude, which at times is identified with having goods and at others with not having or even not knowing goods or technologies. Things are chiefly present through syntactic negation as amplification: "no man yit knew" (l. 12). People living in an idyllic Golden Age ate "mast, hawes, and swich pounage" and drank water of the "colde welle"; they didn't know "mader, welde, or wood"; edge or spear didn't know flesh; men didn't know counterfeit coins; ships didn't know waves; people didn't know nor have trumpets for warfare or towers or walls. The presence or absence of things and the knowledge of how to make them in the primitive world mirror human ethics, which themselves are allied with politics. In the Golden Age, people had "no pryde, non envye, non avaryce / No lord, no taylage by no tyrannye," but instead they had "humblesse and pees, goode feith the emperice," or ruler (ll. 53–55). Misfortune marks the present day: "now may men wepe and crye! / for in oure dayes nis but covetyse, / Doublenesse, and tresoun, and envye, / Poyson, manslawhtre, and mordre in sondry wyse" (ll. 60–63).

Yet rhetorical absence, amplified, becomes presence. Presence and absence of technology, politics, and social ethics, complexly intertwined, presents finally a self-canceling history that critiques both the present world and also the lyric's own fantasies of innocence. In listing what the first age "ne knew," the poem gestures to the pleasures of the present one; by naming "clarre" [spiced wine] and "sause of galantyne" [a sauce] (l. 16) as culinary concoctions that the first age lacked, the poem overrides its own ideology of simplicity through negative naming. Similarly, negatives displace agency onto tools, as in the second stanza where human agency is evoked in a double removal. In the first age, the plough did not wound the ground—as of course, by implication, it must do now—a reversal that imagines the plough as a driverless

---

19. L. O. Purdon, "Chaucer's Use of Woad in *The Former Age*," *PLL* 25 (1989): 217 [216–19].

automaton, gouging furrows on an edenic body. The poem's commentary on the differences between now and then, that is to say, is not nearly as transparent about the ethics of edenic sufficiency and the evils of modern technology as it may at first seem. In the former age people slept on "gras or leves," but while they did so in peace and quiet, the luxuries they lacked may offer far more comforting pleasures: "doun of fetheres" and "bleched shete" (l. 45).

Critical consensus has not been met on how Chaucer is directing his commentary on the present and even when he wrote the poem, though most recent readings have been attentive to the ironies and cancellations in the lyric's overt praise of the past. Norton-Smith and Galloway both argue for a date in the late 1390s, contending that the poem critiques the tyrannies and taxation ("taylage," l. 54) of Richard II. Galloway further argues that the poem engages in a contemporary public debate in both reformist and orthodox circles on the failings of the current world, with its "dangers of professionalism and applied learning."[20] If the poem can be said to level a critique at Ricardian political muscle through a backward or nostalgic glance, perhaps its list-making words may also be understood to further that engagement with periodization.[21] The former age, with or without technology, was narrowly but simply English, and our days have now fallen into French. To see French as the state of the fallen world would also be consistent with a public critique of Richard's famous French extravagance. Reading the poem more as cultural dialogue than political allegory, Ardis Butterfield locates the lyric not by date but by conversation within what she calls the "lyric discourse" of the Hundred Years War, a poetic corpus rich in references to "translation, to English, and Englishing."[22] Some of Deschamps' *ballades,* which may have been sources for Chaucer or written in dialogue with his Boethian lyrics, draw on golden age *topoi* to reflect on nation, such as *Ballade* #1317, which lists the familiar delights of bread, wine, pillows, and "white oak-scented sheets" to praise present-day France: "Tel pais n'est qu'en royaume de France!" (l. 10) [Such a country does not exist except in the realm of France!].[23] However we may account for the English origins of so many of names for things in "The Former Age," Deschamp's praise of French pleasures contrasts markedly with the doleful list of French-derived

---

20. Galloway, "Chaucer's Former Age," p. 549.

21. As Masciandaro reads the poem, its narrator voices a naïve nostalgia, with the poem as a whole expressing Chaucer's "skepticism of the primitivist principle" (*Voice of the Hammer,* pp. 98, 110).

22. Butterfield, *Familiar Enemy,* pp. 135–36.

23. Eustache Deschamps, *Oeuvres Complètes de Eustache Deschamps,* ed. Le Marquis de Queux de Saint-Hilaire and Gaston Raynaud, SATF (Paris: Firmin Didot, 1878–1903), vol. 7, pp. 79–80; in Butterfield, *Familiar Enemy,* p. 136.

social ills listed in the aureate final lines of "The Former Age's" last stanza: *covetyse, doublenesse, tresoun, envye, poyson,* and *mordre,* words whose length bespeaks their sociolinguistic register.

In "The Former Age," language choices thus work to underwrite the poem's commentary on temporality and if not nation—at least Englishness—with past and present conjured in language derived differentially from English and French. Failures of the fallen contemporary world also derive from Nimrod, known both for tyranny and also for the confusion of languages, a connection that would seem to be furthered by the reference to Nimrod's "toures hye."[24] As James Dean notes, this final stanza constitutes Chaucer's major addition to Boethius's lyric:[25]

> Yit was not Jupiter the likerous,
> That first was fader of delicacye
> Come in this world; ne Nembrot, desirous
> To regne, had nat maad his toures hye.
> Allas, allas, now may men wepe and crye!
> For in oure dayes nis but covetyse,
> Doublenesse, and tresoun, and envye,
> Poyson, manslawhtre, and mordre in sondry wyse.
> (ll. 56–63)

Positive material things, it would seem, are to negative ethical abstractions as English is to French. The lyric's rhetorical drivers move teleologically toward a present comprised of all the negatives, in both English and French, that the poem has named. To put that another way, things and the technologies that produce them, listed in a dizzying sweep of self-canceling negatives, may define befallenness as much as French-derived bad behaviors, all that is left in "oure dayes."

2.

"The Former Age," a poem that reflects on technology, mirrors Chaucer's polymathic interests in both technology and also in lists as sociolinguistic

---

24. Norton-Smith, "Chaucer's *Etas Prima,*" p. 121, disputes the equation of this Nimrod with the architect of Babel, arguing that the poem's multiple towers—rather than a single one—is a veiled reference to the tyrant Richard II. Nevertheless, the proximity of the name and towers makes it hard to dismiss the association with Babel as well.

25. Dean, *World Grown Old,* p. 275.

principles of narrative. Chaucer's writings reveal his careful attentiveness to the construction, mechanics, and aesthetic effects produced by many kinds of made things: we can think of his descriptions of textiles (the ekphrasis of Alisoun in the "Miller's Tale"), of armaments (preparations for the tournament in the "Knight's Tale"), of jewelry (the Prioress's brooch), of automata (the flying horse in the "Squire's Tale"), or of the apparatus for distilling as carefully explained in the "Canon's Yeoman's Tale," to name just a few of the manufactured objects that appear in the *Canterbury Tales*. As readers have often noted, Chaucer's writings are full of lists of many kinds. Charles Muscatine has ascribed this predilection to Chaucer's "lay encyclopedism" and sententiousness;[26] Steven Barney, in perhaps the most thorough examination of Chaucer's literary lists, suggests Chaucer's fondness for enumeration also owes something to his Aristotelian and taxonomic scientific interests.[27] Chaucer draws on many traditions of list writing—wisdom literature, oral poetry, rhetoric, satire, encyclopedic literature, moral and homiletic literature, and technical and scientific writing—with lists of all kinds sharing the pleasures of enumeration, or plenitude. As Barney puts it, lists in narrative conjoin metaphor with paradigm: "Here in its multitude is the 'what' I speak of."[28] Items in lists, that is, can be thought of as sets of metonyms, with the category or heading gesturing to the abstract "real." Certainly lists bespeak categories and draw our attention to principles of classification, whether through the taxonomic logic of their ordering or, as in Borges's list of animals—"a) those that belong to the Emperor b) embalmed ones c) those that are trained d) suckling pigs e) mermaids."[29]—through the failure of their items to cohere to familiar or recognizable principles of classifying. In *Shimmering in a Transformed Light*, a study of the written still life, Rosemary Lloyd explores the relationship between catalogue and ekphrasis in narrative, noting that the very plenitude of the catalogue works to serve up its real—the larger category of which an individual item can only be a part: "A catalogue is always merely

26. Charles Muscatine, "*The Canterbury Tales*: Style of the Man and Style of the Work," in *Chaucer and Chaucerians*, ed. Derek S. Brewer (Tuscaloosa, AL: University of Alabama Press, 1966), esp. pp. 94–95 [88–113]; cited in Stephen A. Barney, "Chaucer's Lists," in *The Wisdom of Poetry: Essays in Early English Literature in Honor of Morton W. Bloomfield*, eds. Larry D. Benson and Siegfried Wenzel (Kalamazoo, MI: Medieval Institute Publications, 1982), p. 189 [189–224].

27. Barney, "Chaucer's Lists," p. 214.

28. Barney, "Chaucer's Lists," p. 194.

29. Jorge Luis Borges, *The Analytical Language of John Wilkins*, 1942, *Wikipedia*, s.v. "Celestial Emporium of Benevolent Knowledge's Taxonomy," http://en.wikipedia.org/wiki/Celestial_Emporium_of_Benevolent_Knowledge%27s_Taxonomy.

a segment of its possible self, cut off by the picture frame or by ellipses."[30] Lists also gesture, however paradoxically, to their own insufficiency. As in the list of twenty-one trees in the famous *occupatio* of the "Knight's Tale," there can always be more. Lacking modification, items in lists lack the markers of time and place that are central to ekphrasis, as Akbari's essay and the introduction to this volume both remark. Ekphrasis provides a way "to give order to time," Akbari says, by positioning the viewer of the ekphrastic scene outside of history.[31] In "The Former Age," though, the poem's lists serve up a view of history that is also a kind of temporal ordering. Reader and speaker are both present within the poem's historical frame, participating in temporal distinctions made by lists of objects. Lists ("here in its multitude is the 'what' I speak of")[32] detail both the measured plenitude of the former Golden Age as well as excesses of the modern one, enumerated through negatives. If they had acorns and pig food in the past, they also lacked ships, trumpets, merchants, and towers. Lists in this poem, doing curiously ekphrastic work, account for what the former age had, what it lacked, and what modernity contains.

Yet as Lloyd also notes, in their own radical parataxis, lists in narrative point toward language itself, raising the question, as she puts it, "of why language should be used to create them at all."[33] Stripped of syntax, lists present their terms prior to grammar—words themselves, unmodified by grammatical relation but nevertheless gesturing toward a grammar that would give them spatial or temporal order. It is perhaps not surprising, then, that lists have often been used as mnemonic tools in the acquisition of language skills, with the single item or term serving as a foundational piece to be moved around by grammar. Among such texts circulating in premodern England was Alexander Neckam's popular *De nominibus utensilium* [*Regarding the Names of Tools*], a twelfth-century Latin wordbook that was widely copied into the fifteenth century. Neckam's text offers a fascinating metacommentary on the relationship between words and their referents. According to Tony Hunt, the treatise was designed as a pedagogical wordbook for young boys who were learning the basics of Latin vocabulary. In the text, material objects are set in place in nominal still lifes or ekphrastic scenes in ways that emphasize the plenitude of the household—and even, perhaps, show up words themselves as *things* or tools. Hence this 'description' of the kitchen,

---

30. Rosemary Lloyd, *Shimmering in a Transformed Light: Writing the Still Life* (Ithaca, NY: Cornell University Press, 2005), p. 51.

31. Akbari, "Ekphrasis and Stasis in Christine de Pizan's *Livre de la Mutacion de Fortune*," p. 205.

32. Barney, "Chaucer's Lists," p. 194.

33. Lloyd, *Shimmering*, p. 30.

in which "there should also be jars, a tripod, a hatchet, a mortar and pestle, a roasting spit, a hook, a cooking pot, a copper kettle, a plate, a frying pan, a griddle, a pitcher . . . and knives with which fish—which have been caught by fish trap or net or hook or dart or by a little fork or by basket, in an enclosure or a deep pool—can be gutted."[34] Closer to inventory than to ekphrasis, this passage provides very little information with which a reader can visualize these kitchen tools in relation to each other or optically in relation to him- or herself. This set of directives naming the tools that a well-stocked kitchen ideally should contain does not indicate, for instance, that the cooking pot is likely to hang in the fireplace or that the pitcher sits on a table, nor does it give information organizing these objects as if one were making a visual tour of the room (e.g., "First you see . . ."). Nevertheless this list manages to be surprisingly visual. Things, named in their specificity and accumulation, build a picture of a kitchen. The kitchen is a place of tools. The list furthers the evocation of a kitchen through the step outdoors to a deep pool or enclosure, a site for capturing the fish that is now in the kitchen for gutting. The pool makes the kitchen centripetal as a space that draws in nature and subjects it to craft.

According to Rita Copeland, the *De nominibus* served not only as a Latin word list for schoolboys but also as a transitional pedagogical text that was used to prepare boys for reading the Latin classics. Words and the tools they designate are preliterary, objects that need to be named and known before one can proceed to mastery of literary form: "Words are themselves treated like objects that are linked, by their designative function, to things in the world."[35] Literary form, in contrast, organizes words into syntactic structures that point toward the "immanent idea of form itself" beyond the materiality of words.[36] The wordbook draws attention to human organizing and making—to the relationship between words and things or words *as* things—or even to words as tools themselves.

---

34. "Item sint ibi olle, tripodes, securis, mortarium, pilus, contus, uncus, cacabus, aenum, patella, sartago, craticula, urceoli, discus, scutella, parapsis, salsarium, artavi, quibus pisces extenerari possunt, gurgostio et funda vel fucina vel iaculo vel hamite levi et nassa in vivario sive in stangno depressi." Cited in Tony Hunt, *Teaching and Learning Latin in Thirteenth-Century England*, vol. 1 (Cambridge: D. S. Brewer, 1991), p. 181; English translation: Rita Copeland, "Naming, Knowing, and the Object of Language in Alexander Neckam's Grammar Curriculum," *Journal of Medieval Latin* 20 (2010): 43 [38–57]. Many of the manuscript versions contain extensive Anglo-French glosses.

35. Copeland, "Naming," p. 54. Hunt provides a summary of the text on pp. 180–81. I am grateful to Rita Copeland for sending me her essay when it was a work-in-progress. I also want to thank Jenna Mead for her comments on Neckam's wordlist at the Berlin Ekphrasis Conference.

36. Copeland, "Naming," p. 55.

In its use of lists of things to draw attention to the close relationship between the usefulness of words and the utility of things—words as tools—Neckam's text is similar to other word lists in Anglo-French England. Later texts composed specifically for multilingual language learning in England, among them Walter de Bibbesworth's *Tretiz* and Caxton's *Dialogues,* employ lists for French vocabulary learning as well as for instruction in conduct and daily household management. They equally draw our attention to the close ties between words for things and the plentitude of the well-stocked household (among other categories of worldly exuberance).[37] A measure of worldly well-being may perhaps be not just the things one has but also the number of words, in multiple languages, one knows for those things, with the household squarely at the heart of this particular word/thing economy. Bibbesworth's *Tretiz,* which plays liberally synonyms and homonyms, embeds its lexicon in a set of loose descriptions of the human body; of techniques of farming, brewing, and building; and of beasts, birds, and plants. A late thirteenth-century French wordbook written for a female patron named Dyonise de Mountechensi, the *Tretiz* is designed to instruct English-speaking children in the French they will need to know in order to manage their estates, according to William Rothwell.[38] French rhyming couplets include multiple homonyms, as in a passage from the section on words for the head, which plays on words sounding like "levere": "Vous avez la levere e le levere, / la livere e le livre" with interlinear English glosses, "lippe," "hare," "pount," and "bock" (ll. 61–62) [You have the lip and the hare; you have the pound and the book],[39] or as in the early fifteenth-century *Femina,* a French language primer that adds full Middle English translations to its abridgement of the *Tretiz,* "3e

37. For accounts and inventories in household reckoning, see D. Vance Smith, *Arts of Possession: The Middle English Household Imaginary* (Minneapolis: University of Minnesota Press, 2003), pp. 8–9. For multilingual inventories and language learning, see William Rothwell, "Sugar and Spice and All Things Nice: From Oriental Bazar to English Cloister in Anglo-French," *Modern Language Review* 94 (1999): esp. 648 [647–59].

38. The *Tretiz* survives in two manuscripts from the thirteenth century and eleven manuscripts from the fourteenth and fifteenth centuries, and has been edited by William Rothwell, *Le Tretiz* (London: Anglo-Norman Text Society, 1990), p. 1. The argument that the *Tretiz* voices the need for French among estates officers, managers, and young aristocratic land owners is supported by Richard Ingham, "Mixing Languages on the Manor," *Medium Aevum* 78 (2009), p. 84 [80–92]. Ingham also argues that spelling and code-switching in accounting records on manorial estates indicates a widespread use of oral French until the fifteenth century.

39. For discussion of this passage, see M. T. Clanchy, *From Memory to Written Record: England 1066–1307,* 2nd ed. (1979, repr. Malden: Blackwell, 1993), pp. 197–200; Robert M. Stein, "Multilingualism," in *Middle English,* ed. Paul Strohm, Oxford Twenty-First Century Approaches to Literature (Oxford: Oxford University Press, 2007), p. 27n. [23–37]. See also Butterfield, *Enemy,* pp. 329–30.

haveþ la lir*e* & le lev*e*re, balau*n*ce & þe hare þe book also & þe lyppe (p. 15, ll. 11–12)."[40] Play with language occurs primarily with the French lexis, though it also appears liberally in the English as well, as in the following selection, in the *Femina,* from words for parts of the head:

Di ma teste ou mou*n* chief,	I say myn heved & myn heved.
Et la *gr*eve de mou*n* chief	And þe shode of myn heved.
featez la *gr*eve a tou*n* lever	Make þe shode at þyn upprist
Et manger la *gr*iv*e* a tou*n* dyn*er*	And ete þe feldfare at þyn dyn*er.*
(p. 13, ll. 6–9)	

I say my head or my head / And the part on my head / Put on your greaves/ shoes when you get up / And eat thrush for your dinner.

When possible both French and English in the *Femina* will use equivalent homonyms—"greve" in the French for English "part" and "greave," and "shode" in English for French "part" and "to be shod"—particularly where the terms approximate meaning across languages.

Caxton's phrasebook, a text that promises "ryght good lernyng / For to lerne / Shortly frenssh and englyssh,"[41] reprises, in mid-fifteenth-century French and English, a French/Flemish wordbook dating from the fourteenth century. Far more than just a list of words and phrases, the *Dialogues* is a book of worldly classifying, as much an encyclopedia as a lexicon, and one that seems to equate bilingual competency with mastery of principles of classification—not just detailing the familiar world in its particularity but categorizing it. Composed for multilingual instruction and directed primarily toward merchants traveling from one country to another, the phrasebook also seems to be a guide to cross-cultural urban plenitude, or as Lisa Cooper puts it, a "template for social advancement for the aspiring bourgeois."[42] Giving us daily life in its rich particularities through an inventory of things produced by both craft and nature, the *Dialogues* also doubles the number of

---

40. William Rothwell, ed., *Femina* (Trinity College Cambridge, MS B.14.40). *Anglo-Norman On-Line Hub,* http://www.anglo-norman.net/texts/femina.pdf.

41. William Caxton, *Dialogues in French and English,* ed. Henry Bradley, Early English Text Society, Extra Series, 79 (London: Kegan Paul, 1900), p. 3, ll. 14–16. For a discussion of the *Dialogues* as well as other French language textbooks, see Tim William Machan, "French, English, and the Late Medieval Linguistic Repertoire," in *Language and Culture of Medieval Britain: The French of England,* ed. Jocelyn Wogan-Browne (Woodbridge: York Medieval Press, 2009), pp. 363–72; and Lisa H. Cooper, *Artisans and Narrative Craft in Late Medieval England* (Cambridge: Cambridge University Press, 2011), pp. 32–44.

42. Cooper, *Artisans and Narrative Craft,* p. 35.

those items by listing them, divided by side of the page, in two languages, as in this introductory statement of the book's business purposes:

Qui ceste liure vouldra aprendre   Who this booke shall wylle lerne
Bien pourra entreprendre   May well enterprise or take on honde
Marchandises dun pays a lautre   Marchandises fro one land to anothir,
Et cognoistre maintes denrees   And to knowe many wares
Que lui seroient bon achetes   Which to hym shalbe good to be bou3t
Ou vendues pour riche deuenir.   Or solde for riche to become.
(p. 3, l.37–p. 4, l.5)

The *Dialogues* even opens with an index of its indexes: household furnishings, the names of animals, the names of birds, and so on, moving later to a taxonomy of craft: bridlemakers, tailors, dyers, and drapers, all alphabetized by given names of craftsmen. Much of the phrasebook comprises word lists:

Poires, pommes, prounes,   Peres, apples, plommes,
Cherises, fourd[r]ines,   Cheryes, sloes,
Moures, freses, noix,   Morberies, strawberies, notes,
Pesques, nesples,   Pesshes, medliers,
Figes, roisin,   Fyggis, reysins,
Amandes, dades.   Almandes, dates.
(p. 13, ll. 4–9)

Toward the end of the text, the narrator remarks (perhaps tongue in cheek) that he can't seem to bring his book to an end: "Lordes, who wolde, / This boke shold neuer be ended, / For men may not so moche write / Me shold fynde always more" (p. 50, ll. 25–28)—and indeed, the phrasebook itself, with French words versified in the left-hand column and the English in verse form on the right, bespeaks the conjoined pleasures of material and lexical abundance.

3.

Multilingual lists were also features of Chaucer's own daily work. When Geoffrey Chaucer took on the job as Clerk of the King's Works in 1389, he would have been given an office in Westminster. From this office, a room with a fireplace on the west side of the hall, he may well have looked out on the palace's storehouses, which contained—as we know from the indentures or the contractual inventories that came into his hands along with the job—a large assortment of tools, architectural flotsam, and mechanical equipment.[43] Items on this list include materials for windows: twenty-one panes of glass in iron casements for windows in the King's chamber, twelve Reigate stones for two windows, and fifteen nails called clergynails for use in window glazing.[44] One part of the storeroom seems to have been dedicated to unused architectural ornament: a bronze image, two unpainted stone images, and seven images of kings. Included as well among this "dead stock," or *mortui stauri,* are parts of a carriage that had belonged to Edward III, including iron casements for its window panes; as well as an array of construction materials, some apparently in working order and some "franguntur et devastantur": scaffolding, a windlass with all the equipment, a pile driver with a broken stem, slings for a crane, a woodworking lathe, and a pair of large supporting hinges with four iron bolts; and a pair of double lists for use at the joustings in Smithfield, thirty-two particates in circumference. Mentioned as well are many miscellaneous smaller tools for household use: bowls, rakes, andirons, pickaxes, bottles, scales, cables, and an iron crowbar.

The primary function of The Clerk of the King's Works' inventories was not language learning, of course. Nonetheless, a secondary function of these lists may fall under the rubric of language instruction. Writing of the Clerk of the King's Works Indentures in his 1932 Chaucer lectures, John Livingston Lowes remarks, "only in the laconic Latin of the documents themselves can the blooming welter of these dumbfounding registers be relished to the full."[45] In calling the Latin in these documents "laconic," Lowes seems to mean that the Latin base is inadequate to its freight of nominals, or the "blooming welter" of all that stored stuff—which of course it is. Much of the

---

43. H. M. Colvin, ed., *The History of the King's Works,* vol. 1 (London: Her Majesty's Stationery Office, 1963), pp. 200–201. As Clerk of the King's Works, Chaucer's responsibilities for these objects, and also for building materials stored at the Tower of London, Sheen, and other palaces under his purview, would have been chiefly as overseer. The position, an important one that he held for two years, was chiefly as one of the "grand accountants through whose hands large portions of the king's revenues regularly passed" (p. 196). As noted by Martin Crow and Clair C. Olson (*Chaucer Life-Records* [Oxford: Clarendon Press, 1966], p. 473), Chaucer was also employed as a surveyor, vested with responsibility to see that delegated maintenance and construction were carried out. The detail in the indentures and the emendations to the records as the job changed hands over the years suggest that holders of the position would have had to spend time on a routine basis keeping track of these objects in their comings and goings.

44. Crow and Olson, *Chaucer Life-Records,* pp. 406–8. I am grateful to John Fyler and Jeffrey Forgeng for assistance on language.

45. John Livingston Lowes, *Geoffrey Chaucer and the Development of His Genius* (Boston: Houghton Mifflin, 1934), p. 65.

welter is named in English. Most of the inventories associated with Chaucer's tenure as Clerk of the King's Works, as well as cockets surviving from his earlier and far longer tenure as Controller of the Wool Customs, are written in a trilingual, macaronic business language that superimposes English and sometimes French words over a Latin base.[46] English words, "tricked out with Latin flexions," as William Rothwell describes the lexical overlays of many government records,[47] name crafted objects for which Latin words might may not exist; they also identify objects for readers—such as accountants like Chaucer—who might be expected to have a rudimentary Latin grammar but lack sufficient vocabulary of Latin technical terms. Hence, with Latinized English words in italics [mine]: "i par *andyerns* [andirons] quorum pedes ii franguntur et devastantur," "xv clavi vocati *clergynaill*," "ii *slynges* pro le *crane*," "ii paria *wynches,* and "i *crowe* [crowbar] ferri"—and from the inventory at the Tower, "i *lathe* pro officio *carpentarii*," "C petre rotunde vocate *engynstones*," and wonderfully, "i *fryingpanne.*" Common generic terms, such as nails or iron (*ferrus*), are likely to be in Latin whereas subcategories, such as keys called clergynails and specific tools—andiron, winch, crowbar, lathe, sling, crane, and frying pan—are in English.

The language of these indentures as well as other medieval business accounts, where mixed language is the norm rather than the exception, bespeaks a marked attention to the overlay of grammars and the lexicons of labor and materials; to the relationships among language of origin and tools and manufactured products generally; things are classed not only through grammar but also through language mixing.[48] Studies of late medieval business languages have argued that they follow consistent rules. Business macaronic, the "patois of the custom house,"[49] might even be thought of as a creole, according to William Rothwell, who also argues it was a spoken language; Custance in the "Man of Law's Tale," Rothwell proposes, may be speaking such a language with the Northumbrians in her "Latin corrupt," and if so, I would also add that she is speaking a language of mercantile exchange well-suited for her role in global and specifically devotional trade.[50] Adapted to

---

46. See the "typical records" of Chaucer's work at the wool quay in Crow and Olson, *Chaucer Life Records,* pp. 176–80.

47. William Rothwell, "The Trilingual England of Geoffrey Chaucer," *Studies in the Age of Chaucer* 16 (1994): 48 [45–67].

48. Laura Wright, *Sources of London English: Medieval Thames Vocabulary* (Oxford: Clarendon Press, 1996), esp. pp. 5–15.

49. N. S. B. Gras, *The Early English Customs System* (Cambridge, MA: Harvard University Press, 1918), p. 561, cited in Wright, *Sources,* p. 6.

50. Rothwell, "Trilingual," pp. 54 and 66. As Rothwell notes in "Sugar," p. 658, the French prose version of *Fouke le Fitz Waryn* has a merchant speaking a "latyn corrupt" to the mayor,

serve the needs of a multinational, multilingual trading community, business or chancery creole also draws from English and French differentially to name different types of things. In the Durham Account Rolls, for instance, the words for farm or household implements are generally English, as they are in the Clerk of the King's Works inventories. In the Durham Rolls, things that are produced regionally, such as local fish, farm, and household tools, tend to be named in English. Examples from these Rolls include "dog-drave" [cod]; "stokfysses," "dawghrape," "smalrape," "sowdyngyrns," "grosers," "burdclath," "rostyngyrn," "hamerys," "axilnayl," "muk fork," and so on. On the other hand, fabrics, furnishings, imports, and significant architectural ornaments are named in French.[51] The predominantly French accounts of the Goldsmiths' Company make similar lexical distinctions by using French words for gold and gem work but drawing on English words to name construction materials: "iiii hokes pur le seler, rooftiel, tylpyns."[52]

Code-switching inventories such as these are tantalizing for what they may show about the sociolinguistics of accumulation and global exchange: objects named and categorized by language and also inflected by grammatical relationship to a base. For Chaucer, the flexible language mixing of the business inventories he handled as Customs Controller (1374–86) and as Clerk of the King's Works in some ways parallels the lexical innovation that in the fourteenth century had become, as Christopher Cannon, argues, a "formal principle of Middle English poetics" and a notable feature of Chaucer's poetic practice: using words already brought into English from French or Latin and changing their grammatical form.[53] In the business language that Chaucer read, wrote, and probably spoke on a regular basis for over sixteen years, lexical flexibility, translation, and innovation would seem to be basic principles of composition.

Flexibility, translation, and innovation, of course, could also describe much of Chaucer's literary writing and certainly seem apt for "The Former Age," whose lexicons of accumulation, I have suggested, make pointed uses of French and English language registers. The list-making principles of the

---

"E quanqu'il parla fust latyn corupt, mes le meir le entendy bien" (*Fouke le Fitz Waryn*, eds. Ernest J. Hathaway, Peter T. Ricketts, Charles A. Robson, and A. D. Wilshere, Anglo-Norman Text Society 26–28 [Oxford: Blackwell, 1975], p. 56 [ll. 16–17]).

51. Rothwell, "Sugar," p. 654, esp. n. 38. See also Rothwell, "Trilingual," pp. 48–49.

52. Lisa Jefferson, "The Language and Vocabulary of the Fourteenth- and Early Fifteenth-Century Records of the Goldsmiths' Company," in *Multilingualism in Later Medieval Britain,* ed. D. A. Trotter (Cambridge: D. S. Brewer, 2000), p. 185 [175–211].

53. Cannon, *Making,* p. 77. For a review of recent research on code switching in multilingual Britain, see Mary Catherine Davidson, *Medievalism, Muiltilingualism, and Chaucer* (New York: Palgrave Macmillan, 2010), pp. 81–84.

lyric may brush up against the list-making rules of Chaucer's business language in its attentiveness to tools and the products of craft as specifically English—and marked as English in a close lexical or grammatical relation to Latin or French. As William Rothwell comments of medieval business men, "we cannot afford to forget that the native Englishmen who used French and Latin habitually in their work would in all probability retain the terminology of these languages even when discussing or thinking about their work in English";[54] and as Robert Stein notes about what he calls the "polyglot reality of medieval life," "in the polyglot world, literary language is fissured not only internally by words not spoken but also continuously by always gesturing to the language of the other that inescapably inhabits our own."[55] Crossing between business language and literary language, often through translation and code switching, Chaucer the administrator/bureaucrat dealt on a daily basis with lists of tools and crafted objects that gesture to the language of the other, and even claim that language through a territorial overlay. Perhaps these gestures comprise the language story of "The Former Age": an early English Golden Age followed by a French fallen world of *taylage* and *tyrannye,* and also a present age with English and French uneasily, and imperfectly, at once.

---

54. Wright, *Sources,* p. 7.
55. Stein, "Multilingualism," p. 34.

Chapter 3

SPEAKING IMAGES?

ICONOGRAPHIC CRITICISM AND CHAUCERIAN EKPHRASIS

John M. Bowers

his essay started in Berlin as a presentation with many pictures but little formal text. Now in print, the discussion becomes all text with no pictures but rather the description of pictures according to the commonly recognized sense of ekphrasis as the verbal account of a painting, sculpture, or carved mural. Chaucer, as we shall see, went further by representing visual images "speaking out" according to the Greek etymology of *ek* (out) *phrasein* (to speak).[1] Homer initiated this practice in Book 18 of his *Iliad* when describing the shield of Achilles, and Virgil provided the paradigm for Western medieval writers in Book I of the *Aeneid* when describing what the Trojan leader saw engraved inside Juno's temple at Carthage.[2] "Late antique and medieval poetry used it lavishly," Curtius remarked of

---

1. Grant F. Scott, "The Rhetoric of Dilation: Ekphrasis and Ideology," *Word and Image* 7 (1991): 301–10. The etymology and usages of ekphrasis are examined by Claus Clüver in "Quotation, Enargeia, and the Functions of Ekphrasis," in *Pictures into Words: Theoretical and Descriptive Approaches to Ekphrasis,* eds. Valerie Robillard and Els Jongeneel (Amsterdam: VU University Press, 1998), pp. 35–52.

2. Andrew Sprague Becker, *The Shield of Achilles and the Poetics of Ekphrasis* (Lanham, MD: Rowman & Littlefield, 1995), and Michael C. J. Putnam, *Virgil's Epic Designs: Ekphrasis in the* Aeneid (New Haven, CT: Yale University Press, 1998).

ekphrasis in its rhetorical sense of an exhaustive description.[3] My own shift to the verbal aptly reflects Chaucer's late-medieval anxiety over sensually enticing pagan images, especially those surfacing in Boccaccio's Italy, as well as local anxiety in England at the end of the fourteenth century when "graven images" became the targets of Lollard iconoclasts. Chaucer's responses took many forms, including ekphrastic episodes featuring conspicuously literary, non-Christian images in a progression from *Book of the Duchess,* to the "Knight's Tale" and the *House of Fame,* and finally to the "General Prologue" of the *Canterbury Tales.*

To pose an often overlooked problem with late-medieval visual imagery, I begin with a scene from the film *In Bruges* in which Colin Farrell's character stands in front of a painting in the Groeninge Museum and stares at the details of a man being flayed alive. The camera focuses upon strips of skin being cut from his body with surgical precision, thereby creating its own moment of cinematic ekphrasis as one artistic medium represents another. Farrell moves along to the next painting, but we are left to wonder who was this victim depicted in the grisly portrait of a flaying? Viewers schooled in the basics of Christian hagiography from *The Golden Legend* would assume that the martyr flayed alive was St. Bartholomew.[4]

But the clever gallery-goer would be wrong. The picture is Gerard David's *Judgment of Cambyses: The Flaying of Sisamnes* (1498) based upon an episode from Herodotus's *Histories* (IV, 25): "Sisamnes was one of the royal judges, and as punishment for taking a bribe and perverting justice, Cambyses had him flayed."[5] As a powerful example of W. J. T. Mitchell's "relation of images, violence, and the public sphere,"[6] *The Flaying of Sisamnes* was commissioned for the Town Hall in Bruges as a warning to judges against corruption, although probably nobody simply walking into the Town Hall in 1498 would have known that the picture represented criminal execution, not Christian martyrdom, because Herodotus was almost wholly unknown in the West. Only in the third quarter of the fifteenth century had Lorenzo Valla produced

3. Ernst Robert Curtius, *European Literature and the Latin Middle Ages,* trans. Willard R. Trask (Princeton, NJ: Princeton University Press, 1953), p. 69.

4. Jacobus de Voragine, *The Golden Legend,* trans. William Granger Ryan, 2 vols. (Princeton, NJ: Princeton University Press, 1993), 2:112–13.

5. Herodotus, *The Histories,* trans. Aubrey de Sélincourt, rev. John Marincola (London: Penguin, 1996), p. 288. Different versions of the story of Cambyses were available in the Latin sources *Gesta Romanorum* and Valerius Maximus, *Facta et Dicta Memorabilia* (vi.3); see Hans J. van Miegroet, "Gerard David's *Justice of Cambyses: Exemplum Iustitiae* or Political Allegory?" *Simiolus: Netherlands Quarterly for the History of Art* 18 (1988): 116–33.

6. W. J. T. Mitchell, "The Violence of Public Art: Do the Right Thing," in *Picture Theory: Essays on Verbal and Visual Representation* (Chicago: University of Chicago Press, 1994), p. 371 [371–96].

the first Latin translation of the *Historia,* and the Aldine edition of Herodotus in the original Greek did not follow until 1502. David's painting typifies a hermeticism that resisted public understanding and almost guaranteed misreading his *Flaying of Sisamnes* as the martyrdom of St. Bartholomew.

This confusion troubles the assumption underlying the iconographic method which posited that the original audiences automatically recognized and understood these subjects. Erwin Panofsky himself paused to wonder how viewers understood symbolic meanings and even how they knew which images were symbolic. *Early Netherlandish Painting* hints at a growing crisis of signification in the later Middle Ages when long-standing systems of symbolism collided with an impulse toward greater realism. The challenge for Panofsky became detecting a picture's "concealed or disguised symbolism as opposed to open or obvious symbolism":

> If every ordinary plant, architectural detail, implement, or piece of furniture could be conceived as a metaphor, so that all forms meant to convey a symbolical idea could appear as ordinary plants, architectural details, implements, or pieces of furniture: how are we to decide where the general, 'metaphorical' transfiguration of nature ends and the actual, specific symbolism begins?[7]

His concern for the intrusion of nonsymbolic details anticipates Roland Barthes's "reality effect" in nineteenth-century fiction when superfluous objects intrude into the text without any clear narrative function, a tradition he traces back ultimately to "a craze for ekphrasis" in Alexandria during the second century AD.[8] Panofsky resolved this critical impasse with an appeal to historical resources as part of a methodology that might still fail to save us from misidentifying Gerard David's flayed man:

> We have to ask ourselves whether or not the symbolical significance of a given motif is a matter of established representational tradition (as in the case with the lilies); whether or not a symbolical interpretation can be justified by definite texts or agrees with ideas demonstrably alive in the period and presumably familiar to its artists . . . and to what extent such a symbolical interpretation is in keeping with the historical position and personal tendencies of the individual master.[9]

---

7. Erwin Panofsky, *Early Netherlandish Painting: Its Origins and Character,* 2 vols. (1953, repr. New York: Harper & Row, 1971), 1:141–42.

8. Roland Barthes, "The Reality Effect," in *The Rustle of Language,* trans. Richard Howard (New York: Hill and Wang, 1986), p. 143 [141–48].

9. Panofsky, *Early Netherlandish Painting,* 1:142–43.

Panofsky is asking: when is a lily just a lily? He continues by asking: when does a lily participate in some other local meaning demonstrably alive in the period and familiar to its audiences as well as artists? As a case in point, Chaucer's "G Prologue" to the *Legend of Good Women* introduced a new line describing the "lylye floures newe" (l. 161) adorning the garland of the God of Love. Not Marian imagery, these "new" lilies belong to the historical moment of Chaucer's revision when Richard II's marriage to the French king's daughter in 1396 prompted inclusion of French fleur-de-lis in various artworks of royal commission, such as the Wilton Diptych.[10]

D. W. Robertson in his *Preface to Chaucer* did much to import the iconographic method to literary studies while making scant allowance for "ambiguities, situational ironies, tensions in figurative language," just as he ignored social turmoil such as that following the 1395 posting of the *Twelve Conclusions of the Lollards* when he insisted upon the "quiet hierarchies" of late-medieval England.[11] He was satisfied to describe allegorical understandings as *commonplaces* automatically understood by medieval viewers but recoverable by us only by historical research.[12] These symbolic representations became "conventionally established areas of meaning" even when encountered in realistic-looking works such as the *Canterbury Tales*.[13] Robertson and other critics who employed this iconographic method—including myself in my earliest scholarly publication on Chaucer's *Troilus*[14]—proceeded without pondering how Chaucer's readers would have recognized figural meanings without access to the *Patrologia Latina* and how they suppressed anxiety over pagan idols like Troy's image of Pallas Minerva.

Literary scholars as well as art historians have assumed that medieval spectators operated with an unproblematic understanding of the visual imagery saturating their textual environments. The title *Speaking Images* epitomizes confidence in the quasi-psychic communication between writer and readers already claimed by the volume's dedicatee V. A. Kolve in his "Introduction" to *Chaucer and the Imagery of Narrative* (1984):

---

10. John M. Bowers, *The Politics of* Pearl: *Court Poetry in the Age of Richard II* (Cambridge: D. S. Brewer, 2001), pp. 179–80.

11. D. W. Robertson, Jr., *A Preface to Chaucer: Studies in Medieval Perspective* (Princeton, NJ: Princeton University Press, 1962), p. 51.

12. Robertson, *Preface to Chaucer,* p. 52.

13. Robertson, *Preface to Chaucer,* p. 242.

14. John M. Bowers, "How Criseyde Falls in Love," in *The Expansion and Transformations of Courtly Literature,* eds. N. B. Smith and J. T. Snow (Athens: University of Georgia Press, 1980), pp. 141–55.

I make no claim that Chaucer looked upon any of these pictures, only that he would have understood them, and that he could have counted on some substantial part of his audience to share with him that skill.[15]

Kolve's *Telling Images: Chaucer and the Imagery of Narrative II* (2009) continues expressing his assurance in this shared recognition and easy comprehension:

I think of Chaucer's first audiences as bringing to his art not only a widely shared habit of visual imagining, responsive to both oral and written texts, but also a storehouse of images popular, courtly, and religious in nature— traditional images *known from poems and tales and sermons as well as from the visual arts*—and ready to deepen and enrich their response to narrative.[16]

This appeal to "traditional images" partakes of Robertson's confidence in commonplaces for explaining how original audiences possessed ready access to meanings, along with the insistence that Chaucer's readers "almost certainly knew" these prior texts and "would certainly have understood" these time-honored images.[17]

But for those of us who labor diligently in the classroom to instruct our students in the basics of our own culture, we cannot help wondering whether medieval audiences, too, needed teachers to educate them in this sophisticated and often obscure pictorial language. Tolkien made the same point that specific sorts of learning were needed for *Beowulf*'s first readers: "They were no more born naturally into an Englishman of the seventh or eighth centuries, by simple virtue of being an 'Anglo-Saxon,' than ready-made knowledge of poetry and history is inherited at birth by modern children."[18] Exactly how much training was required to learn the meanings of such images, then, and where did readers go to become proficient in this hermetic system of signs and symbols?

Chaucer's pilgrims never reach Canterbury Cathedral where they would have been confronted with a great richness of religious imagery, but sometime

---

15. V. A. Kolve, "Introduction" in *Chaucer and the Imagery of Narrative: The First Five Canterbury Tales* (Stanford: Stanford University Press, 1984), p. 8 [1–8]. Thomas L. Reed, Jr., suggested the Festschrift's title to Robert F. Yeager and Charlotte C. Morse, eds., *Speaking Images: Essays in Honor of V. A. Kolve* (Asheville, NC: Pegasus Press, 2001).

16. V. A. Kolve, "Preface" in *Telling Images: Chaucer and the Imagery of Narrative II* (Stanford: Stanford University Press, 2009), p. xvi [xv–xxvii] [emphasis in original text].

17. Kolve, *Telling Images*, pp. xxiii–xxiv.

18. J. R. R. Tolkien, "*Beowulf*: The Monsters and the Critics," in *The Monsters and the Critics and Other Essays*, ed. Christopher Tolkien (London: Harper Collins 2006), p. 27 [5–48].

early in the fifteenth century, an anonymous imitator brought the original characters to their sacred destination in the work entitled *The Canterbury Interlude* in its most recent edition. Yet some of these medieval pilgrims show real difficulty in deciphering the stained-glass windows near the shrine of St. Thomas Becket:

> The Pardoner and the Miller and other lewde sotes
> Sought hemselff in the chirch, right as lewd gotes,
> Pyred fast and poured highe oppon the glase,
> Counterfeting gentilmen, the armes for to *blase*, *identify*
> Diskyveryng fast the peyntour, and for the story *mourned* *mused over*
> And *ared* also—right as rammes horned! *interpreted*
> "He bereth a balstaff," quod the toon, "and els a rakes ende."
> "Thow faillest," quod the Miller, "thowe hast nat wel thy mynde.
> It is a spere, yf thowe canst se, with a prik tofore
> To bussh adown his enmy and thurh the sholder bore."
> "Pese!" quod the Hoost of Southwork. "Let stond the wyndow glased.
> Goth up and doth yeur offerynge. Ye semeth half amased."
> (*Canterbury Interlude*, ll. 147–58)[19]

This nameless poet mocks these low-life pilgrims for interpreting "straight as a ram's horn" because the stained-glass figure that draws their attention offers the least possible challenge to understanding. Still visible today, the nearly naked laborer digging with a shovel, itself hard to confuse with a spear, clearly represents the fallen Adam living by the sweat of his brow. The twelfth-century image is actually labeled ADAM in large lettering to dispel any uncertainty.[20] Though we might not expect much exegetic insight from the Miller, the Pardoner's ignorance is more ludicrous in terms of his presumed literacy and routine commerce in relics and sacred images.[21]

Even allowing for its satirical contents, this scene deserves attention for undercutting quite intentionally, I believe, the late-medieval English defense of imagery as books for unlettered men.[22] The *Twelve Conclusions of the Lol-*

---

19. Previously known at *Tale of Beryn*, this text has been newly edited in John M. Bowers, ed., The Canterbury Tales: *Fifteenth-Century Continuations and Additions* (Kalamazoo, MI: TEAMS Medieval Institute Publications, 1992), p. 64.

20. David K. Coley, "'Withyn a temple ymad of glas': Glazing, Glossing, and Patronage in Chaucer's *House of Fame*," *Chaucer Review* 45 (2010): 71–72 [59–84]; fig. 1 shows the window with Adam and his spade.

21. Robyn Malo characterizes the Pardoner as a fraudulent custodian of relics in *Relics and Writing in Late Medieval England* (Toronto: University of Toronto Press, 2013), pp. 125–59.

22. Priscilla Heath Barnum, ed., *Dives and Pauper*, Early English Text Society, Original

lards responded by condemning visual imagery as "the book of error for the uneducated."[23] Not targeting actual relics, Lollards objected to the superstitious worship directed to statues, the wealth wasted through donations, and generally the lavish craftsmanship devoted to these shrines costing large sums that might better have helped the poor.[24]

Increasingly virulent during the last two decades of the fourteenth century, Lollard iconophobia lurks somewhere in the background of Chaucer's own ekphrastic episodes, which in response offered Classical rather than Christian images for avoiding any suggestion of idolatry except for the benighted pagans in the "Knight's Tale" and *Troilus and Criseyde.*[25] James Heffernan notices the poet's neglect of the visual precisely where readers would most expect it in the *House of Fame:* "Chaucerian ekphrasis can be oddly nonpictorial: not just inattentive to features such as composition or to the representational friction between medium and referent, but sometimes less imagistic than descriptions of what his narrators see in the would-be 'real' world."[26]

Instead, Chaucer's passages come loaded with didactic content preempting complaints that pictures could not communicate the finer points of instruction.[27] Even Lollard ekphrasis condemning the lavish architecture of London's Blackfriars in the *Pierce the Ploughman's Crede* (ca. 1393)[28] surpasses

---

Series 275 (London: Oxford University Press, 1976), p. 82: "þey been ordeynyd to been a tokene and a book to þe lewyd peple, þat þey moun redyn in ymagerye and peynture þat clerkys redyn in boke."

23. Anne Hudson, ed., *Selections from English Wycliffite Writings* (Cambridge: Cambridge University Press, 1978), p. 27: "þis forbodin ymagerie be a bok of errour to þe lewid puple."

24. Hudson, *Selections,* p. 27: "þe pilgrimage, preyeris, and offringis made to blynde rodys and to dede ymages of tre and of ston ben ner of kin to ydolatrie and fer from almesse dede."

25. For detailed analyses of Lollard iconophobia and its impact on Chaucer, see Sarah Stanbury, "Visualizing," in *A Companion to Chaucer,* ed. Peter Brown (Oxford: Blackwell, 2000), pp. 459–79; and by the same author, *The Visual Object of Desire in Late Medieval England* (Philadelphia: University of Pennsylvania Press, 2008), esp. pp. 33–75 and pp. 95–116. An insightful discussion of Lollard responses to religious images is offered by Shannon Gayk, *Image, Text, and Religious Reform in Fifteenth-Century England* (Cambridge: Cambridge University Press, 2010), pp. 1–44. For the particular role of the theater and the tournament in ekphrastic negotiations of the visual and the verbal, see Andrew James Johnston, "Ekphrasis in the *Knight's Tale,*" in *Rethinking the New Medievalism,* eds. R. Howard Bloch, Alison Calhoun, Jacqueline Cerquiglini-Toulet, Joachim Küpper, and Jeanette Patterson (Baltimore: Johns Hopkins University Press, 2014), pp. 181–97.

26. James A. W. Heffernan, "Ekphrasis and Rape from Chaucer to Spenser," in *Museum of Words: The Poetics of Ekphrasis from Homer to Ashbery* (Chicago: University of Chicago Press, 1993), p. 62 [61–74].

27. Anne Hudson, *The Premature Reformation: Wycliffite Texts and Lollard History* (Oxford: Clarendon, 1988), pp. 306–7.

28. Helen Barr, ed., *The Piers Plowman Tradition* (London: Dent, 1993), pp. 68–70 (ll. 160–215).

in visual detail Chaucer's columns in the palace of Fame, such as the iron pillar supporting Troy's renown:

> Ful wonder hy on a piler
> Of yren, he, the gret Omer;
> And with him Dares and Tytus
> Before, and eke he Lollius,
> And Guydo eke de Columpnis,
> And Engliyssh Gaufride eke, ywis;
> And ech of these, as have I joye,
> Was busy for to bere up Troye.
> So hevy therof was the fame
> That for to bere hyt was no game.
> But yet I gan ful wel espie
> Betwex hem was a litil envye.
> Oon seyde that Omer made lyes,
> Feynynge in his poetries,
> And was to Grekes favorable;
> Therfor held he hyt but fable.
> (*HF*, ll. 1465–80)[29]

Chaucer's iron pillar is translated back into the text *as text* without images but rather with the naming of authors (perhaps labeled, perhaps intuitively recognized), the description of the strain of holding up the great weight, the drama of envy among these writers, and finally a "speaking image" who accuses Homer of fabricating his history to make it favorable to the Greeks, all without any truly pictorial ingredients. The most mysterious figure has always been the "Engliyssh Gaufride," now thought to be Geoffrey Chaucer himself, whose *Troilus and Criseyde* upholds the fame of Troy in English. Quite probably it is the self-projected image of the dreamer who accuses Homer—in English—of falsifying history by favoring the Greeks.

THE *BOOK OF THE DUCHESS*

The dream vision and the mystical vision formed the mainstream of medieval ekphrasis, and although Chaucer was an exact contemporary of Julian of

---

29. All citations come from *The Riverside Chaucer*, gen. ed. Larry D. Benson (Boston: Houghton Mifflin Co., 1987).

Norwich, he steadily avoided anything resembling the religious visions that troubled the recluse's efforts at making sense of what she saw.[30] The visionary genre is essentially ekphrastic, after all, because the poet uses words for describing what he saw while sleeping, and often his dream landscapes are crowded with artifacts both sculptural and literary that in turn require description. "Whether images generate texts in descriptive ekphrasis, or texts generate images in this sort of intertextual visualization," Jessica Brantley writes of Mitchell's *imagetexts* in dream visions, "oscillations between word and picture provide the mechanism through which these imagetexts work"[31]—as indeed Chaucerian dream visions like *Book of the Duchess* begin with the dreamer reading a book before he falls asleep and sees images.

I begin tracing this desire to make literary images speak for themselves in Chaucer's career by starting with the example of "mute ekphrasis" in *Book of the Duchess* (ll. 321–34). The dreamer finds himself in a bedchamber, bombarded with visual images "wel depeynted" in stained-glass windows showing the whole history of Troy starting with the reign of King Priam and continuing to the arrival of Trojan refugees in Italy:

> For hooly al the story of Troye
> Was in the glasynge ywroght thus,
> Of Ector and of kyng Priamus,
> Of Achilles and of kyng Lamedon,
> And eke of Medea and of Jason,
> Of Paris, Eleyne, and of Lavyne.
> (*BD*, ll. 326–31)

Madeline Caviness considers monumental window cycles not simply designed for religious instruction but rather "transformed into popular romance,"[32] although Chaucer's windows are oddly nonpictorial for achieving any of these ends. We are not actually shown portraits of Hector, Priam, and the other worthies; we are not told about the spatial arrangements of panels within windows; and we get no sense of a historical narrative beyond the naming of characters. And how does the dreamer even know this jumble

---

30. Claire Barbetti, "Inhuman Ekphrasis: The 40(plus)-Year Ekphrasis of Julian of Norwich," in *Ekphrastic Medieval Visions: A New Discussion in Inter-Art Theory* (New York: Palgrave Macmillan, 2011), pp. 123–40.

31. Jessica Brantley, "Vision, Image, Text," in *Middle English*, ed. Paul Strohm (Oxford: Oxford University Press, 2007), p. 319 [313–34].

32. Madeline H. Caviness, "Biblical Stories in Windows: Were They Bibles for the Poor?" in Bernard Levy, ed., *The Bible in the Middle Ages: Its Influence on Literature and Art* (Binghamton, NY: Medieval & Renaissance Texts & Studies, 1992), p. 147 [103–47].

of names? Perhaps there were labels like those in the window at Canterbury Cathedral—or perhaps not—in which case he enacts the wish-fulfilling fantasy of knowing their names in that instinctive manner presumed by iconographic criticism.

Unlike W. H. Auden's meditation upon Brueghel's painting in his "Musée des Beaux Arts," Chaucer offers a "notional ekphrasis" describing an imagined artwork, not an actual one, although chivalric figures of this sort did sometimes intrude into sacred spaces.[33] For instance, Gloucester Cathedral was remodeled to accommodate a massive window program commemorating Edward III's victory at Crécy.[34] David Coley has written at length about the poet's engagements with this extremely expensive artistic medium: "The medieval glazier ideally produced long-lasting works, durable and vibrant texts that communicated vital religious instruction to an unlettered laity, memorialized window patrons, venerated worthy figures both secular and sacred, and illuminated—architecturally and spiritually—the space into which they were integrated."[35] Not artworks on pedestals, these pictures in the *Book of the Duchess* are luxury decorations contributing to the high-status lifestyle that extends to the deer hunt and the extravagant mourning of the Black Knight. Coley continues about aristocratic patronage for Chaucer no less than for the glaziers: "Stained glass becomes not only an eminently logical expressive medium, but an ekphrastic recapitulation of the *Book of the Duchess* itself, an authorial nod toward the memorial function of the poem and a reinscription of the circumstances of its composition."[36]

The poem's figural procession overflows from Virgil's *Aeneid,* with reference to Jason and Medea from his favorite author Ovid, whose account of Ceyx and Alcione from the *Metamorphoses* the dreamer was reading when he fell asleep.[37] Virgil had presented Roman imperial history as a continuation of Trojan history, and the twelfth-century Geoffrey of Monmouth's *History of the British Kings* took this narrative of colonial settlement as a template for the British foundation myth, which Chaucer's anonymous contemporary retraced in the first stanza of *Sir Gawain and the Green Knight.*[38] The Painted Chamber in the Palace of Westminster was well known for its scenes from

---

33. The term "notional ekphrasis" comes from John Hollander, "The Poetics of Ekphrasis," *Word & Image* 4 (1988): 209–19.

34. Robertson, *Preface to Chaucer,* pp. 214–19.

35. Coley, "'Withyn a temple ymad of glas,'" p. 62.

36. Coley, "'Withyn a temple ymad of glas,'" p. 75.

37. Ovid treated this legend of Medea in his *Heroides* (no. XII) and *Tristia* (Book III, no. ix) as well as his *Metamorphoses* (Book VII, lines 1–606).

38. Sylvia Frederico, *New Troy: Fantasies of Empire in the Late Middle Ages* (Minneapolis: University of Minnesota Press, 2003), pp. 1–28, and John M. Bowers, *An Introduction to the Gawain Poet* (Gainesville: University Press of Florida, 2012), pp. 15–17.

the Bible,[39] but Chaucer envisages instead a program of pagan history as if already registering objections from reformers against the motives for commissioning stained-glass images. William Langland was not alone in criticizing wealthy individuals who would "glase þe gable and graue ther name."[40] What Sarah Stanbury has called the "materialist critique of images" in *Piers Plowman* (and elsewhere) focuses upon patrons whose imaged-filled windows became "exclusionary property" laying claims to intercessional privileges on behalf of their souls only.[41] In this regard, it is worth noticing that the windows in the *Book of the Duchess* do not contain the heraldry of John of Gaunt or any other named patron.

In addition to these figures from the Trojan past, the bedchamber's painted walls contained the complete text of the *Roman de la Rose* with glosses (*BD*, ll. 332–34). Medieval artists routinely produced what Peter Wagner calls *iconotexts* or "the use of (by way of reference or allusion, in an explicit or implicit way) an image in the text or vice versa."[42] The Apocalypse murals from the Charterhouse of Westminster Abbey show such pictures framed top and bottom by scriptural texts. This conjunction of words and pictures would later serve Reginald Pecock in his argument that these images were "seeable rememorative signs" affirming doctrines already known from religious writings.[43]

Medieval writers typically worked from their memories of things represented in books rather than from any mimesis of the things themselves, recalling, sorting, and cementing in place what had been read, just as Chaucer has incorporated this French poem into the walls of the bedroom in the dream vision.[44] He may also have been making a joke about his own *Romaunt*

---

39. Michael Norman Salda, "Pages from History: The Medieval Palace of Westminster as a Source for the Dreamer's Chamber in *Book of the Duchess*," *Chaucer Review* 27 (1992): 111–25.

40. George Russell and George Kane, eds., *Piers Plowman: The C Version*, (London: Athlone, 1997), p. 245 (C.3.52); Langland continues his harangue at greater length in C.3.68–74.

41. Sarah Stanbury, "The Vivacity of Images: St. Katherine, Knighton's Lollards, and the Breaking of Idols," in *Images, Idolatry, and Iconoclasm in Late Medieval England*, eds. Jeremy Dimmick, James Simpson, and Nicolette Zeeman (Oxford: Oxford University Press, 2002), pp. 145–47 [131–50].

42. Peter Wagner, "Introduction: Ekphrasis, Iconotexts, and Intermediality—the State(s) of the Art(s)," in *Icons—Texts—Iconotexts: Essays on Ekphrasis and Intermediality*, ed. Peter Wagner (Berlin: de Gruyter, 1996), p. 15 [1–40].

43. Margaret Aston, "The Defence of Images," in *England's Iconoclasts* (Oxford: Clarendon, 1988), pp. 148–49 [143–54].

44. Mary Carruthers, *The Craft of Thought: Meditation, Rhetoric, and the Making of Images, 400–1200*, Cambridge Studies in Medieval Literature (Cambridge: Cambridge University Press, 1998), p. 3; see also Lorraine Kochanske Stock, "'Peynted . . . text and [visual] gloss': Primitivism, Ekphrasis, and Pictorial Intertextuality in the Dreamers' Bedrooms of *Roman de la Rose* and *Book of the Duchess*," in *Essays on Chaucer and Chaucerians in Memory of*

translated from French to English as here it is translated from one medium to another; his English *Romaunt* might also have been a "gloss" expounding the meaning of the original version. In terms of ekphrasis, the poet is certainly making a joke when claiming all 21,750 lines of the *Rose* were inscribed upon the walls, but without any of the images so often found in deluxe manuscripts of this vernacular classic.[45] If anything, the bedchamber threatens the nightmarish breakdown of the viewer's expectations as images appear in the windows without texts, but a huge amount of text crowds the walls without pictures.

In Chaucer's first major English poem, the process of *translatio studii* begins with this ekphrastic episode importing the wartime characters from Classical history and the courtly themes from the French tradition. The *Book of the Duchess* also establishes a norm for Chaucerian ekphrasis by representing artworks not as freestanding, autonomous aesthetic objects. The stained glass and painted texts remain merely decorative. Elaborate architectural details project an aesthetic surplus elsewhere in Chaucer's writings, as if acknowledging the fringe, nonutilitarian nature of his own poetic art.

The Trojan figures and the *Rose* verses anticipate the chivalric identity of the Black Knight as a man who fights and a man who loves his lady. Chaucer's word-pictures of war and amatory aggression recall Mitchell's question—"Is public art inherently violent, or a provocation to violence?"[46]—and this early dream vision invites us to ponder how the poet steadily commemorates forms of knightly violence in all of his ekphrastic scenes while at the same time using artworks to enclose and neutralize these threats. Chaucer's merely decorative framework creates a strategy for containing the debate about images that would erupt in Reformation England, when Chaucer himself would be forced to take sides, as the reigning poet, and his literary authority was pressed into service on behalf of the iconoclasts.

THE KNIGHT'S TALE

The three temples of Venus, Mars, and Diana in the "Knight's Tale" (*CT* I, ll. 1881–2437) derive from Boccaccio's *Teseida,* a source that Chaucer would have recognized as closer to an authentic pagan past than the mythography

---

Emerson Brown, Jr., eds. T. L. Burton and John F. Plummer (Provo, UT: Chaucer Studio Press, 2005), pp. 97–114.

45. John V. Fleming, *The* Roman de la Rose: *A Study in Allegory and Iconography* (Princeton, NJ: Princeton University Press, 1969), surveys the rich tradition of illuminations.

46. Mitchell, "Violence of Public Art," p. 378.

previously available to him in the *Roman de la Rose,* although these shrines also invoked aspects of fourteenth-century material culture and religious controversy. They had been produced by the "portreyour" and "kervere of ymages" hired by Duke Theseus as a royal patron (ll. 1895–1905), and within Michael Camille's taxonomy of idols—painted or sculpted, on pedestals or on pillars, singly or in groups—these images come closest to the freestanding statues that attracted fiercest hostility from Lollards.[47] As with the Trojan pictures in the *Book of the Duchess,* these memorial images became statements of historical affiliation and staked claims upon the cultural past, all freighted with anxiety because that past was pagan: "The figure of the idol—the god, the mythological person, the naked body, or simply the concrete artifact—articulates the anxieties of a highly archival culture about its own textual inheritances, especially the non-Christian ones."[48] David Wallace is certainly right that "medieval poets were thus nervous of the pagan riches in their midst,"[49] but Chaucer would have grown doubly nervous during the last dozen years of his career when London Lollards became bolder in their attacks upon all images.

Chaucer animates these temple scenes in the process of describing them, making background figures actually move in a manner beyond the pictorial medium, so different from the frozen, speechless figures in the temple of Venus in *The Parliament of Fowls,* for example, but dangerously close to the moving, speaking, bleeding statues of saints that haunted the fantasies of fourteenth-century iconoclasts.[50] Henry Knighton's two Lollards, for example, chopped the head off a statue of St. Katherine to see if she would bleed, using the wood for their cook fire when she did not.[51]

The Knight as pilgrim-narrator seems haunted by a history of violence, remembering dead comrades as well as scenes of rape and slaughter as his temple scenes become "the dark storehouse of the Knight's mnemonic

---

47. Michael Camille, *The Gothic Idol: Ideology and Image-Making in Medieval Art* (Cambridge: Cambridge University Press, 1989), esp. pp. 27–49, and Margaret Aston, "Image-Worship," in *England's Iconoclasts,* pp. 109–10 [104–24].

48. Nicolette Zeeman, "The Idol of the Text," in *Images, Idolatry, and Iconoclasm in Late Medieval England: Textuality and the Visual Image,* eds. Jeremy Dimmick, James Simpson and Nicolette Zeeman (Oxford: Oxford University Press, 2002), p. 46 [43–62].

49. David Wallace, "Afterword" in *Images, Idolatry, and Iconoclasm,* p. 208 [207–14].

50. Aston, *England's Iconoclasts,* pp. 235–36; see also Aston, "Graven Images: More Realism, More Danger?" in *England's Iconoclasts,* pp. 401–08. Zeeman, "The Idol of the Text," pp. 58–59, remarks that the gods in the *Parliament of Fowls* are not idols exactly, but personifications or figures striking iconic poses, frozen in sexual desires permanently deferred.

51. Stanbury, "The Vivacity of Images," p. 140, offers a fine account of this episode. Like St. Katherine, Chaucer's St. Cecilia is martyred specifically for her refusal to worship images.

gallery."[52] Besides the orgy of bloodshed on view in the temple of Mars, even the iconography of Diana as goddess of childbirth includes a violent struggle with the audible cry of "Help!" added to the physical movement, denoted by the verb *gan* for ongoing action beyond the capability of statuary or mural painting:

> A woman travaillynge was hire beforn;
> But for hir child so longe was unborn,
> For pitously Lucyna gan she calle
> And seyde, "Help, for thou mayst best of alle!"
> (*CT* I, ll. 2083–86)

Palamon, Arcite and Emelye pray to their separate planetary deities, and each of the two young knights receives an encouraging reply: the one that he will receive victory from Mars and the other that he will receive his lady-love from Venus. Emelye's prayers are answered with much more ambiguous signs from Diana:

> And at the brondes ende out ran anon
> As it were blody dropes many oon;
> For which so soore agast was Emelye
> That she was wel ny mad and gan to crye,
> For she ne wiste what it signified . . .
> (*CT* I, ll. 2339–43)

Apparently blood will be spilled, but will it be bloodshed at the tournament? Chaucerians are schooled to read the drops of blood as prophecy that the Amazon princess will lose her virginity,[53] although these signs elude Emelye, who only weeps in her confusion.

In response to this lady's failure to understand visual signs, Diana animates her own statue as a "speaking image" to explain that Emelye must marry one of the two Thebans (*CT* I, ll. 2351–57). But rather than learn which man she must marry, the Amazon princess hurries home without ever receiv-

---

52. Brooke Hunter, "*Remenants* of Things Past: Memory and the *Knight's Tale*," *Exemplaria* 23 (2011): 140 [126–46]. Robert Epstein, "'With many a floryn he the hewes boghte': Ekphrasis and Symbolic Violence in the 'Knight's Tale,'" *Philological Quarterly* 85 (2006): 51 [49–68], agrees that the Knight's ekphrasis reminds readers of episodes from his dark, violent past.

53. Larry D. Benson, "The 'Queynte' Punnings of Chaucer's Critics," in *Contradictions: From Beowulf to Chaucer,* eds. Theodore M. Andersson and Stephen A. Barney (Aldershot: Scolar Press, 1995), pp. 217–42.

ing the explicit message promised by the goddess. John Fleming has argued that the poet's vocabulary of *ambage* or "ambiguity" provided the philosophical theme in these pre-Christian narratives, because pagans like Emelye were tragically ill-equipped to grasp the meanings of signs such as the "blody dropes."[54] Only a Christian spectator like the dreamer in the *House of Fame* can understand the moral content of a pagan tragedy like Queen Dido's.

THE *HOUSE OF FAME*

Book 1 of the *House of Fame* offers Chaucer's most sustained deployment of ekphrasis as "speaking images" to dramatize the potential for visual representations identifying themselves and disclosing their thoughts and feelings.[55] As a medley of episodes, this dream vision stands as the author's most profound meditation on the relationship between the verbal and visual arts, extending what he had learned from the touchstone passage in Book 1 of Virgil's *Aeneid* when Aeneas gazed at murals in Juno's temple depicting scenes from the Trojan War.[56] That Chaucer's temple of Venus is constructed entirely of glass suggests the brittleness of love and fragility of literary posterity, although a medieval reader might also think about the durability of stained glass as a medium for long-term recollection, like the windows preserving the renown of Troy in the *Book of the Duchess*.

Here Virgil's Latin epic is first translated into English before further translated into visual scenes:

I fond that on a wall ther was
Thus writen on a table of bras:

---

54. John V. Fleming, *Classical Imitation and Interpretation in Chaucer's* Troilus (Lincoln: University of Nebraska Press, 1990), in his chapters "Ambages; Or, The Genealogy of Ambiguity," pp. 45–71, and "Idols of the Prince," pp. 72–154.

55. My placement of *House of Fame* third in discussion follows Chaucer's order of composition since (1) the "Knight's Tale" was composed during the mid-1380s in the version called *The Love of Palamon and Arcite* in the "Prologue" to the *Legend of Good Women* and (2) the *House of Fame* was written in the late 1380s after *Troilus* and after the first draft of *Palamon and Arcite* as well. For revised chronology, see John M. Bowers, "The Naughty Bits: Dating Chaucer's *House of Fame* and *Legend of Good Women*," in *The Medieval Python: The Purposive and Provocative Work of Terry Jones, Essays Presented on the Occasion of His Seventieth Birthday*, ed. R. F. Yeager and Toshiyuki Takamiya (New York: Palgrave Macmillan, 2012), pp. 105–17.

56. Charles Russell Stone, "'And sodeynly he wax therwith astoned': Virgilian Emotion and Images of Troy in Chaucer's *Troilus*," *Review of English Studies* 64 (2013): 574–93, argues that the ekphrasis of the *Aeneid* haunted Chaucer's memories of the fall of Troy.

"I wol now synge, yif I kan,
The armes and also the man . . ."
(*HF*, ll. 141–44)

Imagining the sort of ornamental brass favored by wealthy patrons for memo-rializing themselves in churches, Chaucer confuses the reader whether his dreamer sees words or pictures, or both, as these tableaux come alive with action and audible speech, in effect collapsing the binaries of the two art forms. "The notoriously ambiguous status of this narrative both 'seen' and 'written,'" says Nicolette Zeeman, "is an excellent instance of the text under-stood in imagistic terms—as a graven image or idol."[57]

Greek and Roman practices had long established an interdependence between these "sister arts" by including pictures in their books and basing sculptural works like the Pergamum Altar on literary texts.[58] Ancient temples doubled as museums that kept alive cultural memory, and medieval churches continued to function as elaborate memory-images, fostering the recollection of worthy patrons as well as saints. Chaucer explores ekphrasis as the most iconophilic mode of literary representation while tactfully avoiding outright Christian iconography even when describing these murals as church art: "As I saugh graven in this chirche" (*HF*, l. 473). However much the temple resem-bles a Gothic church with its time-honored images, it is a church without the relics that stirred Wycliffite criticism. And however opulent the shrines, they are not reliquaries, except in the sense of preserving the literary remains of Virgil himself—an important consideration for Chaucer as an author aspir-ing for his own "canonization" within later literary tradition.

Unlike the shrine of Venus in the "Knight's Tale," these programmatic pictures resemble more closely medieval church art while safely substituting literary figures for saintly martyrs. After perhaps seeing actual Roman statu-ary during his travels in Italy, Chaucer engages in cultural archeology without any actual digging. His "museumizing imagination" comes into play when the dreamer finds himself in a building that functions as a repository for art-works as ancient relics imported from abroad for domestic consumption.[59] Looking at an artwork is always, for Chaucer, looking into the past. As the site of an aesthetic experience likened to religious wonder when the murals

---

57. Zeeman, "The Idol of the Text," p. 48.

58. J. J. Pollitt, *Art in the Hellenistic Age* (Cambridge: Cambridge University Press, 1986), p. 107.

59. Benedict Anderson, "The Museum," in *Imagined Communities*, rev. ed. (London and New York: Verso, 2006), p. 178 [178–85].

come alive,[60] the temple of Venus becomes a private space where the dreamer experiences a moment of stillness for the purposes of artistic homage, commentary, and self-discovery. Here Chaucer's dreamer becomes the prototype of "the poet in the museum" in the later English tradition.[61]

Chaucer nonetheless confounds any straightforward understanding of what precisely the dreamer sees, first claiming that he found an English rendering of the opening lines of the *Aeneid* "writen on a table of bras" (*HF*, l. 142) and then that he "sawgh" the destruction of Troy and heard the Trojans crying "Allas and welaway!" (*HF*, l. 170). Chaucer continues with a mixed-media experience as the dreamer *sees* speech synaesthetically: "Ther sawgh I grave how Eneas / Tolde Dido every caas" (*HF*, ll. 253–54). Does he read a text, or does he actually see Aeneas talking? Successive scenes are again animated by repeated use of *gan* to indicate ongoing actions:

> How she *gan* hym comforte thoo (l. 235)
> She *gan* to wringe hir handes two (l. 299)
> In suche words *gan* to pleyne (l. 311)

Like nearly all readers throughout the Virgilian tradition, Chaucer focuses upon the episode of Aeneas's escape from Carthage and Dido's anguish as an abandoned lover, almost as a retort to Lollard objection that dead images "neither thirsteth nor hungereth nor felleth any coldness neither suffereth disease, for they may not feel nor see nor hear nor speak."[62] Dido does indeed feel and speaks her feelings. The dream's spectral murals become what Margaret Aston has termed "idols of the mind" as part of image-centered affective devotion for which Chaucer provides a secular counterpart when picturing Dido as a love-martyr.[63] Centuries ahead of John Keats in his *Ode on a Grecian Urn*, Virgil had already provided a model for meditating upon the relations between human misery and the artistic medium representing that misery. Aeneas weeps at the images he sees at Carthage, but the images themselves seem to weep for his mortal sufferings: "Sunt lacrimae rerum et mentem mortalia tangunt" (*Aeneid* I, l. 462).[64]

---

60. Shannon Gayk, "'To wonder upon this thing': Chaucer's Prioress's Tale," *Exemplaria* 22 (2010): 138–56.

61. Barbara K. Fischer, *Museum Mediations: Refining Ekphrasis in Contemporary American Poetry* (New York: Routledge, 2006), p. 3.

62. Aston quotes from an anonymous treatise on the Decalogues in *England's Iconoclasts*, p. 119.

63. Margaret Aston, "Idols of the Mind," in *England's Iconoclasts* (Oxford: Clarendon, 1988), pp. 452–66.

64. Virgil, *Eclogues, Georgics, Aeneid 1–6*, ed. Henry R. Fairclough, rev. G. P. Goold

Yet for all of the pathos of Dido's desertion and death, Chaucer elicits relatively little emotion, first by slighting the visual, then by abbreviating the original text, and finally by retreating into the bibliographical. The dreamer has little affective engagement with what he witnesses, his emotional life as arid as the desert that he finds outside the temple. With the "refusal of empathy" that Bruce Holsinger finds central in writings criticizing the financial waste of image-making,[65] Chaucer's narrator creates emotional distance by dryly citing his sources. If readers wants to know more about the death of Dido, they should consult "Virgile in Eneydos / Or the Epistle of Ovyde" (ll. 378–79); and if curious for further information about the underworld, they should read "On Virgile or on Claudian / Or Daunte" (ll. 449–50).

His version of iconoclasm is not breaking images but ignoring them. This retreat was shared by others. "With mounting intensity, Lollard polemic was denouncing the use of visual stimuli in favor of textual authority."[66] Ekphrasis remains the most narcissistic trick of literary discourse by substituting its own scripted enticements for the original *objet d'art,* and Chaucer's extended ekphrasis exposes the dreamer's self-regard as a reader of books by reverting to the literary texts from which these animated images ultimately derived. Like the four textual authorities named above, Chaucer harbors an unspoken hope for his own memory to endure and outlive him.

When the past speaks to Chaucer, it speaks in English. The ekphrastic transformation from Latin poetry to English-speaking images also permits a selective focus amounting to the sort of censorship already evident in the original. Chaucer's interest in the historical character of Troilus would have drawn his attention to Virgil's vague account of the Trojan prince's death— "Infelix puer atque impar congressus Achilli" (*Aeneid* I, l. 475). Servius had alerted medieval readers to the Roman author's bowdlerization of Achilles' homoerotic assault: "led by the love of Troilus, Achilles offered him the doves that made him pause with delight to hold them; then seized by Achilles, Troilus perished in his embraces—but the poet changed this disgraceful scene in his heroic song."[67] Chaucer's extensive research into the Troilus story makes this omission from his *Aeneid* précis noteworthy, reversing what Stephen Cheeke has identified as the greater explicitness of the textual

---

(Cambridge, MA: Loeb Classical Library, Harvard University Press, 1999), p. 294.

65. Bruce Holsinger, "Lollard Ekphrasis: Situated Aesthetics and Literary History," *Journal of Medieval and Early Modern Studies* 35 (2005): 75 [67–89].

66. Stanbury, "Vivacity of Images," p. 135.

67. John M. Bowers, "'Beautiful as Troilus': Richard II, Chaucer's Troilus, and Figures of (Un)Masculinity," in *Men and Masculinities in Chaucer's* Troilus and Criseyde, eds. Tison Pugh and Marcia Smith Marzec, Chaucer Studies 38 (Cambridge: D. S. Brewer, 2008), pp. 21–22 [9–27].

over the visual: "The poem *knows* something or *tells* something that had been held back by the silent image."[68] By repressing the homosexual rape of Troilus, the Latin epic feigns to know less than might have been shown on the temple walls, whereas Chaucer's dream vision tells us nothing at all.

Virgilian ekphrasis had been refracted for Chaucer through Canto 10 of Dante's *Purgatorio,* inspired ultimately by Trajan's victory column in Rome, where the scene of the emperor's exemplary humility becomes intensely real-seeming with physical movements, the sounds of dialogue, and even the smells of incense:

Colui che mai non vide cosa nuova
produsse esto *visibile parlare*
novello a noi perchè qui non si trova.
(ll. 94–96)

He who never beheld any new thing wrought this *visible speech,* new to us because here it is not found.[69]

Book II of the *House of Fame* elaborates this notion of *visibile parlare* by having the Eagle explain the physics of sound waves, in effect, reversing ekphrasis to describe the mysterious process whereby the act of speaking generates the image of the person who did the speaking:

Hyt wexeth lyk the same wight
Which that the word in erthe spak,
Be hyt clothed red or blak;
And hath so verray hys lyknesse
That spak the word, that thou wilt gesse
That it the same body be.
(*HF,* ll. 1076–81)

Words "clothed red or blak" indicate theology and philosophy, like the Clerk of Oxford's volumes bound in red and black, whereby replicas of speakers are reified in visible forms as the learned authors who produced these words. These images then become available as the literary idols who materialize in Book III.

---

68. Stephen Cheeke, *Writing for Art: The Aesthetics of Ekphrasis* (Manchester: Manchester University Press, 2008), p. 6.

69. Dante Alighieri, *The Divine Comedy: Purgatorio,* ed. and trans. Charles S. Singleton (Princeton, NJ: Princeton University Press, 1973), 1:104–5 (ll. 94–96). On Dante's purgatorial friezes, see Barbetti, "Inhuman Ekphrasis," pp. 129–30.

The ekphrasis inside Fame's great hall takes the form of a series of pillars, all of them erected as war memorials recalling histories of violence and glorifying military campaigns in what Mitchell has called the "monumentalizing of violence."[70] Statius celebrates the victories of Achilles in his *Achilleid* and the Theban civil wars in his *Thebaid* (one source for the "Knight's Tale"), and then Homer, assisted by Dares and Dictys, sustains the fame of the Trojan War (*HF*, ll. 1456–85). Even Ovid claims his place among the triumphal columns for recounting campaigns of erotic conquest.[71] No longer simply playing one art form against another, Book III's idolatry becomes inseparable from author-worship as a Chaucerian innovation for elevating canonic writers and making possible a literary genealogy, analogous to the series of the royal statues commissioned for Westminster Hall at the end of the fourteenth century.[72] This genealogical model for a literary tradition is, in turn, one in which Chaucer could install himself as a founding father.

The *House of Fame* ends notoriously by introducing a nameless "man of gret auctorite"—perhaps the dreamer confronting his mirror image as a future authority on love stories—but before the text breaks off, some less-noticed events occur. The dreamer is led toward "newe tydynges" by an anonymous guide who speaks at great length about showing him exactly what he is looking for (*HF*, ll. 1912–2026). The role of nameless guides as the medieval predecessors of today's docents and museum guides must be factored into the ways images were "given voice" for visitors to medieval cathedrals. Local experts acted as the custodians explaining iconographic meanings as on-site exegetes who could prevent viewers, for example, from confusing Gerard David's Sisamnes with St. Bartholomew.

In a well-known episode in *The Book of Margery Kempe*, friars operate as tour guides for the pilgrims visiting the sacred sites of Jerusalem:

> Then the friars lifted up a cross and led the pilgrims about from one place to another where our Lord had suffered his pains and his passions, every man and woman bearing a wax candle in their hand. And the friars always, as they went about, told them what our Lord suffered in every place.[73]

---

70. Mitchell, "Violence of Public Art," p. 378.

71. John Watkins, "'Neither of Idle Shewes, nor of False Charmes Aghast': Transformations of Virgilian Ekphrasis in Chaucer and Spenser," *Journal of Medieval and Renaissance Studies* 23 (1993): 346 [345–63].

72. Phillip Lindley, "Absolutism and Regal Image in Ricardian Sculpture," in *The Regal Image of Richard II and the Wilton Diptych*, eds. Dillian Gordon, Lisa Monnas, and Caroline Elam (London: Harvey Miller, 1997), pp. 61–83.

73. *The Book of Margery Kempe*, ed. Lynn Staley (New York: Norton, 2001), p. 50.

Looking back at the *Canterbury Interlude,* we find Chaucer's pilgrims, including the Miller and Pardoner unable to identify Adam in the stained-glass window, now receiving correct information from a monk describing the relics and teaching their significance:

> Then passed they forth boystly, goglyng with hir hedes,
> Kneled adown tofore the shryne, and hertlich hir bedes
> They preyd to Seynt Thomas, in such wise as they couth.
> And sith the holy relikes ech man with his mowth
> Kissed, as a goodly monke the names told and taught.[74]

As the local expert with knowledge of the shrine's history and relics, this monastic custodian may even have been the anonymous poet projecting himself into the action.[75] These shrine-keepers had specific duties to admit pilgrims, supervise their behavior in the crowded confines, and provide a narrative designed to intensify the pilgrims' experience of the relics.[76] Canterbury monks not only knew the particulars of the cathedral but also had a strong motive for championing St. Thomas Becket's relics against increasingly harsh objections from Lollard reformers.

Back again to David's *Flaying of Sisamnes.* Spectators who confront such images of physical suffering are morbidly curious to learn what histories of violence created this scene of agony and victimhood. Who is the man having his flesh knifed off? What crime earned him this grisly punishment? There are many kinds of suffering, to be sure, spiritual as well as physical. All of pilgrims in the *Canterbury Tales* are supposed to feel contrition as penitents, or in other cases (maybe most cases) these pilgrims feel the insidious pain of sins unacknowledged and unshriven. The trajectory of the poet's career led him to the "General Prologue" where the nameless narrator serves as tour guide describing these figures gathered at the Tabard Inn. In a ploy inspired by the *Roman de la Rose*'s description of the wall carvings outside the garden, Chaucer freezes his characters like statues positioned at the entry to his

---

74. Canterbury Tales: *Fifteenth-Century Continuations,* ed. Bowers, p. 64 (ll. 163–67).

75. Peter Brown, "Journey's End: The Prologue to *The Tale of Beryn,*" in *Chaucer and Fifteenth-Century Poetry,* eds. Julia Boffey and Janet Cowen, King's College London Medieval Studies 5 (London: King's College, Centre for Late Antique and Medieval Studies, 1991), p. 149 [143–74]. This work's implied defense of relics and images is discussed in my book *Chaucer and Langland: The Antagonistic Tradition* (Notre Dame, IN: University of Notre Dame Press, 2007), pp. 173–79.

76. Malo, *Relics and Writing,* pp. 92 and 205n44. She doubts the accuracy of the shrine visit in *Tale of Beryn,* p. 38.

great poem.[77] Yet his famous portraits go beyond what any eyewitness could have known by merely looking at these characters or chatting them up, such as their personal histories and secret vices, in a manner consistent with the fantasy of instant recognition and innate understanding dramatized in prior episodes of ekphrasis.

Just as the dreamer in the *House of Fame* knows things about Dido's love-sufferings that no carvings could express, Chaucer the pilgrim knows things about his fellow travelers beyond what could have been learned during tavern conversations: the Knight's fifteen mortal combats, the Squire's sleepless nights, and the Prioress's emotional upset over bleeding mice and beaten puppies. The Pardoner, the Wife of Bath, and the other characters are not verbal artefacts until rendered as such, first frozen statue-like as objects of the narrator's gaze and then animated with all the talking, singing, laughing, and tale-telling that belongs to the bustle of real, living people. These pilgrims become Chaucer's most sophisticated version of "speaking images" coming to life to offer their stories of lust and violence, the tales themselves constrained within the larger pilgrimage narrative—from Palamon and Arcite battling each other for the love of Emelye in the "Knight's Tale" to Phoebus killing his wife in a jealous rage in the "Manciple's Tale."

---

77. J. Lawrence Badendyck, "Chaucer's Portrait Technique and the Dream Vision Tradition," *English Record* 21 (1970): 113–25.

PART II

THE DESIRE OF EKPHRASIS

Chapter 4

VISION AND DESIRE IN *MARY MAGDALENE* AND *THE WINTER'S TALE*

Claudia Olk

⁂he enigmatic encounter between the resurrected Christ and Mary Magdalene in the garden of the tomb (Jn. 20:11– 18) is one of the most intriguing scenes of *The Digby Play of Mary Magdalene*.[1] This scene is not only a culminating moment in the medieval theatrical tradition but has, since early Christianity, stood at the center of a broad range of pictorial narratives.[2] Numerous paint-

---

1. *The Digby Play of Mary Magdalene* was composed at the end of the fifteenth century and was then, perhaps as late as 1520, copied into the MS that became Digby 133 at the Bodleian Library. Apart from the canonical Gospels, Jacobus de Voraigne's *Legenda Aurea* is acknowledged as one of its main sources, alongside the *South English Vernacular Legendary*. *Mary Magdalene* traces the life of the legendary saint, depicting her youth and her temptation by curiosity and luxury. It presents her conversion and repentance, her various meetings with Christ, and her work as a disciple in France, where she performs miracles for the King and Queen of Marseilles. Finally, the play stages her life as a hermit in the wilderness of Provence, her last Eucharist, and her ascent into heaven.

2. The widespread popularity of Mary Magdalene in the fifteenth century and beyond is amply documented. See Clifford Davidson, "The Digby *Mary Magdalene* and the Magdalene Cult of the Middle Ages," *Annuale Mediaevale* 13 (1972): 70–87; Helen Garth, *Saint Mary Magdalene in Mediaeval Literature* (Baltimore: Johns Hopkins Press, 1950); Katherine Ludwig Jansen, *The Making of the Magdalen: Preaching and Popular Devotion in the Later Middle Ages* (Princeton, NJ: Princeton University Press, 2000); Susan Haskins, *Mary Magdalen: Myth and Metaphor* (New York: Harcourt Brace, 1993).

ings of the episode capture the moment in which Christ forbids Mary to touch him since he has not yet returned to his father. His famous words "noli me tangere" mark a site of transition between desire and fulfillment, between the natural and the divine body, and between time and space as they gesture towards eschatology.[3] Further, the scene seems paradoxical in that it stages both an intimate encounter as well as an irreducible distance.[4] Since the scene's paradoxical structure is grounded in the visibility of the divine logos itself it conflates the presence of transcendence with momentary evidence; the encounter unifies heterogeneous realms in a sublime, if not disturbing, intensity of the gaze that effects a merging of the not yet with the no longer.[5]

Barbara Baert describes the tension of the scene as sustained by the unattainability of almost but never quite touching, as "tak[ing] place in the deictic void. There, in the pulsating lacuna of hands that seek and recede, is where the mysterious merger of speech and gaze takes place. *Noli me tangere* is an iconography of direct speech. . . . The gaze of the *Noli me tangere* is an insight-generating gaze."[6] Holding a promise of immediacy, union, and presence, the scene played a central role in medieval devotional practice. Poignantly, the episode achieves its heightened role in medieval culture because it presents this promise of immediacy as unattainable in the present.[7] Crucial for the context of the present volume, it presents a visual

---

3. We may note that the original Greek text, "me mou haptou," implies not only the tactile act but also the metaphorical sense of "to grasp," "to hang on to," so that the words may also mean "do not cling to me," or rather: "you must let go of me." Likewise, in the Vulgate's Latin "noli me tangere" says "do not wish to touch me," which stresses the intensity of the desire to do so all the more (Barbara Baert, "'Noli me tangere': Six Exercises in Image Theory and Iconophilia," *Image & Narrative* 15 [2006]: n.p.).

4. Georges Didi-Huberman, *Fra Angelico: Dissemblance and Figuration,* trans. Jane Marie Todd (Chicago: Chicago University Press, 1995), p. 14.

5. The episode is frequently connected to that of the doubting Thomas. Thomas, in contrast to Mary, recognizes Christ by seeing him but still remains incredulous. As Glenn Most has argued, there is, however, no biblical evidence for Thomas actually touching Jesus' wounds: "We are told that it can be seen (20:20, 29). But we shall never know whether it could have been touched. What kind and degree of materiality Jesus' risen body really has, John has been careful not to reveal" (*Doubting Thomas* [Cambridge, MA: Harvard University Press, 2005], p. 55).

6. Barbara Baert, *Interspaces between Word, Gaze and Touch: The Bible and the Visual Medium in the Middle Ages* (Leuven: Peeters, 2011), p. 16.

7. When Nicholas Love describes the episode, he seeks to alleviate this sense of impossibility and reassuringly adds: "And forthemore þou oure lorde so straungely as it seemeth answered hir at the biginnyng hir that she sulde not touch him, neuereles I may not trowe, bot that afterwarde he suffrede hir to touch him, & sto kysse bothe handes & feete, or thei departeden. . . . That he wolde not thereby in any maner disturbe hir or heuye hir, bot rather in alle poyntes confort hir" (*The mirrour of the blessed lyf of Jesu Christ,* ed. Elizabeth Salter [Salzburg: Institut für Englische Sprache und Literatur, Universität Salzburg, 1974], p. 201).

and a verbal encounter of the religious and the secular spheres, highlighting further tensions: tensions between dialogue and action, word and image, as well as sight and touch. Speech is accompanied by gesture, and seeing describes both an inward and an outward motion, a moment of simultaneous introspection and desire for another, because for Mary to recognize Christ is also to recognize herself.

It is as an "iconography of direct speech" that the scene articulates its ekphrastic potential. Christ's sacred presence is established through a mere three words. The insight Mary gains through her gaze being returned by Christ can create immediacy and figure as a kind of touch, not least because medieval conceptions of sight shared affinities with optical theories that had developed since antiquity, where seeing was understood as a form of touch.[8] Nevertheless insight must remain limited; ultimately it is not through sight that Mary recognizes Christ, but again through his words, when he addresses her by her name.

Articulating the need to see, the scene emphasizes the eyewitness's role as do "public and devotional images, dramatic re-enactments of Biblical stories; the exhibition of relics and other cultic objects; the elevation of the host within mass."[9] Simultaneously, the scene offers a reflection of the theater as medium. As Jean-Luc Nancy observes, the scene is analogous to the relation between the work of art and the viewer.[10] According to Nancy, it creates a model of analogy for the medium of art, which is not to be touched but only looked at. As with the work of art, the prohibition to touch is an invitation to see, to gaze, connecting the revelation of the voice with the manifestation of the visible, corporeal image. The "noli me tangere" episode relates both to painting and drama, since both art forms depend on visibility and corporeality to create artistic presence. The episode highlights the interplay of pictorial and ekphrastic narratives and of discursive and dramatic dialogue, offering a reflection on the status of art and artistic representation.

Mary Magdalene's potential to inspire self-reflection in various media is manifold: she has been taken as a model discourse for expressing religious experience in aesthetic form.[11] She still inspires poetic practices of

8. See Suzanne Conklin Akbari, *Seeing through the Veil: Optical Theory and Medieval Allegory* (Toronto: University of Toronto Press, 2004) and Dallas G. Denery II, *Seeing and Being Seen in the Later Medieval World: Optics, Theology, and Religious Life* (Cambridge: Cambridge University Press, 2005).

9. Suzannah Biernoff, *Sight and Embodiment in the Middle Ages* (Houndmills: Palgrave Macmillan, 2002), p. 133.

10. Jean-Luc Nancy, *Noli me tangere: On the Raising of the Body,* trans. Sarah Clift, Pascale Anne-Brault, and Michael Naas (New York: Fordham University Press, 2008), pp. 66–67.

11. Patricia Badir, *The Maudlin Impression: English Literary Images of Mary Magdalene 1550–1700* (Notre Dame, IN: University of Notre Dame Press, 2009), p. 3.

image making[12] and also articulates the potential of art to be both in and out of touch with the sacred.[13] Scholarship has pointed to Mary Magdalene's composite nature, embodying a number of paradoxes. While she could be regarded as a paragon of beauty and eroticism, or an exemplar of asceticism and the contemplative life, she also served as a model of the sinful but penitent female. As a devoted disciple present at crucial moments of Christ's life and first witness to his resurrection, she was an essential symbol for the Medieval Church, which promoted her as an intercessor and, in her role as a model of penance and redemption, also as an *exemplum*.[14]

Her enormous popularity lasted into the Renaissance and well beyond.[15] She retained her extraordinary importance in early modern religious culture, while the numerous pictorial representations of Mary Magdalene illustrate a process in which she increasingly gained artistic presence. Patricia Badir notes that in the Renaissance, "the Magdalen stood in the middle of controversies over likeness and presence—that is, amidst a precarious and uncertain polemic on the nature and power of illustration and image—and in this tentative location she served . . . 'to resurrect old meanings and generate new ones along with new and unforeseeable connections.'"[16] By the seventeenth

---

12. Images of Mary Magdalene have been shaped by centuries of sermons and paintings, poetry and saint's legends, romance novels and Bible movies, in which she was in turn anathematized or praised as a role model after which women such as Margery Kempe patterned their lives (Theresa Coletti, *Mary Magdalene and the Drama of Saints. Theater, Gender, and Religion in Late Medieval England* [Philadelphia: University of Pennsylvania Press, 2004], p. 145).

13. Badir, *Maudlin Impression*, p. 8.

14. The first mention of Mary Magdalene appears in the Canonical Gospels of the New Testament. The legendary figure of the Saint of Mary Magdalene, however, was composed of several women mentioned in the Gospels: the woman who anointed Christ's feet, the sister of Martha and Lazarus, and the woman Mary who was present at the crucifixion. The evolution of the Magdalene legend is very complex, and the Middle English corpus of writings on Mary Magdalene is very large indeed. Versions of the legend in verse include the Auchinleck *Mary Magdalen* (fourteenth century), the *South English Legendary* (c. 1276–79), the *Northern Homily Collection* (c. 1350), the *Scottish Legendary* (c. 1375–1400), and the "Lyf of Marye Maudelyn" in Osbern Bokenham's *Legendys of Hooly Wommen* (c. 1392–1447). Versions of the Magdalene legend in Middle English prose include John Mirk's *Festial* (c. 1400–1425), the *Speculum Sacerdotale* (c. 1500–1525), the anonymous *Gilte Legende* (c. 1483), and William Caxton's *Golden Legende* (1483). Mary Magdalen also appears as a character in a number of plays in medieval England: *The Cornish Mystery Play of the Three Maries*, *The Mystery of Mary Magdalene and the Apostles*, the Townley play of *Mary Magdalen*, the Chester *Christ's Ministry*, the York plays *The Raising of Lazarus* and *Jesus Appears to Mary Magdalen after the Resurrection*, *The Life and Repentance of Mary Magdalen* by Lewis Wager, the Digby *Christ's Burial and Resurrection*, and the Digby *Play of Mary Magdalen*.

15. Badir, *Maudlin Impression*, passim.

16. Badir, *Maudlin Impression*, p. 4.

century, Mary Magdalene was not merely established as a major figure of devotion, but she had also inspired a rich literary and artistic tradition.[17]

Mary Magdalene is at the center of the works of many of Shakespeare's contemporaries, such as Thomas Robinson's epic poem *The Life and Death of Mary Magdalene* (1620), or Robert Southwell's prose meditation *Marie Magdalen's Funeral Tears* (1591). In *The Winter's Tale,* Shakespeare, far less explicitly than his contemporaries but most poignantly in the resurrection of Hermione, draws on features of the Magdalene story, and he does so particularly at instances when he departs from his primary source, Robert Greene's *Pandosto*.[18] Shakespeare's familiarity with the traditions of medieval drama has been widely acknowledged.[19] Andrew James Johnston has recently shown how Shakespeare's later plays, *Pericles* in particular, configure elements of the ancient novel along with medieval sources to arrive at a model of literary history that allows for a productive coexistence of different levels of temporality while questioning unilinear models of periodization.[20]

In looking at *The Digby Play of Mary Magdalene* and Shakespeare's *Winter's Tale,* I will be concerned with the theater's strategies of actualizing the in-between space between sight and touch. Interested in the theater's presentation of, and reflection on, vision as well as its ways of materializing the immaterial in performance, I shall first explore the nexus of ekphrasis, vision, and performance. Second, I will examine how *The Digby Play of Mary Magdalene* stages the relationship between corporeal and spiritual presence.

---

17. Jane Schaberg, *The Resurrection of Mary Magdalen: Legends, Apocrypha and the Christian Testament* (New York: Continuum, 2002), p. 68.

18. Many of Shakespeare's plays actually explore the link between desire, sight, and touch in scenes explicitly drawing on both religious and theatrical contexts. Lucio in *Measure for Measure* urges the nun Isabella to touch the rigid Angelo: "Ay, touch him; there's the vein" (*MM* 2.2.73). Hoping for the release of her brother Claudio, Isabella does as she is told but must consequently fear for her virginity. Rosalind in *As You Like It* similarly conflates the spiritual and the erotic when she muses that "his kissing is as full of sanctity as the touch of holy bread" (*AYL* 3.4.12–13). *Twelfth Night* features a scene reminiscent of the prohibition to touch as narrated in the Magdalene story: the newly reunited twins resolve to postpone their embrace until Viola has cast off her "manly usurped attire": "Do not embrace me till each circumstance / Of place, time, fortune do cohere and jump / That I am Viola" (*TN* 5.1.244–46).

19. Glynne William Gladstone Wickham, *Shakespeare's Dramatic Heritage: Collected Studies in Mediaeval, Tudor and Shakespearean Drama* (London: Routledge, 1969). And more recently, Ruth Morse, Helen Cooper, and Peter Holland, eds., *Medieval Shakespeare* (Cambridge: Cambridge University Press, 2013).

20. Andrew James Johnston, "Sailing the Seas of Literary History: Gower, Chaucer, and the Problem of Incest in Shakespeare's *Pericles*," *Poetica* 41 (2009): 381–407. For a discussion of romance elements in Shakespeare, see also my "The Musicality of *The Merchant of Venice*," in *Medieval Shakespeare*, ed. Christina Wald (London: Routledge, 2013), pp. 386–97.

In a final step, I will contrast *Mary Magdalene* with *The Winter's Tale*, focusing on the plays' structures of vision, desire, and theatrical presence.

STAGING VISION, TOUCH, AND DESIRE IN *MARY MAGDALENE*

Drawing on a rich iconographical heritage, the Digby *Mary Magdalene* is typical of medieval drama in that it displays numerous parallels to the composition and themes of other contemporary art forms. As Clifford Davidson contends, the play not only "attempts to make visible in an imaginative way the events of her life for all to see,"[21] but it also shares many iconographic features with visual art: "It is possible to see the Digby *Mary Magdalene* . . . as consistent somehow with the traditions of art from the region of its origin."[22] Davidson lists the *Holkham Bible* (presumably originating from East Anglia), Lucas van der Leyden's *Dance of Mary Magdalene,* and Albrecht Dürer's *Mary Magdalene in Ecstasy* as visual analogues to the play text. In the same vein, he acknowledges the lifelike qualities of medieval drama when he explains that the theatrical images "attempted in what was felt to be a very real way to reactualize moments in sacred history."[23] Davidson, amongst others, also explores the immense significance of church windows as an inspirational source for the playwrights of the Cycle Plays to visualize sacred history.

If we understand medieval ekphrasis, as it is traditionally done, as aiming at descriptive lifelikeness,[24] whereby the audience is drawn into the narrative as eyewitnesses, then drama constitutes a special case within the medieval ekphrastic tradition.[25] V. A. Kolve is one of the first modern critics to consider the liveliness of the Corpus Christi plays: "They image more vividly and more unforgettably than any other art form of their time."[26] As Kolve points out, the plays' medieval critics already regarded them as "quike bookis," as images coming to life, aiding the imagination. As speaking pic-

21. Clifford Davidson, *Drama and Art: An Introduction to the Use of Evidence from the Visual Arts for the Study of Early Drama* (Kalamazoo, MI: The Medieval Institute, 1977), p. 4.

22. Davidson, *Drama and Art,* pp. 3–4.

23. Davidson, *Drama and Art,* p. 8.

24. See Introduction to this volume, p. 2.

25. See Ruth Webb, *Ekphrasis, Imagination and Persuasion in Ancient Rhetorical Theory and Practice* (Farnham: Ashgate, 2009), p. 88.

26. V. A. Kolve, *The Play Called Corpus Christi* (Stanford: Stanford University Press, 1966), p. 5. In 1922, Émile Mâle was the first to articulate the theory that religious art and drama of the Late Middle Ages are intricately connected (*The Gothic Image: Religious Art in France of the Thirteenth Century* [New York: Harper and Row, 1972]).

tures, the plays were regarded as furnishing special habits of seeing.[27] In the eyes of medieval observers, the visual is thus not simply a means of attaching iconographical significance to the verbal. Similar to contemplation as described in mystical and devotional literature, visual elements prompt the imagination through which the details of a scene are vividly recalled. Further, through the lifelikeness of a scene, the viewer can identify with a certain character or take up imaginary roles. Both theatrical performance and ekphrasis (the latter understood in its broad sense as vivid description) are forms of "speech that [bring] the subject matter vividly before the eyes;"[28] both therefore produce images in the mind's eye. The theatrical performance makes signs visible so that they become accessible to the senses, to experience, and to interpretation.[29] In a dramatic text, ekphrasis not only participates in the negotiations of relations between images and texts, but it assumes a metarepresentational character that at the same time exhibits and questions the notion of lifelikeness. Analogous to ekphrasis that articulates the ancient hope of mimesis to capture a visible referent, Mary Magdalene in the *noli me tangere* scene foregrounds both the desirability and the impossibility of this attempt.

Ekphrasis hence includes a comment on mimesis itself that becomes particularly critical when the representation of the divine is at stake, the word of God that is at the same time the *imago dei,* the central icon of Christianity. Both *The Winter's Tale* and *The Digby Play of Mary Magdalene* draw on this paradigm of ekphrasis as metarepresentation when they perform the transition from a work of art to a lifelike figure, the moment of recognition of the intangible divine that appears in human form.

Staging the visible, showing the invisible, and exploring the role of touch in negotiating questions of belief are essential concerns of *The Digby Play of Mary Magdalene.* The play situates itself between text and image and stresses its visual impact when it concludes: "Thus enddyt þe sentens / That we have playyd in yower syth" (ll. 2131–32).[30] Drawing on familiar iconographical material and presenting itself as a visual commentary on a scripturally authorized truth, the play is a visualization of a text that invited viewers to contemplate it. Its very nexus of vision and desire links the *Digby Play* to the earliest forms

---

27. Kolve, *Play Called Corpus Christi,* pp. 6–7.

28. Webb, *Ekphrasis,* p.1.

29. Sarah Beckwith, *Signifying God: Social Relation and Symbolic Act in the York Corpus Christi Plays* (Chicago: University of Chicago Press, 2001), pp. 153–57.

30. All quotations from *Mary Magdalene* are taken from Donald C. Baker, John L. Murphy, and Louis B. Hall Jr., eds., *The Late Medieval Religious Plays of Bodleian MSS Digby 133 and E Museo 160,* Early English Text Society 283 (Oxford: Oxford University Press, 1982).

of vernacular theater. Like the *quem quaeritis* trope that was part of the Easter Liturgy, and in which members of the clergy enact the *Visitatio sepulchri* by the three Maries, the *Digby Play* acknowledges absence as a condition of faith.[31]

Suzannah Biernoff examines the link between vision and desire as "a state of suspension on the threshold between self and other and a condition of active desiring permeability."[32] It is this very impossibility to hold on to something, to capture the presence of the unattainable forever, which all the more generates the desire to see. Hans Belting regards this dialectics of presence and absence as fundamental to the mediating role of images as such.[33] Like ekphrasis, images present what is absent as present. They suggest evidence and immediacy where there can be no immediacy, creating an effect of presence and immanence. It is the very encounter between Christ and Mary that encapsulates vision and desire as a kind of seeing on the verge of invisibility, whereby the divine object of desire is about to disappear from sight.

Mary Magdalene's gaze thus presents an iconography charged with the topos of mystic love,[34] an iconography that presents eye contact as creating a physical link between subject and object.[35] At the same time, however, her gaze creates what Aby Warburg terms the "iconology of an in-between space,"[36] an area where seemingly irreconcilable polarities are exhibited.

The iconology of in-betweenness is, however, not restricted to the reciprocal gaze between Mary and Christ, but strongly relies on romance topographies, too. The play covers at least nineteen different locations ranging between Heaven and Hell, the various palaces of worldly rulers, Rome, Marseilles, the Castle of Magdalen, and the wilderness. It also includes the tavern, the garden, and the tomb and features the most important of all romance means of transportation: the ship. The play emphasizes its scenic extravagances through dazzling visual effects, such as heavenly apparitions, clouds in motion, and pagan temples conveniently incinerated to exemplify the supremacy of the Christian God. It might have been its sumptuous and chal-

---

31. On the "productivity" of grief and loss, see Anke Bernau's essay in this volume, pp. 100–123.

32. Biernoff, *Sight and Embodiment,* p. 132.

33. Hans Belting, *Bild-Anthropologie. Entwürfe für eine Bildwissenschaft* (Munich: Fink, 2001), p. 143. For Belting, the relationship between presence and absence is created through the experience of death.

34. Biernoff, *Sight and Embodiment,* p. 150.

35. Akbari, *Seeing through the Veil,* p. 122; pp. 148–49.

36. Aby Warburg, "Einleitung zum Mnemosyne-Atlas (1929)," in *Die Beredsamkeit des Leibes. Zur Körpersprache in der Kunst,* eds. Ilsebill Barta Fliedl and Christoph Geissmar (Salzburg: Residenz Verlag, 1992), p. 171 [171–73].

lenging setting that caused the scribe of the Digby MS to give vent to his exasperation in one of the marginalia: "Jhesu mercy,"[37] and its early editor, F. J. Furnivall in 1882, to regard it as an example of "early Sensationalism."[38]

The sensationalist topographical display has method, however. Exaggeration is already part of the play's expository scenes, when the first words we hear are the ranting speeches of the Imperator, Herod, Pilate, and also of Mary's father Cyrus indicating their vanity and blasphemy, and marking them as late medieval villains grotesquely usurping God's divinity: "I woll it be knowyn to al þe word vnyversal / That of heven and hell chyff rewlar am I" (ll. 3–4). In their flamboyant self-presentations, these characters direct the audience's gaze at what they are *supposed* to see and point to their own luxurious attire. Pilate boasts of his "robys of rychesse" (l. 229), and Mary's father asks the audience to "behold my person, glysteryng in gold" (l. 53). Apart from illustrating the fatal hubris of these characters and their hollow rhetoric, which a contemporary audience would have been well attuned to, the play also exhibits the eminent theatricality of these scenes, in which the theater presents its semiotic strategies in spectacular deictic acts and reflects on them at the same time.

It is, above all, the scenes of Mary's temptation and fall into sin that are rendered in particularly lively terms, exhibiting lavish entertainment and worldly splendor. The allegorical figures of Flesh and Sensuality appear like apothecary peddlers and display their rich array of exotic treats and mundane remedies: "Dya galonga, ambra, and also margaretton— / Alle þis at my lyst, aȝens alle vexacyon! / . . . / Zenzybyr and synamom at euery tyde—" (ll. 339–44). Likewise, the scene in the tavern where Mary is led by Luxuria mixes the historical with the allegorical when the Taverner shows off his copious variety of wines and encourages Mary to drink what is "To man and woman a good restoratyff" (l. 486).

Verbal and visual signs interact when temptation and change of heart are persuasively illustrated by a change in diction and register that couples ornate dress with ornate style, for instance when Mary is flattered by Lechery and Luxuria's courteousness and adapts to their embellished rhetoric: "Mary: Your debonarius obedyauns ravyssyt me to trankquelyte!" (l. 447) or when Lady Lechery is addressed as the "flowyr fairest of femynyte" (l. 423), which uneasily echoes the earlier presentation of Mary by her father: "Here is Mary, ful fayur and ful of femynyte" (l. 71). The register and *decorum* of the characters'

---

37. "Introduction," *The Late Medieval Religious Plays of Bodleian MSS Digby 133 and E Museo 160*, p. xxxii.

38. F. J. Furnivall, ed., *The Digby Mysteries*, (London: The New Shakspere Society, 1882), p. x.

speeches comment on the visual nature and codes of courtly culture, and foreground the deceptiveness of appearances as they warn against an over-reliance on one's sight.

Mary is shown as being easy prey for the deceptiveness of appearances when she falls for the gallant Curiosity and is led astray by his good looks and his flattering words, which compliment her on her colorful and luxurious attire:

> Coryoste: A, dere dewchesse, my daysyys iee!
> Spendavnt of colour, most of femynyte,
> Your sofreyn colourrys set wyth synseryte!
> Consedere my loue into yower alye,
> Or ellys I am smet wyth peynnys of perplexite!
> (ll. 515–19)

The audience is made witness to Mary's fall in a metatheatrical setting, in which visual appearances are presented and commented on by other figures on stage, such as the Bad Angel who interprets Mary's gullibility to the audience when he sneeringly observes: "To here syte, he [curiosity] is semelyare þan ony kyng in tronys!" (l. 554).

When she misinterprets the signs and is misled by outward show, Mary is not characterized as inherently immoral or wicked, but rather as an innocent and impressionable girl whose sin is primarily of an epistemological nature. The play thus cautions the audience against entirely trusting their senses, because these potentially lead to deception and confusion.

A further aspect of Mary's misinterpretation of visual signs points towards allegory as a form of seeing. Through its now iconic garden scene—that is, by having Mary mistake Christ for Simon the gardener—the play teaches viewers that the truth is very often conveyed in allegorical form. The scene is clearly not about love at first sight: it is not through the use of her eyes but through hearing his voice that Mary eventually recognizes Christ. Nevertheless, she has *seen* the allegorical sense of their encounter, since Christ explains to her that he is indeed the gardener of man's soul. Christ's corporeal appearance as gardener is charged with allegorical significance, just as objects as they appear to the senses are potentially enriched with transcendental meaning.

Crucially, the visible points towards the invisible when, throughout the play, clothes and outward appearances are staged as the visible signs of a spiritual status. For example, after her conversion, Mary no longer wears colorful clothes but is now associated with the color white. Explaining the meaning behind her white garments, she states:

> O gracyus God, now I vndyrstond!
> Thys clothyng of whyte is tokenyng of mekenesse.
> Now, gracyus Lord, I woll natt wond,
> Yower preseptt to obbey wyth lowlynesse.
> (ll. 1607–10)

Further, vision acquires a paraenetic dimension when it is linked to light and illumination, and contrasted with blindness and darkness. Light and illumination accompany Mary's conversion and guide the audience's attention as her outward appearance changes.

The dramatic appeal of the scenes from Mary's life relies on their pictorial arrangement, their liveliness, and rhetorical vigor. The play self-consciously presents various kinds of seeing and the ways in which these interact, and, at the same time, teaches the audience how to see.

In staging what have become iconic scenes—Mary's waiting in the arbor or her washing Christ's feet with her tears—the play makes images of the sacred available in corporeal form and inspires a love of seeing as *visio corporalis* that engages the viewer in a form of physical communication with the divine.[39] At the same time, the play promotes a kind of vision that is potentially revelatory as an apprehension of spiritual truths.[40] Spiritual truth is linked to the bodily dimension of spirituality inherent in the viewer's gaze. Hence the play's religious level juxtaposes, or even superimposes, the semiotic and epistemological aspects of vision—as expressed in the anxiety about trusting one's senses—and the corporeal element of vision (sight as touch) in a manner typical of medieval Christianity. Like the Eucharist, seeing proves to establish both a symbolic relationship to the divine and one that insists on the believer's experience of the godhead's physical presence. As Mary Magdalene sees Christ, she touches him—regardless of his prohibition—just as the communicant not merely remembers the Savior through the symbolism of the Eucharist, but bodily tastes and ingests him.[41] This insistence on the physical experience of the divine also becomes manifest in her veneration of relics. When Mary Magdalene recognizes her lord in the garden, however, her desire to anoint him and to "kesse þou from my hartys bote" (l. 1073) is not granted to her as Christ replies: "Towche me natt, Mary!" (l. 1074).

---

39. Biernoff, *Sight and Embodiment*, pp. 135–40.

40. Biernoff, *Sight and Embodiment*, pp. 25–26.

41. Lee Palmer Wandel, *The Eucharist in the Reformation: Incarnation and Liturgy* (Cambridge: Cambridge University Press, 2006). Sophie Read, *Eucharist and the Poetic Imagination in Early Modern England* (Cambridge: Cambridge University Press, 2013).

In the play, the physical communion through touch is transformed into an ocular one when Christ addresses the audience in metatheatrical fashion, making them potential witnesses to his resurrection if only they look for him with the "fervor of love": "I woll shew to synnars, as I do to þe, / Yf þey woll wyth veruens of love me seke" (ll. 1092–93).

SHOWING THE INVISIBLE

As the play demonstrates time and time again, seeing and understanding depend on performance. In a homily delivered to Mary and Martha, Jesus points to the finitude and limitations of human understanding:

> JHESUS: . . . .
> For of all peynnys, þat is impossyble
> To vndyrestond be reson; to know þe werke,
> The joye þat is in Jherusallem heuenly,
> Can nevyr be compylyd be covnnyng of clerke—
> (ll. 803–6)

He rejects the "covnnyng of clerke" and insists on the power of revelatory showing. He makes visible what cannot be understood by words alone and demonstrates his divine power and the grace of God in miraculous signs. When he raises Lazarus from the dead, he thereby proleptically evokes his own death and resurrection: "The agrement of grace here shewyn I wyll" (l. 898). Showing through miracles provides evidence and turns the spectators into witnesses and therefore into believers of his godly sovereignty.

In her apostolate overseas, Mary, too, performs miracles in imitation of Christ and thereby creates evidence of God's powers. In the process of converting the heathen king of Marseilles, she, for instance, prevails in a competition staged—again—as a dazzling visual spectacle. She asks the king to give her license to perform a miracle and, upon a brief prayer, her mission is efficiently accomplished. As the stage direction informs us, a cloud promptly arrives and sets the pagan temple ablaze: "*Here xall comme a clowd from heven, and sett þe tempyl on afyer, and þe pryst and þe clerk xall synke*" (ll. 1562–64). When Mary appears to the King of Marseilles at night, Christ directs her like a stage manager from up above. He is also concerned with the creation of visual effects when he commands his angels to "goo yow before hyr wyth reverent lyth" (l. 1593). Moreover, his angels show an awareness of props and costume "we xal go before yow wyth solem lyth; / In a mentyll of whyte xall be ower araye" (ll. 1603–4). When she sends the King to St. Peter and the Holy Land, Mary emphasizes the spiritual importance of physical contact zones with the sacred, such as the intercession of saints, the sacrament of baptism, and the adoration of central relics like the cross. St. Peter performs the baptism on stage, and in support of Mary's earthbound spirituality, the saint, too, advocates "very experyens" (l. 1846) and advises the King, "To Nazareth and Bedlem, goo wyth delygens, / And be yower own inspeccyon, yower feyth to edyfy" (ll. 1849–50).

In *Mary Magdalene*, vision is not merely spiritualized as transcending the corporeal, but it remains tied to the visible, material referent, or rather, it celebrates physical presence in spiritual experience. Although the play consistently returns to the power of showing, it also challenges a merely materialist hermeneutics in which seeing would be equated with believing. Significantly, it presents a chiastic vision that creates a balance between the corporeal and the spiritual. For example, Jesus promises his disciples that they will be able to see him: "Bodyly, wyth here carnall yye" (l. 1124), but he also exhorts them that: "Blyssyd be þey at alle tyme / That sen me nat, and have me in credens" (ll. 699–700). In doing so, he points to the limitations of sight as a reliable way to grace and emphasizes that vision as insight depends on revelation, too.

The play thus stages a kind of vision that lies on the threshold between visibility and invisibility. Mary is the ideal figure through which to construct this threshold, since she is not only among the few who are in touch with Christ's physical body but also the first to experience the absence of Christ's body. In the Digby *Mary Magdalene*, the tensions between the visible and the invisible, separation and union, presence and absence culminate in her reception of the Eucharist by Jesus' command at the end of the play. The Eucharist, however, is not just a point of convergence, but it rather creates a counterpoint to the "noli me tangere." The play's many parallels and typological patterns that govern its reflection of vision are set within the magnetism of these two poles: the Eucharistic communion and the "noli me tangere." Instead of offering transubstantiation as a resolution, the play stages a paradox within Christian belief in which the presence of the "Hoc est enim corpus meum" is qualified by the distance of the "noli me tangere." And here the "noli me tangere" also promises another kind of presence, one in which visual immediacy points beyond itself and promises an infinity that reaches beyond the duration of the flesh. In *Mary Magdalene*, Jesus appears again to assert his presence for those who desire it: "To shew desyrows hartys I am full nere, / Women, I apere to yow and sey, 'Awete!'" (ll. 1110–11).

Mary Magdalene is, indeed, set in a time where the final *parousia* is still to be awaited, and when sensory contact with Christ was no longer possible.

This could be seen as a reason why Mary Magdalene survived well into the Reformation. She is, after all, the only female saint who remained in the 1549 *Book of Common Prayer,* and her feast was still included in the Protestant calendar. She provided both a point of identification for Catholics whose physical contact to Christ in the Eucharist was limited after the Reformation, as well as an articulation of the reformed faith relying on the symbolic quality of presence.[42] As the original witness of the transubstantiated body, she also provided a model for the act of seeing as a way of participating in the commemorative celebration of the Eucharist[43]—when it is the priest who touches the host, and not the believer, who touches it only with his eyes.

PERFORMANCE AND EKPHRASIS IN *THE WINTER'S TALE*

Like the Magdalene story, *The Winter's Tale* is a tale of transformation; it is about the end of ignorance and sin and the beginning of new wisdom and insight. Presenting a promise of reunion it gestures towards reforging original unities that have been broken: the unity between Leontes and Polixenes dating back to their childhood friendship, between Leontes and Hermione, between Hermione and Perdita, and between Perdita and Florizel, as well as the unity between art and nature, the replica and the original in the figure of Hermione herself.

The Winter's Tale shares many Romance elements with *Mary Magdalene*: the fulfillment of prophecies, rough sea voyages and shipwrecks, resurrections from the dead, spectral appearances in dreams, and foundlings miraculously surviving in distant lands. Like *Mary Magdalene, The Winter's Tale* centers on a type of synoptic vision in which two perspectives and two modes of being coexist at the same time. The play establishes parallel worlds, double identities, and constant shifts of perspective, and hence engages the viewer in a process of seeing in which distance—between father and son, mother and daughter, nature and artifice—is both created and suspended. As the play introduces secondary presences to reflect the original, it inspires a notion of difference in which something is to be seen in terms of an other. It is not the totality and completeness of a unity that *The Winter's Tale* attempts to reach, but a way to explore two identities simultaneously at play.

---

42. "Pastoral literature produced by and for English Catholics of this period . . . used Mary Magdalene as a symbolic vehicle to guide the faithful to the realization that Christ was still present with believers even in the absence of the physical body" (Lisa McClain, "'They have taken away my Lord': Mary Magdalene, Christ's Missing Body, and the Mass in Reformation England," *Sixteenth Century Journal* 38 [2007]: p. 78 [77–96]).

43. Badir, *Maudlin Impression,* p. 47.

When Leontes compares himself to Mamillius ("we are / Almost as like as eggs" [1.2.129–30]),[44] or when he likens Polixenes' image to that of Florizel ("Your father's image is so hit in you / His very air, that I should call you brother" [5.1.126–27]), he refers to these likenesses as a form of self-differentiation and repetition, while he is also fatefully deluded by his own jealous projections. Neither words nor images can convince him, and seeing for him is no longer believing as he rejects the apparent, ocular proof when Paulina presents him with his newborn daughter: "Although the print be little, the whole matter / And copy of the father—eye, nose, lip, / . . . / And thou, good goddess Nature, which hast made it / So like to him that got it" (2.3.98–104).

Whereas Polixenes has retained the ability to view the other as a potential mirror of the self ("Your chang'd complexions are to me a mirror, / Which shows me mine changed too" [1.2.376–77]), Leontes fatally depends on his own sight imprinted on the mind as in a mirror ("I have drunk and seen the spider" [2.1.45]), and as a consequence, is hopelessly deluded by his senses: "You smell this business with a sense as cold / As is a dead man's nose; but I do see't and feel't" (2.1.151–52). He tries but fails to convince others of his viewpoint: "Who mayst see / Plainly as heaven sees earth and earth sees heaven, / How I am gall'd" (1.2.310–12). His "plain vision," however, remains pathologically one-sided and willfully blind to the truth. His self-absorption in which he twice refers to himself as the center ("thy intention stabs the centre" [1.2.137]; "The centre is not big enough to bear / a schoolboy's top" [2.1.102–3]) conforms with the reformed notion of sin as blindness to others and a form of idolatry of the self.[45]

Leontes reads the situation as the audience reads him, and the play engages the viewer in the process of seeing opposites, like two sides of the same coin, something that Leontes deems impossible: "Canst with thine eyes at once see good and evil, / Inclining to them both" (1.2.300–301). Much of the play's dramatic impact relies on visual structures of desire pointing towards what is not there, or not there yet. As in *Mary Magdalene*, these structures of desire include having to wait for the impossible: the return of the daugh-

44. William Shakespeare, *The Winter's Tale*, eds. Susan Snyder and Deborah T. Curren-Aquino, The New Cambridge Shakespeare (Cambridge: Cambridge University Press, 2007). All references to *The Winter's Tale* are to this edition.

45. On *The Winter's Tale*'s staging of Jewish, Graeco-Roman, Catholic, and Protestant discourses of idolatry, see Julia Reinhard Lupton, *Afterlives of the Saints: Hagiography, Typology, and Renaissance Literature* (Stanford: Stanford University Press, 1996), pp. 177–90. Also, for instance, Tyndale in his *Obedience of a Christian Man* (1527) writes that "nothing bringeth the wrath of God so soon and so sore on a man, as the idolatry of his own imagination" (Henry Walter, ed., *Doctrinal Treatises and Introductions to Different Portions of the Holy Scriptures by William Tyndale* [Cambridge: Cambridge University Press, 1848], p. 292).

ter and the wife, forgiveness through grace, and the resurrection of the dead who are clad in Paulina's almost fairy-tale prophecy: "Unless another / As like Hermione as is her picture, / Affront his eye" (5.1.72–74).

Like *The Tempest*, *The Winter's Tale* seems to be prompted by the question: "What impossible matter will he make easy next?" (*Tempest*, 2.1.87)[46]. Shakespeare's play explores the notion of impossibility when it departs from its principal source *Pandosto*. At the end of Greene's novel, the protagonist welcomes the return of his daughter and her husband after having spent sixteen years of mourning and daily visiting his dead wife, for whose death he is responsible. He falls in love with his daughter whom he takes to be a refugee, but who reminds him of his dead wife. When he learns that his guest is his daughter, he commits suicide out of shame. His mourning, it seems, has no effect whatsoever. In *The Winter's Tale*, Shakespeare changes the ending to have the wife, who had hidden for sixteen years, come back to life: first as a statue Leontes admires that then comes miraculously to life on stage to reunite the family.

Hermione's reappearance in the likeness of a statue is an instance of resurrection, in a scene equally bewildering to the audience as to the characters. It is one of the most intense moments on Shakespeare's stage, and indeed, one of the last scenes that he is presumed to have written. It presents an ekphrastic moment par excellence: an image coming to life through words.

Hermione's sensational revitalization occurs in a setting that is at once sacral, artistic, and theatrical. Paulina's "chapel" (3.2.236) that Leontes vouched to visit "once a day" is the "gallery" (5.3.10) in which she exhibits Hermione's ekphrastic performance. Hermione's divinity is suggested in several ways: first by her apparent victory over death, her "holy looks" ("That e'er I put between your holy looks / My ill suspicion" [5.3.148–49]) that Leontes praises in repentance; second by the many Marian allusions of the scene, when for instance Perdita is asked by Paulina to "kneel / And pray your mother's blessing" (5.3.119–20), and also when Polixenes, early in the play, had called her "most sacred lady" (1.2.75).[47] But alongside these references to Catholic practices, Hermione also epitomizes a quasi-replica of the Oracle at Delphi represented by a statue.[48]

The statue scene revolves around looking at, but not immediately touching, the one who is newly brought back from death. Taking up the role of a

---

46. William Shakespeare, *The Tempest*, ed. by David Lindley, The New Cambridge Shakespeare. Updated Edition (Cambridge: Cambridge University Press, 2013).

47. For the Marian associations of this scene, see Lupton, *Afterlives of the Saints*, pp. 176–78; pp. 206–18.

48. Lupton, *Afterlives of the Saints*, pp. 207–11.

stage manager and speaking for the silent Hermione, Paulina both torments and entices Leontes and Perdita with the possibility that Hermione might be alive. In a prologue to her revelation—a gesture similar to that of Christ raising Lazarus from the dead—she addresses the audience and the characters on stage alike:

As she liv'd peerless,
So her dead likeness I do well believe,
Excels whatever yet you look'd upon,
Or hand of man hath done; therefore I keep it
Lonely, apart. But here it is: Prepare
To see the life as lively mock'd as ever
Still sleep mocked death. Behold, and say 'tis well!
(5.3.14–20)

When she urges the viewers to "awake" their "faith" (5.3.95) so that Hermione may also awaken, and tells Hermione that "[she]'ll fill your grave up" (5.3.101), Paulina calls to mind Christ's encounter with Mary in the garden. In both passages, faith in resurrection itself is "requir'd" (5.3.94). This certainly recalls the reformed faith in things not seen, but it also suggests, as Richard Wilson has argued, faith in "the imponderable that was produced mechanically on this stage."[49] Since Paulina's magic is a magic of the theater, her appeal to faith also calls for a willing suspension of disbelief that does not merely center on the invisible, but is also inspired by the visible, Pygmalion-like transformation of what can be seen on stage. Paulina orchestrates and directs the gaze of the characters on stage and that of the audience. She relies on the visual impact of the scene and also fulfills her much earlier assumption that "The silence often of pure innocence / Persuades when speaking fails" (2.2.40–41).

Paulina instigates a desire for seeing in which the effort of the viewer is needed to activate the power of the maker, and the overwhelming effect of the statue coming alive under their eyes in return also animates the viewer: Leontes, and with him Perdita, indulge in the moment: "So long could I / Stand by a looker / on" (5.3.83–85). Paulina, however, calculatedly prolongs the moment of recognition. She makes self-deprecating remarks about "the sight of [her] poor image" (5.3.58), and her metatheatrical threat to draw the curtain and to end the performance enhances Leontes' desire to gaze more in wonder of the statue's lifelikeness and increases the audience's attraction to the statue.

---

49. Richard Wilson, *Secret Shakespeare. Studies in Theatre, Religion and Resistance* (Manchester: Manchester University Press, 2004), p. 258.

Paulina twice prohibits others from touching the statue, first by telling Perdita, who longs to kiss Hermione's hand, to have "patience! / The statue is but newly fixed, the colour's / Not dry," and second, by warning Leontes that he will "mar" the statue's lips and "stain" his own with paint if he dares to kiss it (5.3.46–48, 80–83). Similar to Mary Magdalene's encounter with the risen Christ, this refusal to be embraced on the spot is both a rejection and a reassuring delay, as *The Winter's Tale* is driven by the impetus to feel "the future in the instant" (*Macbeth,* 1.5.408)[50] and to make the moment last. The play is driven by the idea of longing for the paradox of an eternal here and now. Early on, Polixenes had mused what it might be like "to be boy eternal" (1.2.63). And when Florizel gazes at Perdita, he desires her presence to last forever:

> What you do,
> Still betters what is done. When you speak, sweet,
> I'd have you do it ever:
> . . . .
> When you do dance, I wish you
> A wave o'th'sea, that you might ever do
> Nothing but that, move still, still so,
> And own no other function. Each your doing,
> So singular in each particular,
> Crowns what you are doing, in the present deeds,
> That all your acts are queens
> (4.4.135–46)

Florizel articulates the paradox of motion in standstill, a state in which the present perpetually surpasses itself. He describes a creative mechanism of continuous self-enhancement in which being is never free from becoming, and his description also anticipates the living statue of the final scene.

A statue realizes a moment frozen in time that endures in an eternal here and now. It fixes a transitional space in which death and immortality become inseparable—to become a work of art is both to die and to become immortal at the same time. The artwork, however, infinitely aspires toward life and this desire also manifests itself in the very materiality of the sculpture. Marble, in this respect, was considered particularly apt to create a convincing lifelike effect of soft surfaces and delicate tissues.[51]

---

50. William Shakespeare, *Macbeth,* ed. by A. R. Braunmueller, The New Cambridge Shakespeare (Cambridge: Cambridge University Press, 1997).

51. Franz von Kutschera, *Ästhetik,* 2nd ed. (1998, repr. Berlin: de Gruyter, 2010), p. 327.

Hermione's redemptive statue is attributed to "that rare Italian master Giulio Romano, who (had he himself eternity and could put breath into his work) would beguile nature of her custom, so perfectly he is her ape" (5.2.82–85). Shakespeare uses this reference to the historical (albeit already deceased) Renaissance artist and notorious illustrator of pornography to comment on Hermione's "renaissance," which presents the interplay of life and death, and the impurity latent in a seemingly pure work of art that "from the all that are took something good / To make a perfect woman" (5.1.14–15).

The ekphrastic statue scene reflects on processes of making and breaking of the image, processes that coincide with a cathartic moment of repentance. The transformation of the stone effigy into a dramatic image challenges any one-sided approach to the image. It undermines potential idolatry and image worship by the statue coming to life, and it counters potential iconoclasm by the creation of the dramatic image in performance. What lies at the heart of the ekphrastic moment of Hermione's resurrection is a self-destruction of mimesis that goes hand in hand with the assertion of theatrical immanence.

As Perdita's return moved the onlookers ("Who was most marble there changed color; some swooned, all sorrowed" [5.2.76–77]), the statue, when it does "move indeed" (5.3.88) in both physical and emotional terms, also demonstrates the power of the object of art to animate the viewer. Even though Hermione has been "preserved" (5.3.127), her emergence is, as Richard Wilson has argued, not merely to be explained naturalistically: "The twist is that this creaturely creation *really is a work of art,* 'now newly performed' by a boy but scripted by that rare . . . 'master' William Shakespeare (5.2.87; emphasis in original)."[52] The ideas of resurrection and transubstantiation, of bringing the dead image to life, are revealed as a theatrical masterstroke.

This resurrection, though charged with Christian allusions, clearly differs from the biblical narrative of Christ's resurrection. Not only are the gender roles reversed, but once Paulina calls for "music" to "awake her," she invites touching, urging Hermione to "present" her "hand" to the husband who wooed her in his youth (5.3.107–8). Leontes, coming close enough to her to sense her "warmth," wishes the "art" that has brought Hermione back to life to prove "as lawful as eating" (5.3.109–11). Polixenes, who had initially been accused of having "touched his queen / Forbiddenly" (1.2.411–12), delivers a stage direction for Hermione: "She embraces him!" (5.3.11), and Camillo adds the remark, "She hangs about his neck!" (5.3.112) reversing Leontes' earlier suspicion: "Why he that wears her like a medal, hanging / About his

---

52. Richard Wilson, "'To excel the Golden Age': Shakespeare's Voyage to Greece," in *Vollkommenheit. Ästhetische Perfektion in Mittelalter und Früher Neuzeit*, eds. Verena Lobsien, Claudia Olk, and Katharina Münchberg (Berlin: de Gruyter, 2010), p. 197 [181–204].

neck, Bohemia" (1.2.304–5). Leontes sees and touches, and the reunion is not referred to eschatology but takes place in the present. Similar to *Antony and Cleopatra*, *The Winter's Tale* realizes the eternal in the sensuous here and now "[e]ternity was in our lips and eyes" (*Antony and Cleopatra* 1.3.35)[53], and not unlike Cleopatra, who can make "defect perfection" (*Antony and Cleopatra* 2.2.241), Hermione is perfect in and through her imperfections.

The Winter's Tale offers a model of theatrical presence. It gestures toward perfection and immediacy and fulfills it in the performance.[54] The microcosm of the theater creates a kind of perfection that lies in the imperfect and can be conceived as a process of transcending and negating the very boundaries within which it operates. At the same time, the theater becomes a medium of transformation and the place where the impossible can be actualized as a possibility.

In the performance of Hermione's ekphrastic resurrection, *The Winter's Tale* recasts a religious poetics into an aesthetics of theatrical immanence, one in which the work of art generates its own truth in its materiality. It no longer stands in relation to something outside and beyond itself but has its *raison d'être* in a reflection of itself. In *The Winter's Tale,* this mode of reflection manifests itself in the many parallelisms, the mirroring structures, and the iterative patterns of repetition and variation. Hence the end of the play refers to its beginning: "Dear Queen that endeth when I but began" (5.3.45). However, the reunion at the end of *The Winter's Tale* comes at a cost. Even though there is resurrection, there is no redemption, no Paradise regained: A son, a husband, and sixteen years have been lost, and the viewer, once again, is permitted to see both sides of the same coin. Like an image that always signals an absence even as it conjures the sense of a presence, these absences and losses poignantly evoke a reunion that is itself preceded by a process of partition and self-differentiation, and that finally occurs through the appearance of a likeness—the return of the daughter, and the resurrection of Hermione as statue.

Whereas *Mary Magdalene* is an affirmation of the theater's capacity for both presenting and analyzing the visible at the same time, and for including the audience in the experience of touching with one's own eyes, it also relies

---

53. William Shakespeare, *Antony and Cleopatra,* ed. by David Bevington, The New Cambridge Shakespeare. Updated Edition (Cambridge: Cambridge University Press, 2005).

54. In contrast to Cynthia Lewis's reading of this scene, I would suggest that Shakespeare does not discard art and "earthly trappings" in favor of "the true identity" of a character, but that he, quite on the contrary, affirms the status of art that questions any notion of a "true identity" ("Soft Touch: On the Renaissance Staging and Meaning of the 'Noli me tangere,'" *Comparative Drama* 36 [2002]: 70 [53–73]).

on a promise of presence and immediacy yet to come.[55] *The Winter's Tale,* by contrast, fulfills this promise in the mortal and finite here and now of the theatrical moment. "Paulina re-creates art as life, and life as art,"[56] and Leontes is finally able to embrace his resurrected wife. Unlike Shakespeare—the maker of this moment of fulfillment—Mary remains a spectator, and her way of seeing and desiring may also find its extension in the theatrical experience where the dramatic text comes to life in the performance, which we have looked at, and loved, and must part with again.

55. On the intersection of universal history and time, see Suzanne Conklin Akbari's essay in this volume, pp. 194–205.

56. Marjorie Garber, *Shakespeare after All* (New York: Anchor Books, 2004), p. 851.

Chapter 5

FEELING THINKING

PEARL'S EKPHRASTIC IMAGINATION

Anke Bernau

he fourteenth-century dream vision poem, *Pearl,* presents the reader with an odd but little commented-on passage embedded in the opening lamentation of the sorrowing "jeweler" for his lost pearl, "that dos bot thrych my herte thrange, / My breste in bale bot bolne and bele" [that does nothing but pierce my heart sharply, swell and burn my breast painfully].[1] It constitutes a momentary shift in tone that introduces a calmer—even peaceful— voice, in which he remembers meditating upon his loss in an inspirational and artistically productive silence:

> Yet thoght me never so swete a sange
> As stylle stounde let to me stele;
> Forsothe, ther fleten to me fele
> To thenke hir color so clad in clot.
> (ll. 19–22)

---

1. Sarah Stanbury, ed., *Pearl* (Kalamazoo, MI: TEAMS Medieval Institute Publications, 2001), ll. 17–18. All future references will be to this edition; line numbers will be given parenthetically in the text. Glosses and translations are also taken from Stanbury's edition (with line breaks removed in the translations). Translations should only be taken as indicative; the ambiguity of the original vocabulary is central to my argument at numerous points throughout the essay.

Yet I thought never so sweet a song as a still time let steal over me; indeed, there flew to me many [songs], to imagine her colour so clad in dirt.

Although the narrator soon returns to the mode of lament and the description of emotional turmoil, these lines provide a curious and intriguing hiatus. The pearl's loss, it seems, is not associated exclusively with grief—or, rather, grief is shown to be a complex emotion: unpredictable, capacious, and imaginatively productive.[2] Indeed, the many sweet songs that come to him specifically emerge out of the combination of his memory and his imagining of her new condition.[3] The contrast between the past and the present that memory makes possible results in powerful emotion and the emergence of "swete . . . sange"; one might say that the latter is made possible by the former.

Nicolette Zeeman has urged medieval scholars to take more seriously "'imaginative' articulations of literary theory." Her argument is that we can find in medieval vernacular imaginative texts a literary theory that privileges figural rather than the "analytical and explicit terms" provided by the philosophers of the schools.[4] I will be reading *Pearl* in light of this possibil-

---

2. The sweetness of the songs presumably echoes the one-time ability of his pearl to "devoyde my wrange" (l. 15), thus introducing the idea that sorrow existed for the narrator even before this loss. "Wrange," from "wrong," can also mean "that which is morally wrong" or "error" (*MED,* s.v. "wrong"). And while "color" can mean "complexion," it can also refer to "paint," a "stylistic device," or an "argument" (*MED,* s.v. "colour"). The behavior the pearl ameliorates ranges from sorrow to more serious sins, while her "color" brings into play associations with human physicality, painting, rhetoric, and reason.

3. On the poetics of loss in elegy, see Peter M. Sacks, *The English Elegy: Studies in the Genre from Spenser to Yeats* (Baltimore: Johns Hopkins University Press, 1985). I am not, however, focusing on *Pearl* as elegy.

4. Nicolette Zeeman, "Imaginative Theory," in *Oxford Twenty-First Century Approaches to Literature: Middle English,* ed. Paul Strohm (Oxford: Oxford University Press, 2007), pp. 222 and 239 [222–40]. See also Steven F. Kruger, "Dreams and Fiction," in *Dreaming in the Middle Ages* (Cambridge: Cambridge University Press, 1992), pp. 123–49. For a consideration of imagination in relation to *Pearl,* see Thorlac Turville-Petre, "Places of the Imagination: The *Gawain*-Poet," in which he looks at the *Gawain*-poet's exploration of "the psychological and spiritual condition" of his protagonists and highlights the sense of "progression, a physical movement that mirrors psychological development towards some sort of reintegration" (in *The Oxford Handbook of Medieval Literature in English,* eds. Elaine Treharne and Greg Walker [Oxford: Oxford University Press, 2010], p. 596 [594–610]). See also Sandra Pierson Prior, *The Fayre Formez of the* Pearl *Poet* (East Lansing: Michigan State University Press, 1996); J. J. Anderson, *Language and Imagination in the* Gawain-*Poems* (Manchester: Manchester University Press, 2005); and most recently, Linda Tarte Holley, *Reason and Imagination in Chaucer, the* Perle-*Poet, and the* Cloud-*Author: Seeing from the Center* (New York: Palgrave Macmillan, 2011). Tarte's reading and mine overlap in places (we share an interest in poetic theory), but we approach the poem from different perspectives. For an excellent discussion of medieval theories of memory and imagination, see Alastair Minnis, "Medieval Imagination and Memory," in *The Cambridge History of Literary Criticism, Volume 2: The Middle Ages,* eds. Ian Johnson and Alastair Minnis (Cambridge: Cambridge University Press, 2005), pp. 239–74.

ity, considering the ways in which it conceptualizes the *craft* of imaginative composition—primarily in its use of ekphrasis, through which it explores the complex and shifting relationships between memory and wonder. I will begin, as *Pearl* does, with grief.[5]

Grief is a potent and potentially transformative emotion—the nature of its experience and its quality or intensity are difficult to predict or regulate. At the same time as it affects the individual in private and specific ways, modes of grieving are also communally and historically determined.[6] In the late Middle Ages, grief posed an ethical as well as social problem, for it was perceived to be a response to loss (particularly the death of a loved one) that was both appropriate and uncontrollable, inevitable yet always in danger of being excessive.[7] The balance between remembrance of the loss, and the forgetting needed in order to ward off despair, was delicate and uneasy. Overwhelming

---

5. Throughout this essay I will be using the terms *emotion* and *affect* interchangeably. In this, I am aligning myself with Alex Houen's recent assessment that "there's still no consensus about how we can make clean distinctions between the terms" (Alex Houen, "Introduction: Affecting Words," *Textual Practice: Special Issue: Affects, Text, and Performativity* 25.2 (2011): 218 [215–32]).

6. There is a considerable—and rapidly expanding—body of work on emotions in a wide range of disciplines. For a critique of *emotions historiography* from a medievalist's perspective, see Barbara H. Rosenwein, "Worrying about Emotions in History," *The American Historical Review* 107.3 (2002): 821–45. See also Sarah McNamer, "Feeling," in *Oxford Twenty-First Century Approaches to Literature: Middle English,* ed. Paul Strohm (Oxford: Oxford University Press, 2007), pp. 241–57; Simo Knuuttila, *Emotions in Ancient and Medieval Philosophy* (Oxford: Oxford University Press, 2004); Dominik Perler, *Transformationen der Gefühle: Philosophische Emotionstheorien 1270–1670* (Frankfurt: Fischer, 2011).

7. Throughout this essay, I will be considering the Dreamer's expression of loss as being indicative of grief rather than melancholia. Medieval definitions of melancholia differ from our understanding of the term, and while *Pearl* can be usefully considered as representing a melancholic narrator figure, I am interested here in the way the poem is thinking through the emotional effects of concrete loss. Although it could be argued that the Maiden is trying to redefine the Dreamer as a melancholic of Freud's description, she actually does not say that his loss is imaginary; according to her, it is the *nature* of what he has lost (a rose, not a pearl) that the Dreamer misunderstands and misrepresents. For the classic essay on the distinction between the two, see Sigmund Freud, "Mourning and Melancholia," in *The Standard Edition of the Complete Psychological Works,* trans. J. Strachey, 24 vols. (London: Hogarth, 1953–1974), 14:243–58. For historicist perspectives on melancholia, see, for instance, Stanley W. Jackson, *Melancholia and Depression from Hippocratic Times to Modern Times* (New Haven, CT: Yale University Press, 1986); Juliana Schiesari, *The Gendering of Melancholia: Feminism, Psychoanalysis, and the Symbolics of Loss in Renaissance Literature* (Ithaca, NY: Cornell University Press, 1992); Rudolf Wittkower and Margot Wittkower, *Born under Saturn: The Character and Conduct of Artists: A Documented History from Antiquity to the French Revolution* (New York: Random House, 1963). On a discussion of the difficulty of clearly distinguishing between mourning and melancholia, and their complex manifestations in Chaucer's elegies as well as in medieval studies, see L. O. Aranye Fradenburg, "'Voice Memorial': Loss and Reparation in Chaucer's Poetry," *Exemplaria* 2 (1990): 169–202.

grief could threaten the psychological and spiritual destruction of the grieving individual, especially by placing in doubt his or her faith in God. This, in turn, had implications for the wider social networks in which that individual was embedded. Codified expressions and rituals of grief were there to offer safe passage through the mourning process, but the outcome of that process was never certain. Thus, grief was viewed as simultaneously "necessary and efficacious" *and* "excessive and subversive."[8]

The concept of Purgatory exemplifies the memorial impulse inherent in officially sanctioned processes of grieving: relations between the living and the dead continued, made possible by remembrance. By praying for the dead, the living could affect the afterlives of those residing in Purgatory; in turn, the departed souls required and were grateful for such intervention. As Jean-Claude Schmitt has shown, socially produced practices of memory and commemoration were the means by which individuals and communities could safely negotiate the potentially overwhelming emotion of grief. Through approved rituals of death, burial, and mourning, grief's treacherous depths (and the troubling energy of the recently dead) could be negotiated safely. At the same time, forgetting should not happen too quickly: this was inappropriate emotion in surviving relatives and a danger to the one languishing in Purgatory. As Schmitt concludes, surviving autobiographical accounts of loss from this period show that "what is most important is the conflict between the desire to forget and the impossibility of doing so, between the fragility of memory and the will to remember."[9]

Appropriate social performances as well as literary representations of grief were intricately coded, or scripted, according to class, gender, and the individual's level of religious faith, for instance. As some scholars have noted, literary and artistic depictions of grief "often counter or transgress cultural

---

8. Katharine Goodland, "'Vs for to Wepe No Man May Lett': Accommodating Female Grief in the Medieval English Lazarus Plays," *Early Theatre: A Journal Associated with the Records of Early English Drama* 8.1 (2005): 90 [69–94]. For a reading of *Pearl* that draws on Kubler-Ross's "five psychological stages of loss" in response to death, see Karen A. Sylvia, "Living with Dying: Grief and Consolation in the Middle English *Pearl*," Honors Projects Overview, Paper 45 (2007), p. 41, *Digital Commons @RIC,* http://digitalcommons.ric.edu/honors_projects/45.

9. Jean-Claude Schmitt, *Ghosts in the Middle Ages: The Living and the Dead in Medieval Society,* trans. Teresa Lavender Fagan (1994, repr. Chicago: University of Chicago Press, 1998), p. 9. Medieval homilists and sermons often referred disapprovingly to family members who forgot their dying/dead loved ones too soon; see G. R. Owst, *Literature and Pulpit in Medieval England: A Neglected Chapter in the History of English Letters and the English People* (1961, repr. Whitefish, MT: Kessinger, 2003). On the demand of ghosts to be remembered, see Dawn Hadley, *Death in Medieval England: An Archaeology* (Stroud: Tempus, 2001), p. 75.

limitations placed on how [to] grieve or mourn."[10] Imaginative writing both reflected and produced models for the ways in which grief and memory might (or ought to) be experienced and negotiated; what Sarah McNamer, writing about affective meditation, has called "intimate scripts."[11] Certainly there was a wide range of imaginative writings that addressed or represented grief: laments, elegies, romances, drama, lyrics, and ghost stories are some of these.[12] In exploring the nature and effects of grief, such writings are often explicitly commemorative: in their subject matter (Christ's passion or the loss of a loved one), their iteration of other discourses, and even in the fact of their existence. Indeed, grief, literary invention, and memory are all shown to be closely associated with powerful emotions: dangerous such emotions might be, but also indispensable to the very processes that made thought, feeling, and identity possible. Rather than just being descriptive, prescriptive, or indeed proscriptive, such imaginative engagements also explore the affective and cognitive processes and responses that they produce and are shaped by; that is, they imagine what it means to think, feel, and write imaginatively. Grief can be, in this sense, a particular way of thinking and imagining, as well as feeling.

Critical responses to *Pearl* have tended to emphasize opposed and incompatible ways of knowing offered by the poem. In her 1972 overview of scholarly approaches to *Pearl*, Marie Hamilton notes that critics read it either as a personal elegy or as an allegory, where the former is associated with the personal, experiential, and affective, and the latter with the formal, theoretical, and cognitive.[13] In 2000, J. Allan Mitchell reiterated this assessment when

10. Jennifer C. Vaught, Introduction in *Grief and Gender, 700–1700*, eds. Jennifer C. Vaught and Lynne Dickson Bruckner (New York: Palgrave Macmillan, 2003), p. 2. See also Goodland, "'Vs for to Wepe.'"

11. Sarah McNamer, *Affective Meditation and the Invention of Medieval Compassion* (Philadelphia: University of Pennsylvania Press, 2010), p. 1. She bases this on William Reddy's term *emotion scripts*; see William Reddy, *The Navigation of Feeling: A Framework for the History of Emotions* (Cambridge: Cambridge University Press, 2001). See also Silvan Tomkins, "Script Theory and Nuclear Scripts," in *Shame and Its Sisters: A Silvan Tomkin Reader*, eds. Eve Kosofsky Sedgwick and Adam Frank (Durham, NC: Duke University Press, 1995), pp. 179–96.

12. See Velma Bourgeois Richmond, *Laments for the Dead in Medieval Narrative*, Duquesne Studies Philological Series 8 (Pittsburgh: Duquesne University Press, 1966).

13. Marie P. Hamilton, *The* Pearl *Poet, A Manual of the Writings in Middle English, 1050–1500*, ed. J. Burke Severs, vol. 2 (New Haven: Connecticut Academy of Arts and Sciences, 1970), pp. 339–53. Ad Putter sees in the poem a "tension between doctrine and experience" (*An Introduction to the* Gawain *Poet* [London: Longman, 1996], p. 188); and Jennifer Garrison concludes that the poem's difficult conclusion exemplifies the Dreamer's recognition that "rigid control of one's emotional state is essential if one is to accept the profound state of lack that defines human earthly life" ("Liturgy and Loss: *Pearl* and the Ritual Reform of the Aristocratic Subject," *Chaucer Review* 44.3 [2010]: 322 [294–322]). Helen Barr sets out to

he refers to the "notorious 'elegy versus allegory' debate," which shaped the critical reception of *Pearl* "for the first half of [the twentieth] century."[14] While later critics did not necessarily invoke these terms, they often still read the poem in the light of conflicting modes or referential frameworks. Thus Sarah Stanbury, in *Seeing the Gawain-Poet* (1991), writes that "*Pearl* dramatizes the aporia between visual experience and other ways of knowing, such as the instruction by doctrine the Maiden provides,"[15] and David Aers (1993) reads the poem as presenting the reader with two kinds of memory.[16] According to Aers, the Dreamer's "unregenerate memory" is a response to the "crushing pain we experience in the loss of those we love" and is used by him "as a defense against our real acknowledgement of change." This is set against the Maiden's memory, which is apocalyptic and future-oriented.[17] The purpose and quality of these two kinds of memory echo the oppositions set out by other critics in relation to form or ways of knowing. Yet while these readings of oppositional cognitive and affective modes undoubtedly raise important and valid questions about the poem, and offer valuable insights into its complexity, medieval theories of memory do not easily allow for a clear opposition between experience and doctrine, or between feeling and knowing.

As work by Mary Carruthers and Janet Coleman has shown, memory—understood both as natural capacity and as trained mental skill—was cen-

---

"continue recent moves to break out of a closed hermeneutic system of juxtaposing the heavenly and the earthly" in *Pearl,* reading it instead as exploring contemporary social concerns ("*Pearl*—Or 'The Jeweller's Tale,'" in *Socioliterary Practice in Late Medieval England* [Oxford: Oxford University Press, 2001], pp. 40–62).

14. J. Allan Mitchell, "The Middle English *Pearl*: Figuring the Unfigurable," *Chaucer Review* 35.1 (2000): 86 [86–111]. He reads the poem as offering a "critique of typology" that "qualifies improper homage to verbal revelation" (p. 108). This is not to overwrite the diverse interpretations the poem has attracted, not least of which in recent years.

15. Sarah Stanbury, *Seeing the Gawain-Poet: Description and the Act of Perception* (Philadelphia: University of Pennsylvania Press, 1991), p. 14.

16. David Aers, "The Self Mourning; Reflections on *Pearl,*" *Speculum* 68.1 (1993): 55–56 [54–73]. Here Aers offers a brief overview of what he sees as the two main critical responses to the poem: one that reads it as privileging clerical authority, and one that focuses "on the dramatic and rhetorical movements of the poem," mainly concerned with human emotions and motivations, Aers also identifies a third, "deconstructive" strand, but aligns his reading of the poem most closely with the second (p. 56). Gregory Roper, writing in 1993 also, notes, "Most readings, it seems, now concentrate on the dreamer's progress in knowledge (or lack of it); the poem is seen as a dynamic process leading from the dreamer's ignorance to his greater understanding. This, of course, is where my reading is headed, though I will try to show it as a penitential journey" ("*Pearl,* Penitence, and the Recovery of the Self," *Chaucer Review* 28.2 (1993): 183, n. 1 [164–86]. My reading is not concerned as much with evaluating the nature of the Dreamer's understanding, or his successful (or failed) "progress"; I am looking at how the poem presents the ways in which thought and feeling *work,* and how this is related to imaginative writing.

17. Aers, "Self Mourning," pp. 68, 58, and 62.

tral to medieval understandings of selfhood and of community.[18] It lay at the heart of theories of what we now would consider psychology as well as ethics. Indeed, whether a memory was based on personal experience (thus rooted in the past), or on textual knowledge, or on a dream vision (and thereby possibly focused on the future, but nonetheless encountered in a moment that is now past), the formation and impression of the memory in the individual followed similar processes, particularly in that each memory was thought to be necessarily attached to (or "colored by") a specific, often powerful, emotion.[19] *All* knowledge was thus thought of as originating in sensory processes and in experience for, as late medieval philosophers such as Thomas Aquinas noted, "There is nothing in the intellect that was not first in the senses."[20]

It is therefore difficult to make a distinction between feeling and knowing, or the knowledge gained from experience and that gained in other ways. As McNamer reminds us, the Middle English term *felen,* which can mean both "to feel" and "to know," "serves as a reminder of the integration of the somatic, affective, and cognitive in a pre-Cartesian universe."[21] I am not arguing that there are *no* distinctions between different kinds or uses of memory, or different kinds of knowledge, in medieval thought, but that the poem can fruitfully be read as exploring imaginatively their overlapping complexities, since they draw on shared mental and affective processes. It is in the

---

18. See, for instance, Mary J. Carruthers, *The Book of Memory: A Study of Memory in Medieval Culture* (Cambridge: Cambridge University Press, 1990); Mary J. Carruthers, *The Craft of Thought: Meditation, Rhetoric, and the Making of Images, 400–1200* (Cambridge: Cambridge University Press, 1998); Janet Coleman, *Ancient and Medieval Memories: Studies in the Reconstruction of the Past* (Cambridge: Cambridge University Press, 1992).

19. See Mary J. Carruthers and Jan M. Ziolkowski, Introduction in *The Medieval Craft of Memory: An Anthology of Texts and Pictures,* eds. Mary J. Carruthers and Jan M. Ziolkowski (Philadelphia: University of Pennsylvania Press, 2002), p. 8 [1–31]: "Memories themselves are *affects* of the soul and mind." See also Mary J. Carruthers, "[E]very memory image is emotionally colored. It is never neutral" ("Invention, Mnemonics, and Stylistic Ornament in *Psychomachia* and *Pearl*," in *The Endless Knot: Essays on Old and Middle English in Honor of Marie Borroff,* eds. M. Teresa Tavormina and R. F. Yeager [Cambridge: D. S. Brewer, 1995], p. 204 [201–13]).

20. Cited in Michael Camille, "Before the Gaze: The Internal Senses and Late Medieval Practices of Seeing," in *Visuality Before and Beyond the Renaissance: Seeing as Others Saw,* ed. Robert S. Nelson (Cambridge: Cambridge University Press, 2000), p. 200 [197–223]. See also Cynthia Hahn: "Vision is a central element of later medieval epistemology. It is not only the noblest of the senses, but the corporeal origin and requirement of intellectual vision" ("*Visio Dei:* Changes in Medieval Visuality," in *Visuality Before and Beyond the Renaissance: Seeing as Others Saw,* ed. Robert S. Nelson (Cambridge: Cambridge University Press, 2000), p. 188 [169–96].

21. McNamer, "Feeling," pp. 241–57. See also Houen, "Affecting Words," p. 218: "What it [affect] does comprise are emotional compounds of bodily feeling and cognition, where cognition can include imagination no less than reasoning."

poem's ekphrastic passages that the interrelationships of cognition and affect in memory are explored most insistently; it is here that we see the Dreamer negotiating questions of knowing, feeling, and creating through encounters with both memory and wonder.[22] Indeed, if there is a cognitive and affective counterpoint to memory in the poem, it is represented by the astonishing, unfamiliar nature of the marvelous that the Dreamer encounters. Yet memory and marvel (or wonder, as the response to marvel) are also characterized by similar features, and both are necessary for imaginative creativity.

Ekphrasis is a visual, affective, and cognitive mode.[23] Carruthers notes that in a medieval context, ekphrasis was considered a "typ[e] of the cognitive, dispositive topos called *pictura*," central not only to rhetoric and poetic composition, but more generally to what she terms the "craft of thought."[24] Used in medieval monasticism to aid meditational practice, it provided the mind with detailed descriptions or images on which to linger and ruminate. Detailed description stimulated the imagination, harnessing or stirring emotions that could be fed back into the meditation. By incorporating visual clues and cues for the reader or practitioner, it suggested connections to other themes, texts, experiences, or emotions that could, in turn, be brought to bear on the description at hand, thereby extending its meanings by linking it to a web of associations. One of its discursive functions was to "provide[ ] a meditative occasion within a work," since it "slows down, even interrupts, the established *ductus* . . . and often sends the reader in a new direction."[25] Roland Recht comments on its frequent use by preachers, in order to contextualize or embed doctrinal truths within "the fabric of listeners' daily experiences."[26] While the details ekphrases provided might slow down the pace of a narrative or sermon, their proliferation also provided further narrative possibilities. Ekphrasis, then, is concerned with detail—with *ornament*—which is memorable but also inventive, familiar but open to the new, encouraging cognitive engagement through affective appeal.[27]

---

22. For an insightful, recent reading of *Pearl* that touches upon questions of memory and wonder in its consideration of the poem's exploration of prudence and subjectivity, see Corey Owen, "The Prudence of *Pearl,*" *Chaucer Review* 45.4 (2011): 411–34.

23. See, for instance, Simon Goldhill, who notes: "In short, ekphrasis is designed to produce a viewing subject" ("What Is Ekphrasis For?" *Classical Philology: Special Issue on Ekphrasis* 102.1 [2007]: 2 [1–19]).

24. Carruthers, *Craft of Thought,* p. 200.

25. Carruthers, *Craft of Thought,* p. 199.

26. Roland Recht, *Believing and Seeing: The Art of Gothic Cathedrals,* trans. Mary Whittall (Chicago: University of Chicago Press, 2008), pp. 78–79.

27. On ekphrasis as ornamental, see Carruthers, *Craft of Thought,* p. 223. One recent definition notes that originally "the true use of ekphrasis was not to simply provide astute details of an object, but to share the *emotional experience* and content with someone who had never

According to St. Augustine, there were three kinds of vision a human subject could experience: corporeal vision, at the lowest level, in which one sees with one's bodily eyes; spiritual vision, which relates to "images in dreams or the imagination"; and "intellectual vision, occurring in the highest levels of the mind," the only place where one could perceive "divine truths."[28] *Pearl* takes place at the second level, spiritual vision, which concentrated on the imaginative part of the soul, "the intermediary and mediatory power between *sensus* and *mens,* which received and transformed images" before they were stored in memory.[29] In this imaginative context, ekphrasis provides a commentary on the poetic process even as it presents the mind's eye with carefully crafted images. In their introduction to a special issue on ekphrasis for *Classical Philology,* Shadi Bartsch and Jaś Elsner outline the myriad (and at times contradictory) impulses of this rhetorical trope, many of which can usefully inform a reading of *Pearl.* They refer to its tendency to "play[ ] with the tension between . . . stillness and narrative," and to its imbrication with a range of sensory perceptions.[30] Most importantly for my argument here, they state that one of the "effects that much ekphrasis strives to create" is "a sense of wonder and of the immediacy of the described object or scene," encouraging in the reader "an emotive response . . . and a degree of immersion into the imagined visual."[31]

---

encountered the work in question" ("The University of Chicago: Theories of Media: Keywords Glossary," s.v. "ekphrasis," University of Chicago, http://csmt.uchicago.edu/glossary2004/ekphrasis.htm, [emphasis mine]).

28. Cynthia Hahn, "*Visio Dei,*" p. 171. See also Schmitt, *Ghosts,* pp. 22–25. Stanbury expands on the process of spiritual ascent as theorized by Augustine, Hugh of St. Victor, and Bonaventure, relating their ideas of the problematic status of sensory experience to the "dreamer's spiritual progress" in *Pearl* (*Seeing the* Gawain-*Poet,* p. 15). Two key studies of the medieval dream vision form are A. C. Spearing, *Medieval Dream-Poetry* (Cambridge: Cambridge University Press, 1976) and Kathryn L. Lynch, *The High Medieval Dream Vision: Vision, Philosophy, and Literary Form* (Stanford: Stanford University Press, 1988).

29. See Schmitt, *Ghosts,* p. 24. See also Kruger, *Dreaming,* p. 131: "Involved in the middleness of imagination, the poetic, like the oneiric, dwells in a region between body and intellect, wedding ideas to a sensible and pleasurable form."

30. Shadi Bartsch and Jaś Elsner, "Introduction: Eight Ways of Looking at an Ekphrasis," *Classical Philology: Special Issue on Ekphrasis* 102.1 (2007): ii [i–vi]. They note that while "drawing us to interpretation," ekphrasis also highlights the contingency of any reading by reminding us of the "subjectivity of the interpreter." The vividness that characterizes ekphrases encourages the reader to identify with the narrator (or with the object of description), while also alienating the reader (from the narrator, from herself) through the proliferation of "multiple" perspectives (iii).

31. Bartsch and Elsner, "Introduction," p. v. Much has been written recently on the fraught and contested late medieval context in relation to the status of the visual and of images in particular. See, for instance: Jeremy Dimmick, James Simpson, and Nicolette Zeeman, eds., *Images, Idolatry, and Iconoclasm in Late Medieval England: Textuality and the Visual Image,* (Oxford: Oxford University Press, 2002); Sarah Stanbury, *The Visual Object of Desire*

Ekphrasis enacts the close connection between memory and imaginative composition, as both are necessary for its creation and both work through emotionally charged images that draw on subjective experience as well as shared knowledge. Both were conceived of as "compositional art[s],"[32] requiring the subject's capacity for invention; both, if done well, presupposed a level of skill and craftsmanship.[33] And the ekphrastic passages in *Pearl* draw, too, on that other component noted by Bartsch and Elsner, for they contrast the image of the craftsman—someone who displays mastery, appropriates and makes his own a subject or material through his skill, experience, and knowledge—with marvel, or wonder, gesturing toward that which lies beyond, and proves resistant to, mastery. If memory is based on experiences already had, or knowledge already internalized, then wonder marks their limit. Both memory and wonder, however, are inextricable from subjective experience and powerful emotions. In a sense, then, imaginative writing can be said to incorporate the possibilities and resources of memory and wonder; it depicts and enacts wonder.

Whereas the *Pearl's* opening is marked by loss, grief, and ultimately, prostration, the dream vision introduces the Dreamer to new sights and movement.[34] Taken out of his familiar surroundings, he is re-placed in a setting that

---

in *Late Medieval England* (Philadelphia: University of Pennsylvania Press, 2008); and Shannon Gayk, *Image, Text, and Religious Reform in Fifteenth-Century England* (Cambridge: Cambridge University Press, 2010). While I am not concerned with material images here, figurative language was of course also suspect due to its perceived seductive potential.

32. On memory as "compositional art," see Carruthers, *Craft of Thought*, p. 9. She adds, "The arts of memory are among the arts of thinking, especially involved with fostering the qualities we now revere as 'imagination' and 'creativity.'"

33. Carruthers notes that "any person thinking is fundamentally a craftsman" ("Invention," p. 203). On the poet as, or in relation to the category of, craftsman, see, for instance, Lois Ebin, *Illuminator, Makar, Vates: Visions of Poetry in the Fifteenth Century* (Lincoln: University of Nebraska Press, 1988); and Lisa H. Cooper, *Artisans and Narrative Craft in Late Medieval England* (Cambridge: Cambridge University Press, 2011). On craftsmanship (either figural or literal) in relation to *Pearl,* see, for instance, Felicity Riddy, "The Materials of Culture: Jewels in *Pearl*," in *A Companion to the* Gawain-*Poet,* eds. Derek Brewer and Jonathan Gibson (Cambridge: D. S. Brewer, 1997), pp. 143–55; Helen Barr, *Socioliterary Practice in Late Medieval England* (Oxford: Oxford University Press, 2002), esp. ch. 2: "*Pearl*—Or 'The Jeweller's Tale,'" pp. 40–62; Seeta Chaganti, *The Medieval Poetics of the Reliquary: Enshrinement, Inscription, Performance* (New York: Palgrave Macmillan, 2008); and Elizabeth Harper, "*Pearl* in the Context of Fourteenth-Century Gift Economies," *Chaucer Review* 44.4 (2010): 421–39. See also Carruthers, who notes that: "The *Pearl* Dreamer . . . is depicted as a jeweler because he is an inventor, using ornaments (in his dream) to make more ornaments (in the poem) which in turn will initiate meditational invention in his readers" ("Invention," pp. 201–13). Carruthers's reading does not, however, take into account the personal grief that is also a central strand in the poem's consideration of artistic production, affect, and cognition.

34. Many critics comment on this; for cognitive and emotional effects of this on the Dreamer, see in particular Turville-Petre, "Places," p. 606.

is the subject of the first ekphrastic passage in the dream vision. When he tells us that his "goste is gon in Godes grace, in aventure ther mervayles meven" (ll. 63–64) [spirit is gone in God's grace in quest where marvels happen], we are being alerted to this change, which is locational but also experiential and cognitive: "aventure" signals a quest and "mervayles" are, by definition, novelties—the generically anticipated but nevertheless unfamiliar that one encounters on quests into the unknown.

Terminology related to the marvelous, or to the response of wonder to it, occurs only a few times in *Pearl*: each time it is part of an ekphrastic passage, and each time it marks a significant moment in the Dreamer's affective and cognitive state.[35] Caroline Walker Bynum has shown that by the late Middle Ages, "theorists . . . understood wonder (*admiratio*) as cognitive, non-appropriative, perspectival, and particular."[36] Wonder resides in the interstices between self and other; always subjective and contextualized, "only that which is really different from the knower can trigger wonder." Bynum identifies three medieval discourses of wonder: the "theological-philosophical," the religious, and that found in "literature of entertainment."[37] The tone of the opening scene of the Dreamer's vision seems to belong in the final category, though it also participates in the second; its reference to "aventure" and description of the exotic landscape are reminiscent of travel literature as well as romance. The Dreamer's initial response to the visionary setting is to forget his grief and relinquish the memory of his loss. While the landscape appears, in its compositional elements, to be like a natural topography, featuring a forest, hillsides, cliffs, trees, birds, and streams, its material makeup is not: the cliffs are crystalline, the tree trunks blue as indigo, the leaves burnished silver, the gravel "precious perles of Oryente" (l. 82). The description of the landscape is thus also a description of a work of art, and different kinds of artistic productions are alluded to, such as tapestries, jewelry, and illuminations. It is specifically the materiality, and the crafted detail or adornment—the "adubbemente"—that "garten my goste al greffe forgete" (l. 86) [caused my spirit all grief to forget].[38] This crafty, marvelous

---

35. The first time is when the Dreamer begins his "aventure," anticipating "mervayles"; the second when he sees the Maiden across the stream for the first time; the third when he describes her and encounters the "wonder perle" set in her breast. After this, the next five references are all clustered together closely and relate to the vision of the New Jerusalem. The final reference comes at the end of that vision, when the Dreamer tries to cross the stream.

36. Caroline Walker Bynum, *Metamorphosis and Identity* (New York: Zone Books, 2005), p. 39. She adds: "We wonder at what we cannot in any sense incorporate, or consume, or encompass in our mental categories" (pp. 52–53).

37. Bynum, *Metamorphosis*, p. 39.

38. Brigitte Buettner points out the centrality and importance of "sumptuous objects"

setting situates the Dreamer anew; and this re-placement is both affective and cognitive.

On the one hand, the marvelous landscape allows the Dreamer to forget his sorrow and loss by introducing novelty and beauty to his experience; on the other, it allows him to exercise his own skills and judgment as a "jeweler" or craftsman. He marvels, but he also assesses, and is able to conclude that "webbes that wyyes weven" [fabrics that people weave] "wern never . . . of half so dere adubbemente" (ll. 71, 72) [were never . . . of half so precious adornment]. Here, then, the Dreamer encounters superior craftsmanship (which also alludes—though not yet explicitly—to a religious significance), whose creativity and *inventio* move him in new directions, physically as well as affectively.[39] This idea of the healing and soothing qualities of artistic works is also relevant in relation to literature. Glending Olson has shown that thinkers such as Thomas of Chobham discussed the "psychological rather than didactic benefits" of stories, for instance. Outlining medieval notions of the medical, ethical, and affective benefits of stories, Olson suggests (not unlike Zeeman in her discussion of imaginative literature) that what emerges is a "more tolerant" approach to the "non-didactic than 'official' medieval culture is often thought to be"—to the extent that it "furnish[es] the basis for more self-consciously literary reflections."[40] This can be read in relation to the first ekphrastic passage of the Dreamer's vision: the "artistic" pleasure he feels might soon give way to more uncomfortable feelings and desires, but it is what brings him "out of himself" and makes what follows possible in the first place. Novelty, beauty, and adornment, in particular, offer through ekphrasis a "new direction."[41]

The focus on the materiality of these surroundings foregrounds the affective and cognitive possibilities of craft and adornment; their aesthetic

in the medieval period: "Sumptuous objects were the locus of an intensive investment—aesthetic, financial, functional, and otherwise." She notes that the "only artist ever to attain sainthood was a goldsmith, Eligius (Eloy)" and sees this as "proof of the high status that his craft enjoyed during the Middle Ages" ("Toward a Historiography of the Sumptuous Arts," in *A Companion to Medieval Art: Romanesque and Gothic in Northern Europe,* ed. Conrad Rudolph [Oxford: Wiley-Blackwell, 2006], p. 467 [466–87]).

39. On the wonder-inducing effects of human artistic productions (and the narrative potential of costly materials) in the late medieval period, especially within a religious context, see Recht, *Believing and Seeing,* esp. ch. 3, "The Seen and the Unseen," pp. 69–107.

40. Glending Olson, "The Profits of Pleasure," in *The Cambridge History of Literary Criticism, Vol. II: The Middle Ages,* eds. Alastair Minnis and Ian Johnson (2005, repr. Cambridge: Cambridge University Press, 2009), p. 276 [275–87]. See also his *Literature as Recreation in the Later Middle Ages* (Ithaca, NY: Cornell University Press, 1982). On the pleasure of "art for art's sake," see also Stanbury, *Visual Object,* p. 104.

41. Carruthers, *Craft of Thought,* p. 199.

pleasures reside for the Dreamer both in surface beauty—the multiple sensory delights and distractions they offer—as well as in his connoisseur's appreciation of the exquisite skills that produced them. The artfully crafted achieves what the natural garden in which the Dreamer falls asleep hints at but cannot fulfill. It:

> Bylde in me blys, abated my bales,
> Fordidden my stresse, dystryed my paynes.
> (ll. 123–24)

> Built up bliss in me, abated my sorrows, abolished my distress, destroyed my pains.

He keeps moving, his "braynes" "bredful" (l. 126) [brimful]. Although criticism of what Brigitte Buettner calls the "sumptuous arts" was expressed in the high and late Middle Ages, she points out that even its critics, most famously Bernard of Clairvaux, acknowledged that certain kinds of audiences (especially laypeople) could be led to greater devotion through "material ornaments." Defenders, such as Abbot Suger, expounded on the affective and meditational effects of beautifully crafted objects and gems.[42] In *Pearl*, ekphrastic ornamentation initially functions to expand the Dreamer's range of experience and affective possibilities.[43] The inner turmoil, which results in the Dreamer's swoon-like prostration in the garden, is momentarily displaced by delight; grief, and the thoughts and feelings it brings into ferocious play, are briefly forgotten or stilled. The generic associations of "aventure"—that is, of the movement entailed by a quest, and the promise of marvels that necessarily comes with it—combine the familiar and the new, allowing the Dreamer to draw on his own skills while encountering the unknown. This interplay of new and old, which is also an interplay of memory and marvel, is encapsulated and made possible by ornamentation: both in the sense of poetic technique (ekphrasis) and effect (the visualized landscape).[44]

---

42. Buettner, "Toward," pp. 470 and 472.

43. As L. O. Aranye Fradenburg has noted, the "function" of ornamentation is to "extend[ ] our sentience by drawing out our enjoyment" ("Making, Mourning, and the Love of Idols," in *Images, Idolatry, and Iconoclasm in Late Medieval England: Textuality and the Visual Image,* eds. Jeremy Dimmick, James Simpson, and Nicolette Zeeman [Oxford: Oxford University Press, 2002], p. 32 [25–42]). Heather Maring speaks of the "experiential education" of the Dreamer ("'Never the Less': Gift-Exchange and the Medieval Dream-Vision *Pearl,*" *Journal of the Midwest Modern Language Association* 38.2 [2005]: 10 [1–15]).

44. As Carruthers notes, "Ornamentation is no mere frill, but plays an essential role of initializing and orienting the procedures of cognition and recollection" ("Invention," p. 204).

It is significant that the theme of this ekphrasis is a landscape in which the Dreamer awakes and moves through, since it points toward the importance of *setting* to memory, affect and craft (or composition). By finding himself in a new *place*, the Dreamer must reconsider his own position, both physically and psychologically. The poem has already identified spot-lessness as the ambivalent stimulus to grief and creativity in the opening stanzas,[45] the dream continues and develops this theme by introducing a new place. Identity and situatedness are thus shown to be intimately connected.[46]

A change of one's place can bring about a change of perspective, and change of heart: it re-places us. It is not, then, the jeweler who sets the pearl, but the dream which re-sets the Dreamer-Jeweler. This replacement, however, can have repercussions for the Dreamer's relationship not just to himself, but to others also. Affect and craft emerge here as relational and situated processes; once the context in which one finds oneself changes, there is a possibility of change in one's affective and cognitive state, too—in the way one relates to the object of one's sorrow/creativity. This is a dynamic process: the craftsman can shape his materials, but his situatedness (which includes his experience, knowledge, emotional state, and the nature of his materials or subject) also determines the possibilities of what can be made, and how. It is no coincidence, then, that *Pearl* draws on a range of discursive and generic registers, including dream vision, lament, elegy, allegory, romance, and travel writing. Yet the Dreamer's change of place results not just in a glittering array of new sensory impressions, or in a momentary absence of grief—it ultimately leads from bliss and wonder to a less unambiguously pleasurable state. The longer he moves through "those floty vales" (l. 127) [those watery vales], the

Carruthers does not here address the affective impact of ornamentation or the response to marvel, which I argue are central to the Dreamer's experience. See also Carruthers, *Craft of Thought*, pp. 116–17: "If a thinking human mind can be said to require 'machines' made out of memory by imagination, then the ornament and decoration, the 'clothing,' of a piece will indicate ways in which these mental images are to be played."

45. While the first stanza begins with the image of a set pearl, it ends with its loss and the narrator's expression of sorrow: "I dewyne, fordolked in luf-daungere" (l. 11). In the second stanza, this loss leads to a kind of static placement as the narrator waits and longs for the pearl's return. Yet it is also here that many sweet songs first come to him. The link between poetry and place is indicated a number of times, for instance in line 37, when he refers to "that spot that I in speche expoun," or the many sweet songs that come to him "in that spote" (l. 13).

46. It is no coincidence that memory was understood to be locational; memories were "stored as images in places." Indeed, losing one's place due to an exclusive focus on the images themselves (rather than on an orderly progression through their places) was seen as a "vice of dilettantism" and of *curiositas*. See Mary J. Carruthers, "Reading with Attitude, Remembering the Book," in *The Book and the Body*, eds. Dolores Warwick Frese and Katherine O'Brien O'Keeffe (Notre Dame, IN: University of Notre Dame Press, 1997), p. 18 [1–33].

"more strengthe of joye myn herte straynes" (l. 128) [the more the strength of joy my heart strains]. This *excess* of joy (akin to his earlier excess of grief) is troubling; this is indicated in the ambivalent term "straynes," which can mean "to stir," as well as "to bind, fasten, restrict," or even to "torment."[47] As he ponders that a man wishes always to have more of what Fortune sends him, "whether solace ho sende other elles sore" (l. 130) [whether she sends solace or else sorrow], he uncovers the essentially illogical, unpredictable nature of human desire.

The outcome of this "aventure," this encounter with "mervayles," is thus far from certain; it has put him on a new path and introduced new movement, but the goal is indeterminate. Within this first ekphrasis, then, it is the shifting of the Dreamer's subject position (from conflicted, immobilized mourner to blissful, then troubled, but active "quester") that provides the matter. The vividness of the ekphrastic landscape draws him (and the reader) in and onwards—the new emotions he feels and the stimulus to his desire may be ambivalent, but they are also the condition of new possibilities.[48] This is a crucial point: if we read it as a commentary on imaginative writing, or on artistic production, we can see that it makes no claim to didactic probity, but demonstrates (and enacts in this demonstration) the powerful affective and cognitive effects of skillful invention, requiring both memory and marvel.

Marvel and memory return again in the Dreamer's encounter with the Pearl Maiden. As he approaches her, the "nwe note" "meved" his "mynde ay more and more" (ll. 155, 156) [new matter . . . moved . . . mind ever more and more]. In its close association with the faculties of memory, as well as imagination, affect, and reason, "mynde" is a particularly appropriate term to be used in anticipation of the coming meeting.[49] Its significatory capaciousness allows it to signal intentionality, emotional register, and the active, creative engagement of reasoning and imaginative modes of thought. It captures the Dreamer's fully engaged attempts to "place" or identify the Maiden, as well as to work out what this situation—and she herself—means, not least in relation to, and for, him.

---

47. See *MED*, s.v. "strayne."

48. On medieval imaginative representations of remembering and forgetting as movement through material (as well as conceptual) space, see Seeta Chaganti, "The Space of Epistemology in Marie de France's *Yonec*," *Romance Studies* 28.2 (2010): 71–83.

49. It is also a capacious term; see *MED*, s.v. "mynd[e]," which can refer to "the human mind as seat or instrument of memory, thought, reason, will, imagination, emotion"; to "the faculty of memory" more specifically, or to "individual remembrance or remembering"; to the "thinking process, mental attention, thought, consideration"; or to "reason, understanding" and "will, purpose, inclination, intention." It underlines McNamer's ("Feeling", pp. 241–57) point about the perceived unity of cognitive, somatic, and affective processes in medieval psychology and also indicates the Dreamer's engagement with the new experience he is involved in.

Even as his "mynde" is "meved," his "dom" (reason or judgement) is immediately "adaunt" (stunned, overcome) because of "more mervayle" (l. 157).[50] There are two movements and forces at work in the Dreamer. While the marvelous landscape allowed the Dreamer to respond in fresh ways, literally and metaphorically moving him along, this marvel stops him in his tracks. As memory and marvel meet within "mynde," his ability to make judgements based on knowledge is "adaunt." Marvel here does not bring about bliss and delight; its effect is much more powerful and perhaps even threatening to the Dreamer's "mynde." *All* cognitive and affective faculties are potentially useless in the face of such wonder—one might even say that the marvel is excessive, not unlike the intense sorrow that threw his mind and heart into such disarray at the outset of the poem.

And at this moment memory returns to the Dreamer; while his wonder initially seems a response to nothing that is specified with any certainty, it is soon related to his recognition of the "faunt" (l. 161) [young child] sitting on the other side of the stream: "I knew hyr wel, I hade sen hyr ere. / . . . / On lenghe I loked to hyr there—/ The lenger, I knew hyr more and more" (ll. 164, 167–68) [I knew her well, I had seen her before . . . For a long time I looked at her there—The longer (I did so), I knew her more and more].[51] Memory and wonder cause a disjunction in his affective state: while his examination of her leads him to feel a rare "gladande glory" (l. 171) [gladdening glory], the unfamiliar setting in which he finds her ("I sey hyr in so strange a place" [l. 175] [I saw her in so strange a place]) causes "baysment" [shock] to give his heart a "brunt" [blow]—a "burre" [blow] that makes it "blunt" [stunned] (ll. 174, 176). This paradoxical effect of heightened and stunned response proceeds from his inability to reconcile what he (thinks he) knows with the changed context. This is a perfect "wonder-response," for as Bynum notes, "wonder was . . . associated with paradox, coincidence of opposites."[52] Or as Jones and Sprunger put it: "Marvels unsettle established certainties," which make them "'symbolically impure.'"[53] It also underlines

---

50. See *MED*, s.v. "dom." This is another capacious term related to cognition; it can refer to "mental faculties" quite generally, but can also mean, more specifically, the "ability to make judgments," "the imagination," even "the ability to control (dreams)." The verb "adaunten" indicates a powerful, even violent, act, meaning to "conquer, subdue" or to "overcome," even to "destroy" (*MED*, s.v. "adaunten").

51. Here recognition is a partial and uncertain process. Rather than conveying certainty, memory is shown to be fragile and dependent on context (which is also a kind of narrative).

52. Bynum, *Metamorphosis*, p. 43. She also notes that this places them in close proximity to the monstrous in medieval categorizations of the marvelous.

53. Timothy S. Jones and David A. Sprunger (citing Mary Douglas), "Introduction: The Marvelous Imagination," in *Marvels, Monsters, and Miracles: Studies in the Medieval and Early Modern Imaginations,* eds. by Timothy S. Jones and David A. Sprunger (Kalamazoo, MI: Medieval Institute Publications, 2002), p. xiii [xi–xxv].

the subjective nature of the wonder experience: for the Dreamer, the Maiden in this setting does not make sense.

It is not so much her ontological purity that is at issue here as the epistemological and affective challenge she poses *for him*. His knowledge of her depends on a particular, familiar situatedness, which is not just locational (she is not in the garden in which he lost her), but also relational (their relationship to each other is also dependent on, and conditioned by, place). What Bynum calls the "non-appropriative" nature of the "wonder-response" as it was theorized in the Middle Ages—we can only wonder at that which we cannot grasp, consume, or assimilate—works against the impulses of memory, "natural" but also trained memory, which is precisely about internalizing, categorizing, and making one's own (*placing*) an experience or knowledge.[54] If memory can be said to be "individual and particular," marvel, though also subjective, is that which refuses to be recognized and assimilated.[55] The Dreamer therefore cannot be sure of *what* he thinks, knows, or feels—this is the *point* of wonder, but also its danger.[56] Affective intensity and possibility mark the wonder moment; it is, as Mary Baine Campbell notes, "rich with ambivalence and undecidability."[57]

When the Maiden raises her face to him, the Dreamer's heart is "stonge . . . ful strai atount" (l. 179), which can mean either that his heart is stunned by bewilderment, or that he is "led mentally astray"—or both.[58] His profound disorientation results from the mismatch between his expectations and the new event: he *thinks* he recognizes her, but cannot be quite sure.[59] Wonder

---

54. See Carruthers and Ziolkowski, Introduction, on how *memoria* is about fitting new information into one's "existing networks of experience" (p. 8). The Maiden, because of her familiarity, is not recognized by the Dreamer to represent something new. He is trying to negotiate her current "place," as it is defined by his experience, with her new place, which is outside of his experience. In this position she functions as a marvel.

55. Carruthers and Ziolkowski, Introduction, p. 8. Wonder does, however, share with memory a close association with both cognition and affect, leading Lorraine Daston and Katharine Park to call it a "cognitive passion" (*Wonders and the Order of Nature, 1150–1750* [New York: Zone Books, 1998], p. 14).

56. Daston and Park point out the unpredictable and diverse affective responses that marvels could bring forth: "Vernacular terms for wonder, like the Latin, admitted a spectrum of emotional tones or valences, including fear, reverence, pleasure, approbation, and bewilderment" (*Wonders*, p. 16).

57. Mary Baine Campbell, *Wonder and Science: Imagining Worlds in Early Modern Europe* (Ithaca, NY: Cornell University Press, 1999), p. 2.

58. *MED*, s.v. "atount." It can also mean "senseless."

59. This is reminiscent of the story recounted in *The Book of John Mandeville*, in which a traveller does not recognise his homeland because it is not where he expects it to be: "And he / wende so longe by londe and by see seynge aboute the worlde, and he fonde an yle / where he herde his owen speche, and dryvynge beestys saynge soch wordes as men / dyde

initially appears to be his response: he tells us that he dare not call out to her, and describes himself as standing "wyth yyen open and mouth ful clos" (l. 183). He soon takes up position in relation to her, however, pushing away "ambivalence and undecidability": he "stod" "as hende as hawk in halle" (l. 184) [as courtly as hawk in hall]. The use of the hawk analogy reveals his silence to be not that of a "non-appropriative" response to marvel, but strategic: he does not speak out lest "ho me eschaped that ther I chos" (l. 187) [she escape me whom there I looked at].[60] That he is both a bird of prey watching his quarry and a craftsman selecting his "theme of discourse" is suggested by the use of the term "porpose," when he "hoped that gostly was that porpose" (l. 185).[61] What follows is the second ekphrasis of the dream vision: a detailed *effictio* of the Pearl Maiden, in which the hawkish Dreamer-Jeweler marshals and displays his skills: he observes, assesses and "sets" her for the reader.[62]

After a couple of stanzas, however, the ekphrasis is interrupted by the return of wonder, when the Dreamer comes to the "wonder perle" that is "inmyddes hyr breste . . . sette so sure" (ll. 221, 222). This pearl renders impossible the very skills required by ekphrasis, both verbal and experiential:

A mannes dom moght druyyly demme
Er mynde moght malte in hit mesure.
I hope no tonge moght endure,
No saverly saghe say of that syght[.]
(ll. 223–26)

A man's judgement might be utterly baffled before his mind might take its measure. I believe no tongue could manage, nor describe that sight in fitting speech.

This marvel can only be described by recourse to the inexpressibility topos, a rhetorical equivalent of the "non-appropriative" wonder-response.[63] Ekphra-

---

in his owen contré, of whych he hadde gret mervayle for he wiste noght how / that myghte be" (Tamarah Kohanski and C. David Benson, eds., *The Book of John Mandeville* [Kalamazoo: Medieval Institute Publications, 2007], ll. 1735–39. Available online at *TEAMS Middle English Text Series,* http://www.lib.rochester.edu/camelot/teams/tkfrm.htm).

60. See *MED*, s.v. "chesen," meaning not just to "see," but also to "select" or "pick."

61. See *MED*, s.v. "purpos."

62. There is another self-conscious reference to artistic production here when he describes her "semblaunt sade for doc other erle," where "semblaunt" can refer either to her appearance or manner, or to a "representation of a person . . . a portrait" (see *MED*, s.v. "semblaunt").

63. On the poem's use of the inexpressibility topos, see, for instance, Ann Chalmers

sis here, then, cleverly combines memory and marvel in its fluctuation between *effictio* and its assertion of the inadequacy of language (its disavowal of mastery) to depict the "wonder perle." Precise, intricate detail is followed by a rhetorically articulated "silence": ekphrasis stages its own limitations, or failure, and in this sense ekphrasis and the Maiden are alike in that they are both rendered visible through craftsmanship and adornment, yet bear at their very center that which resists or escapes "mynde" and "tonge." Even in its silences, then, the poem portrays the Maiden. The Dreamer's response remains ambivalent: although he stops his ekphrastic rendition of her, he does so with a final attempt at "placing" her: "Ho was me nerre then aunte or nece" (l. 233) [She was nearer to me than aunt or niece]. Whereas the ekphrastic description of the landscape incorporates marvel in order to represent and perform the new cognitive and affective possibilities it occasions, this ekphrasis focuses on the limits of "mynde" when an emotionally charged memory meets with wonder. He tries to claim her still (she "was me nerre"), but can only do so imprecisely, approximately. She escapes his categories, but obliquely, for she is not entirely unrelated to them.

The marvelous-yet-familiar Maiden resists the Dreamer's claim several times over. Firstly, she does not exactly correspond to the memory-image he has of her (is she a "faunt" or a young woman?) He recognizes her, but this recognition seems to be triggered by something more—or other—than her appearance. Secondly, she denies that she is in any way "marked" by memories of a life with him: she is, as she says, "spotless," which is why she is where she is. Having died so young, the Maiden is not only unstained by experience and sin, but arguably, also by memory. Having bypassed Purgatory, that place which connected and aided both the living and the dead through reciprocal remembrance, she has no need of his memories. Her close association with the pearl, a gem thought to be created by miraculous self-generation, also resists his claims of kin- and ownership. All of this throws into question his version of the past and the memories that define him and his grief. If death gives rise to memories, and if, as Aers argues, memories are about fixing the past, then the Maiden clearly exceeds and stymies that function. Ekphrasis, and its failure, mark the Dreamer's shift from "hawk" to questioner. If

Watts, "*Pearl*, Inexpressibility, and Poems of Human Loss," *PMLA* 99.1 (1984), pp. 26–40. Watts's understanding and identification of moments of inexpressibility in the poem to some extent overlaps with my identification of marvel and wonder in it. However, our reading of the effect of such instances differs, as Watts sees them as moments that trouble the poem through their "vocabulary of faint heart that finally breaks the dream" (p. 26). See also Teresa Reed's argument in "Mary, the Maiden, and Metonymy in *Pearl*," *South Atlantic Review* 65.2 (2000): 134–62 and Theodore Bogdanos, *Pearl: Image of the Ineffable: A Study in Medieval Poetic Symbolism* (University Park: University of Pennsylvania Press, 1983).

ekphrasis allows the Dreamer to display his mastery, and reveals his appro-priative stance, then its faltering through wonder opens him up to engage-ment through dialogue.

Although the Dreamer's ekphrastic description of the Maiden falters, he describes a different kind of "ornamentation" in his following conversation with her. Alone at night, he tells her, he has "playned," and "much longeyng" has he "layned" [concealed] for her (ll. 242, 244). He depicts himself as a "joyles jueler" (l. 252) who has secreted his grief, lamenting repeatedly alone "on nyghte" (l. 243). Grief is also care-full composition: the product of sus-tained meditation and mental energy. The stanza enacts this for the reader by proliferating and elaborating (ornamenting) the terms used to describe his remembered grief: "Pensyf, payred, I am forpayned" (l. 246) [Sorrowful, broken, I am wasted away], he says, and laments his "del and gret daunger" (l. 250) [sorrow and great heartache]. This kind of adornment, which con-centrates on evoking the nuances within a single emotional register, offers an intricate, elaborate, but also contained, self-referential image. Unlike the marvelous landscape and the "wonder perle" (l. 221), it is not characterized by "ambivalence and undecidability,"[64] or the openness of "aventure" (l. 64).

The Maiden denies his careful composition, telling him that he has his "tale mysetente" (l. 257) [tale distorted] and has chosen a "mad porpose" (l. 267). Their perspectives, unsurprisingly, are utterly different, since they are, both experientially and ontologically, coming from different places. In their ensuing dialogue, the Maiden eventually returns to the "wonder perle" that disrupted the Dreamer's ekphrasis previously, in order to prepare the ground for the final and most detailed ekphrasis of the dream: the vision of the New Jerusalem. She likens the pearl to the "reme of hevenesse" (l. 735) [realm of heaven]: it is "commune to alle that ryghtwys were" (l. 739), and the Lord has placed it "even inmyddes my breste" as a "token of pes" (ll. 740, 742). The pearl, then, is a memorial as well as a marvel, and she is its setting.[65] In a sense, she is like the Dreamer in his grief: she is utterly certain and her terms allow for no other interpretation. I am not suggesting that the poem presents the Dreamer and the Pearl Maiden as equals, but it does show that meaning, derived from memory and emotion, is (for humans at least) always relational.

This time the Dreamer responds to the Maiden's words by opening him-self up to new knowledge and meanings, even though he remains interested primarily in the Maiden herself rather than the wondrous pearl she explicates:

---

64. Campbell, *Wonder and Science*, p. 2.

65. See *MED,* s.v. "token," which can signify a "visionary image with symbolic import," an "omen," "portent," or "marvel." It can also be a "memento" or "memorial."

Quo formed thee thy fayre fygure?
That wroght thy wede, He was ful wys.
Thy beauté com never of nature;
Pymalyon paynted never thy vys,
Ne Arystotel nawther by hys lettrure
Of carpe the kynde these properties.
(ll. 747–52)

Who formed your fair figure? The one who made your clothing was most skillful. Your beauty never came from nature; Pygmalion never painted your face, nor does Aristotle in his learning speak of the nature of these properties.

These questions focus on craftsmanship ("wis" plays on both "art" and "wisdom," for instance) and on different kinds of production and knowledge (nature, art, and natural philosophy), as he adjusts his claims to kinship and, with that, his memories. Yet he does this *in relation to her as he sees her.* Her words may be true in an absolute sense, but the poem shows us that this only takes on *felt* meaning (that is, they only become fully meaningful) once the Dreamer can *incorporate* her words into his own networks of meaning. The Dreamer has clearly undergone a transformation of sorts: wonder has moved him into dialogue, which has in turn made him willing and able to reconsider the significance of his memories. But what motivates and conditions his learning is still necessarily embedded in particular and subjective affective and cognitive associations, for he needs to think from a position, from a point of subjectivity, even as he reviews it. Unlike the "spotless pearl," he is not a blank slate. His references to craftsmanship show him negotiating what he already knows with what he strives to incorporate into his understanding. He works from the familiar, towards the unfamiliar, with the tools (the *modes* of knowing) available to him. This is a *process*—a quest—not unlike invention or composition.

The ekphrasis of the New Jerusalem exemplifies this process, which, while open to the new, always remains contiguous with the Dreamer's inevitably and even necessarily *partial* capacities and memories. John's authoritative, scriptural, vision becomes the framework and reference point for the Dreamer's experience. Like the Maiden, the New Jerusalem is not unfamiliar (either to the Dreamer or to the poem's audience), even as this poetic account of the Dreamer's experience of it extends (adorns, elaborates on) John's earlier, authoritative experience. The poem's ekphrastic depiction of the New Jerusalem, then, represents once more a fusion of marvel and memory; by ordering his vision in accordance with John's, the Dreamer improvises on an established pattern, reconfirming the tendency of ekphrases to be simultaneously "alien" and "home."[66] He is also enacting *memoria* by integrating personal experience with a wider set of associations and sources. As a result, he—and we, through him—see as John sees, *again*. Toward the end of the ekphrasis, the Dreamer's position towards his "material" has changed, which in turn reflects and reinforces a change in him, from "hawk" to "dased quayle" (l. 1085) [dazed quail]. The appropriative stance has been transformed to a pure wonder-response.[67] Marvel marks every aspect of his vision: it is "so gret merwayle / No fleschly hert ne myght endeure" (ll. 1081–82); the city's "fasure" [appearance] is "ferly" [marvelous] (l. 1084) and his response mirrors it, for he is as a dazed quail "for ferly of that freuch figure" (l. 1086) [in amazement at that vivid vision].[68] This, then, is the setting for the Lamb and his followers, and for his own "lyttel queen" (l. 1047).

The authority and order provided by the memory of John's account stabilize but do not render safe (in an emotional or cognitive sense) the effect on the Dreamer. Bynum argues that the response to marvel encouraged by medieval thinkers was *admiratio*: because wonder was associated with the limits of human knowledge, it was (particularly in a religious context) thought of as a "response to 'majesty,' to 'hidden wisdom' or significance."[69] It is also, as the poem suggests, dangerous to the subjectivity of the individual encountering it. Each experience of wonder, framed by a succession of ekphrases, has brought the Dreamer to new knowledge and new affective possibilities— but each instance also ratchets up the intensity of that experience. Were the Dreamer to assimilate the vision, it would no longer be marvelous—and this cannot be possible in the logic of poem. Although wonder enables new experience and knowledge, each time the Dreamer moves closer to a *pure* wonder response, he is also closer to the brink of annihilation.

The Dreamer is right in noting that "no fleschly hert ne myght endeure" (l. 1082) this wondrous vision. To be able to endure it would be to suggest a

---

66. Carruthers comments on the familiar-yet-unfamiliar nature that characterizes many medieval ekphrases, citing the New Jerusalem as a representative example of this: "Though the artifacts of medieval ekphrases are marvelous, like the jeweled Heavenly City, . . . they are not alien, they are familiar, home" (*Craft of Thought*, p. 223). On the city as "ideogram," see Sarah Stanbury, "The Body and the City in *Pearl*," *Representations* 48 (1994): 30–47.

67. This stanza offers the poem's most insistent and dense use of terminology related to marvel and wonder.

68. *MED*, s.v. "ferli." As an adjective, "ferly" connotes something "terrifying," "strange," "marvelous," "miraculous" or "wonderful." As a noun, it signifies "astonishment," "surprise," "wonder."

69. Bynum, *Metamorphosis*, p. 55.

different kind of "hert" and a capacity for comprehending and feeling fully its significance (of comprehending wonder).[70] While the final ekphrasis does mark and exemplify a change in the Dreamer, it also signals the *necessary* limits to that change. The delight he feels just before he attempts to cross the water threatens him with disintegration: "My manes mynde to madding malte" (l. 1153) [My human mind to madness dissolved]. This likens his mind to a crafted object, or to the materials out of which they are made: like coins, jewelry, or gold it can be shaped, impressed, adorned—but also melted down.[71] The Dreamer is relinquishing craftsmanship, or mastery, for the first time—yet his overwhelming desire to achieve an impossible unity with what has to remain the object of his wonder (and, however imperfectly, his inventive skill) is also shown to be a (forbidden) movement towards death. His mad lunge shatters the mode of the preceding ekphrasis, for it seeks to break through it, to the Real beyond. Ekphrasis is as close as he (and we) can get; imaginative writing mediates the wonder that a human subject could not otherwise bear (and would most likely never experience).[72] The poem, in this sense, *is* the stream, dividing the known from the unknown, but touching the bank on either side.

---

70. My reading here is in agreement with Jessica Barr's argument that "to read *Pearl* with the expectation that it will show the dreamer achieving *unio Christi* . . . may not be appropriate," for "the Jeweller is not, in fact, unequivocally invited into a unitive experience of the divine" (*Willing to Know God: Dreamers and Visionaries in the Later Middle Ages* [Columbus: The Ohio State University Press, 2010], p. 123). She concludes: "His love for the Maiden is what enables him to have the vision of the divine truth; attachment therefore *can* lead to a glimpse of the divine" (p. 150). My argument has been, in addition, interested in the way the poem suggests the impossibility of thinking, remembering or understanding, without emotion.

71. See also Carruthers on how medieval theorists saw the well-stocked memory as necessary to the laborious processes of thought and understanding: "We need our inventory well-stored, our memory fully attentive, and we work and work away at the text in the way that a jeweller (or other master craftsman) works gold" ("Reading with Attitude," p. 25). Here it is not just the text that can be likened to worked gold, but the mind itself; in a sense, the crafting of the poem is the outcome of the crafting of the mind that composed it. And the reader's mind also engages dynamically with the text it attends to.

72. Bartsch and Elsner point out that ekphrases enable both the construction and rethinking of subjectivities (see Introduction, iii). For a discussion of the relationship of ekphrasis (and its history) in relation to the recent "turn to the real," see Larry Scanlon's essay in this volume. Scanlon's essay probes the category of the "unknowable" in order to question "the modernist break" and to critique the "vanguardism" that always privileges a desired (and imagined) "new." Whereas Scanlon is interested in the effect of the real on either side of a posited medieval/modern rupture, my essay has suggested that the poem explores an "imaginative" way of knowing that is made possible by poetic form and invention. Yet we both discuss *Pearl* to argue for the complexity and ongoing importance of medieval epistemological theories; for the "histories," as Scanlon argues, of "names."

In her article "Making, Mourning, and the Love of Idols," L. O. Aranye Fradenburg argues that the things we make—craft—are integral to our civilization, especially in relation to sentience and ethics. She notes that "*Tekhné,* coming from the Greek, means 'skill' but also 'art.' We make tools—or develop skills and arts—with which we shape our sentience and our world: our embodied, sensual encounter with the world."[73] This, inevitably, raises ethical questions. By attempting to cross the stream, the Dreamer momentarily rejects *tekhné* in favour of pure, unmodulated sentience: this is, in fact, shown to be an act akin to self-annihilation. *Tekhné,* though limited and problematic, is thus shown to be the (only?) way of approaching the divine. *Tekhné,* in this context, is a crafting of the poem (most self-consciously in its ekphrastic passages), and also, as these passages have shown, of the self: of the Dreamer's "mynde" and "hert."

In Rev. 21:4, the end times are characterized by the absence of the very things that structure the concerns of this poem:

And God shall wipe away all tears from their eyes, and death
shall be no more, nor mourning, nor crying, nor sorrow shall be
any more, for the former things are passed away.[74]

This elimination of certain kinds of sentience is not possible for the Dreamer, who must live in the world, that "doel-doungoun" (l. 1187) [sorrow-dungeon]. It is *this* life that he must return to and negotiate, even as he remembers his vision (which is never, in Augustine's terms, an intellectual vision, but which explores the possibilities of imaginative vision). The poem's difficult ending, which has been commented on and puzzled over by many of its critics, is an acknowledgement of the possibilities and limitations of sentience and *tekhné.* Both lie at the heart of subjectivity—and civilization. The Dreamer does not (cannot) reject his memories, but he has "adorned" them—recrafted them in the light of wonder, within the framework provided by ekphrasis.[75] This does not magically bring about a new subject, but it traces the *process* (gradual, difficult, uncertain, partial) of imaginative invention—with all the ethical and affective problems and possibilities that entails.

---

73. Fradenburg, "Making," p. 26.

74. See *Douay-Rheims Catholic Bible,* http://www.drbo.org/chapter/73021.htm.

75. This is arguably repeated at the level of the poem; as Larry Scanlon points out in his essay in this volume, *Pearl* is the work of a poet who "use[s] . . . convention unconventionally," p. 267.

Chapter 6

FROM ENSLAVEMENT TO DISCERNMENT

LEARNING TO SEE IN GOTTFRIED'S *TRISTAN*

Kathryn Starkey

*G*ottfried von Strassburg famously distinguishes in his prologue to *Tristan* between the "edlen Herzen" (l. 47) [noble hearts] who will be able to appreciate and correctly interpret his poem, and those other readers and listeners who will not.[1] Implicit in this privileging of an elite subgroup of audience members is a challenge or an invitation to the reader/listener to attempt to belong to that select group. Indeed, Gottfried's *Tristan* has, among many other facets, a strong pedagogical one in that it seeks to train its audience to fully comprehend the concept of love that it presents. The pedagogical program in *Tristan* attempts to educate the audience to become noble hearts. Key to understanding *Tristan*-love, I will argue, is developing a particular way of viewing the world in which the lovers reside. As part of his pedagogic program, Gottfried presents models of seeing in which he enables his audience to view the world of the lovers discerningly. Ekphrasis is one strategy for cultivating discernment. This essay investigates two key ekphrastic scenes that draw a contrast between the uncritical courtly gaze and a more reflective and distanced vision,

---

1. All citations of *Tristan* are from Gottfried von Strassburg, *Tristan*, vols. 1–2 (Stuttgart: Reclam, 1987). Translations based on Gottfried von Strassburg, *Tristan with the 'Tristran' of Thomas*, trans. A. T. Hatto (London: Penguin, 2004).

and a third one that provides a model of viewing to which to aspire: Tristan's flaying of the stag, Isolde's entrance at the court of Ireland, and the presentation of the little dog Petitcreiu.

Despite recent interest in ekphrasis, there has been little attention paid to Gottfried's use of the technique.[2] This is rather surprising since, on the one hand, visuality and seeing play such an important role in the story, and on the other, ekphrasis has been acknowledged as a highly productive technique generally in medieval German literature.[3] The technique was widely used in sources available to medieval German poets and authors, including works from antiquity, such as those by Homer and Ovid, and the legends of Alexander and Aeneas, as well as the medieval French romances. Well-known examples of ekphrasis in German medieval literature abound, including Enite's horse in Hartmann von Aue's *Erec,* Lancelot's painted cell in the *Prose Lancelot,* Helmbrecht's cap in Werner der Gartenaere's *Meier Helmbrecht,* Blanscheflur's tomb in Konrad Fleck's *Flore und Blanscheflur,* and Camille's mausoleum in Heinrich von Veldeke's *Enaesroman.* These and other ekphrases have been addressed at length in scholarship, albeit not typically under the heading of ekphrasis. Yet, as James A. W. Heffernan points out, ekphrasis is a literary mode, and in order to discuss that mode across genre and throughout literary history, it is important to identify it and agree on a name for it.[4] Indeed, as Haiko Wandhoff shows in his extensive work on ekphrasis in the medieval German romance, placing these highly descriptive passages in this rhetorical tradition not only deepens our understanding of their function in their respective texts but also allows us to identify specifically medieval preoccupations.[5] Whereas, for example, some medieval

---

2. Marianne Kalinke, "Tristams saga ok Ísöndar, ch. 80: Ekphrasis as Recapitulation and Interpretation," in *Analecta Septentrionalia: Beiträge zur nordgermanischen Kultur- und Literaturgeschichte,* eds. Wilhelm Heizmann, Klaus Böldl, and Heinrich Beck (Berlin: de Gruyter, 2009), pp. 221–37, examines the ekphrasis of the Hall of Statues in the Old Norse version of the story, making the case that it provides an interpretation of the story from the perspective of Tristan.

3. See, for example, Haiko Wandhoff, *Ekphrasis. Kunstbeschreibungen und virtuelle Räume in der Literatur des Mittelalters* (Berlin: de Gruyter, 2003).

4. James A. W. Heffernan, "Ekphrasis and Representation," *New Literary History* 22.2 (1991): 298 [297–316]. Heffernan makes a case for identifying ekphrasis as a pan-historical mode in order to identify characteristics that, according to him, all ekphrases share, namely an implicit commentary on representation and misrepresentation, and a concern with the boundaries between graphic and verbal representation.

5. See, for example, Wandhoff, *Ekphrasis,* and ibid, "Bilder der Liebe—Bilder des Todes. Konrad Flecks Flore-Roman und die Kunstbeschreibungen in der höfischen Epik des deutschen Mittelalters," in *Die poetische Ekphrasis von Kunstwerken: eine literarische Tradition der Grossdichtung in Antike, Mittelalter und früher Neuzeit,* ed. Christine Ratkowitsch (Vienna: Verlag der Österreichischen Akademie der Wissenschaften, 2006), pp. 55–76.

ekphrases are a continuation of the antique tradition, others, according to Wandhoff, "are characterized by a [particularly medieval] fascination with architectural and technical marvels for which there are no models in the classical epics of antiquity."[6]

The neglect of *Tristan* in the context of studies on ekphrasis may be explained by scholars' inclination to define the term as the description of an artwork. And yet as Janice Hewlett Koelb reveals, this narrow understanding of the term is a twentieth-century invention stemming from John Dewar Denniston's entry in the 1949 *Oxford Classical Dictionary*.[7] This in and of itself need not prevent us from using it to discuss ekphrasis in medieval texts.[8] The greater problem is rather that this narrow definition is grounded in a particularly nineteenth- and twentieth-century understanding of the artwork that cannot be assumed for the Middle Ages. The medieval German romance is not so much concerned with artworks as it is with artistry and artifice. These may well find their expression in a composed work or piece of art, but more often they are found in more tangible constructions, such

---

Page Dubois's landmark study examines ekphrases from four historical periods, suggesting that it is possible to identify historically distinct renderings of the technique of ekphrasis (*History, Rhetorical Description and the Epic: From Homer to Spencer* [Cambridge: D. S. Brewer, 1982]). Wandhoff, too, identifies specifically medieval preoccupations in the medieval ekphrases of "artworks" that he examines. Yet despite these important studies there remain many open questions not only about the function of ekphrasis in medieval German literature but also regarding the specificity of medieval ekphrasis.

6. Wandhoff, "Bilder der Liebe," pp. 71–72, writes: "Die Unterscheidung dieser beiden Traditionsstränge, die sich in der poetischen Praxis stets mehr oder weniger stark durchmischen, vermag ein Licht darauf zu werfen, in welcher Weise man sich im Mittelalter einerseits des antiken Erbes der epischen Kunstbeschreibung bediente, um sie andererseits jedoch mit Blick auf das eigene Epochenbewusstsein aus- und umzubauen." Similarly, but more specifically, Werner Wunderlich, "Ekphrasis und Narratio: Die Grabmalerei des Apelles und ihre 'Weiberlisten' in Walters von Châtillon und Ulrichs von Etzenbach Alexanderepen," in *Erzählungen in Erzählungen: Phänomene der Narration in Mittelalter und Früher Neuzeit*, eds. Harald Haferland and Michael Mecklenburg (Munich: Fink, 1996), pp. 259–71, examines the intersection of the antique and medieval traditions, making the argument that the ekphrases by Walter von Châtillon and Ulrich von Etzenbach "sind Beispiele für die Autorität einer klassischen Erzähltradition, die im Mittelalter unter heilsgeschichtlichen Aspekten erneuert wurde" (p. 271).

7. Janice Hewlett Koelb, *The Poetics of Description: Imagined Places in European Literature* (New York: Palgrave Macmillan, 2006), p. 2. She and others attribute the broad acceptance of this definition to a 1955 essay by Leo Spitzer, "The 'Ode on a Grecian Urn,' or Content vs. Metagrammar," in *Comparative Literature* 7 (1995): 1–2 [203–25]. See also Ruth Webb, "Ekphrasis Ancient and Modern: The Invention of a Genre," *Word and Image* 15.1 (1999): 16–17 [7–18] and Ruth Webb, *Ekphrasis, Imagination and Persuasion in Ancient Rhetorical Theory and Practice* (Burlington, VT: Ashgate, 2009), p. 7.

8. Wandhoff, for example, despite his argument for the specificity of medieval ekphrasis, insists on maintaining this twentieth-century definition of ekphrasis as a description of a work of art in his analysis of medieval texts. See Wandhoff, *Ekphrasis*.

as an object of utility (goblet, tent, shield, plate, blanket, hat), a carefully choreographed event (arrivals, departures, feasts), the beautiful body and adornment of a lovely lady or valiant knight, a superior castle, a wondrous animal, or anything else that has been artfully crafted by man, God, Lady Love, magicians, or fairies, to name just a few examples.

Formalist redefinitions of ekphrasis from the 1960s on might appear to be helpful for analyzing this mode in medieval literature, as they foreground vivid description. Recently, for example, the term has been interpreted quite broadly to mean very vivid description, or in Murray Krieger's words, "any sought-for equivalent in words of any visual image, inside or outside art; in effect the use of language to function as a substitute natural sign."[9] James A. W. Heffernan defines it as "the verbal representation of visual representation."[10] According to this view, whether or not something is ekphrastic does not depend on the quality or status of the thing seen, or the technique of description, but instead has to do with the process of transition from seeing to verbalizing. Yet, if the understanding of the term ekphrasis as a description of an artwork is too narrow for discussing medieval ekphrasis, then the formalist understanding of the term is too expansive. In an environment in which literary culture was primarily oral and performed, and narrators repeatedly emphasized that they had witnessed the events they were about to relate, every literary experience was a verbal representation of a visual experience—or at least framed as such—and hence an example of ekphrasis, according to this broad understanding of the term.

Those who were familiar with the mode of ekphrasis in the Middle Ages almost certainly understood it in the sense handed down by the rhetorical tradition of classical antiquity, namely as a technique that could be used to visualize all manner of objects or events.[11] Indeed, while *Tristan* contains no paintings, murals, or other objects that one might categorize as traditional artworks, it does contain several ekphrases that describe particularly visual experiences, spaces, and objects. In classical antiquity, when the term was first defined and the technique developed as a rhetorical mode, the descrip-

9. Murray Krieger, *Ekphrasis: The Illusion of the Natural Sign* (Baltimore: Johns Hopkins University Press, 1992), p. 9.

10. James A. W. Heffernan, *Museum of Words: The Poetics of Ekphrasis from Homer to Ashbery* (Chicago: University of Chicago Press, 1993), p. 3. Earlier, in "Ekphrasis and Representation," Heffernan defined it as "the verbal representation of graphic representation" (p. 299).

11. See Simon Goldhill, "Refracting Classical Vision: Changing Cultures of Vision," in *Vision in Context: Historical and Contemporary Perspectives on Sight,* eds. Teresa Brennan and Martin Jay (New York: Routledge, 1996), pp. 17–18 [15–28], for a discussion of the changing discourse on visuality in antiquity.

tion of artworks was considered at most a subgenre of ekphrasis, which is more accurately identified not by the nature of the object described but by the technique of description and its impact on the audience.[12] The formal definitions of ekphrasis that appear in the *Progymnasmata,* a collection of four handbooks from the first to the fifth century CE containing introductory rhetorical guidelines and exercises, identify it as a technique of creating an illusion.[13] Aelius Theon, the earliest rhetorical theorist represented in the collection, writes, "Ekphrasis is descriptive language, bringing what is portrayed clearly before the sight."[14] Other authors in the *Progymnasmata* reiterate this definition, explaining that ekphrases may be composed of such things as "places, times, persons, festivals, [and] things done."[15] Indeed as classicist Ruth Webb explains, "An ekphrasis can be of any length, of any subject matter, composed in verse or prose, using any verbal techniques, as long as it 'brings its subject before the eyes.'"[16] The aim is, according to the fifth-century description by Nicolaus of Myra, to "make the hearers into spectators."[17]

Recent work on classical ekphrasis has explored both the pedagogical uses of the mode and the danger inherent in its persuasiveness.[18] One means by which ekphrases can take on a pedagogic function is by drawing attention to the act of looking, thus providing its audience with a model of seeing. Classicist Jaś Elsner writes:

> Ekphrasis, insofar as it provides a pedagogic model for the gaze, may be
> seen as both its enabler (in helping the viewers it is training to see) and

---

12. Webb, *Ekphrasis,* p. 7. On the description of art as a subgenre of ekphrasis, see Jaś Elsner, "The Genres of Ekphrasis," *Ramus* 31 (2002): 1–18, a special edition of *Ramus* on *The Verbal and the Visual: Cultures of Ekphrasis in Antiquity* edited by Elsner.

13. The standard edition of the *Progymnasmata* is Leonardus Spengel, *Rhetores Graeci,* 3 vols. (1854, repr. Frankfurt a. M.: Minerva, 1966). George A. Kennedy, *Progymnasmata: Greek Textbooks of Prose Composition and Rhetoric* (Leiden: Brill, 2003), provides the English translation that I have cited here. James A. Francis, "Metal Maidens, Achilles' Shield, and Pandora: The Beginnings of 'Ekphrasis,'" *American Journal of Philology* 130.1 (2009): 1–23, warns "we should not overplay the evidence in the *Progymnasmata.* These are textbook definitions, after all, useful in their own way but hardly the last word" (p. 4). Nonetheless these handbooks offer us important evidence for a classical perspective on the definition and function of ekphrasis. On the use and usefulness of the *Progymnasmata,* see Ruth Webb, "The *Progymnasmata* as Practice," in *Education in Greek and Roman Antiquity,* ed. Yun Lee Too (Leiden: Brill, 2001), pp. 289–316.

14. Kennedy, *Progymnasmata,* p. 45. Goldhill, "What is Ekphrasis For?" *Classical Philology: Special Issue on Ekphrasis* 102.1 (2007): 3 [1–19].

15. Kennedy, *Progymnasmata,* p. 166.

16. Webb, *Ekphrasis,* p. 8.

17. Kennedy, *Progymnasmata,* p. 166.

18. See, for example, the special issue on ekphrasis of *Classical Philology* 102.1 (2007), edited by Shadi Bartsch and Jaś Elsner. Of particular interest in my thinking about the use of ekphrasis in *Tristan* are the contributions by Goldhill and Elsner.

its occluder (in the veil of words with which it screens and obscures the purported visual object). But when, in its own performance, ekphrasis demonstrates a clear self-awareness of both these qualities (enabling and occluding), then one might say that its true subject is not the verbal depiction of a visual object, but rather the verbal enactment of the gaze that tries to relate with and penetrate the object.[19]

Ekphrases can thus tell us as much about notions of seeing as they do about their subject of description. In Gottfried's *Tristan*, the gaze is indeed the focus of some of the ekphrastic passages, but as we will see, Gottfried addresses other modes of viewing as well, distinguishing between the gaze, which is characterized by a viewer's desire and longing, and the emotionally distanced vision of the more discerning viewer.[20] In so doing, he recognizes the power of the visual experience to persuade and manipulate the listener. Indeed as this essay attempts to show, Gottfried uses ekphrasis to warn the discerning listener about the seductive power of the gaze.

In drawing attention to the process of seeing, then, ekphrasis goes beyond envisioning an object for its audience. Drawing on ekphrastic poems of classical antiquity, Simon Goldhill observes, "ecphrasis is designed to *produce a viewing subject* [original emphasis]. We read to become lookers, and poems are written to educate and direct viewing as a social and intellectual process."[21] He points out that the technique is often used to dramatize "the moment of looking *as* a practice of interpreting, of reading—a way of seeing meaning."[22] Many of Goldhill's examples draw attention to the process of viewing by depicting a critical observer who sees himself seeing. This "critical gaze . . . creates and regulates the viewing subject."[23] While not all medieval ekphrases are designed with pedagogical purpose in mind, I contend that Gottfried's ekphrases in *Tristan* are designed specifically to instruct his audience on how to view the story of Tristan and Isolde. As we will see below, these key ekphrastic passages in *Tristan* are consistently constructed in a

19. Jaś Elsner, "Viewing Ariadne: From Ekphrasis to Wall Painting in the Roman World," *Classical Philology* 102.1 (2007): 20–44.

20. Stephen G. Nichols, "Ekphrasis, Iconoclasm, and Desire," in *Rethinking the Romance of the Rose: Text, Image, Reception,* eds. Kevin Brownlee and Sylvia Huot (Philadelphia: University of Pennsylvania Press, 1992), p. 146 [133–66], productively distinguishes between the gaze versus vision in his analysis of Book I of the Aeneas, in which Aeneas views the murals in the temple of Juno. Nichols identifies "Aeneas' longing backward look and expressed desire to see and hold his mother" as an example of the gaze, while vision refers to the forward and prophetic looking presented in Books VI and VIII.

21. Goldhill, "What Is Ekphrasis For?" p. 2.

22. Goldhill, "What Is Ekphrasis For?" p. 2.

23. Goldhill, "What Is Ekphrasis For?" p. 2.

manner that draws the reader/listener into a visual experience only to then impose a critical distance to the ekphrastic subject. This forces the reader/listener to see not only the object itself but to observe the text-internal viewers and the effect that the visual experience has on them.

Implicit in the classical notion of ekphrasis is an understanding of the danger inherent in the technique. In creating a convincing illusion, ekphrasis engages our emotions, and our emotional response, in turn, inhibits our ability to think clearly and critically. Goldhill has worked extensively on this intersection between vision (*phantasia*), emotion, and the classical perception of the danger inherent in the rhetorical ability to create persuasive illusions.[24] He explains that, according to the rhetorical theorists, "visualization is a means of violent distraction of the audience away from facts or proof and towards emotion."[25] The ability to make something visible "is a rhetorical weapon to get around the censor of the intellect, to cut the listener off from the facts, to leave him or her not just 'as if a viewer at events,' but with the destabilizing emotions of that event."[26] Indeed, as Goldhill points out, Longinus's treatise *On the Sublime* expresses the concern that vivid visualization had the power to enslave its listeners: "Now what is rhetorical imagery able to accomplish? It is equally able to bring into our speeches and writings what is characteristic of the courtroom and what is emotional, and when joined with attempts at practical arguments, it not only persuades the audience, it also enslaves it."[27] Ekphrasis—rhetorical visualization—thus combines rational thought and emotion, and it is this combination that is so powerful and so persuasive. Goldhill writes: "This is the constant threat of rhetoric—to emasculate, defeat, humble its audience. A good listener knows to resist, to be critical."[28]

In my view, two related aspects of the classical understanding of ekphrasis are key to the manner in which Gottfried uses the technique in *Tristan*. The first is the idea that visualizing rhetoric is manipulative, as a visual experience

---

24. See, for example, Goldhill, "What Is Ekphrasis For?"; Goldhill, "The Naïve and Knowing Eye: Ecphrasis and the Culture of Viewing in the Hellenistic World," in *Art and Text in Ancient Greek Culture,* eds. Simon Goldhill and Robin Osborne (Cambridge: Cambridge University Press, 1994), pp. 105–24; and Goldhill, "The Erotic Eye: Visual Stimulation and Cultural Conflict," in *Being Greek under Rome: Cultural Identity, the Second Sophistic, and the Development of Empire,* ed. Simon Goldhill (Cambridge: Cambridge University Press, 2001), pp. 154–94.

25. Goldhill, "What Is Ekphrasis For?" p. 19.

26. Goldhill, "What Is Ekphrasis For?" p. 19.

27. Longinus, *On the Sublime,* trans. with a commentary by James A. Arieti and John M. Crossett (New York: Edwin Mellen Press, 1985), p. 94 (ch. 15.9). This passage is also cited in Goldhill, "What Is Ekphrasis For?" p. 4.

28. Goldhill, "What Is Ekphrasis For?" p. 4.

created through rhetoric can inhibit its audience's ability to think critically. The persuasive power of the visual experience, be it an actual experience or an ekphrastic one, derives from a combination of the rational and the emotional. On the one hand, a viewer/reader/listener will try to make sense of what is seen, but on the other, the experience is sensory and seductive and can override the rational process. The second aspect is the ability of ekphrasis to construct a critical viewer by highlighting the process of seeing and drawing attention to the manipulative power of visualization. I have referred to this above as its pedagogic function.

Gottfried was certainly aware of the power of the visual, particularly its emotional power and ability to manipulate and persuade its viewer. When introducing his protagonists, as will be shown below, he uses ekphrasis in combination with a commentary on the effect of the visual experience on its viewers to warn the discerning listener about the danger of visualization and its ability to enslave the listener to the power of such beauty. The ekphrastic introductions of the two lovers and the little dog Petitcreiu suggest that Gottfried associates his protagonists with a highly visual literary mode and that visualization is necessary to perceive their story. The focus of the present investigation is thus not the ekphrastic subjects in *Tristan* but the narrative function of the ekphrastic passages. Gottfried uses ekphrasis, I argue, to create models for viewing his protagonists, to reflect on the effect of their splendid appearance and to instruct his audience to look discerningly and not be seduced by what they see. He does this by means of creating beautiful and sensual descriptions of his protagonists, providing persuasive visual experiences, and then drawing attention to the power of those experiences on the undiscerning viewer. The ekphrasis of Petitcreiu by contrast shows readers and listeners the model of vision necessary to fully appreciate an object of beauty—namely, close, careful, and critical observation from different perspectives. The model of vision depicted in the Petitcreiu ekphrasis demonstrates how to both appreciate and withstand beauty.

EKPHRASIS AND ENSLAVEMENT: THE FLAYING OF THE STAG

Tristan's first public appearance is composed in the ekphrastic mode. Tristan has been abandoned on the coast of Cornwall by the Norwegian merchants who kidnapped him and has just met up with Mark's hunting party, which has killed a stag and is about to quarter it.[29] The boy steps in, expresses his aston-

---

29. On the motif of the hunt in *Tristan* as an allegory for love, see John S. Anson, "The Hunt of Love: Gottfried von Strassburg's *Tristan* as Tragedy," *Speculum* 45.4 (1970): 594–607.

ishment at the hunters' unrefined practice of merely quartering their bounty, and offers to flay the stag in the tradition of his own country. This flaying is a highly visual and ritualistic art, explicitly and repeatedly referred to in the poem both as a *list* (l. 2816) and as *künste* (l. 2997), two Middle High German terms for "art."[30] The ekphrasis describes it in excruciatingly vivid detail over 223 verses (ll. 2843–3080), starting as one might expect, by placing the listener squarely in the position of eyewitness and virtually uniting him or her with the text-internal audience by focusing everyone's attention on Tristan as he prepares to flay the stag:

> Tristan der ellende knabe
> sînen mantel zôch er abe
> und leite den ûf einen stoc.
> er zôch hôher sînen roc;
> sîn ermel vielt er vorne wider.
> sîn schoene hâr daz streich er nider,
> ûf sîn ôre leite er daz.
> (*Tristan*, ll. 2843–49)

Tristan, the boy so far from home, removed his mantel, and placed it on a tree stump. He hitched up his robe, and rolled up his sleeves. His beautiful hair, that he smoothed down and tucked it behind his ears.

But rather than allow the listener to become fully engulfed in the visual experience of watching Tristan, the narrator then inserts a passage that focuses on the experience of the text-internal onlookers and thus reminds the listener that he is only a secondary eyewitness to the flaying:

---

30. Margaret Brown and C. Stephen Jaeger discuss the importance of courtly ritual in Tristan with respect to the procession to Mark's court immediately following the flaying of the stag ("Pageantry and Court Aesthetic in Gottfried's *Tristan*," in *Gottfried von Strassburg and the Medieval Tristan Legend*, eds. Adrian Stevens and Roy Wisbey [Cambridge: D. S. Brewer, 1990], pp. 29–44). The flaying itself, however, is also a highly aesthetic performance. Interestingly with respect to the on-going debates about the definition of ekphrasis, Gottfried often refers to his ekphrastic objects as *list* (art). Whether he is talking about Tristan's flaying, Isolde's body, Petitcreiu, or the love grotto, he refers to them as artfully constructed objects, available for our aesthetic pleasure. The central role of art and artfulness in Gottfried's *Tristan* is well documented, and it is beyond the scope of this essay to revisit that discussion here. On the use of the term *list* in Gottfrieds *Tristan*, see Evelyn Jacobson, "The *Liste* of Tristan," *Amsterdamer Beiträge zur älteren Germanistik* 18 (1982): 115–28 and Wolfgang Jupé, *Die List im Tristanroman Gottfrieds von Strassburg: Intellektualität und Liebe oder die Suche nach dem Wesen der individuellen Existenz* (Heidelberg: Winter, 1976).

nu besâhen si'n baz unde baz,
die dâ zem baste wâren.
sîn gelâz und sîn gebâren
daz nâmen s'alle in ir muot
und dûhte sî daz also guot,
daz sî'z vil gerne sâhen
und in ir herzen jâhen,
sîn dinc waere allez edelîch,
sîniu cleider vremede unde rîch,
sîn lîp ze wunsche getân.
si begunden alle zuo z'im gân
und sîner dinge nemen war.
(ll. 2850–61)

Those present at the flaying of the stag eyed him ever more intently. They all inwardly considered his bearing and behavior, and it pleased them so much that they delighted to watch it, and they were convinced in their hearts that everything about him was noble, his clothes rare and magnificent, his figure of perfect build. They all began to gather around him and watch what he would do.

Mark's men respond to Tristan's artful flaying with astonishment, awe, and the conviction that Tristan is utterly noble. For the text-external listener/reader, the flaying, however, becomes a visual experience of a visual experience; the poem offers a reflection, on the one hand, of the power of the visual and, on the other, of the uncritical nature of the courtly gaze that is so quickly captivated by Tristan. Once Tristan has skinned the stag, he tells Mark's men to take over, but they insist that he continue, literally, to recall Longinus, enslaving themselves to Tristan in payment for his dazzling performance: "volvüere dîne meisterschaft! / wir sîn dir iemer dienesthaft" (ll. 2933–34) [Display your skill to the full! We shall forever be in your service]. Tristan obliges and continues with the *furkie,* the practice of skewering and binding the liver and testicles on a forked stick. When Tristan interrupts his performance again and asks Mark's men to continue the process themselves with the so-called *curie,* his enraptured audience again begs him to continue showing them his artistry:

swîc unde sage uns niht hie van.
swaz ez sî, daz lâ geschehen,
daz wir'z mit ougen ane sehen.

diz tuo durch dîne hövescheit!
(ll. 2966–69)

Be silent and don't say a word of explanation—do the thing itself so that we can see it with our eyes. Do this for the sake of your courtliness!

Tristan obliges and continues by separating the head and antlers, disposing of the spine, and chopping up the heart, spleen, and lungs and spreading them over the skin for the dogs. In response, Mark's men gather more closely and watch more carefully: "dar gie diu companîe / und nâmen sîner künste war" (ll. 2996–97) [the company went there and watched his artistry]. They are utterly convinced of the virtue of Tristan's performance: "wir sehen wol, dise liste sint / bracken und hunden ze grôzen vrumen vunden" (ll. 3040–42) [We clearly see that these arts were devised to the great good of blood-hounds and pack]. Finally Tristan tells them to ride ceremoniously to court carrying the stag. Mark's men insist that Tristan show them this too: they beg him to *show* them how to ride to court in the customary manner of his country so that they may *see* his performance to its conclusion (ll. 3073–77).

As Mark's men ride toward the court, the full effect of their visual experience of the flaying is revealed. The poem tells us that they can hardly wait for this opportunity to speculate about Tristan's story:

Nu s'also mit ein ander riten,
nu haeten jene vil kûme erbiten
der state unde der stunde.
ir iegelîch begunde
entwerfen sîniu maere,
von welhem lande er waere
und wie er dâ hin waere komen.
sî haeten gerne vernomen
sîn dinc und sîn ahte.
(ll. 3081–89)

Now they were all riding together; they had scarcely been able to await the opportune moment. They all began to speculate on his affairs—where he was from and how he had come there. They would have liked to hear about his affairs and his circumstances.

And it turns out that Tristan carefully planned his performance to have this powerful and emotional effect on his audience:

diz nam in sîne trahte
der sinnesame Tristan.
vil sinneclîche er aber began
sîn âventiure vinden.
(ll. 3090–93)

And this is just what Tristan was shrewdly considering. He proceeded very
subtly to fabricate his story.

The visual experience has rendered Mark's courtiers putty in Tristan's hands.
For the discerning listener, the dangers of becoming thoroughly persuaded
by the beauty and fascination of a visual experience should be apparent in
Tristan's evident manipulation of his admirers. Through the series of breaks
in the description of the flaying, the text-internal audience's response of utter
persuasion, of enslavement to the image, becomes the topic of this ekphrasis.
Mark's men are thoroughly caught up in the dazzling display and are robbed
of their critical abilities. Tristan has set out to manipulate them, and he has
succeeded. The listener is first drawn into the performance and then becomes
witness to the response of Mark's men and their careful manipulation, so that
ultimately, the representation of the uncritical courtly gaze in this ekphrasis
is a source of ironic distance.

EKPHRASIS AND EMOTION: ISOLDE'S ENTRANCE

Whereas the flaying of the stag is Tristan's first public appearance within the
poem, Isolde's initial public appearance is her entrance at the court of Ireland,
and it is similarly described in ekphrastic mode. She appears as a vision of
loveliness, and those who see her become so enthralled by her beauty that
they lose themselves in the visual experience. As in the Tristan-ekphrasis,
Gottfried draws attention to the viewers' emotional response to the protagonist and the manipulative effect of their visual experience.

When the queen Isolde leads her daughter, "die liehten maget Îsôte" (l.
10889) [the radiant maiden, Isolde] into the court, the narrator describes her
in objectifying terms. She is:

suoze gebildet über al,
lanc, ûf gewollen unde smal,
gestellet in der waete,
als sî diu Minne draete

ir selber z'einem vederspil,
dem wunsche z'einem endezil,
dâ vür er niemer komen kan.
(ll. 10893–99)

beautifully formed everywhere, tall, well-molded, and slender, formed in
her attire as if Lady Love had molded her to be her own falcon, a complete
fulfillment of desire that nothing could surpass.

The extensive description of Isolde's clothing that follows emphasizes her
sexuality and frames her body as the object of the courtly gaze. The ekphrasis masterfully leads the listener's or reader's eyes all over Isolde's body, from
her feet to her head and back again, sometimes pausing at the most titillat-
ing parts:

si truoc von brûnem samît an
roc unde mantel, in dem snite
von Franze, und was der roc dâ mite
dâ engegene, dâ die sîten
sinkent ûf ir lîten,
gefranzet unde g'enget,
nâhe an ir lîp getwenget
mit einem borten, der lac wol,
dâ der borte ligen sol.
der roc der was ir heinlîch,
er tete sich nâhen zuo der lîch.
ern truoc an keiner stat hin dan,
er suohte allenthalben an
al von obene hin ze tal.
(ll. 10900–10913)

She wore a mantel and robe of purple samite, cut in the French fashion.
There where on the side it covered her hips, the robe was fringed and pulled
snug, cinched tightly to her body with a belt that sat there where a belt is
supposed to sit. The robe fit her like a glove; it clung to her body. It bulged
nowhere but rather fitted tightly everywhere, from top to bottom.

Objectifying descriptions of beautiful women are commonplace in medieval literature. Both romance and lyric poets use the ekphrastic mode to

present women's bodies as the objects of voyeuristic pleasure.[31] In that sense, Gottfried's visualization of Isolde is not original. What is striking, however, is the juxtaposition with Tristan's ekphrastic introduction in the hunting scene and the self-referential passages in both scenes that draw attention to the act of seeing. This vivid description of Isolde continues over many lines of verse, but as with the Tristan-ekphrasis, Gottfried interrupts it to tell us what effect the sight of Isolde has on those watching her:

> gevedere schâchblicke
> die vlugen dâ snêdicke
> schâchende dar unde dan.
> ich waene, Îsôt vil manegen man
> sîn selbes dâ beroubete.
> (ll. 10957–61)

> Predatory feathered glances flew thick as snowflakes, preying here and there.
> I expect that Isolde robbed many a man of his senses there.

The narrator thus compares the courtly audience watching Isolde's arrival to birds of prey, greedily and rapaciously observing her. As in the flaying of the stag the focus of all the courtiers is on the ekphrastic subject, in this case Isolde, and their gaze is an emotional one that robs the audience of their critical abilities. The bird of prey might be seen as a metaphor for a strong, active, masculine gaze, but in fact in this instance, the predator itself has been ensnared. Isolde's effect on the courtiers is to create joy. She provides a stunning vision as she enters the hall and looks around her:

> daz dâ vil lützel ougen was,
> in enwaeren diu zwei spiegelglas
> ein wunder unde ein wunne.
> diu wunnebernde sunne
> si breite ir schîn über al,
> si ervröute liute unde sal
> slîchende neben ir muoter hin.
> (ll. 11003–9)

---

31. A. C. Spearing, *The Medieval Poet as Voyeur: Looking and Listening in Medieval Love-Narratives* (Cambridge: Cambridge University Press, 1993). Spearing discusses specifically Mark's voyeuristic enjoyment of Isolde's body when gazing into the love grotto (p. 64).

that there was not a single eye that did not consider these two mirrors (i.e., her eyes) to be a wonder and a joy. The joy-bringing sun (i.e., Isolde), she spread her luster everywhere, she brought joy to the hall and the people as she entered quietly next to her mother.

The subject of the Isolde-ekphrasis is thus not only her beauty and her nobility but also her effect on her viewers. As with the flaying of the stag, the listener/reader is first drawn into the scene by means of its visualization and then abruptly shown the effect of the visual experience on the text-internal courtiers. There is no doubt that Isolde's entrance is choreographed to specific purpose and that it is successful in manipulating her audience's emotions: they are filled with joy by watching her.

The continuation of the scene supports the argument that visualization is essential to the lovers and their bond. Immediately after Isolde's entrance, there is an exchange between the steward and Queen Isolde in which the steward is not described at all. Following this, we are witness to Tristan's entrance, which is described in ekphrastic mode. This Tristan-ekphrasis is similar to the flaying episode in that his exquisite appearance and splendid comportment both convince the onlookers of his nobility and make them curious about his identity. The protagonists' parallel ekphrases and the stark juxtaposition to the steward who is introduced with no attempt at visualization underline the fact that Isolde's true partner in nobility is Tristan. The Isolde-ekphrasis thus functions not only to provide a model of the gaze but also to demonstrate the power of the visual and establish visualization as a common bond between the lovers.

EKPHRASIS AND DISCERNMENT: PETITCREIU

Gottfried's ekphrasis of Petitcreiu is arguably a minor passage in the text inserted between the episode of Isolde's ordeal and Tristan's return to Mark's court, and yet for understanding the importance of a particular kind of seeing in the poem, it is crucial. After he returns briefly to Cornwall to play his pivotal role in Isolde's carefully devised public oath of fidelity, Tristan flees to the kingdom of Swales where he resides with Duke Gilan, but he is deeply saddened to be separated from Isolde. Noticing his guest's sorrow, Gilan brings out his prized possession, the tiny dog Petitcreiu:

> daz was mit solher wîsheit
> an den zwein dingen ûf geleit,
> an der varwe und an der craft,

daz zunge nie sô redehaft
noch herze nie sô wîse wart,
daz sîne schoene und sîn art
kunde beschrîben oder gesagen.
(ll. 15811–17)

It had been conceived with such ingeniousness with respect to its two qualities, namely its color and magic power, that there was never a tongue so
eloquent nor heart so discerning that they could describe its beauty and its
nature.

Petitcreiu is a wondrous thing, conjured up in the fairyland of Avalon and
given as a gift of love to the Duke of Swales by an Avalonian goddess.

    Gottfried's introduction of the ekphrasis suggests that he is familiar with
the classical tradition that often incorporates the making of the object, its
poiesis, into the description—Petitcreiu has been conceived or conjured
up *mit wîsheit,* with intelligence or with ingenuity, rather than whelped.[32]
Despite Gottfried's gesture of humility in which he tells us that the little dog
has been created so cleverly that it is impossible to describe, he proceeds to
describe Petitcreiu in minute detail, and it immediately becomes apparent
that we are dealing with more of a work of art than a house pet. The dog is a
prized object, displayed by Duke Gilan on a rare purple cloth. Similarly when
Isolde receives the dog, she places it in a splendid golden casket. Petitcreiu
apparently neither eats nor drinks; it tolerates anything one might do to it
(ll. 15886–88); and it is mute.[33] Its only noise is the sound of the little golden
bell around its neck, which banishes all trouble from its hearer's heart.[34]

---

32. Aaron E. Wright, "Petitcreiu: A Text-critical Note to the *Tristan* of Gottfried von
Strassburg," *Colloquiua Germanica* 25.2 (1992): 112–21, discusses the significance of Petitcreiu's
undoglike origin and nature. On the importance of the narration of the creative process
in ekphrases, see James A. W. Heffernan, *Museum of Words: The Poetics of Ekphrasis from
Homer to Ashbery* (Chicago: University of Chicago Press, 1993), p. 9.

33. Wright, "Petitcreiu." Interestingly the manuscript variation in the description of Petitcreiu suggests that medieval redactors were also concerned with Petitcreiu's canine qualities. In the 1240 Munich manuscript cgm 51, the two verses that inform us that Petitcreiu
needed neither food nor drink are omitted. This manuscript also omits the allegorical interpretation of the love grotto and in general is more concerned with telling a more concrete
and less ambiguous story of love. It is therefore significant that the only manuscript variation
in this episode involves these lines, which escalate the dog to an impossible perfection. On
manuscript variation of Gottfried's *Tristan,* see Martin Baisch, *Textkritik als Problem der
Kulturwissenschaft: Tristan-Lektüren* (Berlin: de Gruyter, 2006). For his discussion of the
Petitcreiu episode, see pp. 217–28.

34. As Christoph Huber has pointed out, Petitcreiu is both acoustically and optically
unique (*Gottfried von Strassburg,* Tristan und Isolde: *Eine Einführung* [Munich: Artemis,
1986], p. 90). I focus here on the visual aspect of the dog's description. For a recent study of

Petitcreiu is traditionally interpreted as a symbol of Tristan and Isolde's love.[35] According to Christoph Huber, it documents the intimacy, selflessness, and perfection of this love.[36] Tristan wins Petitcreiu with no concern for the danger that he must put himself in to do so, and Isolde destroys the dog's little bell, which was intended to make her feel better, because she will not allow herself to be comforted when Tristan is miserable.[37] The dog's ability to survive without food prefigures the lovers' isolation in the love grotto, the cave in the woods to which Tristan and Isolde retreat when they are banished from Mark's court. There they are able to subsist on love alone.

But Petitcreiu is also an object of fascination in the world of the poem, and its ekphrasis comments at length on its visual reception, thus presenting us with a model of seeing. The dog's color is one of its most remarkable characteristics:

> sîn varwe was in ein getragen
> mit alsô vremedem liste,
> daz nieman rehte wiste,
> von welher varwe ez waere.
> (ll. 15818–21)

Its color had been compounded with such rare skill that none could really tell what it was.

Further this amorphous shimmering color varies depending on one's perspective:

> ez was sô missehaere,
> als man ez gegen der bruste an sach,
> daz nieman anders niht enjach,

---

the dog's acoustic significance, see William Layher, "'Sô süeze waz der schellen klanc.' Music, Dissonance and the Sweetness of Pain in Gottfried's *Tristan*," *Beiträge zur Geschichte der deutschen Sprache und Literatur* 133.2 (2011): 235–64.

35. For a synopsis of the older scholarship on this episode, see Louise Gnädinger, *Hiudan und Petitcreiu: Gestalt und Figur des Hundes in der mittelalterlichen Tristandichtung* (Zurich: Atlantis, 1971), esp. pp. 26–48.

36. Huber regards the dog as a surrogate for love for Duke Gilan, an "Ersatzobjekt der Minne" (*Eine Einführung*, p. 90); see also Christoph Huber, *Gottfried von Strassburg: Tristan* (Berlin: Schmidt, 2000), pp. 94–95.

37. Silke Philipowski, by contrast, views the breaking of the bell as a point of conflict between the lovers ("Mittelbare und unmittelbare Gegenwärtigkeit oder: Erinnern und Vergessen in der Petitcriu-Episode des *Tristan* Gottfrieds von Strassburg," *Beiträge zur Geschichte der deutschen Sprache und Literatur* 120 [1998]: 29–35).

ezn waere wîzer danne snê,
zen lanken grüener danne clê,
ein sîte rôter danne grân,
diu ander gelwer dan safrân.
unden gelîch lazûre,
obene was ein mixtûre
gemischet alsô schône in ein,
daz sich ir aller dekein
ûz vür daz andere dâ bôt.
dane was grüene noch rôt
noch wîz noch swarz noch gel noch blâ
und doch ein teil ir aller dâ,
ich meine rehte purperbrûn.
daz vremede werc von Avalûn
sach man ez widerhaeres an,
sone wart nie kein sô wîse man,
der sîne varwe erkande.
si was sô maneger hande
und sô gar irrebaere,
als dâ kein varwe waere.
(ll. 15822–44)

When you looked at its breast it was so multi-colored that you would not
have said otherwise than that it was whiter than snow; but at the loins it was
greener than clover; one flank was redder than scarlet, the other yellower
than saffron; underneath, it resembled lapis lazuli, but above there was a
mixture so finely blended that no one hue stood out from all the others—
for here was neither green, nor red, nor white, nor black, nor yellow, nor
blue, and yet a touch of all, I mean a true purple. If you looked at this rare
work from Avalon against the grain of its coat, no one, however discerning,
could have told you its color. It was as bewilderingly varied as if there were
no color at all.

Ursula Liebertz-Grün has regarded Petitcreiu's shimmering fur as a paradigmatic example of multiperspectivalism in Tristan: "Like the wondrous dog
Petitcreiu, [Gottfried's *Tristan*] invites different reactions. . . . The romance of
Tristan is conceived as an open composition that challenges the interpreter to
conduct different and contrary experiments in its interpretation."[38] The text as

---

38. Ursula Lieberz-Grün, "Pluralismus im Mittelalter: Eine polemische Miszelle," *Monatshefte für deutschen Unterricht, deutsche Sprache und Literatur* 86 (1994): 4 [3–6].

a whole, she argues, reflects different perspectives and diverse points of view. The little dog could thus be regarded as emblematic of the idea developed in Gottfried's *Tristan* that what you see depends on how you look at it.

More importantly in the context of ekphrastic theory, however, this presentation of multiple perspectives emphatically rejects the notion of an objective and authoritative point of view. Petitcreiu appears to be situated between an objective material thing and a subjective mental image.[39] Like Tristan, each listener must determine not only from which perspective to examine the dog but also how the image is transformed in the mind's eye. Rather than persuade and enslave a passive, uncritical listener, the appearance of the dog and this ekphrasis of it force him or her to actively engage with the story, becoming not only an eyewitness but a participant in a particular model of seeing. Viewing the little dog at Duke Gilan's court may be a communal courtly activity, but what one sees is individual, subjective, and requires interpretation.

The Petitcreiu ekphrasis is an introduction to the mode or model of viewing necessary to see the love grotto and in turn to contemplate Tristan and Isolde's love, which is made manifest in these objects that are situated between the listener's imagination and the material world of the poem. By simultaneously enabling the listener to see the dog and occluding his vision, to recall Elsner, this ekphrasis becomes as much about seeing as it is about the little dog. It also demonstrates the power of the visual both for the listener and in the world of the poem. Tristan becomes so obsessed with the dog, that he tricks his friend into giving him his prized and beloved possession. At issue in these ekphrases is the distinction between a courtly gaze, which is revealed to be gullible and uncritical, and the more critical vision of the discerning viewer who looks more closely and interprets what he or she sees. The focus in the Petitcreiu episode is on a model of vision that requires interpretation. It is not possible to view the dog passively. Rather the viewer is tasked to see both the ekphrastic subject and its effect on its viewers.

VISUALITY AND *TRISTAN*-LOVE

The emphasis on the visual is not limited to these ekphrases. Rather, Tristan and Isolde's love is described throughout the poem in predominantly visual

---

39. As Mario Klarer has pointed out, "The medieval notion of a picture, not as a painting [or in this case, an object] but as an immaterial mental image is . . . very much a product of classical philology and theory of sense perception" ("Ekphrasis, or the Archeology of Historical Theories of Representation: Medieval Brain Anatomy in Wernher der Gartenaere's *Helmbrecht*," *Word and Image* 15 [1999]: 36 [34–40]).

terms: it is experienced and transmitted primarily through the eyes.[40] When Tristan and Isolde first fall in love, the narrator tells us:

> si blicte underwîlen dar
> und nam sîn tougenlîche war.
> ir clâren ougen und ir sin
> diu gehullen dô wol under in.
> ir herze unde ir ougen
> diu schâcheten vil tougen
> und lieplîchen an den man.
> der man der sach si wider an
> suoze und ineclîchen.
> (ll. 11841–49)

(Isolde) glanced at him now and again and watched him covertly; her bright eyes, her mind, and her heart preyed secretly and lovingly on the man, while the man looked back at her sweetly and intimately.

And the more the lovers look at one another, the more their visual perception changes. Once they are in love: "die gelieben dûhten beide / ein ander schoener vil dan ê" (ll. 11856–57) [the lovers seemed to each other fairer than before]. Their love not only makes them perceive one another differently but it also visibly marks them:

---

40. Christopher R. Clason, in "'Good Lovin': The Language of Erotic Desire and Fulfillment in Gottfried's *Tristan*," in *Sexuality in the Middle Ages and the Early Modern Times: New Approaches to a Fundamental Cultural-Historical and Literary-Anthropological Theme,* ed. Albrecht Classen (Berlin: de Gruyter, 2008), pp. 257–78, argues that, whereas Gottfried describes the sexual relations of Marke with Brangaene and Isolde, and Rivalin with Blanscheflor graphically, he resorts to allegory and metaphor when describing the love-making between Tristan and Isolde: "The more profane the relationship, the more the audience is permitted to visualize via concrete, descriptive language" (p. 278). With Tristan and Isolde there "is little visual description, and what the lovers do in private is communicated symbolically or allegorically" (p. 272). Clason suggests that this mode of allegorical and metaphorical description "forces the reader to consider the lovers non-visually, i.e., not through their superficial physicality, but rather as a 'mythic presence,' better comprehended through symbol and metaphor" (p. 276). I disagree with Clason, however, that "Gottfried's allusions and metaphors place [the lovers'] activities beyond the reader's inner eye" and instead view Gottfried's portrayal of sexual relations between Tristan and Isolde as an extension of the visual code that is apparent throughout the poem whenever the lovers interact. As with Petitcreiu, the reader/listener is invited to imagine the lovers, and what each person sees will be subjective and individual. The point is that these sexual descriptions are not narrated by an authoritative voice that determines how we see them. While the language describing Tristan and Isolde's sexual acts may not be concretely descriptive, it is highly visual, presuming an elevated level of seeing.

sô s'eteswenne tougen
mit gelîmeten ougen
ein ander solten nemen war,
sô wart ir lîch gelîche var
dem herzen unde dem sinne.
(ll. 11903–7)

When from time to time they tried to observe each other secretly through
eyes which Love had limed, their flesh assumed the hue of their hearts and
minds.

Gottfried personifies love as a painter who colors the lovers' faces first red,
then white, then red again (*Tristan*, ll. 1190820). It is through these visible
signs that the lovers see their own feelings of love reflected:

hie mite erkande ietwederez wol,
als man an solhen dingen sol,
daz eteswaz von minnen
in ietwederes sinnen
zem anderen was gewant
(ll. 11921–25)

From that each of them recognized what one recognizes from such things,
that something of love in each of their minds was turned toward the other.

Love is thus described as a visual code that the discerning listener/reader
(with the help of the narrator) is able to see and identify.

As I have shown, several key moments in Gottfried's *Tristan* address viewing explicitly, providing a model of vision for the audience. These moments
are ekphrastic passages in which the listener has the opportunity to participate in the story as an eyewitness, to watch, see, interpret, and imagine concrete manifestations of love.

CONCLUSION

In *Tristan,* the first public appearances of Tristan, Isolde, and the little dog
Petitcreiu, are described in minute detail in the ekphrastic mode: Tristan's artful carving of the stag, Isolde's appearance before the Irish court after the slay-
ing of the dragon, and Petitcreiu's wondrous shimmering fur. These passages

suspend the linear progression of the narrative and involve the listener/reader as a participant in the events of the story by unfolding before his or her eyes detailed visual descriptions of the two lovers and their little dog. In effect, these passages create a virtual three-dimensional space in which the reader/ listener is integrated into the story as an eyewitness to a wondrous visual experience. But these are also dynamic passages in which the malleability and gullibility of the watching courtiers are revealed and the reader/listener is challenged to take a critical perspective on what he or she is viewing.

By examining these three key scenes in *Tristan* as examples of ekphrasis, I am not attempting to make claims about Gottfried's investment in the classical techniques of rhetoric. I am, however, suggesting that he was familiar with the mode, and that his description of Tristan, Isolde, and Petitcreiu follow the principles of (classical) ekphrasis in order to draw attention to the way in which visual experience, and particularly visual beauty, is able to persuade and deceive viewers. Ekphrasis in *Tristan* shows the power of visual experience to alter a viewer's perception. Implicit in Gottfried's ekphrases is another type of viewer, however, one who is able to recognize the seductive persuasiveness of a beautiful visual experience and yet resist it, a critical viewer who watches as others are manipulated by the scene brought so vividly before their eyes. This critical distance between the text-internal courtly viewers and the discerning projected audience of the story is crucial to Gottfried's literary project to cultivate noble hearts that are able to fully understand Tristan-love.

In the context of his medieval German contemporaries, Gottfried expands the use of ekphrasis in an important way. Most medieval German ekphrases provide a single authoritative perspective and seek to incorporate the listener into the text, thus eliding the boundary between the fictional world of the text and the world of the audience. Indeed this authoritative or foundational perspective has been viewed as one of the characteristic features of medieval ekphrasis.[41] Gottfried, however, uses ekphrasis, on the one hand, to distance the audience from the events and characters in the text and, on the other, to invite the reader/listener not to passively watch as the narrative unfolds before his mind's eye but to actively construct visual objects in his or her imagina-

---

41. See Mary Carruthers, *The Craft of Thought. Meditation, Rhetoric, and the Making of Images, 400–1200, Cambridge Studies in Medieval Literature* (Cambridge: Cambridge University Press, 1998), p. 197. Her discussion of *Bildeinsatz* is in effect a discussion of the technique of ekphrasis and its role in the art of memory. See also Wandhoff, "Bilder der Liebe," pp. 66–70, who argues that the ekphrases in Konrad Fleck's *Flore und Blanscheflur* provide a foundational but imperfect model of pagan antique love that the Christian protagonists ultimately surpass. The ekphrases in this romance are thus presented from a single authoritative perspective but are revealed to be inadequate.

tion that will enable him or her to reflect on and remember the concept of love developed in the text. The ekphrases I have discussed above are particularly significant because they evoke one of the larger central thematic concerns of the poem, namely the distinction between those who are able to fully appreciate the love story, and those who are not.[42] Like the story's prologue, which warns the audience that only an elect group, the noble hearts, will truly be able to appreciate the story, the ekphrases draw a distinction between those who watch and are persuaded and those who are truly able to see.

---

42. As Ruth Webb, points out in "The Model Ekphraseis of Nikolaos the Sophist as Memory Images," in *Theatron: Rhetorische Kultur in Spätantike und Mittelalter—Rhetorical Culture in Late Antiquity and the Middle Ages,* ed. Michael Grünbart (Berlin: de Gruyter, 2007), pp. 463–75, "one particular function of ekphrasis within the larger rhetorical system [is] the evocation of a larger narrative context from the inclusion of a few telling details" (p. 464).

PART III
THE EPISTEMOLOGY OF EKPHRASIS

Chapter 7

EKPHRASIS AND RELIGIOUS IDEOLOGY IN SPENSER'S *LEGEND OF HOLINESS*

Darryl J. Gless

$\mathcal{O}$ ver the centuries, Spenser's *Faerie Queene* has seemed, to many readers, pervasively ekphrastic.[1] That statement becomes immediately convincing only if one adopts the broad definition of ekphrasis employed by influential rhetoricians of the classical, medieval, and early modern periods—as well as by other authors in this collection. Throughout its early history, ekphrasis meant "an extended description of something, such as a person, place, battle or work of art."[2] Spenser's great poem does of course incorporate striking

---

1. Describing Spenser's poetry as "a gallery of pictures" has been a persistent feature of his reception history. For useful précis and analysis of this tradition, see John B. Bender, *Spenser and Literary Pictorialism* (Princeton, NJ: Princeton University Press, 1972) and Ernest B. Gilman, "Spenser's 'Painted Forgery,'" in *Iconoclasm and Poetry in the English Reformation: Down Went Dagon* (Chicago: University of Chicago Press, 1986), ch. 3.

2. Quotation from Clark Hulse, *Metamorphic Verse: The Elizabethan Minor Epic* (Princeton, NJ: Princeton University Press, 1981), p. 177. For a recent history and analysis of the ancient understanding of the term, see Ruth Webb, *Ekphrasis, Imagination and Persuasion in Ancient Rhetorical Theory and Practice* (Farnham: Ashgate, 2009). "In the Greek schools of the Roman empire," she demonstrates, students were taught that ekphrasis is "'a speech that brings the subject matter vividly before the eyes.' . . . at no point in antiquity (or Byzantium) was ekphrasis confined to a single category of subject matter, nor can every text about images

ekphrastic passages more narrowly defined—detailed depictions of works of visual art. These include, to mention only the most obvious examples, the ivory-gated entry to the Bower of Bliss in *The Faerie Queene;* an elaborately described tapestry picturing the tale of Venus and Adonis; and the still more elaborate tapestries and golden engravings of "monstrous shapes" of love on the walls of Busyrane's castle in *The Faerie Queene,* Book III.[3]

Far more often, however, Spenser's poetry is ekphrastic in the broad traditional sense. This feature of his work has led readers over the past four centuries to "locate Spenser within the realm of the literary-pictorial" and to make "pictorialism" a recurrent topic in Spenser studies.[4] I will argue in this essay that when Spenser offers pictorial description—as he certainly does—

be claimed as ekphrasis in the ancient sense" (pp. 1–2). For studies of Spenser's ekphrases based on a much later narrow definition, a verbal description of a visual work of art, see, *inter alia,* Page Dubois, *History, Rhetorical Description and the Epic from Homer to Spenser* (Cambridge: D. S. Brewer, 1982) and James A. W. Heffernan, *Museum of Words: The Poetics of Ekphrasis from Homer to Ashbery* (Chicago: University of Chicago Press, 1993), p. 3. Murray Krieger, *Ekphrasis: The Illusion of the Natural Sign* (Baltimore: Johns Hopkins University Press, 1992), pp. 6–8, proposes explanations for the gradual reduction of the term's reach, including the striking quality of Homer's description of Achilles' shield in *Iliad* 18 and the influence of the powerful imitations of it in subsequent epics by Virgil, Dante, Tasso, *inter alia.* For the broad definition of the term, Krieger (*Ekphrasis,* p. 7, n. 8) cites Hermogenes' *Elementary Exercises (Progymnasmata)* in Charles S. Baldwin, *Medieval Rhetoric and Poetic* (Gloucester, MA: Peter Smith, 1959), pp. 35–36: "In Hellenistic rhetoric . . . it referred, most broadly, to a verbal description of something, almost anything, in life or art." He then notes that this definition "would seem to overlap, almost totally, the rhetorically encouraged virtue of *enargeia,* which is also defined as vivid description addressed to the inner eye."

3. Edmund Spenser, *The Faerie Queene,* ed. A. C. Hamilton, textual eds. Hiroshi Yamashita and Toshiaki Suzuki (London: Longman/Pearson, 2001). All citations are to this edition, hereafter cited parenthetically in my text. The ekphrases mentioned above occur at II.xi.43–46, III.i.34–38 and xi.28–49. These ekphrases have been often discussed. See, among others, Dubois, *History,* pp. 71–94 and Judith Dundas, *The Spider and the Bee: The Artistry of Spenser's* Faerie Queene (Urbana: University of Illinois Press, 1985).

4. Claire Preston, "Spenser and the Visual Arts," in *The Oxford Handbook of Edmund Spenser,* ed. Richard A. McCabe (Oxford: Oxford University Press, 2010), p. 684 [684–717]. On pp. 685–86, Preston suggests the kinds pictorial elements that pervade Spenser's works:

> descriptions of art-objects (pictures, emblems, heraldic devices, tapestries, architecture, costume, jewels, sculpture, and ornamental landscapes with grottoes and fountains), episodes set in and dependent on the displays of such objects (for example, the tapestries and bas reliefs in the house of Busirane and in Castle Joyous in *Faerie Queene* III; the chamber of Phantastes, "dispainted" with "infinite shapes" in the Castle of Alma; and the minutely rendered artifice of the Bowre of Blisse in *Faerie Queene* II); and the frequency of deictic signals such as "there you might see," "the sight whereof" (*TW*), and "painted," "portrayed," and "enwoven" (*FQ*), which invite the mind to inspect verbal images as if they were present to the eye, together with verbs of display ("show," 'portray/pourtraict," "figure," "shadow," "picture," "image").

he often does it so cleverly that readers perceive far more visual specificity in the poem than it actually provides. We fall easy prey, that is, to the pleasing illusion that we "see" more than we do.[5] What we think we see in such cases is an illusion generated when relatively sparse linguistic details in the poem activate memories of commonplace visual images that we have seen before. This is the unavoidable perceptual process E. H. Gombrich memorably named "the etc. principle."[6] Sometimes that illusion is so strong that memories override the empirically verifiable features of the text and impede our noticing significant modifications the poet has made to the expected image. My primary focus in this essay will be such moments: passages of *The Faerie Queene, Book I, or The Legend of Holinesse,* that seem to promise detailed description of commonplace works of visual art (ekphrases in the narrow sense) and create the illusion of doing so, but actually offer much more, or something quite different, from what the author induces his readers at first to anticipate.

Partly because readers grant Spenser more credit for detailed pictorial representation than he legitimately earns, readers over the centuries have offered up vague comparisons of Spenserian scenes to great works by Titian, Rubens, Rosa, Claude, Carracci, Michelangelo, *inter alia,* or some other old master of the Italian Renaissance. Claire Preston has recently offered a comprehensive list of such comparisons, noting that "there is hardly an artist of note in the period 1300–1600 who has not been 'found' in Spenser."[7] Ernest B. Gilman helpfully summarizes the interpretive tradition: "It was Warton who praised Spenser for rivaling Rubens; Hazlitt, for his 'high picturesque character'; and Yeats, for his seeming 'always to feel through the eyes, imaging everything in pictures.'" Echoes of this enthusiasm reappear in varying guises and with differing degrees of usefulness in the work of many later scholars, including Josephine Waters Bennett, James Nohrnberg, Alastair Fowler, Angus Fletcher, Jane Aptekar, Graham Hough, Robert Kellogg, Oliver Steele, and Northrop Frye. As Gilman wryly concludes concerning one of these efforts, "What precision lacks in such comparisons ingenuity supplies."[8]

---

5. When I speak of "we," I think primarily of Spenser's earliest readers and of scholarly or at least well-educated and travelled ones today, people who know something of the visual material on which Spenser's poetry draws and which many, if not all of his earliest readers, would have encountered as visible features of their daily lives.

6. "The assumption we tend to make that to see a few members of a series is to see them all" (E. H. Gombrich, *Art and Illusion: A Study in the Psychology of Pictorial Representation,* Bollingen Series XXXV.5, 2nd ed. [Princeton, NJ: Princeton University Press, 1960], p. 219).

7. Preston, "Spenser," p. 688.

8. Gilman, *Iconoclasm and Poetry,* pp. 62–63.

However imprecise comparisons between Spenser's poetry and visual arts might often be, they can become useful for interpreters of the poem at moments when Spenser invites his readers to imagine an image or sequence of images that those readers would in reality have seen before—in illuminated manuscripts, in civic or court pageantry, on tapestries, on murals in parish churches, private chapels, great halls, or indeed on painted clothes in less exalted surroundings, including inns and taverns. Many religious images in these places had by 1590 been whitewashed over or otherwise obliterated, but many others escaped unscathed, and more would have lived on in readers' memories if not in artifacts that had escaped the iconoclasts' enthusiasm. As Margaret Aston's history of iconoclasm in England abundantly demonstrates, it took more than a century of image-breaking campaigns to erase most of the visual richness of England's medieval religious heritage.[9]

The intermittence, long duration, and imperfect scope of that process enabled Spenser to count on a broad spectrum of his readership's vivid memories or recent observations of that rich visual culture. And as Preston points out, "it is not only the comfortably-off classes who used hangings as a form of insulation as well as of decoration, but also the great households which displayed spectacular collections of them."[10] More particularly, Spenser is virtually certain in 1579–80 to have been in some form of service at Leicester House and thus to have known Robert Dudley's collection of illuminated manuscripts, which contained various "'histories' of the gods." As Rosemond Tuve and Frederick Hard established long ago, a number of aristocrats who had connections with Spenser valued and collected such manuscripts.[11]

This inference can help us understand why in salient passages Spenser tends less to describe than to hint at description.[12] He does this, for instance,

9. On the long history of iconoclasm in England, which began with the Lollards in the late fourteenth century, violently intensified by government action under Henry VIII, Edward VI, and Elizabeth I, and achieved completion by Parliamentary forces and local enthusiasts during the Civil War, see Margaret Aston, *England's Iconoclasts, Vol. 1: Laws against Images* (Oxford: Clarendon Press, 1988).

10. Preston, "Spenser," pp. 689–90.

11. See Frederick M. Hard, "Spenser's 'Clothes of Arras and of Toure,'" *Studies in Philology* 27 (1930): 162–85, and Rosemond Tuve, "Spenser and Some Pictorial Conventions with Particular Reference to Illuminated Manuscripts," *Studies in Philology* 37 (1940): 149–76.

12. See Bender, *Spenser and Literary Pictorialism*, pp. 8–9, for the important rhetorical distinction between *enargeia*, faithful rendering of surfaces, and *energeia*, inner coherence that represents life, liveliness. See also Gilman, *Iconoclasm and Poetry*, p. 79, who notes that a variety of critics, including Paul Alpers, John Bender, and others, have noted and sought to understand this phenomenon of an illusory rather than an actual presentation of the visual. Jane Grogan also recurrently notes this absence of realized description (*Exemplary Spenser: Visual and Poetic Pedagogy in* The Faerie Queene [Farnham: Ashgate, 2009]). See ch. 3, "'Bad Art' or Good Readers? Spenserian Ekphrasis," pp. 103–36.

when evoking what would have been exceptionally commonplace images, such as the Seven Deadly Sins and the Seven Corporal Works of Mercy, images to which I will return. In these cases, our mind's eye both "sees" the traditional image, and at the same time, we can perceive still more emphatically meanings that exceed or differ from those the traditional image itself suggested. The pageant of the Seven Deadly Sins in *The Faerie Queene*, Book I, canto iv, is my first case in point. This familiar sequence anticipates another with which it would normally have been paired in frescoes and wall paintings throughout Spenser's England, the Seven Corporal Works of Mercy. This second set of images provides an even more striking revision of the norm, a highly significant ekphrastic depiction at the symbolic center of *The Legend of Holinesse*.

In order to assess the ideological weight of the passages I have mentioned, however, we need to review some of the broad doctrinal contexts upon which Spenser's poem persistently draws. As I have argued elsewhere, *The Faerie Queene* deploys its images, scriptural echoes, and theological diction with remarkable doctrinal precision.[13] It invites readers, especially those of Calvinistic or, more accurately, "Reformed" biases, to construe the poem in far more complex and engaging ways than I (and many others) had previously noted. It also recurrently allows comfort to those who, at the end of the sixteenth century, were clinging, as many apparently were in Spenser's time, to the Old Faith.[14]

Spenser's precise use of doctrinal terms begins with the alternative title he provided for *The Faerie Queene, Book I: The Legend of the Knight of the Red Crosse, or of Holinesse*. Despite immense complexity and many real or apparent contradictions within the broad range of orthodox opinion in Elizabethan England, the term *holiness* tended to be used with notable consistency. It names, precisely, the consequence of sanctification. And sanctification, as Protestant theologians defined it, is an inevitable consequence of the moment when the elect soul, predestined from all eternity to salvation, receives the "call," finds itself gripped by the irresistible power of grace, and has "righ-

---

13. The doctrinal exposition that appears in the next several paragraphs derives from my *Interpretation and Theology in Spenser* (Cambridge: Cambridge University Press, 1994), pp. 26–37 and 44–45.

14. Pauline Croft, *King James* (Houndmills: Palgrave MacMillan, 2003), p. 162, reports that an estimated 40,000 Catholics remained in England at the end of Elizabeth's reign (1603). Scholars variously class such people as "recusants," "crypto-Catholics," or "Church papists." For a useful treatment of the persistence of Catholicism and the tribulations of its adherents under Elizabeth, see Christopher Haigh, "From Resentment to Recusancy," in *English Reformations: Religion, Politics, and Society under the Tudors* (Oxford: Clarendon Press, 1993), pp. 251–67.

teousness" imputed to it. According to the authorities of the Elizabethan Church as well as their Continental mentors (Calvin, Bullinger, Bucer, Luther, Melanchthon, *inter alia*), the arrival of that irresistible power "justifies" the soul, granting it the faith that alone, without good works, yields salvation.

At the same time, justifying grace renews the hitherto utterly corrupt human will, enabling the soul to "cooperate"—this is a key idea, usually omitted from modern summaries of Reformed doctrine—with persisting impulsions of grace to achieve good works. These good works are necessary consequences of justification, but because they result from a collaborative endeavor of grace and human will, such works can never be good enough to earn any increment, however small, of merit toward salvation. According to a favorite Protestant analogy, good works issuing from a grace-renewed and grace-impelled human will are like the waters of a spring, which are pure at the source, but immediately suffer corruption from the channel through which they run. Good works, in this theology, manifest one's saving or, in the common phrasing, one's "lively faith." They make one's saving faith visible.

Although the justified soul remains certainly justified, its pursuit of holiness through the process of sanctification will always be halting and uncertain. That pursuit will bring with it moments of sinful backsliding, episodes of doubt or even terror at the possibility that the soul's continuing and unavoidable sinfulness will in the end prove to have been evidence of "reprobation," an eternal sentence of damnation. For this reason Protestant theologians often draw upon the Pauline idea that the saved are "baptized" both into Christ's death and his resurrection, and that their lifelong pursuit of holiness will consequently take the shape of a persistent spiritual sensation of death and of resurrection. The faithful will alternately suffer "mortification," which occurs when divine law teaches them how completely they fail to live up to God's demands. But they will then find relief in moments of "vivification," as they regain confidence that their salvation depends not on their own efforts but on the perfect atonement the Savior made on their individual behalf, which has been "imputed" to them.

Equipped with such basic doctrines of the Elizabethan Church and its Continental mentors, readers can achieve a deeper understanding of the climactic cantos of *The Legend of Holinesse*. As Red Cross Knight approaches the House of Holiness in canto x—the ekphrastic section of the poem on which I will concentrate most fully—his confidence that the Savior's atonement was indeed made on his behalf remains deficient. The knight has reason for diffidence. He has just escaped the temptation to suicide offered to him by that most effective tempter, Despaire. And Despaire's temptation has confronted him with the frightening Protestant understanding of sin that has appeared so far in vivid ekphrases during salient episodes in the poem.

The pageant of the Seven Deadly Sins in Book I, canto iv, stanzas 18–36, illustrates this point while at the same time demonstrating that a vivid feature of the poem—one that readers incline to remember primarily as images—appears under scrutiny to offer more nonvisual details than visual ones.[15] As A. Craiger-Smith has demonstrated, images of these sins and their counterpart virtues were among the most common of murals and had migrated to church walls from their original locations in illuminated manuscripts. They would ordinarily have appeared as a tree with seven branches rooted in the original sin of pride, sometimes enlivened by images of men or women expressing the sinful behavior in question, an avaricious man with his pile of gold, for instance, or a glutton drinking from a pitcher.[16] Although such images suggest motion, and like all works of visual art, as W. J. T. Mitchell argues, are not *either* spatial *or* temporal, but rather "structures in space-time," Spenser fully exploits poetry's superiority to painting in representing actions in time.[17] He makes the sins counselors to Queen Lucifera and sets them off on a strikingly static progress. He also provides each sin with an impressive array of descriptive detail. Idleness, for instance, the first of Lucifera's six "Counsellours" (iv.18), rides "a slouthfull Asse" (iv.18), wears a "habit blacke, and amis thin, / Like to a holy Monck" (iv.18), carries a worn "Portesse" (iv.19), has trouble lifting up his head, and suffers from a "shaking feuer" (iv.19). Such details provide a sufficient foundation for a vivid mental representation of surfaces. For Spenser's early readers, and for modern ones familiar with commonplace medieval representations of the Seven Deadly Sins, recollections of paintings and tapestries can supplement the visual details the passage itself provides. Yet the visual materials actually presented in the portrait require but six or seven lines of a 22-line depiction (iv.18–20). Most of the passage in fact describes rationalizations for slothfulness, items like this:

From worldly cares himselfe he did esloyne [withdraw],
And greatly shunned manly exercise,
From everie worke he challenged essoyne,
For contemplation sake.
(iv.20)

---

15. Because all my quotations and citations of *The Faerie Queene* hereafter concern Book I, *The Legend of Holinesse*, I will cite in parenthesis only the canto and stanza numbers in most cases hereafter. When citing from a single canto several times in close proximity, I will provide the stanza number only, at times adding line numbers, as the precision of my commentary demands.

16. A. Craiger-Smith, *English Medieval Mural Paintings* (Oxford: Clarendon Press, 1963), pp. 49–55.

17. W. J. T. Mitchell *Iconology: Image, Text, Ideology* (Chicago: University of Chicago Press, 1986), p. 103.

That final sarcasm neatly captures the vitriol characteristic of Protestant literary treatments of the Catholic regular clergy. What we "see" of Idleness proves to be matters more of mind and spirit than of body.

A similar preponderance of moral and spiritual commentary over visual description characterizes Spenser's portraits of the five other sins that comprise Lucifera's entourage. Yet this combination of the visual and the explanatory, what Clark Hulse has called an "emblematic" version of ekphrasis, proves rhetorically powerful.[18] Red Cross Knight does not miss the point. Moved by a conviction of knightly superiority, "that good knight would not so nigh repaire, / Him selfe estraunging from their ioyaunce vaine, / Whose fellowship seemd far vnfitt for warlike swaine" (iv.37).[19] His avoidance itself reminds us of the persuasive power the visual exerts upon him, a power both the iconoclasts and the iconophiles of the era had acknowledged and, for that reason, either applauded or deplored as aids to faith.[20] Before reaching the pageant of the sins, Spenser's readers will already have witnessed the knight's susceptibility to the visual and auditory allure of Catholicism. He has been easily captivated by Duessa, "a goodly Lady clad in scarlot red, / Purfled with gold and pearle of rich assay." Even her "palfrey" appeals garishly to eye and ear: "overspred / With tinsell trappings, woven like a wave, / Whose bridle rung with golden bels and bosses braue" (ii.13). The knight, "busying his quicke eies" (ii.26), slips readily under Duessa's spell. But in canto iv, those quick eyes warn him away from seven sources of immediate spiritual danger. The poet's tendency to provide commentary that readers nonetheless perceive and remember primarily as visual depiction does not apply, however, to the six counselors' leader, the root sin of Pride embodied in Lucifera.

> High aboue all a cloth of State was spred,
> And a rich throne, as bright as sunny day,
> On which there sate most braue embellished
> With royall robes and gorgeous array,

---

18. Hulse, *Metamorphic Verse*, pp. 28–29.

19. Although it is common to refer to the procession as a pageant, it might more fruitfully be compared to a "triumph." Spenser's sins, like Petrarch's varied victors, march over a landscape of death: "And vnderneath their feet, all scattered lay / Dead sculls and bones of men, whose life had gone astray" (I.iv.36).

20. This shared acknowledgement of the power of visual imagery emerges repeatedly in Aston's *England's Iconoclasts*. For Thomas More's argument that "'images painted, graven or carved' might 'naturally, and much more effectually represent the thing than shall the name either spoke or written,'" see p. 181. The argument More was refuting is explained on pp. 178–80. Sean Kane provides a useful summary statement about Spenser's representations of idolatry in *The Spenser Encyclopedia* (Toronto: University of Toronto Press, 1990), s.v. "idols, idolatry," pp. 387–88.

A mayden Queene, that shone as *Titans* ray,
In glistring gold, and peerelesse pretious stone:
Yet her bright blazing beautie did assay
To dim the brightnesse of her glorious throne,
As enuying her selfe, that too exceeding shone.
(iv.8)

So proud she shyned in her Princely state,
Looking to heauen; for earth she did disdayne,
And sitting high; for lowly she did hate:
Lo vnderneath her scornefull feete, was layne
A dreadfull Dragon with an hideous trayne,
And in her hand she held a mirrhour bright,
Wherein her face she often vewed fayne,
And in her selfe-lou'd semblance tooke delight;
For she was wondrous faire, as any liuing wight.
(iv.10)

This usurping queen's castle, courtiers, ladies-in-waiting, throne, clothing, person, behavior, and "coche" collectively prove almost to overwhelm the viewer's sense of sight (iv.8–17). Spenser makes comprehensive use of this figure's traditional iconography, right down to her attribute, the mirror, and her attendant dragon. In effect, the poet makes her the most readily discernible of the sins—the most discernible, the most insidious, and the origin of all the others.

Most tellingly of all, perhaps, Lucifera inspires behavior the poem's readers or hearers would themselves often have witnessed and most likely performed. Here is Spenser's description of what we can take to be everyday behavior among the denizens of Renaissance courts, whether allegorical or actual: Lucifera's

Lordes and Ladies all this while devise
Themselves to setten forth to straungers sight:
Some flounce their curled heare in courtly guise,
Some prancke their ruffes, and others trimly dight
Their gay attire: each others greater pride does spight.
(iv.14)

Such moments of social satire remind readers that, at root, even unremarkable and pervasive courtly jockeying aligns them with the diabolic. Together with her six counselors, the vividly depicted Lucifera calls on readers who are attentive to theology, that is, to discover here a favored Reformed conception of sin—that a single indivisible evil underlies all particular sins and that sin extends not only to actions and intentions but to corruption so deeply ingrained in the human soul that it operates even below the level of consciousness.[21] This idea appears again in a strikingly visual passage, in iv.46, near the canto's end. There the knight's companion dwarf observes a "donghill of dead carkases," that stand as a "spectacle" of that "sad house of Pride." The narrative's literal corpses have died spiritually—the eternal death they have earned from participation not in one or two of the sins, but in all seven, which are cleverly and unobtrusively listed in stanza 46. Having by this point presented his services to Lucifera and accepted a place at her side (v.16–17), Red Cross is immersed in sin in its totality.

To fall to pride, then, is to fall to sin in its unitary essence. The individual's unavoidable participation in that terrifying, unfathomable essence rises to consciousness when the sinner acknowledges particular sins. Well before he reaches the House of Holiness, the Red Cross Knight's particular sins have convinced him of his own pervasive sinfulness. In his confrontation with Despaire in canto ix, the knight comes to consider that sinfulness is ineradicable and unforgivable. To drive that message home, Despaire employs the very weapon Protestant preachers themselves recommended, "the sword of the spirit," which according to Eph. 6, "is the Word of God."

> The knight was much emoued with his speach,
> That as a swords poynt through his hart did perse,
> And in his conscience made a secrete breach,
> Well knowing trew all, that he did reherse,
> And to his fresh remembraunce did reuerse,
> The vgly vew of his deformed crimes,
> That all his manly powres it did disperse.
> (ix.48)

Despaire, a projection of the knight's now despairing self-judgment, inevitably knows that his host and victim is susceptible to the power of visual imagery:

> To driue him to despaire, and quite to quaile,
> Hee shewd him painted in a table plaine,

---

21. Gless, *Interpretation and Theology,* pp. 38–40, quotations from pp. 104, 39, and 38.

The damned ghosts, that doe in torments waile,
And thousand feends that doe them endless paine
With fire and brimstone, which foreuer shall remaine.
(ix.49)

This little ekphrasis—reinforced for the knight and for Spenser's readers by recollections of numerous Last Judgment scenes that often accompanied illustrations of the sins—does the trick. "Dismaid" (i.e., unmade spiritually) by "the sight" of ghastly eternal torment, Red Cross trembles on the verge of suicide until Una wrests away his knife and berates him with a sequence of rhetorical questions. Her final one, "Why shouldst thou then despeire, that chosen art?" instills in him an immediate conviction, as the laconic next line demonstrates: "So up he rose, and thence amounted straight" (ix.53).

Recognizing the knight's inclination to slide back into despair, however, Una takes him to a place that appears to promise another ekphrasis, a coherent depiction of a convent or monastery. "There was an auncient house not far away, / Renowmd throughout the world for sacred lore, / And pure vnspotted life." But this monastic establishment differs from its medieval models. The place is devoted, under the direction of Celia, its "matrone graue and hore," to both the active and the contemplative life, for Celia's

> only ioy was to relieue the needes
> Of wretched soules, and helpe the helpelesse pore:
> All night she spent in bidding of her bedes,
> And all the day in doing good and godly deedes.
> (x.3)

This alternation of daytime and nighttime occupations would have suited Erasmus and other reforming Catholics as well as English Protestants—so long as the "bedes" in question denote prayers, not rosaries. The poet emphasizes at the outset, moreover, that Una brings her knight to this house "to cherish him . . . where he chearen might" (x.2). This emphasis on both nourishing him and cheering him up appears repeatedly in the cheery welcomes he receives from the inmates, whose most frequent feeling is one of "joy."

For a time, our anticipation of an ekphrastic description of this setting is sustained. Invited in by the porter Humiltà, the knight and lady enter "stouping low; / For streight and narrow was the way, which he did shew" (x.5). They then enter a "spacious court" and then "to the Hall they came" (x.6). But this is where the place begins to lose physical coherence, as it progressively does thereafter. We visit a dark dungeon-like place, two schoolhouses, a holy hospital, and as the House of Holiness seems to expand ever outward, we find ourselves at last on a lofty mountaintop, observing, not far beyond, the heavenly Jerusalem itself. The framing that had been so definite at the outset of the description utterly disappears by the end.

This contributes to a central feature of Spenser's management of the pictorial features of his poem: Rational reflection gradually takes precedence over the visual reflection, triggered by surprising divergences from visual precedents the poet deliberately invokes. In the House of Holinesse, however, progressive loss of architectural coherence counterbalances a vividly visual presentation of the House's allegorical inhabitants. Their ekphrastic presentation makes them seem, at first, altogether unlike the puzzling and deceptive allegorical figures that predominated in the preceding narrative. Fidelia illustrates this initial transparency:

> . . . the eldest, that *Fidelia* hight,
> Like sunny beames threw from her Christall face,
> That could haue dazd the rash beholders sight,
> And round about her head did shine like heuens light.
>
> She was araied all in lilly white,
> And in her right hand bore a cup of gold,
> With wine and water fild vp to the hight,
> In which a Serpent did himselfe enfold,
> That horrour made to all, that did behold;
> But she no whitt did change her constant mood:
> And in her other hand she fast did hold
> A booke that was both signd and seald with blood,
> Wherin darke things were writt, hard to be vnderstood.
> (x.12–13)

This embodiment of Faith, which we might expect to be by far the most conspicuous element in an allegory founded on Protestant soteriology, is rendered striking by her intimidating brilliance and her Eucharistic cup—with its fear-inducing serpent, itself a surprising Spenserian addition to traditional images of faith. And for all her visual clarity, Fidelia's teaching remains obscure, "darke things . . . hard to be understood."

We soon receive momentary hope that these dark writings will receive clarification, for the Red Cross Knight and for us. At Una's request, Fidelia places the knight in her "schoolehous" (x.18.4), and there, we are told, "she him taught celestiall discipline, / And opened his dull eyes, that light mote in them shine" (x.18.8–9). But the vision that seems to be promised us here also proves dark. Although Fidelia teaches Red Cross out of "her sacred Booke" things "that weaker witt of man could never reach," those teachings remain in Spenser's description merely a list of the most complex, weighty, and contested of theological topics: "Of God, of grace, of iustice, of free will" (x.19).

Although his dull eyes have been opened, the knight finds it possible to respond only to half of Fidelia's teaching, the threatening half. As we are told, "she was hable, with her wordes to kill, / And rayse againe to life the hart, that she did thrill" (x.19). The two consequences Reformed Protestants attributed to faith are manifest here, its mortifying and vivifying effects, the effects of divine law alternating with an awareness of imputed righteousness. This alternation explains why Red Cross Knight continues to lapse into despair. Having been taught by both Fidelia and Speranza, he grew "to such perfection of all heuenly grace . . . That he desirde, to end his wretched dayes: / So much the dart of sinfull guilt the soule dismayes" (x.21). Red Cross Knight remains susceptible to guilt and fear engendered by vivid, visual reminders of Faith's threatening features. He remains only partly conscious, or insufficiently convinced, that he will also enjoy her comforting capacity to "rayse againe to life the hart, that she did thrill."

As I mentioned earlier, such moments of despair are endemic to the pursuit of holiness as contemporary Protestants conceived of it. To go to heaven, according to William Perkins, one must "sail by hell."[22] And as we have also noted, what the believer needs when undertaking that perilous voyage is to shift his attention from the damning accusations of the Law to the promise of salvation through faith. But how might the elect soul reliably and assuredly recognize its election? Or to frame the question in terms William Tyndale seems almost to have devised for my purposes in this essay: "How," Tyndale asks, "shall I see my faith?" His answer to that question is particularly apropos—"I must come down to love again, and thence to the works of love, ere I can see my faith."[23] For this reason, Una delivers Red Cross Knight, after his conscience has been "cured" by Patience, to Charissa. Approaching this figure with such expectations in mind, we might therefore anticipate that the opacity of Faith's teaching will now yield immediately to visual clarity. And so, to a degree, it does.

---

22. William Perkins, *State of a Christian Man*, in *The Works of the Famous and Worthie Minister of Christ in the University of Cambridge*, 3 vols. (Cambridge: Cambridge University Press, 1609), I, Ll3ᵛ.

23. Henry Walter, ed., *Expositions and Notes on Sundry Portions of the Holy Scripture* (Cambridge: Cambridge University Press, 1849), p. 202. Quoted together with additional evidence in Gless, *Interpretation and Theology*, pp. 152–53.

Just before delivering the knight to Charissa, his lady again advises "himself to chearish, and consuming thought / To put away out of his carefull brest" (x.29.5–6). To love others as oneself depends on love of self. The knight, described as an "vnacquainted guest" (x.29) to this personification of *caritas*, is no doubt struck by her alluring portrait:

> She was a woman of the freshest age,
> Of wondrous beauty, and of bounty rare,
> With goodly grace and comely personage,
> That was on earth not easie to compare;
> Full of great love, but *Cupids* wanton snare
> As hell she hated, chaste in work and will;
> Her necke and brests were euer open bare,
> That ay thereof her babes might sucke their fill;
> The rest was all in yellow robes arayed still.
>
> A multitude of babes about her hong,
> Playing their sportes, that ioyd her to behold,
> Whom still she fed, whiles they were weak and young,
> But thrust them forth still, as they wexed old:
> (x.30–31)

As usual, Spenser surprises us with something the visual tradition most likely never provided: Ceasing to care for one's loved ones, thrusting them forth at the appropriate time, also manifests *caritas*. This severely generous lady joyfully (x.33.1) takes the knight into her "schoole" (x.32.6) and there instructs "him . . . in everie good behest, / Of loue, and righteousnes, and well to donne . . . / In which when him shee well instructed hath, / From thence to heauen she teacheth him the ready path" (x.33).

Two things seem particularly striking about this passage: first, it appears to assert that well doing opens that "ready path" to "heauen"; second, it has suddenly reverted, as did the presentation of Fidelia, to a nonvisual and quite abstract list: "Of love, of righteousness, and well to doone." In a characteristic move that violates expectations just aroused, Spenser then points out first that the knight will approach that path, though it is "ready," with unready feet. His "weaker wandring steps" require the guidance of Mercy, "well knowne ouer all, / To be both gratious, and eke liberall." This representative of direct divine aid will guide the knight along a path from which he will always incline to stray, and it is she, or rather the power she represents, not his well doing, that saves his soul: "That Mercy in the end his righteous soule might save" (x.34). Even the "righteous soule" will require forgiveness.

We learn, too, that the ready path is strewn with "bushy thornes, and ragged breares, / Which still before him she remov'd away." And as the knight's feet become entangled, or he shrinks from the effort, or begins to "stray," "She held him fast, and firmely did upbeare, / As carefull Nourse her child from falling oft does reare" (x.35). This infantile weakness, the poetry implies here and elsewhere (e.g., Contemplation's assertion that "blood can nought but sin, and wars but sorrow yield" [x.60]), will prove a lifelong condition, even for a figure we will soon learn to identify as "*St. George* of mery *England*" (x.61). But Mercy provides two antidotes for this condition and the despair it might yet again arouse.

The first of these antidotes is a depiction of the Seven Corporal Works of Mercy, here embodied in seven "Bead-men" who appear in "an holy Hospitall / That was foreby the way" and "spend their daies in doing godly thing" (x.36).[24] "Foreby" registers the beadmens' unmonastic readiness to make their homes near the people they might aid. In yet other ways, Spenser's expected description of the beadmen appears—even more remarkably than his treatment of their evil counterparts the Seven Deadly Sins—to evade rather than to offer visual detail. Instead of the expected visual emblems—loaves of bread or flagons of drink or prison bars or sick people in their beds—we are induced to "see" the inward, mental activity that makes such works of outward generosity authentically charitable.

In a description that removes all potential self-interest from the work of providing shelter "unto all that came, and went," the first beadman lodges "not . . . such, as could him feast againe, / And double quite, for that he on them spent, / But such, as want of harbour did constraine" (x.37). The second, whose office was "the hungry for to feed, / And thirsty giue to drinke . . . feard not him selfe to be in need, / Nor car'd to hoord for those, whom he did breede" (x.38). The third gives clothes designed not for show, "but clothes meet to keep keene cold away." He cares for the naked because they are "the images of God in earthly clay" (x.39). The fourth relieves prisoners, acknowledging "that they faulty were, / Yet well he wayd, / That God to vs forgiveth

---

24. For the biblical origin of this traditional group of seven good works, see Mt. 25:34–46, and Alan Sinfield's summary treatment in *The Spenser Encyclopedia,* s.v. "Bead-men," pp. 80–81. Craiger-Smith, *English Medieval Mural Paintings,* pp. 53–55, discusses a number of still-extant images, and notes: "These two practical schemes of human conduct [the seven deadly sins and the seven corporal works of mercy] were taken to be the chief criteria for the separation of the sheep and the goats at the last day. In the remarkable painting of the Doom at Trotton they are not only opposed in general, but contrast with one another point by point. On the left is the wicked man, surrounded by the Sins; on the right is the good man, with medallions of the Works of Mercy round him" (p. 55). These images can readily be found on Google Image, as can an impressive series of seven painted panels there, from 1504, Master of Alkmar, now in Rijksmuseum.

euery howre, / Much more then that, why they in bands were layd" (x.40). The fifth comforts the dying, "for them most needeth comfort in the end, / When sin, and hell, and death doe most dismay" (x.41). The sixth, who buries the dead, does so to honor "the wondrous workmanship of Gods own mould" even in death. The seventh, generously and without self-interest, protects the orphans and widows of the dead (x.43).

By presenting those works as an ekphrasis that promises more of the traditional visual detail than it actually delivers, Spenser calls on his readers' memories to supply much of what they see. What he actually provides is material akin to that of casuistry, that is, ethical thinking applied to particular cases and actions. This combination of allusive depiction and meticulous commentary provides Red Cross Knight with his most apprehensible, comprehensible, and convincing evidence of his assured salvation. Never again does he fall into the degree of despondency that proved potentially self-destructive even after his instruction by faith and hope. These word-centered images stand as a counterweight that supersedes the evidence of sinfulness the knight encountered more graphically in the pageant of the seven deadly sins and in his own soul, as anatomized and visually represented to him by his indwelling Despaire. The most vivid visual depictions in *The Legend of Holinesse,* it seems, prove especially memorable and rhetorically powerful enough to convince anxious souls like Red Cross Knight of their assured damnation—most dangerously for souls who have no Una to remind them and no impulse of grace that enables them to hear that they "chosen art." The saving Truth comes to mortals in *The Legend of Holinesse* by means of words that draw on or, even better, directly echo the Word.

This brings us to the second antidote Mercy supplies to counteract the knight's ever-encroaching despair. This is a vision of the Heavenly Jerusalem, once again presented as a depiction readers must in the main provide for themselves by remembering medieval visual depictions or, preferably for the Protestants of the time, the text of the Revelation of St. John. Spenser's earliest readers would have recognized that the biblical passage qualifies as ekphrasis: the heavenly Jerusalem has a great and high wall; twelve gates labeled with the names of the twelve tribes of Israel; a square layout; specified measurements; materials of jasper, gold, glass, sapphire, emerald, and other precious stones (Rev. 21:10–27). In contrast to this elaborate visual specificity, Spenser simply tells us that it was "a goodly Citty . . . Whose and strong / Of perle and precious stone, that earthly tong / Cannot describe, nor wit of man can tell; / Too high a ditty for my simple song" (x.55). Yet he does mention one quite distinct visual detail, "Blessed angels . . . in gladsome companee . . . with great ioy into that Citty wend, / As commonly as frend does with his frend" (x.56). That detail offers Red Cross a simple, forthright expression of spiritual community achievable by well-meaning knights in this world.[25] By contemplating this largely nonvisual vision with the light of faith shining "in" his dull eyes and consciously authentic charitable works cheering his memory, the knight receives proof sufficient that he is himself a current and future inhabitant of the heavenly Jerusalem. Hereafter, he knows his name, his earthly nation, and his spiritual community (x.61–66). The great dragon of canto xi presents a frightening challenge and inflicts painful wounds, but the knight no longer seems in serious jeopardy.

Ekphrastic passages in *The Legend of Holinesse* make sin and the sensation of incorrigible sinfulness so vivid that only an elaborate, visually memorable—but at the same time a word-centered antidote—can counter it, a word-vision, we might say. That makes it possible for Spenser's knight, finally, "to see his faith." On this account, I believe we might conclude that Spenser seems both to highlight the importance of the Word read and understood, as his Reformed contemporaries wished, but also to recognize not only the dangers but the pedagogical usefulness of visual imagery. But visual imagery shorn of interpretive commentary, as the poet presents it in *The Faerie Queene,* Book I, appears more suited to induce fear than to inspire hope. If we can discern a preference here, Spenser appears to favor images, whether rendered in poetry or paint, that are drawn directly from and carefully interpreted by means of the Word. Despite its grounding in the Bible, so balanced a preference seems to fall short of the Protestant iconoclastic impulse that has sometimes been attributed to the national poet of the Elizabethan age. In this, his ideological commitment seems closer to the reforming zeal of Erasmus or even to Luther's qualified endorsement of religious imagery than to the fervor aroused by Zwingli and the many later iconophobes who deprived most English buildings of their medieval splendor.

---

25. For the contrast between salient medieval and later Catholic notions of contemplation and that Spenser presents here, see Gless, *Interpretation and Theology,* pp. 158–63.

Chapter 8

FACING THE MIRROR

EKPHRASIS, VISION, AND KNOWLEDGE IN
GAVIN DOUGLAS'S *PALICE OF HONOUR*

Andrew James Johnston
and Margitta Rouse

*I*n this essay, we wish to examine Gavin Douglas's ekphrastic engagement with the concept of honor in his *Palice of Honour* with respect to the tension-ridden relationship between the poet and power. We argue that Douglas employs ekphrasis as an enigmatic device to make visible, transmit, and potentially critique, the violent aspects of the concept of honor and its implications within a specifically courtly setting.

Gavin Douglas's Middle Scots dream allegory *The Palice of Honour* not only explores literary fame through a fabulous display of literary allusions, the most famous of which is to Chaucer's *House of Fame,* but also juxtaposes the poet's struggle for literary fame with the courtly concept of honor.[1] Written at the turn of the sixteenth century and dedicated to King James IV of Scotland, the *Palice* ambitiously fuses the fantastic dream narrative with the more overtly political "mirror" of the *speculum principis*-tradition that conventionally claims to provide advice and counsel on the appropriate conduct of a king. This blending

---

1. For a brief analysis of the *Palice* in specifically Chaucerian terms, see Ruth Morse, "Gavin Douglas: 'Off Eloquence the flowand balmy strand,'" in *Chaucer Traditions: Studies in Honour of Derek Brewer,* eds. Ruth Morse and Barry Windeatt (Cambridge: Cambridge University Press, 1990), 107–21.

of the genres of dream allegory and mirror-for-princes is evidently not Douglas's invention. Crucially however, Douglas's poem appears to self-reflexively examine the *speculum* tradition in a highly significant ekphrastic scene where, in the course of his allegorical journey, the narrator suddenly chances onto a mirror: Having fallen asleep in a beautiful garden, he finds himself on a dream pilgrimage to seek the palace where Honour resides. Before he proceeds to view the all-powerful monarch, he sees Venus's circular mirror and is encouraged to take a look at what it represents. Through the aid of this mirror, he can

> . . . se at a sycht
> The dedes and fetes of euery erdly wycht,
> All thinges gone lyk as they wer present
> (ll. 1495–97)[2]

> . . . see at a glance the acts and heroic deeds of any earthly person, all the things past appearing as if they were present

Venus's magical mirror is encyclopedic, as well as costly, and the images it holds are described at length. Gazing into this mirror permits an extensive view, over twenty-eight stanzas (ll. 1468–728), of any honorable deed ever done: "euery famus douchty deid / That men in story may se, or cornakyll reid" (ll. 1693–94). These are deeds as presented by famous writers and historians: "as Stacius dois tell" (l. 1583), "as Virgill weil discriuis" (l. 1631), or "as wryttis Leuius" (l. 1658).

Although the mirror scene is prominent within the poem, it seems surprising that such a little-discussed text like Douglas's *Palice* should actually be one of the few medieval texts (and the only Scottish one) that, on the onset of the recent upsurge of interest in ekphrasis and visuality in medieval British studies, was examined for its use of ekphrasis.[3] Yet where pioneering studies of ekphrasis in medieval English literature, such as that of Margaret Bridges, have uncovered the potential of ekphrasis to function generally "as an inset reflexion of the problematic of the whole work of fiction,"[4] scholarship on

---

2. All references to *The Palice of Honour*, unless stated otherwise, are to the London print of the poem c. 1553, Priscilla J. Bawcutt, ed., *The Shorter Poems of Gavin Douglas*, Scottish Text Society, Fifth Series 2, 2nd ed. (Edinburgh: Scottish Text Society, 2003); all translations from the Middle Scots are ours.

3. John Norton-Smith, "Ekphrasis as a Stylistic Element in Douglas's *Palis of Honoure*," *Medium Aevum* 48 (1979): 240–53.

4. Margaret Bridges, "The Picture in the Text: Ecphrasis as Self-Reflectivity in Chaucer's *Parliament of Fowles, Book of the Duchess* and *House of Fame*," *Word and Image* 5 (1989): 151 [151–58].

the *Palice* has consistently ignored the poem's potential in that respect. John Norton-Smith's reading, for instance, confirms a common view of Douglas as a "mere" imitator, a minor poet not quite capable of reaching the lofty heights of his predecessors. "The passages of *ekphrasis* in the *Palis of Honoure* are not many," he writes, "nor do they contribute much toward the allegorical meaning of the poem."[5] Thus Norton-Smith dismisses the *Palice* as less than an original poem but more of a future provost's exercise in rhetoric: designed to secure a job in the clergy, the work is supposedly content with trying to impress its audience with an outmoded taste in the language of plenitude. Norton-Smith's negative judgment of the poem seems to be taking its cue from the long-held scholarly prejudice against the supposedly turgid and derivative nature of fifteenth-century English poetry that was recently subjected to a scathing critique by Robert Meyer-Lee, amongst others.[6]

Thinking of ekphrasis as a mere stylistic device, Norton-Smith overlooks its ideological function in the *Palice*, where it supports a complex argumentative structure that teases out the political possibilities of allegorical writing. On close inspection, it will become apparent that the mirror scene within the dream allegory *does* provide crucial allegorical insight not only into the concept of honor but also into the ways a courtly poet may actually deal with it. Far from being simply decorative and derivative, Douglas's metaekphrastic approach towards the genre of allegory has a pivotal role to play in this project.

Although the mirror scene is not ekphrastic in the widely agreed modern and narrow sense of evoking a visual work of art, say, a painting, sculpture, or ornamented vase,[7] it follows a familiar ekphrastic topos in that it appears to squeeze rather a lot of sequential narrative information into the description of a single visual image.[8] As a "verbal representation of [a] visual

---

5. Norton-Smith, "Ekphrasis as a Stylistic Element," p. 240.

6. Robert Meyer-Lee, *Poets and Power from Chaucer to Wyatt* (Cambridge: Cambridge University Press, 2007), pp. 1–11.

7. This view of ekphrasis is based on Leo Spitzer's highly influential definition of the concept as "the poetic description of a pictorial or sculptural work of art" ("The 'Ode on a Grecian Urn,' or Content vs. Metagrammar," *Comparative Literature* 7 [1955]: 207 [203–25]). This essay, along with Jean H. Hagstrum's (*The Sister Arts: The Tradition of Literary Pictorialism and English Poetry from Dryden to Gray* [Chicago: University of Chicago Press, 1958]), sparked off the twentieth-century debate of the concept. On the theoretical legacy of the term from antiquity to the present, see Haiko Wandhoff, *Ekphrasis. Kunstbeschreibungen und virtuelle Räume in der Literatur des Mittelalters,* Trends in Medieval Philology 3 (Berlin: de Gruyter, 2003), pp. 2–15; Ruth Webb, "Ekphrasis Ancient and Modern: The Invention of a Genre," *Word and Image* 15 (1999): 10 [7–18].

8. The mirror scene can be regarded as an allusion to a Chaucerian ekphrasis in *The House of Fame,* which describes brass tablets in Venus's temple depicting scenes from Virgil's

representation"[9] that is itself a representation of several verbal narratives, Douglas's mirror shows scenes from the Old and New Testaments as well as from the histories of Thebes and Troy, and it even depicts popular literary favorites such as Robin Hood. What is more, the mirror's frame, borne up by three golden trees in the courtyard of Honour's palace, is lavishly decorated with various gems, and Douglas takes great care to describe not only the images reflected in the mirror, but also the beautiful frame that contains them. What we have here, then, is one costly mirror reflected within another, in the style of intricately ornamented Chinese boxes, where a smaller one is hidden inside a larger one: The three golden trees mirror the poem's division into three books, that is, the three-part structure of the narrative, while the mirror's bejeweled frame represents the decorative style of the rhetorical tradition itself. As Gregory C. Kratzmann puts it in his comparative reading of the *House of Fame* and the *Palice of Honour,* the mirror "itself illustrates what is meant by [the poem's] earlier description of poetry as 'ioyous discipline, / Quilk causes folk their purpois to expres / In ornate wise' (ll. 846–48)."[10] Further, in its self-reflexive embodiment of the rhetorical tradition itself, the mirror scene fuses a narrow, modern, sense of ekphrasis with a wider, classical one: the mirror appears to be a work of art and therefore merits (artful) description, while the verbal description of the images in the mirror has the aim of "bring[ing] the subject before the eyes," making "the listener see the subject described in his or her mind's eye"[11] and breathing life into things that have long passed. Whereas the first sense of ekphrasis concentrates on the subject matter represented (a visual or ornamental work of art), the second focuses on the description's "detail and the visual impact which should flow from it."[12] The first sense is evidently present in classical and medieval literature but was conceptualized only in the twentieth century, whereas the latter

---

Aeneid. This similarity between the two texts has been noted in a different context in Gregory C. Kratzmann, "*The Palice of Honour* and *The Hous of Fame,*" in *Anglo-Scottish Literary Relations 1430–1550* (Cambridge: Cambridge University Press, 1980), pp. 113–14 [104–28].

9. This is James A. W. Heffernan's significant reworking of the concept with a shift in emphasis towards "visual representation," rather than descriptions of artworks; see his *Museum of Words: The Poetics of Ekphrasis from Homer to Ashbery* (Chicago: University of Chicago Press, 1993), p. 3.

10. Kratzmann, "*The Palice of Honour* and *The Hous of Fame,*" p. 114. In this context Kratzmann aptly observes that in Chaucer's *House of Fame,* images from the *Aeneid* are framed in a similar way as the images in Douglas's mirror, in that they are "contained and illuminated by the richly formal setting of the temple."

11. This is Ruth Webb's definition of ekphrasis as it is conceived in antiquity. See her *Ekphrasis, Imagination and Persuasion in Ancient Rhetorical Theory and Practice* (Farnham, England: Ashgate 2009), p. 75.

12. Webb, *Ekphrasis,* p. 75.

sense is firmly rooted in classical and medieval discourses of *enargeia,* the art of re-presenting absent things in a vivid, lifelike fashion.[13]

There is, however, more to Douglas's mirror than its intricate, redoubled presence of two ekphrastic modes. The beautiful gems on the mirror's frame possess the power to staunch blood, and whoever is wounded—in tournament or battle, for instance—is instantly healed by looking into the mirror—"For quha that wound wes in the tornament / Wox hale fra he apon the myrrour blent" (ll. 1484–85). The healing power of stones was widely accepted in the late Middle Ages.[14] The mirror, described in the poem as a "riall rillik" (l. 1486) [royal relic], not only represents and celebrates life itself in its representation and reanimation of historical deeds, but it also points towards its own royal/divine claim to lifelikeness in that it literally *gives* life, or *restores* life to all wounded worthies setting eyes on it. The narrator cannot say of what substance the gems precisely are: "Quhare of it makyt wes, I haue na feil, / Of beriall, cristall, glas or byrnyst steil, / Of Diamant or of the Carbunkill Iem. / Quhat thing it wes diffyne may I not weil" (ll. 1477–80). Whatever their substance, medieval gems, as reflectors of light, were frequently regarded as mirrors themselves, and they were believed to contain divine energies. As Marjorie O. R. Boyle points out, the carbuncle was habitually regarded as a "reflector of eternal light" because it was seen as self-luminous, and hence understood "allegorically [as] a natural mirror of God"; similarly, Christ himself was regarded as a mirror, and it was common "to set the wounds on crucifixes with five carbuncles, whose deep red color symbolized blood."[15] Douglas's mirror ekphrasis, then, stages itself as a complex spiritual meta-ekphrasis within an allegorical engagement with the courtly concept of honor.

---

13. Claire Barbetti insists that the notion of ekphrasis must be conceived of in such a way that it avoids binary conceptions of text and image. For her, ekphrasis is essentially "vision translated into writing," whereby "vision" is artful "composition" of any kind. "The name for [the] verbal translation of composition is ekphrasis." For the Middle Ages, this means that the dream vision genre itself is, by definition, rendered ekphrastic (*Ekphrastic Medieval Visions: A New Discussion in Interarts Theory* [New York: Palgrave Macmillan, 2011], p. 2). Although the broad concept of "vision" avoids binaries, the problem with this definition is that the concept of "translation" is not specified—if one medium can be "translated" into another it appears that the opposition of "seeing" and "writing" is reintroduced through the back door.

14. For a brief account of the healing powers of stones in the Middle Ages, see Corinne J. Saunders, *Magic and the Supernatural in Medieval English Romance* (Cambridge: Brewer, 2010), pp. 102–4; the seminal study on the magic of gems in the Middle Ages is still Joan Evans, *Magical Jewels of the Middle Ages and the Renaissance Particularly in England* (Oxford: Clarendon Press, 1922).

15. Marjorie O. R. Boyle, *Loyola's Acts: The Rhetoric of the Self* (Berkeley: University of California Press, 1997), pp. 130–31.

Curiously, this abundant, multilayered evocation of the mirror within the mirror as encyclopedic, ornamental, lifelike, healing, and potentially soul-saving, appears to create a stark contrast with the poem's sparse and enigmatic pointers as to what the mirror's particular significance might actually be within the narrative economy of the dream itself. As a matter of fact, the poem tells us little about *why* the narrator encounters this mirror at all: While the dreamer looks into it, watching the past "made present" as if reading a book, Venus observes him and knows him by what she sees in his face: "And as I wondryt on that grete ferlye, / Venus at last, in turning of hir E, / Knew weil my face" (ll. 1732–34) [And as I was contemplating this great marvel, Venus, at last, in a turning of her eye, knew well my face]. Later, the narrator's guide, a nymph, explains to him that

> 3one myrrour clere,
> The quhilk thow saw afore dame Venus stand
> Signifyes nothyng ellis till vnderstand
> Bot the gret bewty of thir ladyis facis
> Quhairin lovers thinkis thay behald all gracis.
> (ll. 1760–64)

that clear mirror, the one you saw standing in front of dame Venus, signifies nothing else to understand but the great beauty of the ladies' faces, wherein lovers think they perceive all grace.

It is precisely this ostensibly evasive explanation of the way Venus's mirror is to be understood by the dreamer that has prompted John Norton-Smith to generally perceive descriptive detail in Douglas's poem as "super-abundant, or obscure, or perplexing" and to diagnose a certain "weakening of the allegorical sensibility in the late Middle Ages."[16] The term "weakening" as it is used here in the wake of Huizinga's notorious analysis of the later Middle Ages' supposed cultural decline,[17] undeniably implies that Douglas's ekphrastic passages are of an inferior nature. "Differently shaped from those of Alan of Lille, Jean de Meung or Chaucer," they suggest "interesting, detailed significance without actually providing any."[18] According to Norton-Smith, "the

---

16. Norton-Smith, "Ekphrasis as a Stylistic Element," p. 240.
17. Johan Huizinga, *Autumn of the Middle Ages,* trans. Rodney J. Payton and Ulrich Mammitzsch (Chicago: Chicago University Press, 1996).
18. Norton-Smith refers here to C. S. Lewis—however Lewis does not exactly diagnose a weakening anywhere in his reading of the *Palice*—the phrase he uses is "the poem as a whole illustrates the furthest point yet reached in the liberation of phantasy from its allegorical

description of the events seen in Venus's mirror" serves at best to illustrate Douglas's "copiousness and obscurity."[19] This could perhaps be taken to reflect an older, traditional scholarly approach to ekphrasis that primarily tended to regard the device as digressive or ornamental, contributing little to the work's overall semantics.[20] Yet Norton-Smith is clearly aware of the potential of ekphrasis to invest a narrative poem with more than mere descriptive detail when he claims, "The ultimate object of the poet in the dream allegory is to reach the palace and learn the meaning of honour—but no 'philosophical' definition of honour is to be obtained from the description of the palace itself."[21]

Of the few relatively recent critics who have addressed the curious mismatch of the lengthy mirror scene and the puzzlingly short explanation provided for it, we are aware of merely two— Gregory C. Kratzmann and Antony J. Hasler—who have not found the nymph's explanation irritating, or, to use Priscilla Bawcutt's pithy remark, "lame and unconvincing."[22] For Kratzmann, the nymph indicates that the mirror only "reflects what the beholder wishes to see," and since he apparently wishes to see books, Venus asks him to write one, and "the poet is strengthened and inspired by his contact with books."[23] Similarly, Antony J. Hasler argues that the lover-protagonist sees in the mirror "a compilation that catches up an entire medieval library within the loose and permeable bounds of universal history, which is then named, retroactively, as the face of the beloved. Caught within the reflection of another look, is another archive."[24] Hasler clarifies that this other "archive" is the book that Venus will commission the narrator to write soon after he has looked into

---

justification. . . . What [Douglas] describes is sheer wonderland, a phantasmagoria of dazzling lights and eldritch glooms, whose real *raison d'être* is not their allegorical meaning, but their immediate appeal to the imagination" (*The Allegory of Love: A Study in Medieval Tradition* [1936, repr. Oxford: Oxford University Press, 1990], p. 290).

19. Norton-Smith, "Ekphrasis as a Stylistic Element," p. 240. Even Kratzmann, who seeks to liberate Douglas from his image as derivative imitator and claims that "the Scots poem is arguably a more successful work than Chaucer's [*House of Fame*]," finds that "the Venus's-mirror episode suffers from Douglas's fascination with catalogue and *repetitio*" ("*The Palice of Honour* and *The Hous of Fame*," pp. 128 and 114).

20. On the (misguided) view of ekphrasis as merely digressive, see Bridges, "The Picture in the Text: Ecphrasis as Self-Reflectivity," p. 51.

21. Norton-Smith, "Ekphrasis as a Stylistic Element," p. 240.

22. Priscilla J. Bawcutt, "Introduction—The Palice of Honour," in *The Shorter Poems of Gavin Douglas*, Scottish Text Society, Fifth Series 2, 2nd ed. (Edinburgh: Scottish Text Society, 2003), p. xlv [xv–lii]. For Bawcutt, the mirror "seems to serve chiefly as a decorative digression" (p. xlv).

23. Kratzmann, "*The Palice of Honour* and *The Hous of Fame*," p. 114.

24. Antony J. Hasler, *Court Poetry in Late Medieval England and Scotland: Allegories of Authority* (Cambridge: Cambridge University Press, 2011), p. 105.

the mirror, which critics have generally taken to mean Douglas's translation of the *Aeneid*, a work that was completed twelve years after the *Palice*.

Although these explanations are entirely plausible, we are, however, not wholly convinced by their straightforward neatness. Reducing Douglas's mirror ekphrasis to mere rhetorical excess or conceiving of it as a mere display of the love of books and the dreamer's participation in the literary business, is to miss the political significance of ekphrasis, as well as that rhetorical figure's implications for the concept of allegory itself. Lee Patterson has pointed to George Puttenham's discussion of allegory as "'the courtly figure,' one known not only to 'euery common Courtier, but also [to] the grauest Counsellour.'" As Patterson goes on to explain, according to Puttenham, court poetry was not to be seen as a mere "form of entertainment, but a social practice, the means by which courtiers both learned and displayed the talents needed for success."[25] Seen in Patterson's terms, Douglas addresses the subject of honor through a specifically courtly form of meaning-making that reflects not merely the grace and elegance of the courtly world but also its darker side of ambition and power-struggles and the steep hierarchies that govern it. Whereas the poem might not provide a "philosophical" definition of honor, it does situate its representation of honor in a cultural and rhetorical setting that infuses an aristocratic or even royal ambience of magnificent display and elaborate form with a deep sense of how that very form and display are ineluctably enmeshed in the secret workings of power. Honor thus bears considerable political significance.

Even though their overall approaches differ significantly, Patterson's take on allegory is in remarkable harmony with the line of argument that L. O. Aranye Fradenburg pursues in her study of late medieval Scottish court culture. Fradenburg persuasively shows that Douglas's language of plenitude must be seen in direct relation to the courtly poetics of honor—and we argue that this is particularly true also for Douglas's mirror ekphrasis within the allegory of honor. Fradenburg demonstrates that Douglas's poem takes part in the performative creation of "the arts of rule," such as tournaments and pageantry, whereby the poetics of honor in the *Palice* is dependent on "exhibitionism, theatricalization and phenomenalization."[26] As Fradenburg highlights Douglas's concern with the relations between the body and the image, she draws attention to "his ambitions—for plenty, power, splendor" and the

---

25. Lee Patterson, *Chaucer and the Subject of History* (Madison: University of Wisconsin Press, 1991), p. 56. The quotes refer to George Puttenham's *The Arte of English Poesie* (London: Richard Field, 1589 [printed in facsimile, London: Scolar Press, 1968]), p. 155.

26. L. O. Aranye Fradenburg, *City, Marriage, Tournament: Arts of Rule in Late Medieval Scotland* (Madison: University of Wisconsin Press, 1991), p. 185.

way these "are in accord with his enhanced sense of physical vulnerability. . . . Douglas's language is . . . the overflowing of a constant supply of plenty reinscribed into the space of violence."[27]

And the accusation—as well as defense—of rhetorical excess and obscurity is not just a somewhat cumbersome constant of Douglas criticism but is, in fact, as old as allegory itself and originates in the genre's epistemological function. As J. Hillis Miller has argued in his engagement with Paul De Man's discussion of allegory, the paradox of allegory has always been that

> if you have the key to the allegory, then the esoteric wisdom has been expressed (otherwise), but then you would not have needed to have it said otherwise. If you do not have the key, then the allegory remains opaque. You are likely to take it literally, to think it means just what it says. If you understand it you do not need it. If you do not understand it you never will do so from anything on the surface.[28]

Evidently, allegory and enigma are not opposed to one another, but are closely related. As the nymph explains the mirror's significance to the dreamer, she uses the verbs "signify" and "understand," which implies that at this point in the narrative, readers are indeed presented with a key to understanding not only the mirror ekphrasis but also the narrative's concept of allegory. Importantly, in presenting the key itself as an enigma, the nymph refers to the theological discourse of allegory, since her words also evidently allude to Augustine's famous reading of St. Paul's statement that we know God only through a mirror through an enigma, and not face to face: *Videmus nunc per speculum in aenigmate, tunc autem facie ad faciem* (1 Cor. 13:12). As Suzanne Conklin Akbari reminds us, for Augustine allegorical cognition is indirect and enigmatic—and the figure of the mirror is the appropriate instrument with which to provide allegorical knowledge. Augustine

> associates allegory with enigma, stating that an "enigma is an obscure allegory." . . . By declaring that enigma and mirror are identical, and that enigma is a variety of allegory, Augustine implies that at least some allegories are, figuratively, mirrors. They are not deceptive mirrors, but revealing ones, which allow the viewer to glimpse things ordinarily hidden from

27. Fradenburg, *City, Marriage, Tournament*, p. 187.

28. J. Hillis Miller, "'Reading' Part of a Paragraph in *Allegories of Reading*," in *Reading De Man Reading*, eds. Lindsay Waters and Wlad Godzich (Minneapolis: University of Minnesota Press, 1989), p. 162 [155–70].

human sight; to put it another way, these allegories allow the reader to apprehend meanings normally inaccessible through language.[29]

For Augustine, St. Paul's looking through a mirror is a metaphor of human life following the expulsion from Paradise, where man can look at God no longer face to face but needs to seek knowledge through representation. Our search for the knowledge of God is like trying to make sense of an enigma through shapes in a mirror—knowledge of God can thus only be enigmatic, allegorical. Consequently, Augustine's theory of cognition is founded on the rhetorical arts. For Augustine, knowledge is verbal. Marcia L. Colish explains that "by interpreting all signs as linguistic, Augustine makes it possible for himself to interpret all cognitive intermediaries between God and man as modes of verbal expression."[30]

The "philosophical idea" that underwrites the *Palice* is truly Augustinian in that the reflective device—and by implication its healing power—is associated with the love of knowledge, viewed not face to face but in the enigmatic space of representation, mediated through the grace perceived in the lover's face. If, as Augustine suggests, allegory is a form of cognition, then the epistemological object of desire pursued in the *Palice of Honour* is the knowledge of honor. That Douglas presents us with a mirror within the mirror of allegory, which depicts honorable deeds—a mirror whose ekphrastic description, as we have seen, is meta-ekphrastic even—suggests that the multifaceted ways in which we see this mirror, as art object, healing artifact, and medium of lifelike representation, might provide a clue to understanding Douglas's specifically political poetics of honor.

For Douglas, ekphrasis provides the enigmatic/allegorical/linguistic means through which Honour can be viewed. We can understand this function of the mirror ekphrasis only if we are aware that it is *safe* for the dreamer to *see* the honorable deeds of the past when gazing on the mirror image, and that this mirror-gazing scene takes place at a point in the narrative where the dreamer does not know yet that he will not be permitted to enter the inner sanctum of Honour's allegorical palace—although he will be able to take a brief glimpse at it. From the start, Douglas's poem is

---

29. Suzanne Conklin Akbari, *Seeing through the Veil: Optical Theory and Medieval Allegory* (Toronto: University of Toronto Press, 2004), p. 10. This passage, 1 Cor. 13:12, is discussed frequently by Augustine in *De Trinitate*; the reference cited by Akbari is in Augustine, *The Trinity*, trans. Stephen McKenna, The Fathers of the Church 45 (Washington, DC: Catholic University of America, 1963), p. 471.

30. Marcia L. Colish, *The Mirror of Language: A Study in the Medieval Theory of Knowledge* (Lincoln: University of Nebraska Press, 1983), p. 44.

concerned with the power of sight and the dangers involved in seeing, as well as in verbally representing what has been seen. Repeatedly, this is expressed as a narrative of expulsion from an Edenic space. Singing May's and Nature's praises, the narrator is struck by a violent "impressioun" (l. 105) in the ideal garden that he entered in the Prologue: "And with that gleme so dasyt wes my mycht. / Quill thair remanit nothir voce nor sycht." (ll. 109–10). The narrator loses both voice and sight and finds himself in the hideous wasteland of the first book. He is frightened by the noises he hears there and seeks shelter inside a hollow tree stump. Peeping out of his hiding hole, he realizes that the sound comes from the magnificent pageants first of Minerva, then of Diana, and finally the splendid chariot of Venus, who is accompanied by Cupid, Mars, and several lovers. The dreamer learns that the procession is on its way to Honour's palace. He is particularly interested in Venus's entourage and composes a derogatory lay about the goddess and the inconstancy of love. Subsequently, he is discovered in his hideout and dragged before a Venus tremendously offended by his song. He is severely beaten, hit on the head, and his face is blackened. Having been taken prisoner, he is threatened with death for his blasphemy. Luckily for the narrator, in the second book, the "court rethoricall" (l. 835) rushes to his aid; the poet's court is, amongst others, comprised of such eminent figures as Virgil, Homer, Ovid, Chaucer, Gower, and Lydgate, and "of this natioun . . . Gret Kennedy and Dunbar, ȝit vndede" (l. 923). The poets all support the dreamer's cause, and the Muse Calliope engineers his release. The dreamer then joins the poets on their journey across the world under the tutelage of a nymph, who finally takes him to Honour's palace. The exploration of the palace grounds makes up most of the third book. The nymph takes the narrator to the palace through a lavishly decorated, guarded gate and walks him across a court where knights are engaged in tournament, sometimes even to the point of mortal combat. Broken lances lie around, and wounded knights are knocked to the ground. Venus's throne and mirror are situated here, inside the palace gates but outside the palace's interior—and it is here, that one can take a safe, healing look at the most honorable deeds of all times.

The aspect of safety is crucial because the palace's inner chamber and the monarch who resides in it—the allegorical personification of honor—will be blinding in such a way that the dreamer must actually fear for the loss of his eyesight, even if he only takes a glimpse through a chink of the chamber door. Viewing Honour *inside* the palace, face to face, is harmful. Within the enigmatic space of allegory, the dreamer will not only be temporarily blinded, but he will be struck down by the mere sight of what he sees and suffer severe bodily pain:

Schit wes the dure, in at a boir I blent,
Quhare I beheld the gladdest represent
That euir in erth a wrachit catywe kend.

. . . .

Rial Princis in plate and armouris quent
Of byrnist gold, cuchit with precyus stonys.
Intronyt sat a god armypotent,
On quhais gloryus vissage as I blent,
In extasy be his brychtnes atonys
He smate me doun and byrsyt all my bonys.
Thare lay I still in swoun, with cullour blaucht,
Quhil at the last my Nymphe vp hes me kaucht.
(ll. 1903–26)[31]

The door was shut. I glanced through a chink, where I saw the most pleasing
sight that ever on earth a miserable wretch could see. . . . The Royal Prince
was dressed in plate armor which was made of gleaming gold, and embedded with precious stones.

There sat enthroned a God mighty in arms, whose glorious face I looked
at. Into a trance, through his brightness, suddenly he knocked me down and
bruised all my bones. There I lay still, unconscious, with a blanched complexion, until at last my nymph picked me up.

As Fradenburg has noted, Douglas uses the word "represent" to describe the
scene inside the palace's inner chamber:[32] It mesmerizes the viewer—he feels
both desire and fear while gazing on the alluring image of totalizing power,
and he becomes a wretched captive. It is apparent here that the narrator seems
to have desired the knowledge of something that should have remained hidden, and therefore needs to be punished—yet again.

At such moments of corporal punishment, it may seem that the narrative
model of the dreamer's exclusion from Paradise is closely related to the Platonic theory of vision, whereby the eye emits a fiery ray of light that touches
the object in order for the soul to see it. Interacting with the object, the ray

---

31. Again, precious gemstones play a role in the description of the inner chamber (ll.
1906–16). The gems here are clearly self-luminous, as they illuminate the scene from within.
Although the dreamer guesses he may be seeing a hall made of amethyst, diamond, ruby,
sardonyx, jade, and smaragd, the dreamer cannot identify all of the stones, and their powers
are not entirely clear: "Mycht not behald theair vertuus gudlynes" (l. 1911). For him, they
do not have the healing effect as the mirror. The brightness of the place, as well as that of
Honour himself make the dreamer faint.

32. Fradenburg, *City, Marriage, Tournament*, p. 186.

of light then returns to the viewer. Hence according to Plato, seeing is always to be understood as a reciprocal as well as a mediated action—and vision is touch.[33] The image of the monarch "touches" the viewer who is not powerful enough to withstand the force of this touch, which ultimately suggests that "seeing"/"knowing" is not permitted. In this instance, the power within the act of seeing resides within the object that is seen rather than with the subject who sees.[34] It is only because his guide, his nymph, unceasingly works to revive him that the dreamer survives the visual impact.

It is crucial to remember, however, that at the poem's close, this is already the second time that the poet-speaker is struck down by a blinding force. Earlier, in the prologue, he had been touched by a sudden, blinding flash of light—a light that does not grant insight but that leaves him unconscious in a space that has changed from paradisiacal to infernal.[35] When the dreamer eventually comes to after having seen Honour directly, face to face, he briefly turns into a different man—he is rude and aggressive to his nymph,[36] and she needs to remind him of his actual cowardice and that he, as a cleric, ought to be gentle with women.[37] As Fradenburg has pointed out, the powerful image "remakes the onlooker through devastation."[38]

There is then, in the *Palice of Honour*, a contrast of different ways of seeing and of visually engaging with different allegorical representations of

---

33. On classical and medieval theories of optics and vision, see Akbari, *Seeing Through the Veil*, and Dallas G. Denery II, *Seeing and Being Seen in the Later Medieval World: Optics, Theology, and Religious Life* (Cambridge: Cambridge University Press, 2005).

34. Carolyn P. Colette points out that film and feminist theory has influenced our conception of the nexus of seeing and power in a way that we habitually assume the gaze to be controlled by the gazer: "In contrast, the most influential late medieval thinking about optics assumed a degree of power in the object of vision itself. As a result, the subject one looked at was thought to be as important as the act of looking itself, and the act of looking always a dynamic interchange between viewer and viewed" (*Species, Phantasms, and Images: Vision and Medieval Psychology in* The Canterbury Tales [Ann Arbor: University of Michigan Press, 2000], p. 14).

35. This is similar to the opening lines of John Lydgate's *Temple of Glass*, which also momentarily blinds the narrator. Moreover, this force, at the beginning of both Lydgate's and Douglas's poems, is *not* a source of illumination as might be expected if we are familiar with the story of St. Paul's conversion on the road to Damascus. On Lydgate, see Akbari, *Seeing through the Veil*, p. 236.

36. "On to the Nymphe I maid a bustuus braid. / Carlyng quod I, quhat wes ȝone, at thow said" (ll. 1941–42).

37. While she clearly prefers him placid, she is also glad for him to have found new strength and courage: "Soft ȝow, said sche thay ar not wyse that stryvys, / For kyrkmen wer ay Ientill to ther wyuys. / I am rycht glaid thow art wordyn so wycht / Langere (me thocht) thow had nothir fors, ne mycht, / Curage nor wyll for till have grevyt a fla" (ll. 1943–47).

38. Fradenburg, *City, Marriage, Tournament*, p. 186. This is not of lasting effect however—later faced with another abyss to cross, the narrator is his old fearful self again. Following the nymph across a tree that functions as a bridge, his "spretis woux agast, / Swa peralus wes the passagis till aspy" (ll. 2081–82) and his "harnys trymlyt bissyly" (l. 2085).

honor. Viewing the honorable deeds reflected in Venus's mirror "remakes" the onlooker through healing (he too had suffered bodily harm); this is juxtaposed with an illicit, piercing, direct gaze at the personification of Honour itself that is harmful because it results in physical punishment. In the chamber scene, the viewer's gaze is reciprocated and ultimately leads to exclusion from Honour's palace—narrated as an expulsion from Paradise, which actually also appears to imply an exclusion from the garden of rhetoric.[39] And given the poem's specifically political slant noted earlier, the dreamer's exclusion from the palace also suggests that his encounter with the world of honor has brought him to an understanding of his utter lack of power. The dreamer's near-fatal encounter with Honour is reminiscent of the Prologue(s) to Chaucer's *Legend of Good Women* where the poet-dreamer meets with an authoritarian God of Love who sentences him to death for writing disrespectfully about women.[40]

Leading the narrator to safety, the nymph takes him across the moat surrounding Honour's palace. Walking across the makeshift bridge of a fallen tree, he sees that it connects the palace grounds with the garden where the "swete florist colouris of rethoreis" (l. 2066) bloom, where instead of fruit precious stones grow on trees; indeed, where trees are laden with pearls. However, he falls into the moat and subsequently awakens in the garden where he first fell asleep. On waking, he finds that this Edenic garden has lost its initial attraction for him; neither birdsong nor beautiful flowers console him; indeed, to him it seems like hell in comparison to what he has seen and experienced in the frightening yet overwhelmingly beautiful palace.[41] Having come face to face with the monarch, if only for the briefest of moments in time, the dreamer's poetic experience has become poisoned. The colors of rhetoric have lost their beauty for him because his aesthetic sensibilities have been contaminated by the lure of the ruler's power, even though he has effectively been rejected by that very power.

Since the personification of honor—the allegorical, visual "represent" of an abstract idea—is presented here as the image of a God who must not be viewed directly, the genre of allegory is taken to its limits: it is no longer capable of allowing the reader to access meaning that cannot be communicated through language, but since language is by definition social, allegory is

---

39. Kratzmann rightly stresses that the garden of rhetoric is to be distinguished from the garden where the dreamer falls asleep and later awakes ("*The Palice of Honour* and *The Hous of Fame*," p. 127).

40. A. C. Spearing, *The Medieval Poet as Voyeur: Looking and Listening in Medieval Love-Narratives* (Cambridge: Cambridge University Press, 1993), p. 233.

41. "Me thocht that fare herbere maist lyk to hel, / In till compare of this ye herd me tell" (ll. 2094–95); "All erdly thyng me thocht barrant and vyle" (l. 2100).

nevertheless defined as always already embodied in the realm of power. By contrast, the alternative, ekphrastic view of honor through Venus's mirror stabilizes the allegory both as an instrument of cognition but also as a device that makes it possible for the poet to gaze at and describe the world of power in an idealized manner without actually having to suffer from its murderous effects. The juxtaposition of the healing mirror ekphrasis as an allegory within the allegory and the violent "represent" in the sanctum of the allegorical palace structurally relates to what W. J. T. Mitchell has called the "primal scene" of ekphrasis: the myth of Perseus and Medusa. "Medusa," writes Mitchell,

> exerts and reverses the power of the ekphrastic gaze, portrayed as herself gazing, her look raking over the world, perhaps even capable of looking back at the poet. Medusa is the image that turns the tables on the spectator and turns the spectator into an image: she must be seen through the mediation of mirrors (Perseus' shield) or paintings or descriptions. If she were actually beheld by the poet, he could not speak or write. . . . Both the utopian desire of ekphrasis (that the beautiful image be present to the observer) and its counterdesire or resistance (the fear of paralysis or muteness in the face of the powerful image) are expressed here.[42]

Mitchell's juxtaposition of the figure of ekphrasis with Medusa's gaze underscores the idea that knowledge is dependent on verbal reflection and that the act of seeing that precedes mediation may turn out detrimental for the artist who sees, since, according to the Platonic understanding of sight, the power of the gaze does not belong to the viewer exclusively—and this is especially true in a world where the poet inevitably encounters princely magnificence and royal authority. In Mitchell's terms, the mirror ekphrasis in the *Palice* fulfils a vital narrative function: It pre-empts the poet's typical fear of muteness by offering a narrative model that allows him to transmute the image through the power of words, but it also permits him to approach power in an indirect fashion, rather like Perseus approached the Medusa. Immediately after the mirror-gazing scene, Venus hands the narrator a book and extracts the promise from him to put its forgotten narrative into verse.

Than suddanly in hand a buke scho hynt
The quhilk to me betaucht scho or I went,
Commandand me to be obedient

---

42. W. J. T. Mitchell, *Picture Theory: Essays on Verbal and Visual Representation* (Chicago: University of Chicago Press, 1994), p. 172.

And put in ryme that proces than quyt tynt.
. . . .
Twychand this buke perauentur ȝe sall here
Sumtyme efter quhen I haue mare lasere.
(ll. 1749–57)

Then suddenly she took hold of a book which she entrusted to me before
I left, commanding me to be obedient and put into rhyme that narrative
then quite lost. . . . About this book you shall perhaps hear a little later,
when I have more leisure.

Though commentators generally read these lines as referring to Douglas's
Eneados,[43] this request by Venus to put into rhyme a lost or forgotten narrative
actually refers to any future book and potentially also to the one whose narrative the narrator is unfolding in the moment of speaking. Thus the phrase
"this buke" ambiguously refers to both the book handed to the narrator and
the book he will write. In the context of our argument it is relevant to note
that Venus asks the narrator to do exactly what she had him do when he was
facing her mirror, that is, *re*-view the representation of historical narratives
as sung by poets, in order to put them "in ryme"—and this is also exactly the
function of the ekphrastic passage. If the poet is excluded and expelled from
the actual court of honor by the power of the image, the mirror signifies his
inclusion due to the power of words. The mirror may hold only transitory
images that depend strongly on the viewer's angle of vision, but it is the poet
who fixates whatever the mirror reflects. Through the topos of ekphrasis, the
Augustinian metaphor of the mirror as giving only enigmatic access to the
knowledge of God extends to courtly culture, where man cannot look at the
violence of honor directly but needs to seek knowledge through representation. The search for the knowledge of honor as presented in Douglas's poem
is like trying to make sense of an enigma through shapes in a mirror—the
knowledge of honor can thus only be enigmatic, allegorical, and ultimately
verbal. Structured by the antagonistic struggle of two representational media,
word and image, the mirror ekphrasis thus gains a power to deflect political and social tensions into the sphere of an aesthetic response, whereby the
verbal always wins. And it is no coincidence that Douglas chooses a mirror,
and not a painting, as the medium of reflection. If the "represent" of the God
mighty in arms signifies that language cannot overcome the power of the

---

43. This is of course already suggested in Copland's early print, where the marginal note
to ll. 1756–57 reads, "By thys boke he menis Virgil."

image itself, the mirror ekphrasis signifies the opposite. Through its equation of rhetorical eloquence with historical truth, the mirror scene demonstrates the ideological power of ekphrasis as a mode of aesthetic deflection and idealization. And yet deflection here seems to guarantee that the poet does not become entirely subject to the overwhelming gaze of power. In the *Palice of Honour,* the purely visual seems to equal something close to an unmediated and unconditional subjection to the demands of the courtly world. By contrast, ekphrasis with its emphasis on allegorical mediation and indirect perspectives grants the poet a vantage point from which to face power without utterly succumbing either to its lure or to its violence.

What is so fascinating about Douglas's use of fundamentally different view(ing)s of honor is that the narrative paradigm of the Medusa myth is split apart. Taken on its own, the mirror scene suggests that aesthetic deflection can be successful. Indeed, it seems as if the reflection of honorable deeds is wholly unproblematic, even healing. Allegorically speaking, we could say that the ekphrastic passage is like the ornamental yet healing gemstones that frame the mirror—and which, as we are later led to assume, grow on the wondrous trees in the garden of rhetoric. The violence associated with Medusa's gaze is completely out of focus—like Medusa's reflected image, Honour's image seems entirely harmless, as his violent powers are hidden, or veiled through the mediating effects of verbal representation. Yet viewing the image of Honour face to face brings forth the overwhelming threat emanating from his gaze, a threat that is inherent in the courtly concept of honor. Associated as it is with lethal weapons and state-sanctioned violence but also with the constant jockeying for position in the presence of the prince, the promise of honor motivates as well as masks the elite's privilege to exert violence in the pursuit of its aims. And it also obscures or shrouds the more subtle violence of courtly intrigue or the steep and potentially humiliating hierarchies of courtly patronage—just as it conceals the price paid for aristocratic privilege and inclusion in the charmed circles of the court, as honor is "the veritable currency of chivalric life, the glittering reward earned by the valorous as a result of their exertions, their hazarding of their bodies."[44] But honor is also the keyword capable of excluding from relevance in the courtly world those that do not properly belong to court society, that is, learned poets such as Gavin Douglas.

The *re*-flection of honor in Venus's mirror may facilitate a harmless view of this elite privilege/burden, but the problems involved in de-flecting this

---

44. Richard W. Kaeuper, *Chivalry and Violence in Medieval Europe* (Oxford: Oxford University Press, 1999), pp. 129–30.

(in)sight are made visible only in the palace's inner chamber. Honour's gaze strikes with a vengeance, setting free its violence from within the inner sanctum of the palace within which Honour resides. Douglas's poem is thereby also a comment on the way in which courtly culture suppresses the constant threat of violence through aesthetic deflection—a violence that will always strive to break free from the space within which the harmful aspects of honor are confined.

Ekphrasis as a literary device that simultaneously conceals and reveals, ensures the inaccessibility of the secrets the poem contains even as they are transmitted. Douglas's strategy of collating, imitating, and reworking literary pre-texts that are "mirrored" in this story of a fearful poet on his way to becoming a poet, pre-texts that can even be glimpsed in a literal mirror, is staged as an allegory of collective (inherited) memory and individual composition, where the concept of *topos* is central. Working through the different *topoi*/locations of this poem—from idyll to wasteland, then journeying across the world, reaching Honour's palace, finally taking us back to the idyllic garden after having almost reached the garden of rhetoric—the text privileges ekphrasis as a dynamic literary *topos* that veils the horrors of honorable violence, as well as allowing them to break to the surface. Douglas's allegory, then, shows that the knowledge of honor is one that is made up of both concealment and revelation, of both deflection and the violence of direct confrontation. The framing allegory—the mirror in the Augustinian sense—is one that is not only engaged with the concept of honor itself but it is also a meta-narrative on the processes of deceiving and revealing in writing. And at the same time, the mirror ekphrasis itself becomes the allegorical veil through which the poet can view, represent, and possibly even critique the aristocratic world of honor at whose mercy he would otherwise entirely be. In purely symbolic terms, it appears that the Medusan allusions of Honour's Palace might actually cut both ways. While the direct gaze at Honour's image proves all but fatal, the healing mirror with its verbal mediation of an otherwise unbearable visual experience might contain no less dangerous a threat. After all, Perseus's mirror enabled the Greek hero not merely to cut off Medusa's head but actually to employ that head and its murderous gaze—apparently unimpaired by the act of decapitation—for his own ends as a secret weapon against all enemies. Hidden within the allegory of the allegory there might actually be a violent fantasy of poetic retribution against the powerful.

Chapter 9

EKPHRASIS AND STASIS IN CHRISTINE DE PIZAN'S *LIVRE DE LA MUTACION DE FORTUNE*

Suzanne Conklin Akbari

kphrasis is a rhetorical mode of expression that is found in literature from antiquity to the present, appearing within a wide range of cultural and literary traditions, and most commonly expressed (in the influential formulation of James Heffernan) as "the verbal representation of visual representation."[1] At the same time, ekphrasis takes significantly different forms in different periods and cultural matrices. Medieval ekphrasis has a number of features that separate it from the use of the trope in other periods: for example, as scholars such as Bruce Holsinger and Sarah Stanbury have shown, ekphrasis takes on a distinctive character when deployed in conjunction with iconoclastic literature, such as heterodox Lollard writing in late medieval England.[2] Other features of medieval ekphrasis specific

---

1. James A. W. Heffernan, *Museum of Words: The Poetics of Ekphrasis from Homer to Ashbery* (Chicago: University of Chicago Press, 1993), p. 3. The wavering tension between word and image is highlighted in W. J. T. Mitchell's three aspects of ekphrasis: "ekphrastic indifference," which acknowledges the hopelessly impossible gap that separates the verbal and the visual; "ekphrastic hope," which looks toward the bridging of that gap; and "ekphrastic fear," which reflects an anxiety that the "verbal could displace or replace the visual" (*Picture Theory: Essays on Verbal and Visual Representation* [Chicago: University of Chicago Press, 1994], pp. 152–54).

2. On the distinctive features of ekphrasis in iconoclastic literature, see Bruce Holsinger, "Lollard Ekphrasis: Situated Aesthetics and Literary History," *Journal of*

to the period include its alignment with the genre of allegory. It goes without saying that ekphrasis is commonly found in allegories written during in a wide range of time periods, not just during the Middle Ages; the specific forms of medieval allegory, however, inflect the use of ekphrasis in a number of ways, especially with regard to how the competing claims of word and image relate to the allegorical hierarchy of an alluring integumental surface that conceals a deeper, enigmatic meaning.³

Still other distinctive features can be observed in medieval ekphrasis when it is deployed in historical writing. Dramatic scenes of ekphrasis appear in Latin heroic epics such as the *Alexandreis* of Walter of Châtillon and the *Ylias* of Joseph of Exeter,⁴ romance adaptations of Latin national and imperial histories such as the *Roman de Troie* and the *Roman de Thebes,* and the early fifteenth-century French universal history of Christine de Pizan, which is my focus in this essay. In these texts, as I have argued elsewhere with regard to the *romans antiques,*⁵ ekphrasis serves a specifically temporal function, providing the reader with an apparently static view of history that departs from the linear form of narrative exposition in order to provide a contemplative, synoptic view of the past. In Christine's *Livre de la Mutacion de Fortune,* this static ekphrastic moment provides not only insights into time gone by but also a template for self-improvement and spiritual reform. The first section of this essay, "Shaping the Past," describes the overall structure of Christine's universal history and the crucial role of the "sale merveilleuse" or "marvellous chamber" in organizing the narrative depiction of time upon its magnificently illustrated walls. The following section, "The

Medieval and Early Modern Studies 35 (2005): esp. 75–85 [67–90]; Sarah Stanbury, "The Vivacity of Images: St. Katherine, Knighton's Lollards, and the Breaking of Idols," in *Images, Idolatry, and Iconoclasm in Late Medieval England: Textuality and the Visual Image,* eds. Jeremy Dimmick, James Simpson, and Nicolette Zeeman (Oxford: Oxford University Press, 2002), pp. 131–50.

3. On ekphrasis in medieval allegory, see Rosemond Tuve, *Allegorical Imagery: Some Mediaeval Books and Their Renaissance Posterity* (Princeton, NJ: Princeton University Press, 1966); Suzanne Conklin Akbari, *Seeing through the Veil: Optical Theory and Medieval Allegory* (Toronto: University of Toronto Press, 2004), pp. 3, 157–58, and 209–10.

4. On the commentary tradition concerning the tomb ekphrasis of Darius in the *Alexandreis,* see David Townsend, *An Epitome of Biblical History: Glosses on Walter of Châtillon's Alexandreis 4.176–274* (Toronto: Pontifical Institute of Mediaeval Studies, 2008), pp. 3–14; on the tomb ekphrasis of Teuthras in the *Ylias,* and on the description of Adela's chamber in Baudri's *Carmen 134,* see Christine Ratkowitsch, *Descriptio Picturae: Die literarische Funktion der Beschreibung von Kunstwerken in der lateinischen Grossdichtung des 12. Jahrhunderts* (Vienna: Österreichische Akademie der Wissenschaften, 1991).

5. On tomb ekphrases in the *Roman de Troie* and the *Roman de Thebes,* see Suzanne Conklin Akbari, "Erasing the Body: History and Memory in Medieval Siege Poetry," in *Remembering the Crusades: Myth, Image, and Identity,* eds. Nicholas Paul and Suzanne Yeager (Baltimore: Johns Hopkins University Press, 2012), esp. pp. 153–55 and 160–61 [146–73].

Consolation of History," turns to Christine's integration of Boethian ideas concerning the nature of change not just within her vision of history but also within the ekphrastic epitome itself, as Boethius's personifications of Philosophy and related virtues are juxtaposed with historical events. Finally, "The Ekphrastic Mirror" describes how Christine de Pizan positions Alexander the Great at a climactic—though anachronistic—moment in the historical narrative in order to provide a point of identification and self-reflective reform for the reader. The essay closes with a brief account of the role of materiality in medieval ekphrasis, especially as seen in historical narratives.

SHAPING THE PAST: THE "SALE MERVEILLEUSE"

Although the *Mutacion de Fortune* is most often read for the strikingly original autobiographical allegory featured in its first book, in which Christine recounts how she was transformed from a woman into a man by the goddess Fortune, the vast majority of the work is made up of a versified universal history adapted largely from the expansive *Histoire ancienne jusqu'à César,* a universal history that grafts French national and imperial history onto the rootstock of Orosius's early fifth-century *Historiarum Adversum Paganos Libri VII* (*Seven Books of History Against the Pagans*). In general terms, then, the *Mutacion de Fortune* confronts the intersection of poetics and history by transposing a universal history mainly in prose into verse; in addition, it deals with the intersection of poetics and history in a highly focused and specific way, as the elaborate "sale merveilleuse" or "marvellous chamber" housed within the Castle of Fortune serves as the point of junction between the allegorical opening books of the *Mutacion de Fortune* and the universal history that dominates the latter books.[6]

In structural terms, the *Mutacion de Fortune* is a fusion of Orosian historiography with a Boethian view of the role of Fortune in the life of the individual, and of Providence in the unfolding of time itself. Historiographical and philosophical models of change are integrated throughout the work, expressed through the figures of Fortune and Providence, which act as guiding principles within the effort to understand the nature of the changes that

---

6. On the highly visual presentation of history in the *Mutacion de Fortune,* placing it in the context of ancient and medieval scenes of ekphrasis that include Virgil's *Aeneid,* the *Roman de la Rose,* the *Prose Lancelot,* and Dante's *Commedia,* see Kevin Brownlee, "The Image of History in Christine de Pizan's *Livre de la Mutacion de Fortune,*" in *Contexts: Style and Values in Medieval Art and Literature,* eds. Daniel Poirion and Nancy Freeman Regalado, Yale French Studies, special issue (New Haven, CT: Yale University Press, 1991), pp. 44–86.

take place both on the level of the individual life and on the level of king-doms and empires.[7] Book one is, as noted above, the allegorical autobiogra-phy, which integrates Ovidian and Boethian models of change;[8] books two and three are ekphrastic accounts of the Castle of Fortune, its walls, gates, and pathways, and the inhabitants located in and around the castle. Book four is a transitional book, which will receive extended analysis below. Books five, six, and seven are a sustained exposition of universal history, moving from the empires of Assyria and Babylon to conclude with imperial Rome and rulers of European nations in Christine's own day.

Book four begins with an account of philosophy, the liberal arts, and the sciences, and then moves to a highly detailed ekphrastic account of the creation of the world and the very earliest stages of biblical history. As book four progresses, ekphrasis gradually gives way to historiography in a repeti-tive evocation of the past that emphasizes the repeated dispersal of peoples in the world. Through the integration of universal history and allegory, medi-ated by the poetic mode of ekphrasis, Christine unifies past, present, and future into a single moment, where individual virtue enables the subject—whether the author or the reader—to study the written records of the past, to engage in self-examination, and consequently to live a life of learning and rectitude. The autobiographical allegory of book one enacts the process of self-examination from the perspective of the narrator, positioning her as an authoritative figure whose own "mutacion" enables her to recount the "grandes mutacions" (l. 1460) of history. The counterpart of this authorial self-examination appears in the seventh, final book of the *Mutacion de For-tune,* which disrupts the conventional order of imperial succession by dis-placing the story of Alexander the Great's conquests from its usual place (in Orosian chronicles, just after the rule of Babylon), and then using the figure of Alexander as a model for rule—both the rule of others and the proper rule of one's own self. The reader is encouraged to read the figure of Alexander—and, by extension, all history—as a mirror reflecting the self. As Christine puts it in the closing passages of her Alexander narrative, "Mire toy, mire en ceste istoire" (l. 23274) [Look at yourself, look within this history].

---

7. On the personification of Fortune in the *Mutacion de Fortune,* see Catherine Attwood, *Fortune la contrefaite: L'envers de l'écriture médiévale* (Paris: Champion, 2007).

8. On the integration of Boethian and Ovidian metamorphosis in book one of the *Mu-tacion de Fortune,* see Suzanne Conklin Akbari, "Metaphor and Metamorphosis in the *Ovide moralisé* and Christine de Pizan's *Mutacion de Fortune,*" in *Metamorphosis: The Changing Face of Ovid in Medieval and Early Modern Europe,* eds. Alison Keith and Stephen James Rupp (Toronto: Victoria University Centre for Reformation and Renaissance Studies, 2007), pp. 77–90.

The *Mutacion de Fortune* has a symmetrical structure, with an opening focus (in book one) on the narrator's self-examination counterbalanced by a closing focus (in book seven) on the reader's self-examination, and the generally allegorical framework of the opening three books balanced by the generally historiographical framework of the closing three books. The junction or hinge that links the two halves of this symmetrical structure lies in book four of the *Mutacion*. While we can refer the work as being divided into "two halves," since this bipartite division accurately represents the number of books devoted to allegory and history writing, this division does not accurately represent the overall balance of the work: of its approximately 24,000 lines, more than two-thirds of the work is comprised of the historical chronicle. Allegory serves, therefore, as the preliminary stage or foundation for the exposition of history, with ekphrasis acting as the mediating principle that enables the movement between these two modes. We see this process unfold in book four of the *Mutacion,* as the ekphrasis of the "sale merveilleuse" located within the Castle of Fortune moves the reader from the external perspective of the architectural allegory to the intimate, internal perspective of the reader of narrative ekphrasis. This narrative ekphrasis begins with the Boethian ladder of Philosophy, ranging from theoretical to practical knowledge, through an engagement with all the various branches of knowledge including the Seven Liberal Arts, to an exposition of world history from Creation through the first age of mankind.

Book four opens with a retrospective look back at the architectural allegory of the Castle of Fortune that comprises the preceding two books. Christine states, "Or ay devise grant partie / De ce lieu . . . / Si me convient presentement / Au hault donjon tourner arriere, / Pour mieulx venir a ma matiere" (ll. 7053–62) [now I have described the greater part / Of this place . . . / so that it is now appropriate for me / To turn back to the high castle keep / In order to better approach my matter].[9] This move at the opening of book four repeats the circling-around motion of the first three books of the *Mutacion de Fortune,* in which the phenomenon of change is approached obliquely or, one might say, cyclically: the opening book recounts a series of Ovidian metamorphoses before concluding with an account of the author's own, self-authorizing metamorphosis; the second book describes the architecture of the Castle of Fortune and the landscape surrounding it; the third book describes the figures positioned within the Castle of Fortune, moving

---

9. Quotations from the *Livre de la Mutacion de Fortune* are taken from the edition of Suzanne Solente and are cited in the text by line number; translations are my own (Christine de Pizan, *Livre de la Mutacion de Fortune,* ed. Suzanne Solente, 4 vols. [Paris: Société des anciens textes français, 1955–1961]).

around the internal spaces within the castle. It is significant that, instead of simply penetrating in a linear, direct fashion into ever more interior spaces within the Castle of Fortune, Christine's narrator instead repeatedly tours the same spaces, slowly circling in on the "sale merveilleuse" contained in the castle keep that will mark the final movement into the historiographical mode in book four. This circling progression models a pattern of intellectual progression for the narrator and the reader that proceeds indirectly and obliquely, yet ultimately comes to its destination—like the wandering trajectory of history itself.

In book two, the four gates of the four-sided castle are described, each in turn, before the narrator finally "returns" ("revendray," l. 2885) to describe the first gate. There, she discovers a four-sided courtyard ("court quarree," l. 2893) and four pathways that lead to the summit of the castle; after recounting the nature of these four pathways, the narrator once again "turns around," stating, "Or me convient tourner arriere" (l. 3329), to describe the second gate. After repeating this sequence of description and return for the third and fourth gates, the narrator turns to a fuller account of the various rooms and lodgings within the four parts of the castle before turning to the "plus hault lieu / Du chastel" [very highest place / Of the castle], that is, the "hault donjon" or castle keep (ll. 3696–98). Immediately, however, the narrator turns back outward again, this time to "return" (she states, "Retourner me faut" [l. 3741]) to the figures who are lodged in the various peripheral parts of the castle of Fortune. These figures, described at length in the third book of the *Mutacion de Fortune,* make up a kind of social microcosm, an overview of the various estates that foreshadows the fuller account of late medieval society provided by Christine a few years later in her *Livre du Corps de policie,* or *Book of the Body Politic.*[10]

The introduction of the "sale merveilleuse" (l. 7069) at the opening of book four, then, appears less as the introduction of a new, previously unseen space than as a return to a position previously inhabited. It is said to be in the "dongion dessus dit," the "castle keep described above"—that is, described back in book two, several thousand lines earlier. Yet this movement into an interior space will be quite different from the ekphrastic moves recounted

---

10. On the estates of society in Christine's *Livre du Corps de policie,* see Susan Dudash, "Christine de Pizan and the 'menu peuple,'" *Speculum* 78 (2003): 788–831; on the expression of "vertu" at all levels of society and its ability to unify the body politic ("corps de policie"), see Suzanne Conklin Akbari, "Death as Metamorphosis in the Devotional and Political Allegory of Christine de Pizan," in *The Ends of the Body: Identity and Community in Medieval Culture,* eds. Suzanne Conklin Akbari and Jill Ross (Toronto: University of Toronto Press, 2013), pp. 283–313.

earlier in the *Mutacion de Fortune*, for we never leave the "sale merveilleuse," which is the interior space inhabited by narrator and reader from this point through the very end of the entire work. Its "marvellous" quality resides not simply in its visual opulence and its ability to induce a sense of wonder but in its capaciousness: this space contains all of the universal history of mankind, from the creation of the world through the present day. Yet the space of the "sale merveilleuse" contains still more than this: it begins not, as one would expect, with the creation of the world but with yet another dilatory, cyclical turn, this one focused not on the complexly structured form of the Castle of Fortune but on what we might call the mental furniture of mankind—that is, the branches of knowledge, flowing outward from the central figure of Philosophy.

Christine's opening description of the "sale merveilleuse" emphasizes its enormous scale and its geometrical form: it is "reonde" or round (l. 7090), its perfect circularity emphasizing its essentially microcosmic nature. It is "belle, clere, grande et haulte" (l. 7094), a "fort ouvrage" (l. 7095) [strong piece of work], in spite of the fact that it, like the whole of the Castle of Fortune, is constantly in motion ("toudis tremble," l. 7095). The great chamber is "painte moult richement / D'or et d'azur" (ll. 7104–5) [painted richly with gold and azure], and illustrated with pictorial narratives of the history of the world: "Si sont escriptes les gestes / Des grans princes et les conquests / De tous les regnes, qu'ilz acquistrent" (ll. 7107–9) [And the 'gestes' are also written there, / Of the great princes and of the conquests / Of all the kingdoms that they acquired]. Here, the pictorial quality of the images that are said to be "painted" (cf. "pourtraict," l. 7117) is intertwined with the narrative quality of the "gestes" that are said to be "written" or "escriptes" upon the walls: in other words, text and image are mutually constitutive, united in the ekphrastic writing.

The overwhelming magnificence of the great hall corresponds to the overwhelming abundance of historical materials included on its walls: the images inscribed there are so numerous that the narrator cannot even attempt to recount them all. Christine draws attention to the task of the narrator in selecting which stories to recount, which ones deserve to be translated from the pictorial cues upon the wall into the discursive language of history. This task is centered upon the role of memory, which appears both as a collective, universal quality presided over by the goddess Fortune, and as an individual, personal quality expressed by the narrator. This two-fold character of memory appears in connection with Christine's account of the selective nature of her universal history. In her first reference to the selectivity of her task, Christine declares that she will not attempt to recount everything, "Lonc process seroit a compter / Tout quanque je y vi avenir; / Je vous pourroie trop tenir. / Le plus necessaire diray / Et du seurplus je me tairay" (ll. 7082–86) [because it would be a long task to account for / All that I saw taking place there; / I would hold you back too long. / So I will speak of that which is most necessary / And I will keep quiet with regard to the surplus]. The same concern to explain the basis of her account's selectivity appears later in the same passage, but this time it is accompanied by a fuller account of the principles of selection, as Fortune chooses among the princes who have served her and preserves only those who are worthy of memory: "pour memoire, / Elle fait pourtraire l'istoire / D'eulz, s'ilz sont digne de renom" (ll. 7143–45) [for the sake of memory, / She had the history portrayed / Of those who were worthy of renown]. The narrator promises to "name" ("nommeray," l. 7153) those whose "portraits" ("pourtraitures," l. 7154) appear on the wall, but not all of them:

> . . . car trop seroie
> Lonc, quant trestout deviseroye,
> Mais des principaulx grans seigneurs,
> Qui par elle furent greigneurs,
> Qui tindrent empire ou regné
> Et qui ont par elle regné,
> Et d'autres dignes de memoire,
> Si com vendra a ma memoire.
> (ll. 7155–62)

> . . . for it would be too
> Long, if I were to describe all of them,
> But just the principal great lords
> Who were made greater through [Fortune],
> Who ruled empires or kingdoms
> And who were in turn ruled by her,
> And others worthy of being remembered
> Just as they occur to my memory.

Here, memory appears first with regard to the inscription of historical records upon the walls of Fortune's castle, as those who are worthy of being remembered are etched into the wall by the hand of Fortune; memory appears second with regard to the retrieval of the historical account in the mind of the narrator, as these are cued by the images appearing upon the wall. Memory is thus collective, common to human society and presided over by the goddess, and also individual, filtering the historical knowledge preserved within the mind of the subject as she remembers the past.

THE CONSOLATION OF HISTORY

This equilibrium of the universal and the particular, the collective and the individual, is in keeping with the Boethian principles introduced in the opening books of the *Mutacion de Fortune.* Just as in Boethius's *Consolation,* Philosophy appears both as a transcendent abstraction and as a property within the narrator's own mind, so in the *Mutacion de Fortune,* the function of memory in the generation of historical chronicle appears both on the universal level, in the formation of the historical record, and on the level of the individual, in the writing of Christine's own account of the history of the world. The Boethian substrate of the opening books of the *Mutacion de Fortune* comes most fully into view with the account of the branches of knowledge described in the "sale merveilleuse." Philosophy is the capacious mother of all species of learning, including—remarkably—Theology, which appears as a subset nested within the branches springing from Philosophy. This long exposition of the branches of knowledge appears, again, as yet another cyclical turn preliminary to the final immersion in the universal history that forms the majority of the text. Christine highlights the abrupt, disruptive quality of this account of the branches of knowledge, stating that she must introduce "autre chose," some "other thing," before moving into the historical account itself:

> Pour ma matiere plus complecte
> Faire, ainçois que plus oultre exploite,
> Le propos devant commencié
> Sera cy un pou delaissié,
> Pour d'autre chose racompter,
> Que je volz moult ou lieu notter;
> Bien revendray a mon propos
> Aprés, ainsi com je suppos.
> (ll. 7173–80)

> In order to make my matter more fully complete,
> Before any other undertaking,
> The topic that was begun earlier
> Must now be delayed a little bit
> In order to speak of another thing

Which I would very much like to take note of in this place;
I will then return to my topic
Afterward, just as I have put it forth.

Once again, Christine circles around before "returning" to her central topic in a movement that is characteristic of the mode of exposition of the opening books of the *Mutacion de Fortune* and that perpetuates the earlier books' emphasis on symmetry and order. In books two and three, symmetry appeared repeatedly as an essential feature of formal structures: there were four facades of Fortune's castle, four gates, four porters, and four roads leading to the summit. Here, the principle of symmetry is again shown to be essential to the ordering of abstractions as they are described sequentially, like a series of nested boxes. Philosophy is divided into two parts, practical and theoretical, recalling the two emblematic letters on Philosophy's robe in Boethius's *Consolation of Philosophy*. Because the letters pi and theta on Philosophy's robe anchor the ladder that, in Christine's earlier allegory the *Chemin de long estude,* links heaven and earth, each of the areas of inquiry detailed on the walls of Fortune's "marvellous" room is dedicated, each in a different way, toward facilitating that link: for example, geometry does so in a very practical way, allowing man to measure the "espace / Entre souleil et lune" (ll. 7645–46) [space / Between sun and moon].

The theoretical aspect of philosophy is divided into three: theology, physics, and mathematics; mathematics, representing the quadrivium, is divided into four, the last of which is astronomy. The second aspect of philosophy, "Pratique" or practical knowledge, is divided like theoretical knowledge into three parts: ethics, economics, and politics. Politics is expressed through both words and deeds, Christine explains, and that verbal form is expressed through the "sciences parfaites" or "perfect sciences" of the trivium, made up of grammar, dialectic, and rhetoric. In this account, Christine orders all human knowledge spatially, each area of knowledge containing others within it, just as Fortune's castle contains symmetrically arranged courtyards and rooms. In this sense, Fortune's "sale merveilleuse" is a microcosm of the entire castle, where architectural allegory serves to provide order to memory, and thus to provide an underlying mnemonic structure for Christine's stated purpose in the *Mutacion de Fortune,* the writing of history.[11] Within the highly concentrated space of the "sale merveilleuse," moreover, ekphrasis provides a

---

11. On medieval architectural allegory, see Christiania Whitehead, *Castles of the Mind: A Study of Medieval Architectural Allegory* (Cardiff: University of Wales Press, 2003). On classical precursors particularly important to the medieval tradition, see Alison M. Keith, "Imperial Building Projects and Architectural Ekphrases in Ovid's *Metamorphoses* and Statius' *Thebaid*," *Mouseion,* 3rd series, 7 (2007): 1–26.

jumping-off point for the movement into the historical mode, as the sequence of the various branches of knowledge returns once again to its point of departure in a final turn of the Boethian cycle of exposition. Once again, Christine calls attention to the narrative return to the point of departure. Having recounted the division of Philosophy into its various branches, she writes, "Mais de or suivray ma matiere, / Tirant a la cause premiere" (ll. 8069–70) [From now on I will follow my matter, / Holding to the original topic].

In order to understand the function of this apparently digressive account of the branches of knowledge and their relationship to Philosophy, it is helpful to compare this ekphrastic passage in the *Mutacion de Fortune* with other ekphrastic accounts of the Seven Liberal Arts, especially the very elaborate version that appears in Alan of Lille's *Anticlaudianus*. The expansive account of the Seven Liberal Arts found in this very widely read twelfth-century philosophical allegory is among the most heavily annotated portions of the *Anticlaudianus* in its remarkably rich commentary tradition.[12] Moreover, Alan's account of the Seven Liberal Arts is merely the most fully developed example of a widespread tendency in literature of the twelfth century to focus ekphrases on the depiction of the trivium and the quadrivium: these include the magnificently decorated robe that appears near the close of Chrétien de Troyes' *Erec et Enide,* the chariot of Amphiaraus that appears in the *Roman de Thebes,* and the richly decorated chamber of the Countess Adela of Blois described in the poetry of Baudri of Bourgeuil.[13] In these works, the Seven Liberal Arts appear as the epitome of human "science," that is, the highest summit of learning that is available to human beings outside of the revelatory knowledge that is provided directly by God. For the purposes of a specific comparison with Christine de Pizan's *Mutacion de Fortune,* the most useful point of comparison with the *Anticlaudianus* lies in the nature of the mediating role of the Seven Liberal Arts as depicted in these ekphrases: in Alan's allegorical epic, the Seven Liberal Arts participate in the construction of a magnificent chariot to convey Prudence from earth to heaven. Each of

---

12. An edition of the most substantial commentary on the *Anticlaudianus* can be found in Radulphus de Longo Campo, *In Anticlaudianum Alani commentum,* ed. Jan Sulowski (Wroclaw: Zaklad Narodowy im. Ossolinskich, 1972).

13. For ekphrastic depictions of the trivium and the quadrivium in Chrétien's *Erec et Enide,* the *Roman de Thebes,* and Baudri of Bourgeuil, see the following: Chrétien de Troyes, *Erec et Enide,* ed. Mario Roques (Paris: Honoré Champion, 1970), ll. 6682–728; commentary in Haiko Wandhoff, *Ekphrasis. Kunstbeschreibungen und virtuelle Räume in der Literatur des Mittelalters* (Berlin: de Gruyter, 2003), ch. 3; Guy Raynaud de Lage, ed., *Roman de Thèbes,* 2 vols. (Paris: Champion, 1966–71), ll. 4986–5000 (corresponds to ll. 4749–62 in the edition of Constans); Monica Otter, "Baudri of Bourgeuil, 'To Countess Adela,'" *Journal of Medieval Latin* 11 (2001): 61–142, and the essay by Valerie Allen in this volume, pp. 17–35.

the seven crafts one portion of the chariot: Grammar devises its central pole, Dialectic forms the axle, and Rhetoric carries out the overall decoration.[14] Unlike the trivium, however, the parts of the quadrivium—Mathematics, Music, Geometry, and Astronomy—carry out a slightly different aspect of the chariot's construction: they forge the wheels that will carry the chariot upward.

Here, the powers of the quadrivium are seen to be motive and generative in a way that differs significantly from the powers of the trivium. They are what drive the pursuit of knowledge, moving upward from earth to heaven. In the *Mutacion de Fortune*, by contrast, this motive quality of the quadrivium has been effaced. Christine does not highlight the dynamic powers of the numerical arts; moreover, the descriptions of the Seven Liberal Arts in Christine's text, while lengthy and detailed, lack the elaborately vivid quality of the corresponding ekphrases found in the *Anticlaudianus*. We recognize these passages as ekphrastic only because they have been identified explicitly by Christine as containing "figures estranges" (l. 7183) and "scriptures" (l. 7203), not because of any self-evidently visual quality in the descriptions themselves. To note this disparity does not imply that the account in the *Mutacion de Fortune* is somehow impoverished compared to the *Anticlaudianus*: on the contrary, it illuminates the essential role of structure and hierarchy in Christine's ekphrastic descriptions of the parts of knowledge that together form the bridge that links the architectural allegory of the earlier parts of the work with the historiography of the latter parts. Further, the comparison of these passages in the *Anticlaudianus* and the *Mutacion de Fortune* may also allow us to begin to sketch out the contours of a broader shift from representational to gestural ekphrasis in the later Middle Ages. This shift may also correspond to an increasing emphasis on what Jaś Elsner has called the "pedagogic" function of ekphrasis, insightfully discussed by Katherine Starkey in her essay in this volume.[15]

One of the most striking innovations in Christine's account of the branches of knowledge comprised within Philosophy pertains to the ordering of the Seven Liberal Arts: not only does Christine separate the trivium from the quadrivium, but she also—very unusually—places the quadrivium *prior* to the trivium. For Alan of Lille, writing in the twelfth century, the placement of the trivium preceding the quadrivium was a way to represent the natural sequence of the acquisition of knowledge. As is made explicit in the ubiqui-

---

14. Robert Bossuet, ed., *Anticlaudianus* (Paris: Vrin, 1955); trans. James J. Sheridan, *Anticlaudianus, or The Good and Perfect Man* (Toronto: Pontifical Institute of Mediaeval Studies, 1973).

15. See Starkey in this volume, pp. 124–46.

tous school text of Martianus Capella, the student learns the three parts of the trivium in the first stages of education, then moves on to master the four parts of the quadrivium.[16] In the *Anticlaudianus,* therefore, the movement upward into the celestial regions that Prudence will undertake is foreshadowed in the construction of the chariot: the trivium participates in forming the necessary but less dynamic parts of the chariot's carriage, while the quadrivium participates in forming the wheels that will actually generate motion. In the *Mutacion de Fortune,* the inverted order of the trivium and quadrivium does not undercut the higher nature of the knowledge represented within the four numerical arts; instead, it reflects the inverted nature of the hierarchy of knowledge as presented in Christine's work. Rather than beginning with lower things and moving to higher, as in Alan's allegory, we begin with the highest of all—namely, Philosophy—and then move downward into the more mundane levels of knowing, descending from the theoretical to the practical. Here, Philosophy's ladder is inverted; or, more precisely, we regard the ladder from the top rather than from the bottom—from theta to pi, rather from pi to theta—applying what we have learned in the realm of the theoretical to the real, lived experiences of the practical world.

Having made a final circle through the branches of knowledge, Christine moves at last to the historical mode with an account of the beginning, that is, Genesis. Picking up just after her account of the parts of Philosophy, Christine states that

En la sale, dont j'ay parlé,
Qui fu grande en lonc et en lé,
Avoit tout au commencement
Figuré et paint richement
Comment Dieu forma ciel et terre

---

16. On the use of Martianus Capella's work as a school text, see William Harris Stahl, *Martianus Capella and the Seven Liberal Arts, Vol. 1: The Quadrivium of Martianus Capella, Latin Traditions in the Mathematical Sciences, 50 BC–AD 1250* (New York: Columbia University Press, 1971); the text of the *De nuptiis* appears in William Harris Stahl and R. Johnson with E. L. Burge, trans., *Martianus Capella and the Seven Liberal Arts, Vol. 2: The Marriage of Philology and Mercury* (New York: Columbia University Press, 1977). For a complete edition of the Latin text, see James Willis, ed., *Martianus Capella* (Leipzig: Teubner, 1983). A new edition of the *De nuptiis* is in progress, with books 4, 6, 7, and 9 published so far: Michel Ferré, ed., *Martianus Capella: Les noces de Philologie et de Mercure. Livre IV: La dialectique* (Paris: Les Belles Lettres, 2007); Barbara Ferré, ed., *Martianus Capella: Les noces de Philologie et de Mercure: Livre VI: La géométrie* (Paris: Les Belles Lettres, 2007); Jean-Yves Guillaumin, ed., *Martianus Capella: Les noces de Philologie et de Mercure: Livre VII: L'arithmétique* (Paris: Les Belles Lettres, 2003); Jean-Baptiste Guillaumin, ed., *Martianus Capella: Les noces de Philologie et de Mercure: Livre IX: L'harmonie* (Paris: Les Belles Lettres, 2011).

Et trestout quanque on y peut querre,
Et comme ou firmament assist,
Lune et souleil.
(ll. 8071–78)

In the great chamber, which I've spoken of,
Which was great and long and wide,
There was, right at the beginning,
Figured and richly painted
How God formed the heavens and the earth
And everything else one might seek out there,
And how He established the firmament,
The moon and the sun.

Yet even after moving into the historiographical mode, the circling motion of exposition found repeatedly earlier in the *Mutacion de Fortune* continues to appear, marking the point of transition between the first age of the world and the second. After an account of the Great Flood, Christine describes how the earth was repopulated by Noah and his sons through the "Maintes grans generations / Dont vindrent toutes nacions" (ll. 8341–42) [many great generations / From which come all nations]. Once again, Christine knits together the parts of her work through a promise to "return" to her "matter":

Vous diray, si com j'ay appris
En la sale, dont je raconte,
De trestous les aages le compte,
Affin que vous sachiés le voir,
Car a maint plaist moult a savoir,
Combien que je ysse du propos,
De dire ce qu'ay en propos,
Mais je y retourneray de pres
Et suivray ma matiere après.
(ll. 8346–54)

I will tell you about it, just as I perceived it
In the chamber, which I am describing to you,
The account of all the ages of mankind,
In order to let you know the truth,
For it pleases most people to know a great deal;
For which reason I have departed from the main topic,

To speak of what I have purposed,
But I will return to it shortly
And follow my matter afterwards.

In its emphasis on the fecundity of the sons of Noah, who repopulate the earth after the devastation of the Flood in "maintes grans generacions" [many great generations], this passage recalls the fecundity of Philosophy described in the preceding digressive movement in the *Mutacion de Fortune*.

Immediately prior to her description of the creation of the world, as noted above, Christine places the figure of Philosophy. She is not just the greatest and most capacious of all the aspects of knowledge but their very fountain-head and source:

Or ay devise, en partie,
Com Philosophie est partie
En plusieurs branches et sciences,
Par moult diverses apparences,
Et, a brief parler, d'elle naiscent
Toutes sciences et engraissent;
C'est leur mere, c'est leur nourrice,
N'y a celle qui d'elle n'isse,
C'en est la fonteine et la source,
Dont les autres prennent leur source.
(ll. 8059–68)

Now I have devised, in parts,
How Philosophy is divided
Into several branches and sciences
By many diverse appearances,
And, to speak in brief, from her are born
All sciences, and they grow from her;
She is their mother, she is their nurse,
There is nothing that does not issue from her,
To them, she is the fountain and the source
From which all others derive their being.

This description of Philosophy as "fountain" and "source" of all knowledge sets out a pattern of fecund dissemination that is echoed in the subsequent historiographical account of the ages of man. In other words, the plentitude of Philosophy expressed in the Boethian perspective of the *Mutacion de*

Fortune is the template for the plenitude of successive generations of mankind expressed in the work's Orosian historiography. The initial movement into history in book four takes the form of a synoptic overview of the ages of history that emphases the repeated dispersal of peoples in the world: outward from Eden during the first age; outward into the three known continents of Asia, Europe, and Africa with the migration of the sons of Noah after the Flood marking the second age; outward from Babel following the transgressions of Nimrod and the confusion of languages marking the third age; and so on. The fifth age, for Christine as for Orosius, ends with the Incarnation (*Mutacion de Fortune*, l. 8390) marking the intersection of secular and sacred history. At this point, Christine again halts the forward movement of the progression of history, abruptly shifting from verse to prose to provide an account of diasporic Jewish history after the Crucifixion.[17] She justifies this departure by stating that the "matter" of Jewish history is fundamentally different from that of other nations because the Jews stand outside the economy of Fortune—their fate, Christine states, is determined intentionally by God, not capriciously by Fortune. After this interruption, Christine begins book five of the *Mutacion* with a return to verse and moves into the sequence of world history as presented in the *Histoire ancienne jusqu'à César.*

THE EKPHRASTIC MIRROR

This historiographical mode persists through books five, six, and seven, almost until the end of the entire work; it is halted only in the final book when an abrupt return to the ekphrastic framework serves to punctuate the annals of world history and to introduce a concluding section on Alexander the Great that is at once historiographical and prescriptive, a mirror for princes that seeks to provide guidance to the reader, whatever rank of society he (or she) comes from. In this story of Alexander, as in all narratives recounted in the *Mutacion de Fortune,* the reader can see himself in the mirror of history.[18] Like everyone living in the sublunary realm, Alexander lives at the whim of Fortune, who is sometimes his beloved "amie," sometimes his hateful "ennemye." It is this very mutability that makes Alexander an appro-

---

17. On Christine's use of verse and prose, see Suzanne Conklin Akbari, "The Movement from Verse to Prose in the Allegories of Christine de Pizan," in *Poetry, Knowledge, and Community in Late Medieval France*, eds. Rebecca Dixon and Finn E. Sinclair (Cambridge: D. S. Brewer, 2008), pp. 136–48.

18. On other exemplary heroic narratives in the *Mutacion de Fortune,* see Liliane Dulac, "Le chevalier Hercule de l'*Ovide moralisé* au *Livre de la mutacion de fortune* de Christine de Pizan," *Cahiers de recherches médiévales* 9 (2002): 115–30.

priate focus for the reader, a point made explicitly in the lines that conclude the Alexander narrative of the *Mutacion de Fortune*:

> O tout homme, ou maint vaine gloire,
> Mire toy, mire en ceste istoire,
> Vois se Fortune la perverse,
> En peu d'eure, de moult hault verse!
> (ll. 23273–76)

> Oh, every man, in whom there is so much vainglory,
> Look at yourself, look within this history,
> See how Fortune, the perverse one,
> In short time, from high above, throws down!

These lines evoke two crucial moments in Guillaume de Lorris's *Roman de la Rose*: the narrator's identification of the fountain of Narcissus and his lament concerning Fortune. In the first of these two moments in Guillaume's *Rose*, the narrator recognizes the dangerous nature of the mirroring fountain in the garden: "C'est li miroërs perilleus / ou Narcisus, li orgueilleus, / mira sa face et ses ieuz vers, / dont il jut puis morz toz envers" (ll. 1569–72) [It is the perilous mirror / where Narcissus, the proud one, / looked at his face and his gray eyes, / for which reason he then fell down dead]. Don't gaze at the fountain of Narcissus, Christine warns; instead, "Mire toy, mire en ceste istoire." Look at this, she says, and see yourself as you might become. The Narcissus passage has its counterpart, in Guillaume's *Rose*, in the narrator's closing lament regarding Fortune:

> Ele a une roe qui torne
> et, quant ele veut, ele met
> le plus bas amont ou somet,
> et celui qui est sor la roe
> reverse a un tor en la boue.
> Et je sui cil qui est versez!
> (*Rose*, ll. 3960–65)[19]

> She has a wheel that turns
> and, when she wishes, she places
> he who is the lowest high up at the top,

---

19. Quotations from the *Roman de la Rose* are from the edition of Félix Lecoy, 3 vols. (Paris: Champion, 1965–70); translations are my own.

and he who is on top of the wheel
she throws in one turn into the mud.
And I am he who is turned!

In this passage, as David Hult has persuasively argued, "versez" means both to be turned on the wheel of Fortune and to be immured within poetic verse, to become exemplary for those who will come afterward. A similar pun appears in the earlier passage from the Rose, where Narcissus is said to fall down dead ("envers") or, alternatively, "in verse" ("en vers").[20] In the *Mutacion de Fortune,* Fortune similarly "de moult hault verse," throws people down from on high. They fall, but they too become immured in verse, transformed into examples for the one who can learn from them. The historical mirror of the *Mutacion de Fortune* is, we might say, the *good* mirror of Narcissus: by gazing at the "vrayes histoires" recounted in Christine's verse, it is possible for the reader to make out how he might similarly be tossed on the tides of change.

The concluding turn to Alexander, as a mirror for the reader, is introduced by a return to the ekphrastic mode, a final retrogressive return to the general form of history as seen in the opening historiographical passages of book four. In the earlier book, the ages of mankind served as a kind of epitome or temporal overview of the shape of time; in this final book of the *Mutacion de Fortune,* the parts of the world serve a similar ordering purpose, here providing a geographical overview that corresponds to the temporal overview that opened the initial move into the historiographical mode in book four. At the end of her adaptation of the *Histoire ancienne* and just before her expansive account of Alexander, Christine inserts an epitome of Orosian *translatio imperii.* She writes:

Et, pour revenir a mon conte,
Or avisons des signeuries,
Com commenciees et peries
Furent par espace de temps,
Si com, par ystoires, j'entens.
.IIII. principaulx j'en y treuve. . . .
(ll. 22067–71)

And, to return to my account,
Now we can see the kingdoms,
How they began and they perished

---

20. David F. Hult, *Self-Fulfilling Prophecies: Readership and Authority in the First* Roman de la Rose (Cambridge: Cambridge University Press, 1986), p. 297.

In the passage of time,
Just as I understand it, through histories.
I find four principal ones here . . .

Here, Christine returns to the ekphrastic framework of the *Mutacion*, noting the portrayal of "true histories" or "ystoires . . . voires" (ll. 22059–60) upon the walls of Fortune's castle. The empires depicted there include Assyria in the East; Carthage or Africa in the South; Macedonia in the North; and Rome in the West. This is the Orosian sequence, in which the four cardinal directions align with the four anchoring points of *translatio imperii*.[21] While the passage is adapted from a prose section in the *Histoire ancienne*, Christine displaces it from early in the prose work to a very late point in her own work, just before the climactic account of Alexander. This Orosian epitome corresponds to the sequence of the ages of mankind that begin the move into historiography, one introducing (in book four) and one concluding (in book seven) Christine's adaptation of the *Histoire ancienne*. In each case, the overview of history—whether temporal or geographical—serves to suspend the sequence of chronology, providing the reader with a synoptic glance that represents historical change in a nonlinear form.

These moments of interruption correspond to the ekphrastic moments of interruption described in detail earlier in this essay, suspending the forward movement of the exposition in a temporary state of stasis. In book four, at the opening of her account of Philosophy and the branches of knowledge, Christine describes this state of being in terms of "abstraction":

Par les escriptures, qu'y vy,
Mon esperit y fu ravy
Et astract, si que supposay
D'elle, ainsi qu'icy le posay.
Si vous en diray mon rapport,
Ainsi qu'ay de l'escript recort.
(ll. 7203–8)
By the engravings that I saw there
My spirit was ravished from that place

---

21. On the cardinal directions in Orosius' *translatio imperii*, see Suzanne Conklin Akbari, "Alexander in the Orient: Bodies and Boundaries in the *Roman de toute chevalerie*," in *Postcolonial Approaches to the European Middle Ages: Translating Cultures*, eds. Ananya Jahanara Kabir and Deanne Williams (Cambridge: Cambridge University Press, 2005), esp. pp. 105–15 [105–26]; Fabrizio Fabbrini, *Paolo Orosio: Uno storico* (Rome: Edizione di Storia e Letteratura, 1979), pp. 364–65.

And abstracted, so that I imagined these things concerning
Her, just as I present them here.
So I will tell you my report
Just as I recorded it from the engravings.

This state of being lifted outward from the present moment in a movement
of abstraction (the narrator's spirit is "astract") is the temporal pause that we
have seen repeatedly enacted in the *Mutacion de Fortune*. This takes place
initially in the repeated pauses and then movements of return in the ekphrastic descriptions that make up books two and three and much of book four.[22]
Once the move to historiography takes place in the latter parts of book four,
however, the movement of abstraction is transposed from the state of marvel
induced by ekphrasis into synoptic moments in which great patterns of history are made visible as if they were contained within a single glimpse. These
include the synoptic view of the ages of mankind, in a temporal moment of
stasis, and the synoptic view of the empires of the world, in a geographical
moment of stasis.

LIQUID MATTER

These moments of stasis, both ekphrastic and historiographical, share an
additional common ground: that is, their common reliance on the language
of materiality, which is consistently invoked within the moments of synoptic
vision we have observed in the *Mutacion de Fortune*.[23] In the opening passage
of book four that introduces the "sale merveilleuse," the term "matiere" is used
to refer not just to the materials of history but to the material of ekphrastic
description. Christine makes her characteristic movement of return ("tourner
arriere"), "Pour mieulx venir a ma matiere" [in order to better approach my
matter]. This oblique, cyclical approach to her topic also involves a process
of sifting out the most important historical materials, "Car de matieres y a
moult / Et ne puis tout dire en un mout" (ll. 7053, 7065–66) [because there are
many matters / and I cannot speak of all of them]. In her account of the parts
of Philosophy, Christine uses similar terminology to describe her approach

---

22. In a thoughtful survey of ekphrasis from antiquity to the present, Valentine Cunningham describes ekphrases as "pausings for thought," in which "the linear flow of narrative
slows or even stops" ("Why Ekphrasis?" *Classical Philology: Special Issue on Ekphrasis* 102.1
[2007]: 61 [57–71]).

23. On materiality in ekphrasis, see Stephen G. Nichols, "Seeing Food: An Anthropology
of Ekphrasis, and Still Life in Classical and Medieval Examples," *Modern Language Notes* 106
(1991): 818–51.

to her topic: "In order to make my material ("matiere") more complete," she says, "I will delay speaking of what I had intended in order to recount another thing" (ll. 7173–80). As in the oblique approach to her "matiere" described in the earlier passage, here Christine circles around her topic in order to better approach it, to make it "complete." The same kind of language reappears in each transitional passage, including the one that immediately follows the description of the parts of Philosophy and the one that is sandwiched between the account of the first age, from Creation to the Flood, and the account of the second age. In each case, an account of plenitude and abundance—whether of the "fountain" of Philosophy or the multiple "generations" of the sons of Noah—is immediately followed by a circling return to the narrator's original "matiere." In the last lines of her account of Philosophy's fecundity, Christine promises "from now on I will follow my matter, / Holding to the first cause" (ll. 8069–70); in the last lines of her account of mankind's fecundity, she promises to "return again shortly / And follow after my matter" (ll. 8353–54).

In the simplest sense, these allusions to "matter" simply refer to the stuff of history, as in the common descriptive phrases "Matter of Troy" or "Matter of Rome." On another level, however, in the context of ekphrasis, the repeated allusions to matter touch upon the peculiar quality of poetic language: that is, its ability to express narrative content in static form, to represent the linear movement of time in imagistic nonlinear terms. This quality of ekphrasis is apparent, for example, in the remarkable intaglio image described in canto 10 of Dante's *Purgatorio,* which features an image of the Annunciation in which "visibile parlare," "visible speech," makes manifest the mystery of Incarnation.[24] For Dante, this ekphrastic moment epitomizes the fusion of form and matter, in which the words of the Annunciation are "impressa . . . come figura in cera si suggella" [imprinted . . . as expressly as a figure is stamped in wax],[25] a moment that marks not only the union of God and man but also the temporal hinge of salvation history.

We can find other comparable moments throughout the medieval ekphrastic tradition: for example, in the *Roman de Troie,* the ekphrastic tomb monuments of the fallen heroes are made of the purest, most refined materials imaginable. The super-pure material of these ekphrastic monuments, even more than their beautiful form, causes them to inspire wonder in all those who look at them. For example, the remains of Achilles' body are placed in a

---

24. On Dante's ekphrasis in the *Purgatorio* as a source for the *Mutacion de Fortune,* see Brownlee, "The Image of History," pp. 51–54.

25. *Purgatorio* 10: 43–45, in Dante Alighieri, *The Divine Comedy,* ed. and trans. Charles S. Singleton, 3 vols. (Princeton, NJ: Princeton University Press, 1970–75); on this passage, see Akbari, *Seeing through the Veil,* pp. 157–58.

"cher vaissel" (l. 22470)[26] [costly vessel] made of a single ruby, which is held in the hands of a golden image. This figure is then placed at the summit of a wonderful monument, surmounting "a little sphere made of a single topaz, clear and beautiful." As the poet puts it, "A merveille fu esgardee" (l. 22426) [it was seen as a marvel]. The tomb of Paris is even more precious: instead of being made of gold, his "chier sarquel" (l. 23038) [costly sarcophagus] is made of "un vert jaspe goté: / Ainc en cest siecle trespassé / Ne fu veüz plus cher vaissel" (ll. 23039–41) [a single jasper touched with green: / Never in all the history of the world / Was there a richer vessel].[27]

In contrast to the elaborate ekphrases of twelfth-century literature, including the chariot of Alan of Lille's *Anticlaudianus* and the rich tombs of the *Roman de Troie*, late medieval ekphrasis has a rather different character. The intense focus on monumental ekphrasis common in twelfth-century literature gives way to an interest in the ways in which extended ekphrases can provide structures for the ordering of narrative, and particularly for the orderly presentation of history. This can be seen, for example, in Chaucer's engagement with history in the first book of the *House of Fame*, in which the story of the fall of Troy and foundation of Rome is interwoven from two very different perspectives on Aeneas's journey—Virgil's *Aeneid* and Ovid's *Heroides*—with word and image balanced in an uneasy state of equilibrium. Such use of ekphrasis is also evident in Chaucer's "Knight's Tale," in the descriptions of the amphitheatre and its "oratories" dedicated to the gods, as well as in the monumental "sepulture" of Arcite.[28] In these works, as in the universal history recounted in Christine de Pizan's *Mutacion de Fortune*, ekphrasis provides a way to give order to time—precisely by providing a way to stand outside of it, if only for a moment.

---

26. Quotations are from Léopold Constans, ed., *Le Roman de Troie publié d'après tous les manuscrits connus,* Société des anciens textes français, 6 vols. (Paris: Firmin Didot, 1904–1912) and are cited in the text by line number; translations are my own.

27. For a fuller explication of these tomb ekphrases, see Akbari, "Erasing the Body," pp. 153–55 and 160–61.

28. On ekphrasis in the "Knight's Tale," see Sarah Stanbury, "Visualizing," in *A Companion to Chaucer,* ed. Peter Brown (Oxford: Blackwell, 2000), pp. 459–79; see also the essay of John Bowers in this volume, pp. 55–76.

PART IV

THE BORDERS OF EKPHRASIS

Chapter 10

FACES IN THE CROWD

FACIALITY AND EKPHRASIS IN LATE MEDIEVAL ENGLAND

Ethan Knapp

his essay is concerned with a comparatively simple question about the imagistic vocabulary available to late medieval poets: why is the face an absolutely central image for some of them, while others, even some of those inclined to elaborate descriptive passages, do not take the human face as an object of ekphrastic interest? What is the face for these poets? What does it signify when presented as an image, as something for us to visualize, and what, when it is only discursively constructed as an abstract anatomic assemblage?

It is hard to find a tradition of visual representation in which the human face is not a privileged object. Never merely anatomical, the face has long served a metonymical function as an easily circulating marker of personal identity. We can think here of its function in coinage as the portable sign of sovereign identity, an evocation of the personal authority that stands behind the coin. Or we might consider the massive importance of the face in the tradition of Christian religious imagery, a tradition that crowds medieval paintings with faces of saints and martyrs and fashions the story of Veronica's veil into a perfect allegory for the ambitions of painting to make the sacred visually present in the world. Nevertheless, despite all of these faces, the Middle Ages have also long been considered to be peculiarly resistant to a certain kind of face, namely the verist portrait. Ever since nineteenth-century scholars aligned the development of realistic portraiture with the birth of the individual in the Italian Renaissance, the art of the medieval period has been defined largely by the category of conventionality.[1] And this sense of artistic conventionality, in turn, has been reinforced by the contextualization of many of these facial images within the hermeneutic codes of medieval physiognomy.[2] The result of these tandem influences has been a tendency to read the face iconographically and typologically, leading much interpretive work to skip past the anatomical surface and take these faces, by and large, as allegorical veneers directing us towards something deeper, something hidden beneath the phenomenological object. This approach to reading the history of the face has certainly been productive in Middle English studies—one need only think of the powerful work on the relation of texts and images in the tradition leading from D. W. Robertson to V. A. Kolve.[3] But, at the same time, as with any exercise in allegoresis, the vehicle threatens to become lost, to fade away into pure and abstract signification.

I would like to try to keep our focus on the face itself, to ask what faces mean and how they can mean in ways that are distinct from other visual objects—to ask, in other words, about the function of faciality in the Mid-

---

1. On this point, see Heather McPherson, *The Modern Portrait in Nineteenth-Century France* (Cambridge: Cambridge University Press, 2001).

2. The classic treatment of physiognomy in the context of medieval literature remains that of Walter Clyde Curry, *Chaucer and the Mediaeval Sciences* (New York: Oxford University Press, 1926). For more recent treatments, see John Block Friedman, "Another Look at Chaucer and the Physiognomists," *Studies in Philology* 78.2 (1981): 138–52; Tison Pugh, "Squire Jankyn's Legs and Feet: Physiognomy, Social Class, and Fantasy in the Wife of Bath's Prologue and Tale," in *Medievalia et Humanistica: Studies in Medieval and Renaissance Culture* 32 (2007): 83–101; Douglas Wurtele, "Another Look at an Old 'Science': Chaucer's Pilgrims and Physiognomy," in *From Arabye to Engelond: Medieval Studies in Honour of Mahmoud Manzalaoui on His 75th Birthday*, eds. A. E. Christa Canitz and Gernot R. Wieland (Ottawa: University of Ottawa Press, 1999), pp. 93–111; and Joseph Ziegler, "Text and Context: On the Rise of Physiognomic Thought in the Later Middle Ages," in *De Sion Exibit Lex Et Verbum Domini De Hierusalem: Essays on Medieval Law, Liturgy, and Literature in Honour of Amnon Linder*, ed. Yitzhak Hen (Turnhout: Brepols, 2001), pp. 159–82. On the intellectual backgrounds to medieval physiognomy, see Martin Porter, *Windows of the Soul: The Art of Physiognomy in European Culture* (Oxford: Oxford University Press, 2005).

3. V. A. Kolve, *Chaucer and the Imagery of Narrative: The First Five Canterbury Tales* (Stanford: Stanford University Press, 1984); D. W. Robertson, Jr., *A Preface to Chaucer: Studies in Medieval Perspectives* (Princeton: Princeton University Press, 1969). For more recent and very rich treatments of the theory and practice of medieval iconography, see Suzanne Conklin Akbari, *Seeing through the Veil: Optical Theory and Medieval Allegory* (Toronto: University of Toronto Press, 2004) and Sarah Stanbury, *The Visual Object of Desire in Late Medieval England* (Philadelphia: University of Pennsylvania Press, 2008).

dle Ages. In a fascinating recent issue of *Gesta*, the art historian Stephen Perkinson has laid out two recent versions of an anti-Burckhardtian project, an attempt to understand medieval interest in realistic facial depiction as something other than a teleological foreshadowing of the modern verist (or mimetically accurate) portrait.[4] First, he points to work such as that of Michel Pastoureau and Hans Belting who construe the development of realistic portraiture in the later Middle Ages as an outgrowth of a "crisis" of heraldic representational codes.[5] In the sort of case familiar to literary historians through episodes such as Chaucer's involvement in the Scrope/Grosvenor trial, the proliferation of heraldic insignias in the later Middle Ages led to increased anxiety over identical blazons being used by different parties. In Pastoureau's account, this anxiety led, in turn, to the development of numerous new representational systems meant to differentiate the parties, among which was the verist portrait. Not thus a sign of some new realism, portraiture instead arises, in Pastoureau's words, as "a new form of symbolic representation which takes its place among other forms of representation."[6] The specific interest in the face inspired by this crisis was reinforced, as Perkinson would have it, by a rising vogue for physiognomy, the art of interpreting anatomic features as an expression of both character and destiny. Referring here to work such as that by Willibald Sauerländer, Perkinson suggests that accounts like those in the *Secreta Secretorum* led to an increased interest in anatomical description of all sorts but particularly of the complexion and composition of facial features.[7]

With these two historical influences in mind, I would propose here a third, one that I think was particularly important in the poetry of the period. The face in late medieval poetry is often understood as a particular hermeneutic challenge, or better, it is the privileged site through which the body appears as an object available for hermeneutic analysis. And further, it becomes available in a specific sociological and narratological context. Faciality, for these

---

4. Stephen Perkinson, "Rethinking the Origins of Portraiture," *Gesta* 42.2 (2008): 135–93. See also Perkinson, *The Likeness of the King: A Prehistory of Portraiture in Late Medieval France* (Chicago: University of Chicago Press, 2009).

5. Michel Pastoureau, "L'effervescence emblématique et les origines héraldiques du portrait au XIVe siècle," *Bulletin de la Société Nationale des Antiquaires de France* (1985 [1987]): 108–15; Hans Belting, "The Coat of Arms and the Portrait," in *An Anthropology of Images: Picture, Medium, Body*," trans. Thomas Dunlap (Princeton, NJ: Princeton University Press, 2011), pp. 62–83.

6. Pastoureau, "L'effervescence emblématique," p. 114 (cited by Perkinson, "Origins of Portraiture," p. 136).

7. Willibald Sauerländer, "The Fate of the Face in Medieval Art," in *Set in Stone: The Face in Medieval Sculpture*, ed. Charles T. Little (New York: The Metropolitan Museum of Art, 2006), pp. 2–11.

poets, is a phenomenon conditioned by the experience of the urban crowd and structured by the dialectical opposition between image and narration. My thinking here is very much influenced by Walter Benjamin's meditations on the thematics of urban experience in Baudelaire's allegory, so let me cite his account of the Baudelairean flâneur from convolute "J" of the *Arcades Project* at some length.

> The flâneur plays the role of scout in the marketplace. As such, he is also the explorer of the crowd. Within the man who abandons himself to it, the crowd inspires a sort of drunkenness, one accompanied by very specific illusions: the man flatters himself that, on seeing a passerby swept along by the crowd, he has accurately classified him, seen straight through to the innermost recesses of his soul—all on the basis of his external appearance. Physiologies of the time abound in evidence of this singular conception. . . . But the nightmare that corresponds to the illusory perspicacity of the aforementioned physiognomies consists in seeing those distinctive traits—traits particular to the person—revealed to be nothing more than the elements of a new type; so that in the final analysis a person of the greatest individuality would turn out to be the exemplar of a type.[8]

Benjamin here anatomizes a very specific visual and cognitive experience. The urban crowd is encountered as a sea of faces. The flâneur, the individual who has slipped into the crowd, is, as Benjamin says, open to a particular drunkenness, a particular semiotic illusion, namely the fantasy that the face in front of them can be assigned a precise meaning, a particular individuality. But in a powerful dialectical tension, this illusion of individual and particular meaning is immediately reorganized into the type, the visual caricature, or what we know among the system of tropes as allegory itself. Allegory, in essence, is diagnosed here as an urban art, one derived from the necessarily fleeting glance of the unknown crowd, made knowable only by the instant projection of meaning onto a briefly glimpsed physiognomy. And it is this moment of allegoresis that also isolates the features of a given individual and makes them into a face, an anatomical assemblage that bears meaning.

This experience, this event, is one that left profound traces on late medieval English poetry. I will look here at three of the poets most deeply concerned with these faces in the crowd: Chaucer, Gower, and Hoccleve. As we will see, although the basic structuring experience is, I believe, a shared one,

---

8. Walter Benjamin, *The Arcades Project,* trans. Howard Eiland and Kevin McLaughlin (Cambridge, MA: Harvard University Press, 1999), p. 21.

their responses to it vary widely. For Chaucer, the face serves two functions: it is, first, one of his preferred images for depicting pathos, particularly around women, and around social isolation; second, for Chaucer, the face becomes a structuring device for the particular form of episodic narration, offering, like Benjamin's flâneur, moments where the passage of time, or the movement through the street, is suddenly suspended by the infinite regress of physiognomy. Gower also has two relatively distinct uses of faces: first the face serves, anatomically, as a threshold to the self—it is a set of dangerous boundaries between interior and exterior; second, in a less anatomical sense, it is recurrently treated as a mirroring device, something very much like the vision of modern cognitive science that emphasizes the human propensity to physically mimic the face and expression of other human beings when we engage with them. Finally, for Hoccleve, the face becomes something like a figure for representational art itself, for the poet's ability to project a malleable self into the world.

CHAUCER'S PALE FACES[9]

When we think about faces in Chaucer, the first thing that comes to mind is certainly the physiognomies of the "General Prologue"—the Wife of Bath's gap tooth, the Miller's hairy wart, and so forth. These faces have usually been taken as one of the signs of Chaucer's deep interest in individual personalities, with the physiognomies serving to reinforce the details of clothing, manner and belief that serve to create a sense of specific density in the portrayals. In Jill Mann's words, "The character which is 'symbolized' in the physical detail must accord with what we learn of the pilgrim from the rest of the work."[10] Taken in its own terms, I think that this reading is essentially correct; the faces of the "General Prologue" work in a constellation of pseudoheraldic emblems (clothing, faces, emblematic mottos) very reminiscent of Pastoureau's symbolic representations. At the same time, it is surely significant that even Mann's brilliant eye for realistic and mimetic depiction takes faciality here as an allegorical operation, one in which "physical detail" stands in relation to "character" as a relation of vehicle and tenor. Faces serve to trope the deeper reality of psychological character. Most readings of faces in Chau-

---

9. On the "paleness" of faces in Chaucer, see also the marvelously rich reflections in Carolyn Dinshaw, "Pale Faces: Race, Religion, and Affect in Chaucer's Texts and Their Readers," *Studies in the Age of Chaucer* 23 (2001): 19–41.

10. Jill Mann, *Chaucer and Medieval Estates Satire* (Cambridge: Cambridge University Press, 1973), p. 167.

cer repeat this gesture, relying on the physiognomies of the "General Prologue" and eliding the question of what such faces signify as faces. I will try to avoid this elision by approaching the faces of Chaucer's pilgrims indirectly, by detouring through the less imagistic but more narratologically significant use of faces in two of Chaucer's other works: *Troilus and Criseyde* and the "Man of Law's Tale."

The "Man of Law's Tale," Chaucer's version of the Tale of Constance, has received quite a bit of critical attention lately, focusing largely on the hagiographical elements of the tale and on the depiction of gender in the story of the long-suffering Constance, a competitor to Griselde in her patient martyrdom to Fortune. As should not be surprising, given its hagiographical roots, this story is also one with a persistent interest in the status of the visual. Constance is, of course, beautiful, and in Chaucer's version, it is this beauty that triggers her long peripatetic adventure. In Rome, the Syrian merchants are drawn to both her beauty and her virtue, but the report of the Roman people, surprisingly, subordinates the virtue to the beauty, presenting the virtues as remarkable largely because they are found in someone of such beauty. "In hire is heigh beautee, withoute pride, / Yowthe, withoute grenehede or folye" (ll. 162–63).[11] Contributing further to this subordination of ethical virtue to beautiful image is the fact that the virtues themselves are praised as a "mirror" and metaphorically constructed as emanations of her physical presence. "She is mirour of alle curteisye; / Hir herte is verray chambre of hoolynesse, / Hir hand, ministre of fredam for almesse" (ll. 166–68). Finally, clinching our sense of the priority of beauty over virtue in this hagiography is the fact that when these merchants return to the Sultan, his desire for her is characterized as a desire to possess her image, or "to han hir figure in his remembrance" (l. 187).

If we compare these moments to Gower's treatment of the story, the analogous passages utterly lack this visual emphasis. She is beautiful and virtuous, but there is no sense of coordination or subordination between these aspects. They are simply two admirable features. And there is no sense of a mesmerizing image brought home among the merchandise to capture the Sultan's love. But Chaucer's emphasis on the visual is pervasive, not stopping even after the marriage to the Sultan (as we might think of it as a Romance preliminary to bring her into virtuous marriage). A false oath is punished by the perjurer falling dead with his eyes bursting out of his head, and in another Chaucerian addition, her hidden Christian faith is nearly revealed in a dangerous

---

11. All quotations from Chaucer will be drawn from Larry D. Benson, ed., *The Riverside Chaucer*, 3rd ed. (Boston: Houghton Mifflin, 1987) and will be cited by line number within the text.

moment when a blind man, and fellow secret Christian, calls out to her to ask her to heal him and bring back his sight. The most powerful treatment of her iconic status, however, and the one most important to my argument occurs at a moment of great drama when she has been falsely accused of murder. Living in Northumberland under the protection of a Constable and his wife Hermegyld, Constance has the misfortune of having a knight (the perjurer) fall in love with her. Refused by Constance, the knight takes vengeance by killing Hermegyld and hiding the bloody knife in the chamber shared by the two women. Constance is too grieved to speak in her own defense, so the investigation turns on the testimony of conflicting witnesses. With the king, Alla, serving as judge, the people of the household, with one exception, declare that she loved Hermegyld too much to have slain her. The one exception, the perjurer, insists that the evidence of the knife is incontrovertible and that she is guilty.

Silent in the midst of this trial, Constance is reduced again to what she was at the beginning of the story, an image, but unlike the beginning, this image is now emphatically facialized. In this moment of high drama, the narrator resorts to an extended Homeric simile, comparing Constance to a man condemned to death

> Have ye nat seyn somtyme a pale face,
> Among a prees, of hym that hath be lad
> Toward his deeth, wher as hym gat no grace,
> And swich a colour in his face hath had
> Men myghte knowe his face that was bistad
> Amonges all the faces in that route?
> So stant Custance, and looketh hire aboute.
>
> O queenes, lyvynge in prosperitee,
> Duchesses, and ye ladyes everichone,
> Haveth some routhe on hire adversitee!
> An Emperoures doghter stant allone;
> She hath no wight to whom to make hir mone.
> O blood roial, that stondest in this drede,
> Fer been they freendes at thy grete nede!
> (ll. 645–58)

This simile is meant to depict Constance's tragic isolation, and it does this in two ways, both in its images and in its sudden interruption of the narrative momentum. The signal opposition here is between the "press," the crowd, and the single face that stands out from within it. The face is a condemned one, and it stands out because it has been condemned. The face, in other words, becomes a clear sign when the condemned man is separated from the "press" by his fate, marked out as complete by his imminent death. To return to the passage from Benjamin that I cited earlier, we can see this face plucked out of the crowd because it has now simultaneously become an individual and a type. So Constance has a face at this moment when she is threatened by completion, and as a face she stands still, looking about, just as the narration stands still, interrupted by the lengthy simile. Indeed, noting the reiteration of both the terms "face" and "stant/stondest," one might say that to have a face is to have a stance, that where the crowd is in continual movement, the face is fixed in space and in meaning. The lack of motion thus reiterates her separation from the crowd, imagined to be in motion both physically and hermeneutically, as it is made up of those who are giving testimony, speaking and moving and not themselves frozen into the stasis and silence of faciality.[12]

I would be putting a perilous amount of weight on this simile if not for its eerie similarity to other treatments of the face in Chaucer, especially, perhaps, his depiction of Criseyde in *Troilus and Criseyde*. If we recall the emphatically visual register of the first contact between Troilus and Criseyde, we can see that it produces a very similar sense of an image suddenly separated from a crowd and standing fixed. In the temple, Troilus looks from lady to lady, wondering with each whether they are from the city or not, until, through the crowd, his eye sticks on Criseyde ("thorugh a route / His eye percede, and so depe it wente, / til on Criseyde it smot, and there it stente" [I:271–73]). The focus then shifts to her face, as the narrator tells us that she "let falle / Hire look" as if to say, famously, "What, may I not stonden here?" (I:290–92). We see here the same sense that the face is produced out of the dialectical relation between the mobile and fleeting crowd and the fixed, static individual. Moreover, as the story proceeds, and Criseyde's face begins to fall more and more into paleness, her face and the city appear almost as a diptych of opposed images. Living in the Greek camp, she looks out at "the toures heigh and ek the halles" (V:730) of Troy, and Chaucer describes her in terms that could be neatly inserted into Constance's story:

Ful pale ywoxen was hir brighte face,
Hire lymes lene, as she that al the day

---

12. One might note, of course, that the simile does not quite fit, as *everyone in the household* has already unanimously borne witness that she was too virtuous and loved Hermengyld too much to have killed her (with the single exception of the knight who had killed her and framed Constance for the deed).

Stood, whan she dorste, and loken on the place
Ther she was born, and ther she dwelt hadde ay;
(V:708–11)

The story turns almost immediately, then, to the intricate blazons of Dio-
mede, Troilus, and Criseyde herself. And it is the structural placement of
these descriptions that is so striking. We would normally expect such an
extended *descriptio* to occur at the beginning of a narrative, to introduce a
character, to tell us something about the person before we hear their story.
Ekphrasis in such a context serves as the seedbed of narrative. It produces a
person whose story can be told. But here, in these pale faces, we see the face
as the *end* of narrative, as the expulsion of the individual from the city and
from their place in its history.

Lastly, this effect may also suggest something new about the less pale
faces in the "General Prologue." The portraits in the "General Prologue" are
usually read as beginnings, particularly in so-called "dramatic" readings that
ground the tales in character, as cause and effect. But if we take seriously
this other meaning of the face for Chaucer we might weigh more heavily the
sharp discontinuity between narrative and ekphrasis. As we have known at
least since Lessing, the stillness of the image stands in opposition to the temporality of narration, but the specific problem of the face in Chaucer threatens to add a tragic finitude to the stillness of the image. The portraits in the
"General Prologue" should perhaps be read as an experiment in defeating this
deathly stillness. They are images, but images that will not sit quietly or fall
into paleness.

GOWER: THE FACE ANATOMIZED

Turning now to Gower, the first fact to account for is the radical lack of faces
in his work. There are characters aplenty, hundreds of them, in the proliferating exempla of the *Confessio Amantis,* but, remarkably, we are never told
what any of these characters look like. To a certain extent this lack might
be ascribed to Gower's more abstract, or philosophically inclined, poetics.
Where the substance of Chaucer's world is often visual and concrete, Gower
seems inclined to focus on the structure of things. Ontologically, this seems
an inheritance of the Chartrian world. Nature is not so much a collection of
objects as it is a hidden order behind the things of the world, an order that
sometimes comes down almost to a neo-Pythagorean sense that Nature, truly
revealed, is more number than substance. But this Chartrian world was also

intensely visual. Reading Alain de Lille, we know exactly what Nature looks like, how she wears her hair and what her dress is made of (even where it is torn). With Gower, on the other hand, there is no telling what Genius looks like, or Amans, or any of the other multitude that populate his stories. We see objects and landscapes, but the people who travel in them remain indistinct.

Nevertheless, it would be untrue to say that there are no faces in Gower. Gower uses faces in two ways. First, for Gower, faces often signify a mirroring relationship between individuals, especially moments at which misunderstandings or hostility are resolved into harmony. There are numerous examples of this relationship in Gower. When Paulina realized that she has been seduced not by the God Anubis but by the lecherous Mundus, she tearfully confesses her mistake to her husband. Seeing "Hire fare face and al desteigneth, / With wofull teres of hire ye" (1:966–67), the husband swears that he will not be angry, and husband and wife go together to seek recourse.[13] Similarly, in the "Tale of Three Questions," the anger of the proud young king, angry that a young girl is able to answer the impossible riddles he had manufactured to embarrass the girl's wise father, dissipates when "he began to loke tho / Upon this maiden in the face" (1:3326–27). In a somewhat more extended treatment, Gower ends his own version of the tale of Constance with an elaborate scene of facial recognition. With the perjury of the villainous knight recognized and divine punishment having been meted out, Constance married King Alla and had a son, only then to be again betrayed, this time by the King's mother, who caused her to be set adrift with her son. Protected by her virtue from many other dangers, she eventually makes her way to Rome. Alla, meanwhile, discovers his mother's treachery, has her burned alive, and then, not knowing Constance's fate, himself goes to Rome to seek absolution for his violence. The climactic reunion then takes place, not through a meeting of Alla and Constance, but, rather, through the King's encounter with Moris, the son whom he has never met. As Gower describes the moment, Constance tells Moris to stand before the king

> Bot to Moris hire sone tolde
> That he upon the morwe sholde
> In al that evere he cowthe and mihte
> Be present in the kinges sihte,
> So that the king him ofte sihe.
> Moris tofore the kings yhe

---

13. All quotations from Gower will be drawn from *Confessio Amantis,* ed. Russell A. Peck, (Kalamazoo: Western Michigan University Press, 2000) and will be cited by line number within the text.

Upon the morwe, wher he sat,
Fulofte stod, and upon that
The king his chiere upon him caste,
And in his face him thoghte als faste
He sih his oghne wif Constance.
For nature as in resemblance
Of face hem liketh so to clothe,
That thei were of a suite bothe.
The king was moeved in his thoght
Of that he seth, and knoweth it noght;
The child he loveth kindely,
And yet he wot no cause why.
(II:1365–82)

This is one of the few passages in which Chaucer found a visual emphasis in Gower's version, and Chaucer plays it up further, suggesting that Alla thinks he has a "fantome" in his mind. The unusual visual emphasis here is driven by the narrative's interest in recognition, but Gower has interestingly deflected that moment of recognition into the facial features of the son. The genealogical emblem seems clear: in recognizing Moris's face as that of Constance (and his own as well, as is suggested by the "kindely" love he mysteriously feels), the King has solved a riddle and recovered his wife. All narrative paths, all the seaborne wanderings, come down to this moment of uncanny recognition. The face serves here to reunite the broken family, knitting narrative and genealogy together into a mirroring identity. For a poet as concerned as Gower was with the problem of fragmentation and disharmony, this is a powerful and utopian vision of facial possibilities.

In addition to these mirroring faces, Gower has one other even more striking use for the face. At the beginning of his confession of Amans in Book I, Genius insists that they must proceed in ferreting out the signs of pride by beginning with an examination of his five wits. This investigation is justified by the Latin verses preceding this section, which begin "Visus et auditus fragilis sunt ostia mentis" (I.iv.) [Vision and hearing are the gates of the fragile mind], a sentiment important enough for it to be reiterated in the English verse, "For tho [they—the wits] be proprely the gates, / Thurgh whiche as to the herte algates / Comth all thing unto the feire, / Which may the mannes soule empeire" (I:299–302). Unlike the famously ambiguous usage in *Gawaine and the Green Knight*, in which the five wits might refer either to five inward wits, that is, the senses, Genius is here speaking strictly of the physical senses (sight, hearing, smell, touch, and taste). Genius goes on to examine only the first two of these, sight and hearing, a prioritizing that goes back, as Kolve among others has pointed out, to Plato's establishment in the *Timaeus* of these two as the most important of the human senses.[14]

As Genius begins to explore these two senses, however, he immediately transposes the investigation of the senses into an investigation of the anatomical organs associated with them. In other words, instead of investigating sight and hearing he questions Amans about his eyes and ears. In part, the turn to these anatomical features is a commonplace of medieval treatments of the senses, justifying the division of senses into five by correlating the five with elements of human anatomy. But beyond this, I would suggest that Genius moves immediately to anatomy in order to resituate the metaphor of the senses as the gate to the mind, or to the heart. The gateway now becomes literalized in the face, suggesting that the physicality of the face is significant in that it acts as a threshold and a barrier, protecting the more vulnerable interior. It is an implicit rebuke to the allegorical elision of the face, typical of so much subsequent criticism, in that it is the dense physicality of the organs of faciality that can act as either a potential barrier between the external world and ethically fragile interiority of the subject or as the betraying materiality of the flesh, drawing that subjectivity out into corruption. The relevant exempla set out Gower's point clearly: in considering the use of the eye, Genius tells Amans the stories of Acteon and Medusa; and for the ear, the Sirens. These are stories about danger, about the difficulty of controlling the eyes, which might stray in love or stray towards the figure of the naked goddess, and about the impossibility of controlling the ears, always open to gossip or the lure of a Siren.

And as with the more benign mirroring face we investigated above, this more dangerous face must be understood within the context of Gower's continual concern with fragmentation. As he makes clear in the Prologue's analysis of disharmony in the world, the disharmony of the political and spiritual world is reflected in the microcosmic disharmony of the human being, fragmented fundamentally by the division between body and soul but also now fragmented anatomically into different facial elements that elude the control of the self. Here then, as with Chaucer, the face serves as not just one among many parts of the body but as a privileged site of contestation. Control of the face is control of the self, and lack of such control is the chief entry point for the world's divisions. In preaching against hypocrisy, Genius will later warn that Hypocrisy sets a visor, or mask, upon his face (I:637). But the face, in this second signification, is already a visor set against the world.

---

14. See Kolve's translation and discussion of the Latin hexameter (*Chaucer and the Imagery of Narrative*, p. 24).

Perhaps the most crucial point about these faces in Gower, however, is that the face is always set in relation to another. Whether in the comforting possibilities of the mirror or the threatening perturbation of the visor, the face only appears in a social world. It is all too easy to be misled by the psychological taxonomies of the confessional scheme in Gower into reading his work as some sort of internalized psychomachia. The imperative may be an examination of the lover's conscience, but this conscience is tested always as it moves among a crowded world. And the face appears in this world as one of the pivotal signs of the hopes and dangers of this interpersonal ethics. Genius and Amans, in effect, restage Benjamin's event in an endless sequence of recognitions and misrecognitions, trading the role of the flâneur back and forth as they proceed in a mutual quest to plumb each others' meaning.

HOCCLEVE: THE IMAGE TALKS BACK

I will conclude by turning briefly to Thomas Hoccleve, both because he offers one of the most elaborate descriptions of faciality in Middle English poetry and because his account seems, at first glance, the most insistently private and nonsocial of such accounts, the most foreign to the Benjaminian sense of the face. The relevant scene is a famous one. Complaining in his *Series* that he has been abandoned by his friends, that no one understands or will believe that his madness, his "wylde infirmitee" has passed, Hoccleve finds himself in the street, trying, as he says, to paint a face that will convincingly represent sanity. Failing in this simple endeavor, he retreats from the street and goes home to his own chamber. Here he performs a remarkable self-examination, jumping in front of a mirror to try to find the elusive signs of madness that seem apparent to others.

My spirites labouriden euere ful bisily
To peinte countenaunce, chere and look,
For Þat men spake of me so wondringly,
And for the verry shame and feer I qwook.
Thou3 myn herte hadde be dipped in Þe brook,
It weet and moist was ynow of my swoot,
Wiche was nowe frosty colde, nowe firy hoot.

And in my chaumbre at hoom whanne Þat I was
Mysilfe aloone I in Þis wise wrou3te.
I streite vnto my mirrour and my glas,
To loke howe Þat me of my chere Þou3te,

If any othir were it than it ouȝt,
For fain wolde I, if it not had bene riȝt,
Amendid it to my kunnynge and myȝt.

Many a saute made I to this mirrour,
Thinking, 'If Þat I looke in Þis manere
Amonge folke as I nowe do, noon errour
Of suspecte look may in my face appere.
This countinaunce, I am sure, and Þis chere,
If I forthe vse, is nothing repreuable
To hem Þat han conceitis resonable.'

And therwithal I Þoȝte Þus anoon:
'Men in her owne cas bene blinde alday,
As I haue herde seie manie a day agoon,
And in that same plite I stonde may.
Howe shal I do? Wiche is the beste way
My troublid spirit for to bringe in reste?
If I wiste howe, fain wolde I do the best.'
("Compleinte," ll. 148–75)[15]

We should first notice that this passage is a virtual catalogue of the tropes we have encountered thus far. The image of the face is a mirror, here a physical one, pressing Gower's social image of the *speculum* into a more introspective register. The face is also an assemblage that threatens to escape the control of its bearer, needing to be disciplined into the visor. And as in Chaucer, the face is established in a fixed point in the narrative, when the individual, Hoccleve, is separated out from among the crowd and the movement of the street.

But unlike Chaucer's pale faces, there is a jittery movement about this face that is both disturbing to its bearer and also a protest against the objectifying glance of the crowd. Hoccleve's "spirits" labor to paint a face, and they do so "ful bisily" (one can only imagine the resulting expression). Furthermore, he examines his face in the mirror, but not in some pose of rapt meditation. Rather, he jumps several times, trying to spot something before it vanishes. There is a double paradox here. First, despite the mirroring relationship of the self to the face, the face is peculiarly inaccessible to the self—as Hoccleve says, "Men in her owne cas bene blinde alday." In the imagistic system of this

---

15. All quotations from Hoccleve will be drawn from "My Compleinte" *and Other Poems,* ed. Roger Ellis (Exeter: University of Exeter Press, 2001) and will be cited by title and line number within the text.

passage, the face appears as a blind spot for the subject, the one thing the self most needs to see but the one thing hidden from view. Second, I think we can also read this passage as a careful expression of a paradox also found in Benjamin's account. As the face is isolated, pulled out of the crowd, it is fixed, but fixed only as a mystery. As Benjamin had said, the flâneur is caught in the irresolvable interpretive tension between reading the face as individual and as type. Similarly, in Hoccleve's account, his own face, having been made an object of interpretive scrutiny by his friends, is made into an interminably shifting hermeneutic puzzle. It is a painted thing, a mobile thing, something to be represented in autobiographical art.

And the movement from ekphrasis into verbal art is made explicitly, even polemically, by Hoccleve. After failing to compose his face in the mirror, Hoccleve reconsiders his situation and renounces what I have been calling faciality in this essay. As he says:

> Uppon a look is harde men hem to grounde
> What a man is. Therby the sothe is hid.
> Whethir hise wittis seek bene or sounde,
> By countynaunce is it not wist ne kid.
> ("Compleinte," ll. 211–14)

Rather than reading the face, Hoccleve says, men should turn to "communynge" (l. 21). The image of the face is refused as an interpretive dead end, a failed physiognomy. Instead of the silent regard of physiognomy, Hoccleve insists on speech, on the need of the image to speak back and explain itself. As with Chaucer and Gower, it is clear that Hoccleve saw the face as something very different from other objects. For all of these poets, the human face seems to have been a privileged site at which to work through the hermeneutic difficulties arising from ekphrastic art. As for Benjamin, it was the site at which the friction between crowd and individual was the greatest and the site at which the individual emerged as an uncertain hermeneutic figure, poised between typicality and eccentricity. Most of all, perhaps, the face evoked what I think we could call a near phenomenological sense of the irreducibility of its objecthood. Rather than being the grist for allegorical abstraction, these faces stand out as resistant objects, irresistibly gathering up meaning, but silently refusing any final summation.

Chapter 11

THE SOUL OF EKPHRASIS

CHAUCER'S "MERCHANT'S TALE" AND THE MARRIAGE OF THE SENSES

Hans Jürgen Scheuer

I.

Visiting the Musée d'Art Moderne in Luxembourg (MUDAM) in January 2010, I was struck by an arrangement of pictures devised by the French photographer and video artist Bruno Baltzer. The showcase was something of a miniature digital portrait gallery, as the nineteen pictures of individual children from several primary schools around the city were presented on flat screens. A commentary sheet explained that immediately before the photographs were taken, the children had been asked to imagine their greatest wish. Crucially, the title of the composition, *En vœux-tu en voilà* [all you wish for], indicated that the photographs aimed at the visualization of a complex instance of temporality: the moment in which a wish is *remembered* while its fulfillment is simultaneously being *anticipated,* so that present, past, and future all coincide in one and the same mental image.

At first glance, the arrangement seemed to be governed by a typically modern aesthetics of the "pregnant moment": each picture captures and keeps hold of a brief and highly energetic point in time with the aim of capturing "life" behind the image. Confusingly, however, these were no conventional photographs. Noticeable only when subjected to more than a cursory glance, the technically produced *imagines agentes* did not merely represent a certain "inner" movement but rendered instead a real "outward" motion. More precisely, the pictures actually turned out to be videos showing the briefest of moments, lasting no more than ten seconds in real time, but that had been stretched to a duration of one minute and forty seconds. The effect is remarkable. Presented in slow motion, the children's faces are seized by an agitation hardly to be contained or localized. Through the hint of a smile, through the excessively prolonged blink of an eye or a drifting strand of hair, the briefly entertained wish passes through the image like a breeze, creating a sense of intensity that appears to precede the children's conscious intentions.

Inspired as it obviously is by Bill Viola's video art, Bruno Baltzer's concept actually has affinities with a much older theory of perception and imagination. By means of advanced technology, Baltzer's art simulates the interplay between the physical and the psychic, between internal and external motion in agreement with a model of psychodynamics already expounded in Aristotle's treatise *De motu animalium*:

> Now we see that the movers of the animal are reasoning (*diánoia*) and *phantasia* and choice (*prohaíresis*) and wish (*boúlesis*) and appetite (*epithymía*). And all of these can be reduced to thought (*noûs*) and desire (*órexis*). For both *phantasía* and sense-perception (*aísthesis*) hold the same place as thought, since they all are concerned with making distinctions (*kritikà gàr pánta*). . . . [T]he animal (*tò zôon*) moves and progresses in virtue of desire (*órexis*) or choice (*prohaíresis*), when some alteration has taken place in accordance with sense-perception (*aísthesis*) or *phantasía*. (*De motu,* 700b 17–21. 701a 4–6)[1]

Aristotle claims that any movement of the soul can be observed within the movement of an animated body. Thus, the exhibited tension between conventional (still) photography and (animated) video art is capable of articulating movement in the children's souls as they are driven by fantasy, choice, and desire. Even today, a premodern aesthetics of the mental image is helpful in conceptualizing what might otherwise escape pictorial representation. Significantly, however, the aesthetic power of Baltzer's arrangement does not merely rely on the interplay between photographic and video art but depends also on an implicit, highly condensed kind of ekphrasis: the work's idiomatic title, *En*

---

1. Quoted in Martha Craven Nussbaum, ed. and trans., *Aristotle's* De motu animalium (Princeton, NJ: Princeton University Press, 1978), pp. 38–41.

vœux-tu en voilà, alludes to the psychic processes of desire and wish making. Without this intervention of the verbal, we might not be able to recognize the arrangement of images as a depiction of mental movements at all.[2]

For the same purpose, namely that of making visible inner movement, medieval poetics calls attention to the *descriptio personae,* which we could regard as the written equivalent of the painted portrait. However, medieval poetics does not only aim at depicting the inner movement of the person or creature depicted but also seeks to initiate inner movement within the viewer. Just as every painted work of art seeks to move the soul by depiction, so does every written work of art seek to move the soul by producing mental images (phantasmata, imagines agentes) through description.

In this essay, I wish to argue that medieval ekphrasis is essentially an engagement with the union of language and the inner senses (or soul). My argument will address how ancient and medieval writers—Chaucer in particular—explore this alliance through describing an inner and outer "union" of another kind: marriage. I will show that Chaucer's "Merchant's Tale" is not simply part of a discourse on marriage as a social phenomenon but must be viewed in terms of a general psychological structure characteristic of the premodern poetics of ekphrasis. Chaucer's exemplum on marriage as a whole can evidently be read as an expanded ekphrasis[3] but also, and more importantly, as a treatment *of* ekphrasis. As I will show, in figuring marriage as ekphrasis and ekphrasis as marriage, Chaucer takes recourse to, and com-

---

2. Following Peter Wagner, Baltzer's arrangement can be conceptualized as an "iconotext." In his introductory essay "Ekphrasis, Iconotexts, and Intermediality—the State(s) of the Art(s)" (in *Icons, Texts, Iconotexts: Essays on Ekphrasis and Intermediality* [Berlin: de Gruyter, 1996], p. 16 [1–40]), Wagner proposes this term for works of art in which visual and verbal elements reference one another; iconotexts are "artifact[s] in which the verbal and the visual signs mingle to produce rhetoric that depends on the co-presence of words and images." Resisting the questionable but widely held assumption that text and image are two categorically separate media, an assumption promoted by Romantic notions of "intermediality," we might also speak of an intensified emblematic structure of Baltzer's *En vœux-tu en voilà.* The video installation is emblematic in the sense that the moving *picturae* turn the explanatory power of the missing *subscriptio*'s allegoresis into a vivid physiognomic expression of what drives the human psyche.

3. The foundation for such an expanded concept of ekphrasis, which transcends the boundaries of a rhetorical *descriptio* seen as an amplifying insertion in the description of an object or place within a narrative syntagma toward narrative modality, is discussed in Ruth Webb, "Ekphrasis Ancient and Modern: The Invention of a Genre," *Word and Image* 15 (1999): 7–18. Webb draws attention to the etymology of the Greek term *ek-phrazein* as "intensive" and "complete" vocalization of a set of facts. In relation to rhetorical and poetic practice within the framework of the classical tradition, this means that description and narrative are not strictly separated as they are in modern narratology. See also Webb's monograph, *Ekphrasis, Imagination and Persuasion in Ancient Rhetorical Theory and Practice* (Farnham: Ashgate, 2009), which expands on the topic.

ments on, treatments of mental images by Martianus and Apuleius. I claim that in appropriating these older texts for his purposes, Chaucer proposes to treat ekphrasis as a theater of the psyche. In examining the ways in which ekphrastic moments in the "Merchant's Tale" figure the relationship between physical expression and the psyche, it is helpful first to turn briefly to Matthew of Vendôme's treatment of ekphrasis in his *Ars versificatoria*. Matthew's *Ars* makes relevant, in particular, the nexus of inner motion and the rules of description, while it also motivates "marriage" as the conclusive allegory for this nexus.

Discussing the issue of how a person should appropriately be characterized, Matthew elaborates on the topos of ekphrasis in such a way that it not merely represents affects and passions but that it also sets those passions and affects in motion. As Matthew points out, it is the variety of a person's characteristic traits (*proprietas personarum*) and the diversity of distinctions operating within a description that primarily produce the colors of speech (*colores operum*). In this respect, any *descriptio personae* has the capacity within a given text to channel or unfold the whole repertoire of the imagination. Thus, each description may either actualize this topos in a pointed, highly condensed way (e.g., as a brief reference to a mere name and its epithet) or, by contrast, in a manner so detailed that the whole text itself is turned into a "thick description" (e.g., of a name, as in the case of Gottfried's *Tristan* or Wolfram's *Parzivâl*).[4] No matter which mode of representation— *per complicationem* or *per explicationem*—an author may prefer, by making use of ekphrasis he or she will inevitably enhance the motility of the soul and its phantasms.

In order to understand how deeply this concept of ekphrasis is connected with the idea of the motions of the inner senses, we must turn to one of Matthew of Vendôme's most striking examples: After having portrayed a pope and Caesar, he wonders how someone like Ulysses might properly be depicted—a person less known for his bodily features than for his intellectual activities in both thought and speech:

Ne sit lingua potens sensu viduata, maritat
Se linguae sensus interioris honor.
(*Ars versificatoria*, I.52, ll. 9–10)[5]

---

4. On the relation between ekphrasis and proper names, see Björn Reich: *Name und maere: Eigennamen als narrative Zentren mittelalterlicher Epik. Mit exemplarischen Einzeluntersuchungen zum* Meleranz *des Pleier,* Göttweiger Trojanerkrieg *und* Wolfdietrich D., Studien zur historischen Poetik 8 (Heidelberg: Winter, 2011), pp. 25–91.

5. Franco Munari, ed., *Mathei Vindocinensis Opera: Vol. III: Ars Versificatoria*, Storia e letteratura, Raccolta di studi e testi 171 (Roma: Edizioni di storia e letteratura, 1988).

Lest the powerful language be widowed of sensibility,
the integrity of the inner sense shall be married to his tongue.[6]

When attempting to describe Ulysses, Matthew claims, one has to correlate the character's rhetorical *actio* with his mental foundations. This, however, is only possible if the description captures the movements of his *sensus interior*. For this purpose, Matthew of Vendôme simply opens up Ulysses's cranium in order to observe what is going on in the three ventricles that, according to ancient and medieval anatomy, the human brain consists of. The look inside Ulysses's brain promises deep insights, since *Non cellae capitis in Ulixe vacant*—"the cells of Ulysses'[s] head are not vacant" (V.19). In Ulysses's head, a perceptual apparatus is shown to be at work, which combines the faculties of imagination, judgment, and memory both in an exemplary way and in outstanding perfection:

> Prima videt, media discernit, tercia servat;
> Prima capit, media iudicat, ima ligat;
> Prima serit, media recolit, metit ultima; tradit
> Prima, secunda sapit, tercia claudit iter.
> (*Ars versificatoria*, I.52, ll. 21–24)

> The first perceives, the middle one discerns, the third retains.
> The first comprehends, the middle one judges, the third unites all.
> The first sows, the middle one tills, the third reaps.
> The first reports, the middle one savors, the third holds all.[7]

The first ventricle receives the perceptions of the exterior senses, collects them, strings them together, and further processes them (*videt—capit—serit—tradit*). The second ventricle distinguishes, evaluates, and (by recollection) identifies the perceived images and decides what is worth remembering and what is not (*discernit—iudicat—recolit—sapit*). Finally, the third ventricle stores, retains, joins together, and locks up the incoming phantasms as memory images (*servat—ligat—metit—claudit iter*). These three instances of *imaginatio* (perception), *ratio* (distinction), and *memoria* (retention) constitute the main activities of the psychic apparatus and its image production.

---

6. This translation is mine; Galyon's translation "Lest his mighty tongue be divorced from sound judgement, / He weds the judgment of integrity to the words of the tongue" veils the crucial role of sense perception in this passage. Cf. Matthew of Vendôme, *The Art of Versification*, trans. Aubrey E. Galyon (Ames: Iowa State University Press, 1980), p. 38.

7. Cf. Matthew of Vendôme, *The Art of Versification*, p. 38.

As a basic perceptual structure, they are at work in every ekphrasis whose aim it is to join together speech and inner sense. It is, therefore, by no means a far-fetched metaphor when Matthew speaks of the marriage (*maritat*) of *lingua potens* and *sensus interior*. It is this metaphor that gives expression to the epistemic foundations on which every premodern poetics of ekphrasis must ultimately rest.

II.

Seen against the background of this approach to ekphrasis as a mode of producing and observing mental images, it seems unlikely that in Chaucer's "Merchant's Tale" the topic of marriage is to be understood merely in a literal sense.[8] At the surface level, however, the tale discusses the problem of whether or not a man—especially in his old age—should marry a much younger woman. This discussion proceeds on a plethora of narrative and intellectual levels. On the level of the characters, the arguments are brought forward by January, the elderly suitor, and his brothers Placebo and Justinus, whose names already reveal how the Merchant-narrator judges their attitudes towards the issue in question. Placebo tends to support his older brother's plans and backs his wish to marry (he is the yes-man of the story), while Justinus warns his brother to be extremely careful and thereby represents, as it were, a view shared by the Merchant-narrator himself, whose own marital experience seems to be far from satisfactory. A general discussion of the pleasures and terrors of marriage is followed by a description of events stretching from January's choice of his bride to his wedding and his rival's lovesickness. In the third part of the story, adultery under the eyes of a deceived spouse—a stock feature of popular farce—is staged on a pear tree in the middle of a garden of delights.

Chaucer adds a peculiar twist to his version of this widespread adultery exemplum.[9] He expands and refines the story by bringing four unequal

---

8. Nor can an allegoresis of the Bible exhaust the full scope of medieval interpretations of the marriage *topos*, even if Alexander Neckam remarks on the exegesis of the *Song of Solomon* in his *Commentum super Martianum*: "Quid ergo per Mercurium et Philologiam nisi sponsum et sponsam, id est Christum et ecclesiam, intelligimus?" (II:2, 126). See Alexander Neckam, *Commentum super Martianum*, ed. Christopher J. McDonough, Millenio medievale 64, Testi 15 (Florence: SISMEL, 2006), pp. xiii–xiv.

9. For cross-culturally handed-down analogues of the *Schemaerzählung* [schematic narrative] of the *Buhlschaft auf dem Baume* [courtship on the tree], cf. N. S. Thompson, "The Merchant's Tale," in *Sources and Analogues of the* Canterbury Tales, *Vol. II*, eds. Robert M. Correale and Mary Hamel, Chaucer Studies XXXV (Cambridge: D. S. Brewer, 2005), pp.

couples into the picture instead of merely two. In doing so, he develops a logic of much higher complexity than a simple debate on the pros and cons of late marriages involving a considerable age difference. Instead of forcing the reader to choose between Placebo's and Justinus's points of view, the expanded configuration of couples permits the use of marriage as a general concept for producing and combining ever new contradictory relations.

The first couple, old January and his young bride May, represent an alliance between impotence and sexually passive yet exceedingly libidinous virginity, following the biblical model of a "Josephite marriage."[10] At the same time, the couple's names refer to the cyclic movements of nature. Winter is joined together with spring, the end of the cycle of vegetation with its beginning, in short: death and life merge in a contradictory unity that Chaucer's tale imagines as the cycle of nature.

The second couple, consisting of the sexually frustrated May and a young, highly potent squire in January's service named Damian, commits adultery at the top of a pear tree after January, who has turned blind in the meantime, unwittingly facilitates his wife's ascent to the desired fruits by serving as a human ladder. When January's sight has miraculously been restored, his wife explains to him that the uninhibited sexual intercourse he has witnessed forms part of a magic ceremony intended to restore his vision. In this context, the name of his rival makes perfect sense: Damian is the medieval patron of physicians and pharmacists.[11] Thus, the union of Damian and May mirrors the physical flows and dynamics of sexuality and medical or magical procedures of healing.

The sudden return of January's sight is triggered, observed, and commented on by a third, in this case demonic, couple: Pluto and Proserpina. Once again, the choice of names is crucial, because their origin in mythology—Chaucer's narrator directly refers to Claudian's *De Raptu Proserpinae* ("In Claudyan ye may the stories rede," V.2232)[12]—opens up a field of communicative exchange between the world and the otherworld. On a concrete

---

479–534, and Gerd Dicke, "Das belauschte Stelldichein: Eine Stoffgeschichte," in *Der* Tristan *Gottfrieds von Straßburg.* Symposion Santiago de Compostela, April 5–8, 2000, eds. Christoph Huber and Victor Millet (Tübingen: Niemeyer, 2002), pp. 199–220.

10. See Kenneth Bleeth, "Joseph's Doubting of Mary and the Conclusion of the 'Merchant's Tale,'" *Chaucer Review* 21 (1986): 58–66.

11. See Emerson Brown, Jr., "The Merchant's Damyan and Chaucer's Kent," *Chaucer Newsletter* 13.1 (1991): 5. http://newchaucersociety.org/newsletters/

12. On Chaucer studying Claudian and the contrasting of January and May with Pluto and Proserpina being based on glosses of Claudian, see Mortimer J. Donovan, "Chaucer's January and May: Counterparts in Claudian," in *Chaucerian Problems and Perspectives: Essays Presented to Paul E. Beichner,* eds. Edward Vasta and Zacharias P. Thundy (Notre Dame, IN: University of Notre Dame Press, 1979), pp. 59–69.

level, Pluto, the god of the underworld, represents the miraculous lifting of the old man's blindness. On an allegorical level, Pluto also represents, in a pagan guise, the breakthrough of transcendence into the world. By contrast, Proserpina, bride of Hades and daughter of Demeter/Ceres, represents the principle of innerworldly sagacity,[13] a powerful wish to survive a treacherous world by virtue of betrayal and cunning—hence her bet that May will, by some means or other, find an excuse for her adultery. Miracle and salvation on the one hand, and deceit and cunning intelligence on the other, finally meet in a highly ambiguous model of religious communication and its procedures, as to be witnessed in an unholy and entirely corrupted world.

The fourth couple is not to be found on the syntagmatic axis of the narrative but appears on its paradigmatic level. Among the many learned exempla woven into the "Merchant's Tale," there is one that sticks out because it is used *in loco* of an ekphrasis explicitly omitted by the narrator. In lines 1732–37 of Fragment IV, the marriage between January and May is referred to as follows:

> Hoold thou thy pees, thou poete Marcian,
> That writest us that ilke weddyng murie
> Of hire Philologie and hym Mercurie,
> And of the songes that the Muses song!
> To smal is bothe thy penne, and eek thy tonge,
> For to descryven of this marriage.

Here, instead of claiming the status of an eyewitness, the narrator prefers quoting a learned source: the manual of the seven liberal arts *De nuptiis Philologiae et Mercurii* ('On the marriage of Philology and Mercury') by the late Roman author Martianus Capella.[14] Moreover, he uses this reference to the liberal arts for the purpose of enhancing his hyperbolic speech. Thus, he declares Martianus's encyclopedia and its abundant knowledge a document of failure compared to the task of delivering an appropriate description of a marriage such as the one between January and May. So the ekphrasis of the

---

13. Further implications of this mythical configuration are discussed in Elizabeth Simmons-O'Neill, "Love in Hell: The Role of Pluto and Proserpine in Chaucer's 'Merchant's Tale,'" *Modern Language Quarterly* 51 (1990): 389–407, as well as in Marta Powell Harley, "Chaucer's Use of the Proserpina Myth in the 'Knight's Tale' and the 'Merchant's Tale,'" in *Images of Persephone: Feminist Readings in Western Literature,* ed. Elizabeth T. Hayes (Gainesville: University Press of Florida, 1994), pp. 20–31.

14. Latin edition: James Willis, ed., *Martianus Capella* (Leipzig: Teubner, 1983). English translation: William Harris Stahl, Richard Johnson, and E. L. Burge, trans., *Martianus Capella and the Seven Liberal Arts. Vol. 2: The Marriage of Philology and Mercury* (New York: Columbia University Press, 1977).

first couple (and its unlikely union) is doubly denied: first, because of the narrator's ineptitude, and second, because even the most elaborate ekphrastic model in history would prove incapable of encompassing or even touching on the "merriness," that is to say, the feeling of elation that pervades the festivities. And yet in the end, this figure of a *mise-en-abyme*-like refusal does serve to fire the reader's imagination. It is precisely the ostentatious avoidance of the ekphrastic topos that provokes the activities of imagination, judgment, and memory. In this regard, the allusion to the marriage of Philology and Mercury can be described as a highly volatile, reversible structure, moving back and forth between blindness and insight.

The couple consisting of Mercury and Philologia thus appears to fulfill a particular function, a function reinforced by the repetition of the same narrative gesture later on in the text. Once again in the "Merchant's Tale," we witness Chaucer ostentatiously omitting an ekphrasis where one would naturally expect it. After already refraining from describing the nuptial celebrations, the narrator pointedly passes over the opportunity for a *descriptio* of January's garden of delights, the scene where deception and healing are staged in the presence of all the couples involved:

> He made a gardyn,[15] walled al with stoon;
> So fair a gardyn woot I nowher noon.
> For, out of doute, I verraily suppose
> That he that wroot the Romance of the Rose
> Ne koude of it the beautee wel devyse;
> Ne Priapus ne myghte nat suffise,
> Though he be god of gardyns, for to telle
> The beautee of the gardyn and the welle
> That stood under a laurer alwey greene.
> (ll. 2029–37)

---

15. The phrasing alludes to Gen. 2:8. Immediately after the creation of man, the narrative continues: *plantaverat autem Dominus Deus paradisum voluptatis*. Apart from the obligatory props for a scene of delight—wall, spring, greenery, and tree—any type of descriptive embellishment is lacking in Chaucer. The fact that such descriptive asceticism forms the very foundation of the imaginative productivity of the topos of the garden is attested by the popularity of the topic in Chaucer studies; see Carol Falvo Heffernan, "Wells and Streams in Three Chaucerian Gardens," in *Papers on Literature and Language* 15 (1979): 339–57; Valerie S. Roberts, "Ironic Reversal of Expectations in Chaucerian and Shakespearean Gardens," in *Chaucerian Shakespeare: Adaptation and Transformation: A Collection of Essays*, eds. E. Talbot Donaldson and Judith J. Kollmann (Detroit: Fifteenth-Century Symposium, Marygrove College, 1983), pp. 97–117, as well as Laura L. Howes, *Chaucer's Gardens and the Language of Convention* (Gainesville: University Press of Florida, 1997).

So after the marriage and its unspeakable joy, the garden in its indescribable beauty represents the second of the potential settings that remains visually inaccessible. If even the author of the *Roman de la Rose* has to fall silent, this signals that the most intense stirrings of the human emotions lie outside the limits of representation. After all, it was Guillaume de Lorris's *descriptio* of the spring of Narcissus that famously enlarged upon and outdid Ovid's attempt at mirroring the moment of the first erotic flaring-up of an untouched soul in the *locus amoenus*. If even Priapus—the phallic god of gardens—is rendered speechless, then the desire that overwhelms and propels the bodies of those who sojourn at this particular place outstretches the limits of what can actually be imagined. By activating the topos of the garden in analogy to the topos of marriage via the omission of ekphrasis, Chaucer retroactively makes clear what distinguishes Martianus's couple from all the other couples from the Old Testament or Ovid's *Metamorphoses*, which have been presented in exemplary fashion: its implicit allegorical relation to the psychic principles of perception, which every literary description is first and foremost obliged to pay respect to.

III.

My survey of the four different couples in Chaucer's "Merchant's Tale" highlights the central aspect of the story. As each of the couples turns out to embody some form of contradictory relations, it becomes evident that the text's reference to marriage is not a reference to a mere social phenomenon. Rather, marriage is discussed in terms of a general poetic structure as unequal and opposed elements are united through an ekphrastic mode.[16] The paradoxical images thus generated—images of life and death, sexuality and healing, salvation and deceit, insight and delusion—can be understood as configurations of physical and psychic movements, be it the cycle of nature or a regen-

---

16. In his essay "The Body in Some Middle High German *Mären:* Taming and Maiming" (in *Framing Medieval Bodies,* eds. Sarah Kay and Miri Rubin [Manchester: Manchester University Press, 1994], pp. 187–210), Mark Chinca states the following reason for the preference of marriage stories in popular farce: "Marriage is where centre and periphery meet, the institution in which women are made subject to men in accordance with the biblical teaching that the husband is the head of the wife (Eph. 5:22–24). . . . But marriage is also where the distinction between centre and periphery, lord and subject, is lost. Paul writes in another epistle that 'the wife hath not power of her own body, but her husband: and likewise also the husband hath not power of his own body, but the wife' (1 Cor. 7:4); this was the basis of the canonists' insistence that in marriage husband and wife were completely equal in their right to demand the conjugal debt" (pp. 203–4).

eration accelerated by erotically charged magic and medicine, be it religious communication or the theories of cognition and perception. In this perspective, Chaucer's exemplum on marriage as a whole can be read as an expanded ekphrasis: it describes the elementary distinctions that—for characters and readers alike—establish the perceived world as a theater of irreconcilable contradictions.

To this end, on the syntagmatic axis of his narrative, the narrator treats the matter (*materia*) of his exemplum in an explicative way by putting on display the elements both of the internal and the external process of perception and by demonstrating the principles of how they operate. Accordingly, January's search for the right bride is described as an imaginative process, an interplay of imagination and curiosity within his soul/heart, in the course of which the aged suitor creates the image of his wife-to-be as an erotic phantasm:

> Heigh fantasye and curious bisynesse
> Fro day to day gan in the soule impresse
> Of Januarie aboute his marriage.
> Many fair shap and many fair visage
> Ther passeth thurgh his herte nyght by nyght,
> As whoso tooke a mirour, polisshed bryght,
> And sette it in a commune market-place,
> Thanne sholde he se ful many a figure pace
> By his mirour; and in the same devyse
> Gan Januarie inwith his thoght devyse
> Of maydens whiche that dwelten hym bisyde.
> (ll. 1577–87)

Dream and mirror supply the psychic and physical model of internalization, causing the observed "maydens" to develop from the stage of being perceived as physical shapes ("shap," "visage," "figure") to forming mental impressions ("in the soule impresse") and thoughts circling around them ("inwith his thoght"). January keeps moving them "thurgh his herte" until he passes judgement "bitwixe ernest and game" (l. 1594) and makes his choice.[17]

Not only does Chaucer depict the internal processes, a depiction culminates in the omitted ekphrasis which should have described the marriage of January and May, but he also shows the procedures of external perception. May's explanation for January's discovery of the adultery committed in the

---

17. On the role of medieval psychology and the meaning of internal images in Chaucer, cf. Carolyn P. Collette: *Species, Phantasms, and Images: Vision and Medieval Psychology in The Canterbury Tales* (Ann Arbor: University of Michigan Press, 2001).

pear tree moves the emphasis from a magical deception towards an optical one, from imagination towards illusion:

> But, sire, a man that waketh out of his sleep,
> He may nat sodeynly wel taken keep
> Upon a thyng, ne seen it parfitly,
> Til that he be adawed verraily.
> Right so a man that longe hath blynd ybe,
> Ne may nat sodeynly so wel yse,
> First whan his sighte is newe come ageyn,
> As he that hath a day or two yseyn.
> Til that youre sighte ysatled be a while
> Ther may ful many a sighte yow bigile . . .
> Beth war, I prey yow, for by hevene kyng,
> Ful many a man weneth to seen a thyng,
> And it is al another than it semeth.
> He that mysconceyveth, he mysdemeth.
> (ll. 2397–410)

As Peter Brown has shown, in this passage Chaucer reworks knowledge deriving from medieval compendia (Vincent of Beauvais, Bartholomeus Anglicus) and from specialized treatises on optics (Alhazen, Vitulon). By having May quote the physiological laws governing perfect and debilitated vision in January's Garden of Eden, of all places, Chaucer gives them an allegorical frame in which January's physical blindness is testament to his inner blindness, so that far from opening his eyes, the miraculous return of his vision only renders his delusion more obvious:

> He is never more blind than when his sight is restored and May is able to persuade him that his eyes do not see the truth. They do, but January no longer knows what the truth is. Outer and inner blindness have become as one.[18]

At the same time, it is precisely here, at a point where external and internal blindness coincide, that the narrative's brilliant awareness of the principles of

---

18. Peter Brown, *Chaucer and the Making of Optical Space* (Oxford: Peter Lang, 2007), p. 160. On the pathology of vision in the "Merchant's Tale," see also James M. Palmer, "Your Malady Is 'No Sodeyn Hap': Ophthalmology, Benvenutus Grassus, and January's Blindness," in *Chaucer Review* 41 (2006): 197–205. On the epistemological framework of seeing in Chaucer, see Suzanne Conklin Akbari, *Seeing through the Veil: Optical Theory and Medieval Allegory* (Toronto: University of Toronto Press, 2004).

how the world is perceived both internally and externally becomes manifest. As a kind of totalized ekphrasis, the narrative continuously draws attention to its own (precarious) truth conditions and locates its fictional world in a conceptual frame of physical and mental perception, both of which the tale as a whole shows "in action," that is, in their intrinsic and extrinsic aspects.[19]

Moreover, on the paradigmatic axis, the narrative deploys the mode of *complicatio*. The process of imagination is deepened by merely alluding to ekphrastic *topoi*, which, while remaining undeveloped as far as their argumentative function is concerned, either operate latently and tacitly, or are permitted to rest altogether. In the final step of my argument, I would like to examine more closely the ways in which the topos of marriage might possibly serve to envision such a process. Thus I shall now turn to a more detailed reconstruction of the marriage topos, whose importance in the text, as we have already seen, is especially reinforced by Chaucer's reference to Martianus Capella.

Capella's *De nuptiis Philologiae et Mercurii* is known as a manual of the *septem artes liberales* from late antiquity. Written in the first half of the fifth century in the Numidian city of Madaura, it reaches medieval Europe via Irish monks who made use of it in the context of the so-called Carolingian Renaissance.[20] In this period, the work was already commented on and glossed,[21] and from the twelfth century onwards new copious commentaries

19. This *coincidentia oppositorum* is also evidenced by the fact that Damian's access to January's *hortus conclusus* is made possible by a duplicate key, which owes its existence to a wax print of the original obtained by May: "This fresshe May, that I spak of so yoore, / In warm wax hath emprented the clyket / That januarie bar of the smale wyket, / By which into the gardyn ofte he wente; / And Damyan, that knew al hire entente, / The cliket countrefeted pryvely" (ll. 2116–21). If the external technical procedure is read as an element of a *descriptio* and *tota allegoria* of internal perception, then the *impressio* that unlocks Damian's soul to the erotic phantasm is repeated here in that the narrator alludes to the traditional model of pneumophantasmology used by Plato and Aristotle: external perceptions impress themselves into the substance of the soul like a seal into viscous wax.

20. For a general overview, see Sonja Glauch, "Martianus Capella und die septem artes liberales," in *Die Martianus-Capella-Bearbeitung Notkers des Deutschen*. Münchner Texte und Untersuchungen zur deutschen Literatur des Mittelalters 116, 2 vols. (Tübingen: Niemeyer, 2000), vol. 1, p. 20 [15–25]. Christopher J. McDonough provides a concise summary of the commentary tradition on *De Nuptiis* in his edition of Alexander Neckam's *Commentum super Martianum* (pp. xvii–xxviii), where he states succinctly: "The different cultural and intellectual dynamics of the following centuries moved the spotlight to the introductory mythos of the allegory. From the eleventh to the fourteenth centuries the first two books of the *De Nuptiis* more often than not circulated as a free standing work [. . .] that presented the classical pantheon, decked out in glorious mythological and cosmological dress" (p. xx). On the history of reception of Martian, see also the Italian edition: Ilaria Ramelli, ed. and trans., *Marziano Capella: Le nozze di Filologia e Mercurio: Testo latino a fronte* (Milano: Bompiani, 2001), pp. 1013–67.

21. Cf. Cora E. Lutz, ed., *Johannes Scotti Annotationes in Marcianum*, The Medieval Academy of America Publications 34 (Cambridge, MA: Medieval Academy of America,

were produced that paid special attention to the allegorical and integumental uses of ancient mythology.[22] But already in the eleventh century, Notker of St. Gall wrote an Old High German paraphrase of *De nuptiis*,[23] based on the commentary by Remigius of Auxerre.[24] It is remarkable that Notker—like quite a number of medieval scribes and commentators on Martian's text—does not show any interest in Books III to IX in which personifications of each of the seven liberal arts allegorically present the thematic content of their respective disciplines to the bride Philologia as a dowry. Instead, he singles out the first two books, which are about Mercury's attempts to find a wife and Philologia's preparations for her wedding and her apotheosis. Form and content of these two books are commented on by the first-person narrator with the claim that Satura herself concocted the story: thus, before the thematic concerns of the *artes* are expounded, their epistemological basis is reflected upon in the form of a Menippean Satire.[25]

At the beginning of Book I, Mercury starts looking for a bride, following the example of other deities' *sacra coniugia* (Mart. I.3). In the process, he has to acknowledge that all the women he himself would have preferred have already been given away or are otherwise inaccessible: Sophia, who grew up with his sister Minerva, has decided to remain a *virgo intacta;* Mantike, the personification of prophecy, is already allied to Apollo; and Psyche, introduced as the daughter of Sol and Entelechia, has been caught by the spell of

---

1939) and Cora E. Lutz, ed., *Dunchad: Glossae in Martianum,* Philological Monographs XII (Lancaster, PA: American Philological Association, 1944); on Carolingian glosses, see Sinéad O'Sullivan, ed., *Glossae aevi Carolini in libros I-II Martiani Capellae De nvptiis Philologiae et Mercvrii,* Corpvs Christianorum, Continuatio mediaevalis 237 (Turnhout: Brepols, 2010) as well as Mariken Teeuwen and Sinéad O'Sullivan, eds., *Carolingian Scholarship and Martianus Capella: The Oldest Commentary Tradition.* Digital Edition, 1st ed. (2008), *Huygens Instituut—eLaborate,* http://martianus.huygens.knaw.nl/path.

22. Cf. Haijo Jan Westra, ed., *The Commentary on Martianus Capella's De nuptiis Philologiae et Mercurii attributed to Bernhardus Silvestris* (Toronto: Pontifical Institute of Mediaeval Studies, 1986) and Haijo Jan Westra, ed., *The Berlin Commentary on Martianus Capella's De Nuptiis Philologiae et Mercurii,* Mittellateinische Studien und Texte XX/XXIII, 2 vols. (Leiden: Brill, 1994-98), as well as Neckam, *Commentum super Martianum.*

23. Cf. Notker der Deutsche, *Martianus Capella De nuptiis Philologiae et Mercurii,* eds. James C. King and Petrus Wilhelmus Tax, Die Werke Notkers des Deutschen 4, Altdeutsche Textbibliothek 87 (Tübingen: Niemeyer, 1979) and Evelyn Scherabon Firchow, Richard Hotchkiss, and Rick Treece, eds., *Notker der Deutsche von St. Gallen, Die Hochzeit der Philologie und des Merkur—De nuptiis Philologiae et Mercurii von Martianus Capella. Diplomatischer Textabdruck, Konkordanzen und Wortlisten nach dem Codex Sangallensis 872,* 2 vols. (Hildesheim: Olms, 1999).

24. Cf. Cora E. Lutz, ed., *Remigii Autissiodorensis Commentum in Martianum Capellam. Libri I-II* (Leiden: Brill, 1962).

25. On the question of genre, see Danuta Shanzer, *A Philosophical and Literary Commentary on Martianus Capella's De Nuptiis Philologiae et Mercurii Book I,* University of California Publications, Classical Studies 32 (Berkeley: University of California Press, 1986), pp. 29-44.

Amor. The divine interpreter (*interpres . . . meae mentis* and *nous sacer,* in the words of Jupiter) is thus denied direct access not only to divine *intellectus* and general knowledge concerning the world but also to the human soul. This is why Mercury's brother Apollo strongly recommends the assiduous *virgo docta* Philologia as a substitute and intermediary.[26] In chapters 6 and 7, this substitution is stressed once more by a juxtaposition of Philologia and Psyche. Anticipating the donations to Philologia in the later books, Martianus describes in detail the gifts Psyche is furnished with at her birthday by all the gods of the pantheon: Jupiter crowns her with the diadem of *aeternitas*; Juno adds a golden wedding band to her locks (Notker interprets this as the band of *ratio* that ties together the "hair of virtue"); Pallas fits the virgin with a small veil and a breastband of crimson (Notker again glosses their meaning: wisdom and temperance); Apollo shows her signs of his divinatory and conjectural capacities; Urania presents a mirror that will help Psyche to recognize herself and discover her origin; Vulcanus lights a fire for her that can never be extinguished, the inner fire of her intellect, as Notker puts it; and, finally, Venus equips her with the power of sensuality:

> Omnes vero illecebras circa sensus cunctos apposuit Aphrodite; nam et unguentis oblitam floribusque redimtam halatu pasci fouerique docuerat et melle permulserat et auro ac monare membraque uinciri honorationis celsae affectatione persuaserat. Tunc crepitacula tinnitusque, quis infanti somnum duceret, adhibebat quiesenti. Praeterea ne ullum tempus sine illecebra oblectamentisque decurreret, pruritui subscalpentem circa ima corporis apposuerat uoluptatem.

> Aphrodite added every allure for all the senses. For she had taught her once she was bathed in ointments and crowned with flowers to be nourished and soothed by their breath, and had soothed her with honey, and had persuaded her to gape at gold bracelets, and to put them round her arms in her striving for high esteem. Then Venus added rattles and bells so that she might bring sleep to the resting child. And furthermore, lest any time

---

26. For a discussion of the role of Philologia in comparison with the three other female deities, see Shanzer, *Philosophical and Literary Commentary,* pp. 65–67. Shanzer's suggestion "that she represents the soul of the adept at theurgy or the hieratic arts" (p. 66) underlines Philologia's role as mirror image of the soul. However, a simple identification—"Philologia is Psyche" (p. 70)—seems problematic because the instrumental knowledge of the *artes* that are given to the bride of Mercury clearly mark the difference to Psyche's spiritual and sensual gifts. Remigius of Auxerre's medieval interpretation seems more convincing here: Mercury is interpreted as the personification of *sermo* (speech), Philologia as the personification of *ratio* (reason); cf. Glauch, *Martianus-Capella-Bearbeitung,* vol. 1, p. 253.

should pass without enticement and amusement, she appointed Pleasure to scratch at the itching in the lower portions of the anatomy.[27]

Despite following the rhetorical rules, proceeding from tip to toe, this *descriptio personae* is arrested as soon as it arrives at the seat of sexuality. This sudden interruption is Martianus's way of addressing the double nature of the soul that constantly moves between *rationalitas* and *sensualitas*.[28] The complete setting of the perceptual apparatus is finally imagined by Martianus in the last gift that Hermes/Mercury submits to his beloved Psyche in accordance with his swift comprehension and intelligence:

> [MARTIAN:] But it was Cyllenius himself who gave Psyche a vehicle and flying wheels to run with a miraculous speed, even though Memoria weighed her down and bound her with golden shackles.[29]

> [NOTKER:] Aber selber íro sûocho gáb íro rêit-uuágen mít trâten réderen ûfen démo sî spûotigo fáren máhti Uuánda íro uuíllo uuírt spûotigo gezúcchet êina uuîla ad celestia ánder uuîla ad terrestria. . . . Día snélli gáb er íro doh sia dea memoria mít cúldinen drúhen héftendo suârti. Uuánda daz anima in mûot kenímet táz kebíndet unde gestâtet memoria fílo tîurlicho.

> But her suitor himself gave her a chariot with fast wheels on which she could ride speedily; for her will is swiftly torn hither and thither, either towards the celestial or towards the earthly. . . . He gave her speed even though the goddess Memory bound her with golden fetters and made her heavy; for whatever the soul perceives is bound and fixed in the most exquisite way by memory.[30]

What, then, is the role of this "chariot with fast wheels" (*rêit-uuágen mít trâten réderen*) travelling at a pace that, as Notker knows, corresponds to

---

27. Shanzer, *Philosophical and Literary Commentary*, p. 204.

28. Cf. Georg Heinrich Bode, ed., "Tertius Vaticanus Mythographus," in *Scriptores rerum mythicarum latini tres Romae nuper reperti*, (1834, repr. Hildesheim: Olms, 1968), III, 6,16, p. 182 [pp. 152–256]: "Animae autem duae sunt vires, una superior, altera inferior. Animae superior vis caelestibus adhaeret et incorruptibilibus, et illa concupiscit, vocaturque rationalitas, spiritus, domina, mens, animus. Inferior est, quae voluptatibus corporis consentit, vocaturque sensualitas, animalitas, famula, mens."

29. Shanzer, *Philosophical and Literary Commentary*, p. 204.

30. My translation based on Glauch's modern German translation of the Old German. Cf. Sonja Glauch, *Die Martianus-Capella-Bearbeitung Notkers des Deutschen. Vol. II: Übersetzung von Buch I und Kommentar*. Münchner Texte und Untersuchungen zur deutschen Literatur des Mittelalters 116 (Tübingen: Niemeyer, 2000), p. 340.

the speed at which the will of the soul alternately surges upwards (*ad celes-tia*) and downwards (*ad terrestria*)? The image draws on the concept of the chariot of the soul (*óchēma*), a concept that emerged in the melting pot of North African syncretism and combines elements of the Platonic doctrine of the ascent of souls to a vision of ideas with astrological thinking, the latter of which addressed the soul's passage through the planetary spheres.[31] The significance of this traffic of souls between the terrestrial and the celestial sphere, between microcosm and macrocosm, is twofold. First, the image's syncretism makes it possible to conflate the notion of the soul's chariot with the notion of *pneuma* central to the Aristotelian model of perception. Aristotle conceives of *pneuma* as serving as a medium of communication between the exterior and interior worlds, and therefore also between the stellar sphere and interior images. Second, the chariot of the soul in its func-tion as medium between the outer and inner worlds is connected to Platonic demonology and concepts of eros. Both aspects, the soul as seen in the light of perceptual psychology and in terms of an erotomagical perspective, char-acterize the topos of marriage from Martianus Capella onwards, lending it the particular depth that Chaucer invokes with his ekphrastic omission. Cru-cially, both aspects taken together constitute the perception of the world by the soul as a *theatrum amoris*.

To fully comprehend the narrative function of the *theatrum amoris* as employed by Chaucer, it will be necessary to discuss briefly two authors who both lived in Martianus's hometown and whose work served as a foil for the *De nuptiis:* Augustine (354–430 BC), teacher of rhetoric in Madaura, and Lucius Apuleius (125–180 BC), whose *Metamorphoses* contain the *fabula* "Amor and Psyche," the counterpart to the first two books of the *Marriage of Philology and Mercury*.

IV.

"What, after all, is a demon?" This is a question Augustine raises in Book VIII, chapter 14 of his *De civitate dei,* where he reconstructs the demonol-ogy of his day on the basis of Apuleius's treatise on *The God of Sokrates* (*De deo Socratis*)[32]: "Di excelsissimum locum tenent, homines infimum, daemones

---

31. Cf. Ioan P. Couliano, *Eros and Magic in the Renaissance*, trans. Margaret Cook (Chi-cago: University of Chicago Press, 1987), pp. 53–58.

32. Claudio Moreschini, ed., *Apulei Platonici Madaurensis opera quae supersunt. Vol. III: De philosophia libri* (Leipzig: Teubner, 1991). Cf. the English translation of "On the God of Socrates" by Stephen Harrison in *Apuleius. Rhetorical Works*, ed. Stephen Harrison, trans.

medium. Nam deorum sedes in caelo est, hominum in terra, in aere dae-monum." [The gods occupy the most exalted region, men the lowest, and demons a region between the two. The gods dwell in heaven, men on earth, and demons in the air].[33] The demons' intermediate position becomes evident by the fact that they inhabit the air between the gods in heaven and mankind on earth. Moreover, they share their immortal bodies with the gods but their sensibility and passions with men. As a consequence of this, they are pleased, according to Augustine, by the *ludorum oscenitatibus et poetarum figmentis*, whereas gods are above that kind of obscenity, because they are good and sublime par excellence. In other words, not only are demons susceptible to the phantasms of poetry, theater, and painting, but, moreover, they belong to the same realm of pneumophantasmology (Agamben) in which they are at work as agents for the better or for worse. This is precisely the philosophi-cal pattern at work in the tale of Amor and Psyche. The human soul, whose beauty is embodied in the princess Psyche to such an extent that she rivals Venus and her cult, fascinates Amor who is subject to strong affects. Thus, in Apuleius, Amor-Cupido is nothing else but a demon: He moves through the air on wings and shoots feathered arrows without, however, being immune against their poison and the sexual attraction of Psyche. As a pneumatic entity he is invisible to the soul he communicates with. After he has married Psyche, he sleeps with her under the condition that she will not catch sight of him. Psyche is persuaded by her envious sisters to break his taboo because they tell her that she is having intercourse with a monster that is going to swallow her unless she cuts off her sleeping groom's head *post coitum*.

Of course, problems arise as soon as Amor's identity is uncovered. In the light of the lamp, Psyche recognizes her husband's beauty. At the same moment, she hurts herself with one of his arrows and burns his shoulder with oil pouring out of the lamp. Amor disappears without a word. The rest of the tale relates her growing agony in the absence of Amor, tells of Venus's retali-ations culminating in Psyche's eventual passage through death, and brings us to the happy ending, the marriage of the couple under the auspices of Jupiter. Thus, the tale follows the Platonic structure of the soul's ascent, descent, and re-ascent, as it was signified by the image of the *óchēma* in Martian and Not-ker's comment on the Psyche passage. The end of the tale consists of a short ekphrasis of the marriage and of the news about the birth of Amor's and Psyche's daughter, named Voluptas.

Stephen Harrison, John Hilton, and Vincent Hunink (Oxford: Oxford University Press, 2001), p. 185–221.

33. Augustine, *The City of God Against the Pagans. Vol. III: Books VIII-XI*, trans. David S. Wiesen (Cambridge, MA: Harvard University Press, 1988), pp. 62–63.

Crucial for a reading of "Amor and Psyche" is, however, the fabula's specific contextualization: it is inserted into the adventures of Lucius who metamorphoses into an ass after his beloved has given him the wrong magic potion. This narrative frame connects the movement of the soul in "Amor and Psyche" with the notion that the soul can be misled and manipulated by eros and magic. Ioan P. Couliano defines the relation between eros and magic as follows: "The workings of phantasy in the Renaissance are more or less complex: eroticism is the most important, already apparent in the natural world without human intervention. Magic is merely eroticism applied, directed, and aroused by its performer."[34] By making use of eros the magician exerts influence on the perceptual apparatus and governs the mental images, the phantasmata, *ad libitum*. This results in the notion of a different Amor, who resembles the ancient cosmogonic Eros, even though the world he creates is a purely phantasmatic one. Yet at the same time, this phantasmatic world is the only form of reality that the soul is capable of perceiving. As Aristotle puts it: *diò oudépote noeî áneu phantásmatos hē psychē* (De anima 431a 16–17), or in the words of Thomas Aquinas: *intelligere sine conversione ad phantasmata est praeter naturam [animae]* (Summa theologiae, I, qu. 89, art. 1): "to understand without taking recourse to phantasms is beyond the nature of the soul."[35]

Against this background, it becomes evident what Chaucer makes us see by ostentatiously skipping the ekphrasis of the marriage between Januarius and May and forcefully evoking the depth of the topos "marriage." To put it more precisely: the gap marked out by the narrator's reference to the wedding of Mercury and Philologia is not simply a textual lacuna. Instead, it constitutes an *ou-topos* that must remain vacant and thereby allows us to consider the "Merchant's Tale" to be ekphrastic *in toto*. The paradigm of Martianus's "Marriage" opens up the phantasmatic space that is inhabited by the three other couples that constitute the syntagma of the tale and move the reader to imagine a coherent, but altogether contradictory, world. By touching on the different discursive aspects of nature, medicine, magic, and demonology, the look into the depth of the topos ultimately produces an insight into the soul that must otherwise remain inaccessible to direct visual scrutiny. Chaucer's narrative thus achieves the virtually impossible. By alluding to the power of ekphrasis to allegorically represent the link between the inner motions of the psyche and the sensing of the outside world, the "Merchant's Tale" presents to us the soul's animated portrait as the "soul of ekphrasis."

---

34. Couliano, *Eros and Magic*, p. xviii.
35. My translation.

Chapter 12

EKPHRASIS, TROPE OF THE REAL; OR, WHAT THE *PEARL*-DREAMER SAW

Larry Scanlon

KEEPING IT REAL

Fifteen years into this most uncertain century, it seems safe to say the real has returned. Or perhaps it has just swung back into view as an object of desire. The power of the linguistic turn, for more than fifty years so dominant in nearly every field of humanistic inquiry, has faded. In its place: a "reality hunger," as the title of the novelist David Shields's recent manifesto would have it. More concerned with the broader culture than with academia per se, Shields focuses on such things as reality TV, the new fascination with the memoir—in particular, the spate of counterfeit memoirs and the scandal surrounding them—webcams and blogs, newsiness, Facebook, MySpace, Twitter, hip-hop, Sarah Silverman, and *Kathy Griffin: My Life on the D-List*. Shields recognizes the radical incoherence of reality hunger, but one of the charms of his manifesto is that he embraces it wholeheartedly anyway. He is a little like Octave Mannoni's fetishist: *je sais mais quand même*. "Don't waste your time," Shields urges, "get to the real thing." "Sure," he continues, "what's 'real'? Still, try to get to it."[1] Yet,

---

1. David Shields, *Reality Hunger: A Manifesto* (New York: Knopf, 2010), p. 47.

one can find similar trends in more sophisticated and specialized quarters, and without much trace of Shields's self-effacing sense of irony. Slavoj Žižek's "Introduction" to *The Sublime Object of Ideology,* his first collection to be published in English, provides a prominent early instance. In this version of getting to the real, Žižek rejects both Habermas and most of poststructuralism with the warning, "We must not obliterate the distance separating the Real from its symbolization."[2] More recently, one can cite the philosophical and theoretical trend known as speculative realism, the most thoroughgoing and rigorous of attempts to get to the real. There are lots of others, including in no particular order: thing theory, the return of Bergson and phenomenlogists like Merleau-Ponty, cultural and literary uses of cognitive and evolutionary psychology, the digital humanities, various strands in book history and manuscript studies, and the return of an older historicism with its insistence on the historical record as the anchor for cultural meanings rather than a point of departure. Even the renewed interest in visual culture (in spite of its roots in film theory, semiotics, and Lacanian psychoanalysis) increasingly busies itself with getting to the real. Finally and most recently, there is Frederic Jameson's *The Antinomies of Realism.* A magisterial study by that most magisterial of figures, *The Antinomies of Realism* is a comparative work in the grand style. As it happens, the work also resonates throughout with suggestive echoes of medieval literature and modern medieval scholarship, including a sustained engagement with Jameson's own teacher, the great Erich Auerbach.

The trope of ekphrasis, conventionally defined as a written account of a picture, provides a well-situated window into these developments. If, as Žižek urges, the "the distance separating the Real from its symbolization" must never be obliterated, it is equally the case that the ubiquity of the symbol can never ultimately be evaded. Ekphrasis is a trope that figures this double necessity. It ostentatiously declares its linguistic essence in the course of striving to get closer to the real. It is a trope that takes its job to be to symbolize the distance between symbol and the real in its very irreducibility. As Murray Krieger has argued, ekphrasis finds its motivation in "the semiotic desire for the natural sign, the desire, that is, to have the world captured in the word, the word that belongs to it, or better yet, the word to which it belongs."[3] This "semiotic desire" to capture "the world in the word" is a desire to capture the world as word—to capture the two at once, the *signum* as well as the *res,* to hold on to the difference that gives rise to the *signum,* even as one transcends

---

2. Slavoj Žižek, *The Sublime Object of Ideology* (London: Verso, 1989), p. 3.

3. Murray Krieger, *Ekphrasis: The Illusion of the Natural Sign* (Baltimore: Johns Hopkins University Press, 1992), p. 11.

that difference to reach the *res*. Ekphrasis figures the urge to get to the real as itself semiotic in origin. This essay will explore the relation of this figure to realism and this urge to get to the real. I want in particular to explore the problem's historical and temporal dimension and to suggest that modern idealizations of "the real" owe a good deal to the theological traditions of a medieval past they often see themselves as disavowing. I have chosen a peculiarly literal instance of Krieger's synecdoche, an ekphrasis of the Divine Word from the end of the Middle English poem *Pearl*. But I want to read this text through "L'effet de réel," or "The Reality Effect," of Roland Barthes. Written just as the linguistic turn was reaching its zenith, this essay remains the most searching and rigorous analysis of the semiotics of modern realism. It thus offers a linguistic challenge to the current return to realism that the latter has yet fully to meet.

Almost universally, literary scholarship has viewed realism as a modern phenomenon. That has included medievalists no less than modernists. Thus, in his monumental elegy to medieval culture, Johan Huizinga made a "scrupulous realism," an "aspiration to render exactly all natural details . . . the characteristic feature of the spirit of the expiring Middle Ages." Similarities to later forms of realism were purely illusory. This realism was the product of a "primitive . . . hyperidealist mentality" and "a sign of decline and not of rejuvenation."[4] Huizinga's definitive dismissal seems to have hindered subsequent explorations of late medieval interest in the mimetic, and yet the question persists, even if it rarely attracts sustained or rigorous attention. Curtius also viewed late medieval poetry as radically antimimetic in the realist sense and even cited the period's widespread use of ekphrasis as evidence of this antirealist strain. He notes dryly that ekphrastic accounts of landscape in medieval poetry

> have as little to do with observation of nature as Ekkehart's graces have to do with monastery cooking. Whether the species enumerated could all occur together in one forest, the poet does not care and does not need to care. . . . The ideal of this late rhetorical poetry is richness of décor and an elaborate vocabulary.[5]

Taken on their own terms, both Huizinga and Curtius were largely right. Late medieval poetry relied heavily on traditional rhetorical forms, and it often

---

4. Johan Huizinga, *The Waning of the Middle Ages: A Study of the Forms of Life, Thought and Art in France and the Netherlands in the XIVth and XVth Centuries,* trans. F. Hopman (London: Edward Arnold, 1924), pp. 199, 253, and more generally 182–296.

5. Ernst Robert Curtius, *European Literature and the Latin Middle Ages,* trans. Willard R. Trask (Princeton, NJ: Princeton University Press, 1953), p. 195.

exhibited "a hyperidealist mentality"—though rarely a "primitive" one. Nevertheless, while some serviceability may still remain in such home truths, it is high time we confront the conventional notions underlying them. These are a combination of overly positivist understandings of realism and mimesis, as well as binary, essentialist understandings of the difference between medieval and modern.

Modern writing may strike us as more immediate, as somehow closer to lived experience than its medieval counterpart, but that cannot be on the basis of some putative freedom from rhetorical forms. Ekphrasis provides a particularly compelling demonstration of this too rarely acknowledged fact. Modern novels resort to this trope all the time. Allow me to cite just a few of the most famous instances: *A Picture of Dorian Gray,* the newspaper headlines in *Ulysses,* Lily Briscoe's painting in *To the Lighthouse,* the optometrist's billboard in *The Great Gatsby,* and more recently, the double ekphrasis that opens DeLillo's *Underworld*: A fanciful retelling of the 1951 National League playoff between the New York Giants and the Brooklyn Dodgers, the opening ends with J. Edgar Hoover, his shoes covered with Jackie Gleason's vomit, puzzling over a magazine reproduction of Breughel's *Garden of Earthly Delights*. And that's only the novels. Where would twentieth-century American poetry be without the poem about a picture or other visual construct? It has practically become a compulsory figure. Again, just to cite a few of the most famous: *The Bridge*, "The Man with a Blue Guitar," "At the Musée des Beaux Arts," William Carlos Williams's "Pictures from Breughel," Elizabeth Bishop's "Man-Moth," Adrienne Rich's "Snapshots of a Dutiful Daughter-in-Law," and Ashbery's "Self-Portrait in a Convex Mirror."

Literary scholars have been slow to recognize modern realism's paradoxical dependence on rhetorical convention because such a recognition flies in the face of modernity's most cherished beliefs about itself, namely that it distinguishes itself from the past by its rejection of all idealizations and by its clear-eyed confrontation with reality in its essence. However, as a brief look at the philological evidence suggests, this form of modern self-identification represents less a break with the medieval past than a curious kind of fulfillment. The real derives ultimately from the Latin *realis,* a postclassical adjective itself ultimately deriving from the noun *res,* or thing. The *OED* notes that the Latin word is common in British sources from the twelfth century onward and stresses its use in legal contexts both in Latin and in French and Anglo Norman to refer to things as opposed to people. Its first application seems to have been grammatical, referring to tenses and constructions that indicate actual events as opposed to possible ones. By the time of the scholastics this sense began to be associated with the Eucharist. Aquinas, for instance, uses *realis* and *realiter* liberally in his discussion of the sacrament in the *Summa Theologica*. The usage would ultimately be enshrined in the dogmatic phrase, the Real Presence. It is thus fitting that earliest citation for the adjective in English is also Eucharistic, probably from the end of the fourteenth century but possibly from as early as that century's first quarter. It occurs in *Meditations on the Supper of Our Lord and the Hours of the Passion,* a verse adaptation of the Bonaventure's *Meditationes vitae Christi*:

> Þys soper was real as þou mayst here,
> Foure real þynges cryst made þere.
>
> . . . .
>
> Þe fyrst ys a bodly fedyng,
> Þe secunde ys hys dycyples fete wasshyng,
> Þe þred yn brede hym self takyng,
> Þe fourþe a sermoun of feyre makyng.[6]

Obviously, we cannot draw a single line from such densely theological applications to the modern notion of the real. But it seems even more unlikely that there is no influence at all. The connection certainly helps explain both the authority of this notion and its aspiration to self-evidence. It is not just that Christianity understands its God as the Word, the transcendental signifier, or even that this Word, this pre-eminent *signum,* is simultaneously the pre-eminent *res.* It is the way this cosmic pre-eminence can become ritually available in a banal piece of bread. If for the purposes of analysis, we bracket the Eucharist's complex theological meanings and look at it purely as a signifying structure, we will find it bears a rough resemblance to Lacan's *petit objet a,* a fragment of a transcendent totality that can somehow maintain its connection to the totality's transcendent power. And that may help to explain how the modern notion of the real retains a residual yearning for a form of authority generally taken as antithetical to it. Transubstantiation produces a subject without accidents—a logical monstrosity, John Wyclif complained with a certain amount of justification. But as a spectacle it works by investing an accident, the outward form of the consecrated wafer,

---

6. J. Meadows Cooper, ed., *Meditations on the Supper of Our Lord, and the Hours of the Passion, by Cardinal John Bonaventura* (London: Trübner & Co., 1875), p. 2 (ll. 33–34 and 39–42). This work occurs in three manuscripts, the earliest of which is London, British Library MS, Harley 1701, dating from 1400. In this manuscript, it follows a copy of *Handlyng Synne,* leading Cooper to speculate that Robert Manning might have been the translator. Though there is no other evidence to support this possibility, that would obviously place the date of its appearance before 1330.

with transcendent significance. Shields describes reality hunger at one point as seeking "the lure and blur of the real," which he characterizes as "randomness, openness to accident and serendipity, spontaneity."[7] Is this desire to find aesthetic significance or value in the random and accidental ultimately a profane version of transubstantiation? If so, it is hardly alone. Many of the features modernity takes as differentiating it from the past actually originate in the Middle Ages. Unearthing and interrogating those origins ought to be one of medieval studies' central imperatives.

BARTHES: REALITY OR REGRESSION?

In the introduction to their 2011 collection *The Speculative Turn: Continental Materialism and Realism,* Levi Bryant, Nick Srnicek, and Graham Harman, announce continental philosophy's return to realism with a brief historical narrative:

> The first wave of twentieth century continental thought in the Anglophone world was dominated by phenomenology, with Martin Heidegger generally the most influential figure of the group. By the late 1970s, the influence of Jacques Derrida and Michel Foucault had started to gain the upper hand, reaching its zenith a decade or so later. It was towards the mid-1990s that Gilles Deleuze entered the ascendant, shortly before his death in November 1995, and his star remains perfectly visible today. But since the beginning of the twenty-first century, a more chaotic and in some ways more promising situation has taken shape. Various intriguing philosophical trends, their bastions scattered across the globe, have gained adherents and started to produce a critical mass of emblematic works. While it is difficult to find a single adequate name to cover all of these trends, we propose "The Speculative Turn," as a deliberate counterpoint to the now tiresome "Linguistic Turn." The words "materialism" and "realism" in our subtitle clarify further the nature of the new trends, but also preserve a possible distinction between the material and the real.[8]

It is no particular reflection on the substance of this new philosophical trend to point out that this brief history seems potted, and that its ending is almost a pure evasion. Bryant, Srnicek, and Harman may speak for many when they

---

7. Shields, *Reality Hunger,* p. 5.

8. Levi Bryant, Nick Srnicek, and Graham Harman, eds., *The Speculative Turn: Continental Materialism and Realism* (Melbourne: re-press, 2011), pp. 1–2.

call the linguistic turn "tiresome," but "tiresome" is not much by way of a counterargument. The lack is particularly pronounced in that they actually need the linguistic turn to define their own contrapuntal "Speculative Turn." And of course the phrase itself reveals an entanglement with the linguistic at the very moment it tries to break free into the open air of the real and material. The *turn* in "Linguistic Turn" is a play on the original significance of *trope*. It thus emblematizes the irreducibility of the linguistic in the process of asserting it. By contrast, Bryant, Srnicek, and Harman want the "Speculative Turn" to effect a leap free of any such linguistic irreducibility. In this case, like a tin can tied to the tail of a cat, the play on *trope* drags the linguistic along with it, unwanted but unrecognized.

By default, this failure puts even more temporal pressure on the category of the *tiresome*, and the potted history Bryant, Srnicek, and Harman use to support it. *Tiresome* reduces the movement of ideas through time to a matter of pure duration. Hence: we used to do the linguistic turn. That got boring, and now it's time for the speculative turn.[9] To be sure, there are attractions to such a brutally pragmatic stance. But Bryant, Srnicek, and Harman are not interested in being quite that reductive. They want to present their movement as the result of a historical development. I have called their narrative potted because it follows a very typical pattern: the past was simple, the present is complex. The past of continental philosophy has been dominated by a succession of singular, monumental figures: Heidegger, Derrida, Foucault, Deleuze. The present is radically different: "Since the beginning of the twenty-first century, a more chaotic and in some ways more promising situation has taken shape." We are now in a particularly privileged moment of chaos and promise, framed by the nearly magical invocation of "the beginning of the twenty-first century." We could treat this phrase as simply a piece of information and the timing it conveys as entirely incidental. Perhaps it just so happens that the emergence of the speculative turn coincided with the advent of the new millennium. But that would be to wish away the power of language rather than setting it aside. A slightly stronger reading seems more appropriate, namely that there is some essential, if implicit connection between the beginning of the new millennium and the emergence of this new movement, as if the latter were underwritten by the former, or indeed, as if the former somehow named some particular feature of the latter. This chronological marker certainly corresponds to one of the most basic and paradoxical periodizing conventions of modern historiography, whereby the

---

9. For a concise but compelling analysis of a similar dilemma in current feminism, see Jane Elliott, "The Currency of Feminist Theory," *PMLA* 121 (2006): 1697–703.

measurement of historical time is taken to itself be a fundamental source of meaning. Each century is taken to name a distinct reality, and often the same thing is true of decades.

Later in the essay, Bryant, Srnicek, and Harman will declare that "the various strands of continental materialism and realism are all entirely at odds with so-called "naive realism." That is without doubt as regards the substance of these strands. But it is less true of their sense of their relation to the past. One of modernity's most cherished idealizations of itself is its celebration of its own direct confrontations with reality and its clear-eyed dismissal of the premodern, mired in superstition and unscientific abstraction. This idealization underwrites the characteristic stance of new intellectual movements, which generally present themselves as face to face with whatever issue is at hand, as opposed to the dead letter of the immediately previous movement they are attempting to displace. This programmatic statement by Bryant, Srnicek, and Harman fits the convention perfectly. With its reductive dismissal of the linguistic turn as merely tiresome, speculative realism does not offer an entirely realistic view of its own past. The linguistic turn cannot be so easily wished away.

The Antinomies of Realism provides a wonderful confirmation of this fact in the form of an alternative and more continuous chronological trajectory. Jameson's first two major works, *Marxism and Form* and *The Prison-House of Language,* appearing in 1971 and 1972, respectively, constituted influential early instances of the linguistic turn, yet they turned to structural and formalist conceptions of the linguistic precisely in the interest of a more robust materialism. In that sense, *The Antinomies of Realism* represents no significant deviation. Jameson has been a singular figure, to be sure. But he has hardly been isolated or marginal. His constitutes at least one significant trajectory through the entire duration of the linguistic turn that remained materialist from start to finish. In spite of the grandeur of its *magisterium,* *The Antinomies of Realism* offers itself as an account of the realist novel, a genre it understands in entirely traditional terms as beginning in the early nineteenth century with figures like Balzac and ending in the early twentieth with such high modernists as Joyce, Proust, and Woolf. Jameson declares realism's logical incoherence at the outset: "Realism . . . is a hybrid concept in which an epistemological claim (for knowledge or truth) masquerades as an aesthetic ideal, with fatal consequences for both of these incommensurable dimensions."[10] Jameson regularly notes as one feature of the mode's unstable hybridity a dependence on traditions and motives from the prenovelistic

---

10. Fredric Jameson, *The Antinomies of Realism* (London and New York: Verso, 2013) pp. 5–6.

past that the mode claims to transcend. At one point, he connects realism's demystifying rejection of existing genres to the *sermo humilis* as explicated by Auerbach. At another, he devotes a particularly dazzling chapter to the role of providence in the narrative emplotment of the modern novel, opening up this analysis to show how both Kant's metaphysics and Marxist philosophy recapitulate Christian notions of predestination.

For all of that, Jameson remains frustratingly wedded to a very conventional scheme of periodization, firmly convinced both of the uniqueness of modernity and the epistemological superiority of the novel—wedded, that is, to precisely the same sort of conflation of historical development and aesthetic form he rightly finds so dubious in the work of other critics. Indeed, he even minimizes the importance of the surprising trajectory he demonstrates from Christianity through Kant to Marxism on the grounds that "in this secular and collective version . . . there is a kind of solution, and one not unrelated to the unconvincing theological one in such a way as to demonstrate that the latter was only really a distorted anticipation of the former."[11] With this peculiar piece of special pleading, Jameson himself unconsciously reenacts an even older bit of Christian dogma. He assigns Christianity the role Judaism plays in Paul's famous version of Christian salvation history. Christianity becomes the dead letter to Marxism's living spirit, and Marxism reveals itself as the goal that God, now renamed History, was aiming at all along. Whether this claim is ultimately defensible in the political terms in which Jameson makes it is obviously a question beyond the scope of this essay. What is clear is that once one makes axiomatic this sort of absolute break between modern and premodern literary form, one renders oneself incapable of explaining ekphrasis or any other formal structure that bridges the gap without impoverishing its semiotic potential on both sides of the divide. For that reason, I have chosen to be guided in this essay not by Jameson, rich and suggestive though *The Antinomies of Realism* is, but by the much older "Reality Effect." While conceding the indispensability of this essay, Jameson complains of its "reduction" of realism "to signs alone."[12] Yet this concentration on the semiotic is precisely what makes it so useful for my purposes. It enables a strategic bracketing of the question of historical period and prevents a full exploration of the semiotics of ekphrasis from being blocked by the demands of pregiven historical metanarrative.

"The Reality Effect" remains a compelling account of the semiotic structure of narrative realism. The current resurgence of interest in reality and the

---

11. Jameson, *Antinomies*, p. 201.
12. Jameson, *Antinomies*, p. 36.

real makes this essay more pertinent than it has ever been. Although hardly ignored in its own moment, we might well argue that it never achieved the full influence it might have precisely because it appeared as the linguistic turn was reaching its zenith. As a semiotic analysis of an impulse taken to be obsolescent, the essay may have seemed much more a settling of accounts than the opening of a new direction. The linguistic turn offered itself in relation to realism in exactly the same way the current realist turn offers itself in relation to the linguistic, that is, as a complex, promising present emerging out of the dead letter of a simplistic, discredited past. Indeed, Barthes himself, taking Curtius's account of ekphrasis as a point of departure, locates his analysis within an entirely conventional opposition of medieval to modern. He concludes by describing modern realism as "somewhat regressive." However, as with so much of the best poststructuralist theory, Barthes's argument, almost in spite of itself, overflows the fairly narrow chronological frame to which he confines it. In returning to this argument, I want to look back from it toward the Middle Ages, that is, to demonstrate that Barthes's analysis works as well for late medieval ekphrasis as it does for modern realism. But I also want to look forward to our current moment, to suggest that the conventional, threadbare opposition between medieval and modern is subtended by complicated and compelling continuities, that ekphrasis names one of those continuities, and that as such, it offers a symptomatic instance of reality's ongoing debt to the linguistic.

Citing the "craze for ekphrasis" in the Second Sophistic, which carried forward into the Middle Ages, Barthes sharply distinguishes modern description from that of late antiquity and the Middle Ages.

> As Curtius has emphasized, description in this period is constrained by no realism: its truth is unimportant (or even its verisimilitude); there is no hesitation to put lions or olive trees in a northern country; only the constraint of the discursive genre counts; plausibility is not referential here but openly discursive: it is the generic rules of the discourse which lay down the law.[13]

This distinction should also recall Huizinga. Huizinga and Curtius differ on the applicability of the term *realism*, but for our purposes that is a distinction without a difference. For Curtius (and Barthes), the "openly discursive" character of medieval ekphrasis renders any thought of realism otiose.

---

13. Roland Barthes, "The Reality Effect," in *The Rustle of Language*, trans. Richard Howard (New York: Hill and Wang, 1986), pp. 143–44 [141–48].

Huizinga—correctly in my view—notes a trend in medieval description that gives the term realism a heuristic value. Nevertheless his insistence that such realism derives from a "hyperidealist mentality" brings us very quickly to the same essential difference between medieval and modern. For Barthes this difference means that unlike medieval realism, modern realism depends on the presentation of details that resist all signification. He offers two illustrations: a barometer atop a piano, which Flaubert notes at the beginning of his short story "A Simple Heart," and a knock at the door, which Michelet notes in describing an artist's visit to Charlotte Corday, who is awaiting execution. These details constitute "a kind of narrative *luxury*":

> The pure and simple "representation" of the "real," the naked relation of "what is" (or has been) thus appears as a resistance to meaning; this resistance confirms the great mythic opposition of the *true-to-life* (the lifelike) and the *intelligible;* it suffices to recall that, in the ideology of our time, obsessive reference to the "concrete" (in what is rhetorically demanded of the human sciences, of literature, of behavior) is always brandished like a weapon against meaning, as if by some statutory exclusion, what is alive cannot signify—and vice versa. [italics original][14]

From a post-Derridean standpoint, it might be objected that Barthes's account here lapses into logocentrism. Pure resistance to meaning is a theoretical impossibility. There are no insignificant details, that is, no details that a determined reader cannot ultimately make signify, no matter how resistant to their larger narrative context they may seem. To take the two examples Barthes uses: a barometer connotes scientific precision, the inexorability of the modern. That should not prove too hard to thematize in a story about a woman, the simple heart of the title, whose simplicity is completely overwhelmed by the forces of modernity. As for Michelet's knock at the door, its possible relevance to a narrative that ends with an execution should be even easier to specify. Nevertheless, these objections, in spite of their theoretical validity, miss Barthes's larger point. He is analyzing a form of desire rather than a purely objective historical condition; as he himself concedes, this notion of the real is "mythic" and ideological.

Barthes also treats this desire as transitional. He values modernity's break with the medieval rhetorical norms less for what it was than for what it presages. The essay concludes:

---

14. Barthes, "Reality Effect," pp. 141 and 146.

This new verisimilitude is very different from the old one, for it is neither a respect for the "laws of the genre" nor even their mask, but proceeds from the intention to degrade the sign's tripartite nature in order to make notation the pure encounter of an object and its expression. The disintegration of the sign—which seems indeed to be modernity's grand affair—is of course present in the realistic enterprise, but in a somewhat regressive manner, since it occurs in the name of a referential plenitude, whereas the goal today is to empty the sign and infinitely to postpone its object so as to challenge, in a radical fashion, the age-old aesthetic of "representation."[15]

In sharp contrast to our current intellectual temper, for Barthes the desire to get to the real is already outdated. Realism constitutes the regressive version of a grander, more contemporary desire, that is, the desire "to make notation the pure encounter of an object and its expression." It is no real fault of Barthes that the infinite postponement of reference that he predicts has not come to pass, or to be more precise, that it came to pass for a while and now has subsided. However, while the current resurgence of reality hunger hardly invalidates Barthes's analysis, it does make this part of it even more ripe for interrogation. What is the precise nature of the regression Barthes associates with realism? This parting shot has a paradoxical effect. It intends to affirm the integrity of the break between medieval and modern—between the "new verisimilitude" and the old—from which modern realism arose in the first place. Yet how can modern realism represent both a break with the past and a regression? What would the character of this regression be? Is it ethical or ideological? Is the problem that modern realism has already sensed the imperative for "the disintegration of the sign . . . modernity's grand affair" and, in a failure of political or intellectual will, succumbs to the seductions of plenitude instead? Or is the regression of a more properly psychoanalytic sort, a return to an originary break, a break that can never be transcended, for the break and the desire to transcend it are one and the same?

The sinuous arpeggio that is Barthes's final clause supports the second possibility. If we weight all of its paradoxes equally, we are left with a temporality that defies characterization by metaphors of linear movement. Not regress perhaps, but not progress either, and certainly not some melding of the two. This clause defines the present not by its own, current characteristics, but by its "goal," that is, by its desired future. And while this goal renounces realism's "somewhat regressive" desires for referential plenitude, it may well

---

15. Barthes, "Reality Effect," p. 148.

succumb to a transcendental desire of its own. Its drive "to empty the sign" is no tactical deconstruction but an infinite postponement. What should we make of this surprising and superogatory infinitude? Can it be anything else but a *via negativa*, the self-annihilation of the mystic now displacing the plenitude of the metaphysician? Understood as a "radical" challenge, this infinitude of delay brings the future it desires precisely by holding that future at bay. It also offers a slippage in Barthes's periodizing scheme.

The "new verisimilitude," opposed at the beginning of the paragraph to the old verisimilitude and thereby marking the beginning of the modern, has now been absorbed into the "age-old aesthetic of 'representation.'" The paradoxes of the concluding sentence have displaced the conventional, orderly progress of distinct periods with an all-encompassing, if more evanescent, opposition between the immediate present and everything that preceded it. That present is itself a purely expectant one, defined entirely by its transcendent aspiration for the future. The movement of Barthes's language in this final paradox reveals a dilemma he never quite manages to articulate as such. The regression lurking in modern realism still lurks in the antireferential vanguardism that succeeds realism. That is not simply because, like any *via negativa*, this one ultimately desires transcendence. The vanguardist goal of emptying the sign is not some passive reception of the future. It is a forward projection of the present, a paradoxical desire to freeze the present precisely by recasting it as the future. Like all vanguardisms this one is as much about forestalling the future as it is about escaping the past. It cannot imagine a future to its radical renunciation of the past except in the form of an infinite postponement. It does not know what to ask from the future beyond the preservation of its own transcendent strivings.

Curiously enough, the Speculative Turn and related developments have not in any clear way moved beyond Barthes's postponement. Indeed, they simply reverse its polarity. The basic terms remain the same: the sign and the real. This fact calls into question rather severely any claim to a significant epistemological advance our own intellectual moment might want to make in relation to Barthes's moment. It also, on its face, seems to reinforce the brutally pragmatic view of intellectual trends I have already suggested, namely that they are purely a function of fashion. For a while, we were interested in signs. That got boring, so now we are interested in things. But there is another alternative, which I intend to pursue here. We need to decouple humanistic inquiry from vanguardism—that is, from modernity's characteristic stance toward the past—and the progressivist assumptions about the movement of history this stance entails. There is nothing inherently redemptive in the unrolling of historical time. There is no reason to assume that the movement of history, on its own, brings with it some inevitable epistemo-logical advance. Yet, vanguardism assumes not only that the present always knows more than the past but also that this epistemological advantage is radical and absolute. It is high time we recognize the modernist break for what it is: a form of desire rather than a fact. Like all desires it has large zones of incoherence. We should expose these incoherencies to strict scrutiny rather than allowing them to frame our modes of inquiry. In this case, that means asking whether Barthes's brilliant exposition of the reality effect really only applies to modern modes of mimesis, as he assumes, or whether it can also apply to medieval ekphrases.

Fortunately, Barthes has already begun this work himself, both in the studied ambiguities of his conclusion and in the semiotic character of his analysis itself. Though he treats the examples he cites as historically specific, there is nothing so limiting in the way he analyzes them. He argues that realism works by producing a *"referential illusion"* (italics original). That is, its descriptions work not by denoting specific objects in the world, but paradoxically, precisely by not denoting them:

> Flaubert's barometer, Michelet's little door finally say nothing but this: *we are the real*; it is the category of the "the real" (and not its contingent contents) which is then signified; in other words, the very absence of the signified, to the advantage of the referent alone, becomes the very signifier of realism: the *reality effect* is produced, the basis of that unavowed verisimilitude which forms the aesthetic of all the standard works of modernity. [italics original][16]

At the very moment Barthes declares the details of realistic narration to be empty signifiers, he makes a sudden swerve into the register of the allegorical. Indeed, even to make this claim he has momentarily to convert all these empty signifiers into personifications. Realism is a thoroughly disenchanted realm of empty signifiers; yet to achieve this state of disenchantment it must become so full of meaning that even the most banal, inanimate objects now speak. Barthes leaves this paradox implicit, but it is actually crucial to his analysis. We can unpack the paradox in the following way.

Realist description seeks meaning in pure contingency. It can find the contingency it seeks only to the extent that contingency resists signification. The fuller the resistance, the more fully the description achieves the significance it desires. It is a mistake to view realism as purely a quest for

---

16. Barthes, "Reality Effect," p. 148.

the signified. What it seeks is the signified's resistance to the signifier. It thus seeks the signifier as well, or more precisely, it seeks to inhabit the difference between signifier and signified. That is why in seeking to characterize realism's achievement of this goal Barthes is driven momentarily into the register of allegory, into the mode of narration conventionally understood as realism's antithesis. That is also why he overstates the case when he makes an absolute distinction between realism and ekphrasis. Even if realist description can be said to elude generic constraint in the strict sense—and even in that sense I am not sure it can—something very like the authority of genre lurks in the "referential illusion." Perhaps one should call it "counter-generic." But Barthes's brief allegorical formula accurately expresses an expectation for modern realism held uniformly by writer and reader alike—an expectation, that is, that operates exactly like a generic convention. We might note parenthetically that this fact insures that in literary studies any turn to the real must always be an ironic one. The new speculative philosophers proclaim they are interested in things for their own sake—nothing more and nothing less—and who am I to say no? But that sort of interest differs fundamentally from a literary interest in the real. As Barthes's analysis makes unmistakably clear, in the literary context what matters about Flaubert's barometer or Michelet's door are not their quiddities. It's not about being an actual barometer or an actual door, but rather about how these actualities insure the encounter with the real. That encounter is the ultimate goal. The quiddities are decidedly not ends in themselves. They are intermediaries, important only in so far as they lead to the real. In a word, they are semiotic. They are quiddities that have become signs of their own realness.

All of these paradoxes bring ekphrasis much closer to modern realistic description than Barthes acknowledges. Ekphrasis is a trope that defines itself in part by its incorporation of the extra-rhetorical. As the representation of a representation, it necessarily focuses its readers' attention on the materiality of the signifier. Thus, in the first book of the *Aeneid,* in one of the most famous uses of the trope, Aeneas, spirited into the temple of Hera, suddenly confronts pictures of the fall of Troy. This scene literally offers a sign in the presence of its referent, literally inhabits the difference between signifier and signified. Ekphrasis conflates its mimetic impulse with its insistence on the materiality of the signifier. It thus anticipates both ends of the modern trajectory Barthes suggests, that is, from referential plenitude to referential emptiness. If modern realism regresses by retaining older ideals of representation, it can only do so by repressing this ekphrastic conflation of the mimetic and the deconstructive. That is to say, what modern realism must repress is any temporal dimension to its desire for the real: it must repress not only the possibility that its own desire for the real has a past but that such a desire is not entirely innocent and self-contained, proof against any and all transcendent motives. To find some confirmation of these possibilities, I turn now to *Pearl*. There we can find an ekphrasis that not only fits Barthes's analysis but does so in a thoroughly transcendent context, that is, in a description of the Heavenly City.

SEEING MORE THAN JOHN WROTE

Recent scholarship on *Pearl*, while every bit as lively and variegated as that on other major Middle English poetry, has produced a rare critical consensus: *Pearl* is an intensely visual poem. We can even specify the consensus further. It revolves around a paradox. The poem directs most of its considerable visual energies to exploring vision at its epistemological limits. Thus Sarah Stanbury, in what remains the best book on the *Gawain*-poet ever written, argues that

> sight in this poem is enacted throughout by its twin valences, sight as sensory faculty and as spiritual metaphor, vision and visionary, and perception itself is realized as complex and multivalent experience. Through the subjective voice of the dreamer, *Pearl* dramatizes the aporia between visual experience and other ways of knowing, such as the instruction by doctrine the Maiden provides.

She then concludes:

> The dreamer's vision of the city is a powerful dramatization of the experience of not knowing or of seeing that which cannot be fully grasped. If *Pearl* is intended to describe a contemplative methodology in which the dreamer uses the physical beauties of the world to lead him to anagogical truths, then that process must be said to be a failure.[17]

More recently, J. Allan Mitchell has offered a robust, antitypological reading of the poem, using its recurrent complication of its own revelatory images as a central piece of evidence. As he concludes, "*Pearl* effectively becomes not a confident representation of spiritual reality, nor a total denial of the possibility of its expression, but rather a record of the visionary's dislocation from a 'gostly drem' (796), from a private and incommunicable experience

---

17. Sarah Stanbury, *Seeing the* Gawain-*Poet: Description and the Act of Perception* (Philadelphia: University of Pennsylvania Press, 1991), pp. 13–14 and 35.

that which none greater can be conceived."[18] In spite of this consensus, the poet's use of ekphrasis has gone largely unremarked. As we shall see, ekphrasis enables the poet to give particular rhetorical shape to "the aporia between visual experience and other ways of knowing." Moreover, this rhetorical translation means that the poet's insistence on the limits of vision can double back on itself, unmooring even its devotional certainty from any secure historical placement.[19]

One finds memorable instances of the trope throughout this poet's work. We might cite the extended arming of the hero scene in *Sir Gawain and the Green Knight,* with its distinct and novel interest in textiles and its concluding moralization of the pentangle on Gawain's shield; or the descriptions of Bertilak's castle or the Green Chapel, or indeed, the Green Knight's ax, or his other arms. As a biblical paraphrase, *Cleanness* affords numerous opportunities for ekphrasis, and the poem deploys the trope liberally. Indeed, ekphrasis so dominates the second half of the poem, devoted entirely to retelling the story of Belshazzar, that one could legitimately argue that the trope constitutes the main form of exposition. Ekphrases in *Pearl* include the opening description of the Pearl herself as a gem set in gold (ll. 1–8), her clothing and crown (ll. 195–228), and the Pearl of Great Price (ll. 730–44). Traditionally, the scene for most of the poem, between the opening lament and the final vision, has been read as a *locus amoenus,* the very *topos* that Curtius uses as the representative instance of ekphrasis in the passage to which Barthes refers.[20] Sometimes the topos has been taken to include even

---

18. J. Allan Mitchell, "The Middle English *Pearl:* Figuring the Unfigurable," *Chaucer Review* 35.1 (2000): 108–9 [86–111]. Other important studies of vision in the poem include George Edmondson, "*Pearl*: The Shadow of the Object, the Shape of the Law," *Studies in the Age of Chaucer* 26 (2004): 29–63; Kevin Gustafson, "The Lay Gaze, *Pearl,* the Dreamer and the Vernacular Reader," *Medievalia et Humanistica,* New Series 27 (2000): 57–77; and Sandra Pierson Prior, *The Fayre Formez of the* Pearl *Poet* (East Lansing: Michigan State University Press, 1996), pp. 21–66.

19. On this point, I would enthusiastically align my approach to the *Pearl* with that taken by Anke Bernau in her essay in this volume: we are working opposite sides of the same street. Bernau seeks the poem's "imaginative craft" as a way into its exploration of the complex interdependence between memory and wonder. Following Nicolette Zeeman, she opposes this imaginative craft to the propositional discourses of scholastic philosophy. For me the commonality lies in the deployment of erudition. Students of medieval poetry have long appealed to scholastic tradition as a way of making the poetry more intelligible and easier to understand. They have used the traditions of medieval rhetoric in exactly the same way. Inevitably this approach underplays, or ignores entirely, medieval culture's own manifold investment in the category of the unknowable. I see my essay as exploring this investment from within one of these traditions. I see Professor Bernau's as exploring it in the poetic resources that lie adjacent to another of these traditions.

20. The first to offer this reading was D. W. Robertson, "The Doctrine of Charity in Mediaeval Literary Gardens," *Speculum* 26 (1951): 24–49. See also Derek Pearsall and Elizabeth

the "erbere" (l. 9) or garden of the poem's opening. It certainly includes the indefinite locale to which the Dreamer's vision projects him, with its crystal cliffs, shimmering silvery leaves, pearl gravel, beryl riverside, and crystal clear water with sapphires, emeralds, and other gems—the locale scholars have traditionally termed the Earthly Paradise. Given the ubiquity of the *locus amoenus* in late medieval vernacular poetry, it is not too fanciful to view the subsequent vision of the Heavenly City in part as a meditation on the trope it deploys. In contrast to its frequency elsewhere, ekphrasis does not seem to have been very common in accounts of visionary contemplation, which may be part of the *Pearl*-poet's point.

As both Stanbury and Mitchell demonstrate, the *Pearl* differs from most contemplative accounts in its emphasis on the sinful fallibility—perhaps even spiritual immaturity—of the protagonist. The *locus amoenus* helps dramatize this fallibility by conveying his fascination with visual pleasure. At the same time, the poem's deployment of ekphrasis prevents the visual from being assimilated completely to the side of human fallibility and sin. On the contrary, the poet uses the trope to demonstrate that the desire for visual certainty is as much a gift of divine grace as it is a hard lesson in its limits. The poet effects the shift from the Earthly Paradise to the Apocalyptic vision through an entreaty of the Dreamer. After the *Pearl*-maiden explains the differences between the two Jerusalems, the Dreamer pleads, "Bryng me to þat bygly bylde / And let me se þy blisful bor" (ll. 963–64).[21] In response, the *Pearl*-maiden makes it clear this vision comes as a result of Christ's grace: "Of þe Lombe I have þe aquylde / For a sy3t þerof þur3 gret favor" (ll. 967–68).

The vision will move from the scriptural to the subjective. While watching from the far shore a procession of Christ the Lamb in the midst of one hundred thousand virgins, the Dreamer implicitly refuses to recognize his own guilt in Christ's crucifixion, turning away from the sight of the Lamb's bleeding wound to focus once again on the Maiden. Contravening the Maiden's explicit warning against attempting to enter heaven while still stained with sin, the Dreamer follows his implicit lapse by plunging into the river, and he is expelled from his vision. However, the earlier portions of this vision give these lapses a semiotic dimension, which, at the very least, complicates these subjective devotional lapses. The first two fitts of this portion

---

Salter, *Landscapes and Seasons of the Medieval World* (Toronto: University of Toronto Press, 1973), pp. 56–118.

21. Malcolm Andrew and Ronald Waldron, eds., *Poems of the Pearl Manuscript:* Pearl, Cleanness, Patience, *and* Sir Gawain and the Green Knight (Exeter: University of Exeter Press, 2008), p. 100 (ll. 963–64). All quotations are from this edition; line numbers for subsequent citations will be given in the text.

of the dream set the scene by recapitulating descriptive details from the Book of Revelations. The poet foregrounds this act of paraphrase by repeatedly citing John by name, in the concatenating lines of fitt XVII, for example, "As derely deuysez þis ilk toun / In Apocalyppez þe apostel John" (ll. 995–96) and elsewhere. These citations stage the same confrontation between sign and referent as the ekphrasis I just mentioned from the first book of the *Aeneid*. This passage inhabits the same difference between signifier and signified— the feature I have argued constitutes the common ground between the trope of ekphrasis and modern realism.

But that is not all. Huizinga, Curtius, and Barthes all share a common assumption about the relation between Christian divinity and language, namely that the former inevitably, almost by definition, exerts a stabilizing effect on the latter (this assumption also informs a considerable proportion of *Pearl* scholarship). Here, however, if one temporarily brackets that possibility, if one does not take it as a given—and thereby assumes the very thing one is purporting to prove—if one attends to the movement of the language before attending to the content, one will come to exactly the opposite conclusion. What one finds is not referential plenitude, but absence and aporia. Nor should we find such a conclusion particularly surprising. Referential plenitude as Barthes so lucidly characterizes it, assumes the primacy of the signified. However, the master sign that is Christianity's God confers primacy on the signifier. In John's own famous formulation from the beginning of his Gospel, "*In principio erat Verbum*" (Jn. 1:1) [In the beginning was the Word]. The radically paradoxical effect of this concept is to make absence, deferral, or difference irreducible features of its infinite plenitude. The *Pearl*-poet's highly self-conscious ekphrasis finds a more domesticated version of this radical paradox in his meditations on the peculiarities of John's mimetic praxis.

The poet's vision occupies an impossible middle ground between mundane, embodied vision and the pure, disembodied perception of the redeemed soul. He insists on this impossibility by making his repetition of John itself an instance of unbridgeable difference. Toward the beginning of fitt XVII, he explains, "As John þe apostel, syȝ with syȝt / I syȝe þat cyty of gret renoun" (ll. 985–86). The pleonastic "saw with sight" strongly suggests John experienced the original vision with embodied sight. The lack of pleonasm in the next line leaves the status of the Dreamer's perception slightly more ambiguous. The poet resolves that ambiguity at the end of the next fitt when he declares,

Anunder mone so gret merwayle
No fleschly hert ne myȝt endeure
As quen I blusched vpon þat baly

So ferly þerof watz þe fasure.
I stod as stylle as dased quayle
For ferly of þat frech fygure,
Þat felde I nawþer reste ne travayl
So watz I rauyste wyth glymme pure.
For I dar say with conciens sure,
Hade bodyly burne abiden þat bone,
Þaȝ alle clerkez hym hade in cure,
His lyf wer loste anvnder mone.

Under moon so great a marvel
No fleshly heart might endure
As when I looked upon that city,
So wondrous the form of it was.
I stood as still as a dazed quail
For wonder of that fair figure,
I experienced neither rest not exertion,
So ravished was I with pure radiance.
For I daresay with a sure mind
Had an embodied man experienced that boon
Though all the clerks had him in their care
His life would have been lost under the moon.
(ll. 1081–92)

The Dreamer's vision is the product of a miraculous, inexplicable, temporary disembodiment. Paradoxically, it is John's original vision that is the more carnal; or to put the paradox more precisely, the original vision is at once more carnal and more spiritual, its carnality serving to underscore the thoroughness of its spiritual transcendence.

The Dreamer encounters the details of his transcendent vision not as self-evident quiddities but as confirmations of pre-existent signifiers. The first thing the Dreamer sees is the twelve layers of precious stone that constitute the city's foundation. He knows what they are because he has already read Revelations: "As John þise stonez in writ con nemme, / I knew þe name after his tale" (ll. 997–98). He will recapitulate the list from Revelations 21:19–20: jasper, sapphire, chalcedony, emerald, sardonyx, ruby, chrysolite, beryl, topaz, chrysoprasus, jacinth, and amethyst. His insistence on their intertextual status in his text only underscores the peculiarity of what would seem to be their purely mimetic function in John's original. Unlike most of the other details in Revelations—unlike indeed their numerological significance as an aggregate—there does not seem to be anything portentous or symbolic about these stones. That is not to say subsequent exegetes have not tried. Yet as far as I can tell, none of the many—largely unconvincing—attempts to allegorize the stones has ever denied their literal existence as particular precious stones. And as particular precious stones, they signify only, "We are the celestial." Moreover, in so signifying, they also signify that the celestial is the real in an etymological sense, that is that the celestial is at least partially thing-like, constituted of these precious *rei*. Perhaps not surprisingly, the heuristic power of Barthes's analysis works well on this passage. We can find in its scriptural ekphrasis a quest for the purely contingent, a "resistance to meaning," which, as a rhetorical phenomenon at any rate, is entirely similar to that Barthes finds in the realist depiction of a nineteenth-century interior. In spite of the infinite plenitude of the object being described, the *Pearl*-poet, like John before him, cannot treat the description as complete until he has accounted for the ultimately insignificant or incidental—that is, that part of the scene that is the way it is because that is just how it happens to be.

Indeed, if there is a difference in this respect between this late medieval ekphrasis and modern realism it is that the ekphrasis can acknowledge its semiotic dependence on contingency, can explicitly combine its desire for plenitude with an insistence on its pure contingency as a signifier. The *Pearl*-poet drives this point home in the next fitt, which begins, "As John hym wrytez ȝet more I syȝe" (l. 1033). This line is almost always translated as, "I saw more of what John wrote," as is no doubt appropriate. But it could also mean, "I saw more than John wrote," especially as this fitt will mark the end of the ekphrasis and will interleave details from Revelations with commentary and with other scriptural details. The lines immediately following pick up the paraphrase of Revelations 21 exactly where the previous fitt had left off, describing the city's twelve gates adorned with pearls. But they also add to the gates the names of the children of Israel ("Israel barnez"), a detail drawn from Exodus 12. Without ever relinquishing the authority of scripture, the poet in these lines literally claims to have seen more than is recorded by John. Obviously, this second significance raises the always dicey question of the relation between the Word of God and the insights gleaned by mystical contemplation. Yet even here, the poet can still be seen working within the framework that John himself provides. Sometime after the seventh seal is opened, John hears the seven thunders. But his readers learn no more of them, as he hears a voice that warns, "Seal up the things which the seven thunders have spoken. And write them not" (Rev. 10:4). Thus, Revelations itself views its language as incomplete relative to its object. Accordingly, it makes sense to read the *Pearl*-poet's own claim to greater plenitude as a rhetorical effect rather than as a theological claim. But that is only because the claim actually inhabits an indeterminate boundary between the rhetorical and theological, an indeterminacy that John himself opens up by asserting *he* has seen more than he wrote.

In a similar fashion, the reality effect produced by this ekphrasis of the foundations of the Heavenly City ultimately belongs to John as well. It is John who presents them as celestial things in themselves, who promises his reader that there is a "thingness" to the celestial, a secular, mundane-like solidity where signification stops or comes to rest. In addition to the other delights he promises to his readers, he also promises the textual, rhetorical pleasure of referential, mimetic plenitude—Barthes's "narrative luxury," in this case, pleasure arising from the actual luxury of the Heavenly City's precious foundation materials. While it would certainly be possible to assimilate this pleasure to the finite, limited, essentially fallen character of human language, that would be to underplay the complexity and ambiguity of this pleasure. Human fallenness enters this referential encounter not in the pleasure itself but precisely in the uncertainty of its essence: to what extent is the pleasure the response to a purely human need, and to what extent is it an authentic feature of divine transcendence. To return briefly to Stanbury's point about the failure of the poem's "contemplative methodology": *Pearl* differs sharply from the vast majority of actual contemplative accounts, differs even from less idiosyncratic poetic renditions like Dante's *Paradiso,* in that it seems to want to claim no contemplative privilege whatever. The poem's narrative ends where it started, with the Dreamer still fixated on the loss of the Maiden, whatever consolation purportedly offered in the final two stanzas already undercut by his turning away from Christ in the headlong, impetuous attempt to cross the river and regain her. Moreover this parting disavowal completes the deferral of authority implicit in the poem's ostentatious citation of Revelations. There is nothing unusual in contemplative visions drawing structure or detail from textual antecedents. However, in this case by making the intertextual dependence so explicit, so prominent, and so ostensibly literal, the poet seems to be insisting that the experiential content of this vision is nothing more than a fictional recreation of John's text. The favor that Christ grants to the Dreamer turns out to be little more than the revelations already available to every reader of scripture. But then, that condition also ultimately obtains for even the most revelatory and audacious mystic vision. All Christian contemplation must arise from God's Word, nor can it ever fully transcend the contemplative's individual limitations—not to mention his or her ultimately sinful imperfections. Thus the narrative trajectory of the poem's final vision, from literal

Word of God to the ascent to an actual glimpse of the divine followed by a return to the fallen desires of the Dreamer, possesses an exemplary as well as an individual significance. The descent into "private and incommunicable experience"—to cite J. Allan Mitchell once more—certainly underwrites the poem's disavowal of its own theological authority. Even so, this return to private experience does not ultimately separate *Pearl* from more confident contemplative accounts. The contemplative's condition as fallen human being ensures he or she must always return to contingent human subjectivity after even the most transcendent of mystic ecstasies. In this indirect, entirely deferential manner, *Pearl* achieves a certain measure of theological authority after all.

Such indirect authority extends to the poem's peculiar concern with the mimetic and ekphrastic capacities of scripture, where its very indirection means a shift away from questions both of penitential obligation and theological speculation toward those of God's language and the specific conditions of its intelligibility. Because of its structural liminality, its stubborn grasp of the indeterminate space between sign and referent, the ekphrasis can never be easily consigned to a purely human conventionality. Can divine language be ekphrastic? There is no easy answer, and that is the poet's point. If the possibility cannot be ruled out, then the transcendent reality of the divine will come to humanity anchored in a "thingness" entirely analogous to the solidity of material, terrestrial existence. More to the point, ekphrasis, and by extension poetic figures, generally will retain an epistemological authority distinct from more properly theological discourse. The *Pearl*-poet's particular achievement is to articulate the doctrine of grace as a semiotic dilemma. The Dreamer's desire for the Maiden is a desire that exceeds its object, a predicament allegorized by a pearl that never ceases to be a mundane object, if a precious one. In its literal state, this pearl is a signified that becomes a signifier only by virtue of an excessive desire the poem must ultimately disavow as sinful. The poem's many ekphrases generalize this desire. And the poem's final stanza explicitly connects this ekphrastic dilemma to transubstantiation.

To please the Prince or to be reconciled to Him is "ful eþe to þe god Krystyin," the Dreamer declares, although the narrative that he is bringing to end has just demonstrated precisely the opposite. The Dreamer has found such reconciliation difficult indeed. He then offers a concise summary statement:

Ouer þis hyul þis lote I laȝte,
For pyty of my perle enclyin,
And syþen to God I hit bytaȝte,
In Krystez dere blessyng and myn,

Þat in þe forme of bred and wyn
Þe preste vus schewez vch a daye.
(ll. 1205–10)

Almost by definition, references to the Eucharist are never out of order in the devotional poetry of the later Middle Ages. Still, there is something ever so slightly dissonant about this one. It occurs parenthetically, in a subordinate clause that stresses the quotidian aspect of the sacrament as much as its transcendence significance. The least provocative reading would view this emphasis on the liturgical as reinforcing the Dreamer's acceptance of his loss and his return to a more normal state of piety. But such a reading ignores some obvious complications. The tension between the stanza's opening and the rest of the poem I have already noted. This sentence begins by describing the vision as a contingent event, reminding us it comes to the Dreamer while he lies prostrate over the *Pearl*-maiden's grave. The "syþen" when he entrusts her to God refers perforce to a time after his expulsion from the vision; it seems to announce a passage of time for which there is no other indication. The *Pearl*-maiden has become an "it," receding further behind the literal level of the allegory. And this somewhat offhand mention of the Eucharist emphatically recalls the Dreamer's uncomprehending response to the Lamb's bleeding wound.

These complications all strongly suggest this final stanza should not be taken as a resolution so much as final restatement of the poem's central dilemma. Its parting invocation of the Eucharist brings the reality effect to the problem of transubstantiation. As Aquinas carefully explains, the real presence of Christ in the bread and wine is invisible to the "bodily eye"; apprehensible only by the "intellectual eye."[22] The *Pearl*-poet's conviction that the priest's daily revelation of Christ and His Blessing in the "forme" of bread and wine might seem to overlook this point. In fact, I think he is doing something subtler. He offers the quotidian certainty of the liturgical celebration of the Eucharist as evidence of the certainty of Christ's grace. Yet he locates that certainty not in the transparency of the sacrament, but on the contrary, precisely in its opacity, in the invisibility of the transformed substance of the bread and wine behind the unchanged appearance of their outward accidents. To put the matter in slightly different terms: the poet splits the quotidian banality, the institutionalized certainty of the Eucharist away

---

22. Thomas Aquinas, *Summa Theologiae*, Third Part, Question 76, Article 7 (London and New York: Blackfriars, 1963), vol. 58, 94: "Respondeo dicendum quod duplex est oculus, scilicet corporalis, proprie dictus; et intellectualis, qui per similitudinem dicitur. A nullo autem oculo corporali corpus Christi potest videri prout est in hoc sacramento."

from its outward appearance and links them instead with its inward meaning. The dumbness, the utter insignificance of the appearance of the bread and wine enables Barthes's "resistance to meaning": as pure accidents, their outward appearance signifies only "we are the real." And yet, the stubborn inevitability of this resistance, the inescapability of this blockage at the heart of the sacrament's quotidian certainty, is precisely what guarantees the inevitability of the transformation taking place behind it. The Eucharist's accidental insignificance enters the poem in exactly the same way as the literal level of its allegorical signifiers, that is, as signifiers to whose literal materiality the poem keeps returning. In spite of itself, the doctrine of transubstantiation invests the accidents of bread and wine with an aura of heightened significance, at least as social facts. By foregrounding the celebration of the Eucharist as a regular feature of quotidian reality, the *Pearl*-poet also foregrounds this aura.

Pearl's treatment of ekphrasis is a singular aspect of a singular poem. Indeed, as the author of an unconventional dream vision, an unconventional romance, and two very unconventional biblical paraphrases, the *Pearl*-poet's main claim to fame is his idiosyncratic, unconventional deployment of convention. This distinction is precisely what makes this poet so useful for our purposes. To use a convention unconventionally necessarily reveals its hidden capacities. In ekphrasis, *Pearl* offers a rhetorical logic as the underlay to its juxtapositions of the dream vision, personification allegory and the *locus amoenus* with Christian contemplation and its relation to eschatology. Fittingly, the logic is radically open-ended. As poetic conventions, personification, the dream vision, and the *locus amoenus* stand in relation to the transcendent realities revealed by contemplation and eschatology as sign to thing. More precisely, the poem positions these conventions in the indeterminate space between sign and thing—that is, ekphrastically. Does the final vision record an actual contemplative experience in however mediated a form? Or is it ultimately a poetic fiction, as the poem's generic status as dream vision strongly suggests? Is its portrayal of Christ the Lamb a personification (or depersonification) like the *Pearl*-maiden? And most crucially, is the Heavenly City a *locus amoenus*? The poem's ekphrastic reworkings of the Book of the Apocalypse suggest it is—at least in part, and that is all it takes in this context. *Pearl* characterizes the pleasures of the Heavenly City as possessing a "thingness" coextensive (not to say, consubstantial) with materiality of the most precious of costly terrestrial objects. Yet, none of these confluences definitively indicate a final, global significance. That is, while they annex the poetic to the transcendent, they neither subordinate one to the other nor even hold them in suspension in unmistakable terms. This is not a matter of a simple choice between the two. For even as the poet thoroughly demonstrates the adequacy of poetic convention to the transcendent demands of Christian contemplation, he also insists that this adequacy can itself be seen as a product of Christ's grace. Moreover, we can find ample support for both possibilities in the poem's wider historical context. That is, the postmodern exegete is unlikely to find any a definitive resolution to this indeterminacy via a historical appeal. However, paradoxical as it may seem, this very conundrum constitutes its larger historical value. For it demonstrates—in case the point is still in doubt—that poetic and linguistic indeterminacy cannot be periodized. It also demonstrates that the application of methodology cannot be periodized either. If something works on Flaubert it will work on a medieval dream vision as well. These circumstances obviously mean that medievalists should continue to engage robustly with the most urgent of contemporary theoretical and philosophical debates. But they also suggest that when it comes to the Middle Ages, those debates face a considerable backlog of unfinished business. Although the linguistic turn had a major impact on medieval studies, the ramifications of that transformation have largely escaped the attention of humanistic scholarship more generally. The current turn to the "real"—if that in fact is where we currently are—seems well on its way to rendering this same mistake all the more entrenched. Certainly, its resistance to settling its accounts with its own immediate past does not bode well. The hard lessons of linguistic turn cannot be wished away, no matter how tedious one may find them. There is only one way to get to the real, and that is through the signifiers that give it a name. Nor can the search stop there. The names have histories. And the name of the real takes us back to the Middle Ages, whose shades still walk among us.

Bibliography

Aers, David. "The Self Mourning: Reflections on *Pearl.*" *Speculum* 68.1 (1993): 54–73.

Akbari, Suzanne Conklin. "Alexander in the Orient: Bodies and Boundaries in the *Roman de toute chevalerie.*" In *Postcolonial Approaches to the European Middle Ages: Translating Cultures,* edited by Ananya Jahanara Kabir and Deanne Williams, 105–26. Cambridge: Cambridge University Press, 2005.

———. "Death as Metamorphosis in the Devotional and Political Allegory of Christine de Pizan." In *The Ends of the Body: Identity and Community in Medieval Culture,* edited by Suzanne Conklin Akbari and Jill Ross, 283–313. Toronto: University of Toronto Press, 2013.

———. "Erasing the Body: History and Memory in Medieval Siege Poetry." In *Remembering the Crusades: Myth, Image, and Identity,* edited by Nicholas Paul and Suzanne Yeager, 146–73. Baltimore: Johns Hopkins University Press, 2012.

———. "Metaphor and Metamorphosis in the *Ovide moralisé* and Christine de Pizan's *Mutacion de Fortune.*" In *Metamorphosis: The Changing Face of Ovid in Medieval and Early Modern Europe,* edited by Alison Keith and Stephen James Rupp, 77–90. Toronto: Victoria University Centre for Reformation and Renaissance Studies, 2007.

———. "The Movement from Verse to Prose in the Allegories of Christine de Pizan." In *Poetry, Knowledge, and Community in Late Medieval France,* edited by Rebecca Dixon and Finn E. Sinclair, 136–48. Cambridge: D. S. Brewer, 2008.

———. *Seeing through the Veil: Optical Theory and Medieval Allegory.* Toronto: University of Toronto Press, 2004.

Alighieri, Dante. *The Divine Comedy.* Edited and translated by Charles S. Singleton. 3 Vols. Princeton, NJ: Princeton University Press, 1970–73.

Amsler, Mark. *Etymology and Grammatical Discourse in Late Antiquity and the Early Middle Ages.* Amsterdam: John Benjamins, 1989.

Anderson, Benedict. "The Museum." In *Imagined Communities: Reflections on the Origin and Spread of Nationalism,* 182–90. Revised Edition. London and New York: Verso, 2006.

Anderson, J. J. *Language and Imagination in the* Gawain-*Poems.* Manchester: Manchester University Press, 2005.

Andrew, Malcom, and Ronald Waldron, eds. *Poems of the Pearl Manuscript:* Pearl, Cleanness, Patience, Sir Gawain and the Green Knight. Exeter: University of Exeter Press, 2008.

Anson, John S. "The Hunt of Love: Gottfried von Strassburg's *Tristan* as Tragedy." *Speculum* 45.4 (1970): 594–607.

Appadurai, Arjun. *The Social Life of Things: Commodities in Cultural Perspective.* Cambridge: Cambridge University Press, 1997.

Apuleius. "On the God of Socrates." In *Apuleius: Rhetorical Works,* edited by Stephen Harrison, annotated and translated by Stephen Harrison, John Hilton, and Vincent Hunink, 185–216. Oxford: Oxford University Press, 2001.

Aristotle. *De anima.* Translated by Robert D. Hicks. Cambridge: Cambridge University Press, 1907.

———. *De motu animalium.* Edited and translated by Martha Craven Nussbaum. Princeton, NJ: Princeton University Press, 1978.

———. *Poetics.* Edited and translated by Stephen Halliwell. Cambridge, MA: Harvard University Press, 1995.

Aston, Margaret. "The Defence of Images." In *England's Iconoclasts. Vol. 1: Laws against Images,* 143–54. Oxford: Clarendon Press, 1988.

———. "Idols of the Mind." In *England's Iconoclasts. Vol. 1: Laws against Images,* 452–66. Oxford: Clarendon Press, 1988.

———. "Image-Worship." In *England's Iconoclasts. Vol. 1: Laws against Images,* 104–24. Oxford: Clarendon Press, 1988.

———. "Graven Images: More Realism, More Danger?" In *England's Iconoclasts. Vol. 1: Laws against Images,* 401–08. Oxford: Clarendon Press, 1988.

Attwood, Catherine. *Fortune la contrefaite: L'envers de l'écriture medieval.* Paris: Champion, 2007.

Augustine. *The City of God Against the Pagans. Vol. III: Books VIII–XI.* Translated by David S. Wiesen. Cambridge, MA: Harvard University Press, 1988.

———. *The Trinity.* The Fathers of the Church 45. Translated by Stephen McKenna. Washington, DC: Catholic University of America, 1963.

Bachrach, Bernard S. "The Norman Conquest, Countess Adela, and Abbot Baudri." In *Anglo-Norman Studies XXXV: Proceedings of the Battle Conference 2012,* edited by David Bates, 65–78. Woodbridge: Boydell and Brewer, 2013.

Badendyck, J. Lawrence. "Chaucer's Portrait Technique and the Dream Vision Tradition." *English Record* 21 (1970): 113–25.

Badir, Patricia. *The Maudlin Impression: English Literary Images of Mary Magdalene 1550–1700.* Notre Dame, IN: University of Notre Dame Press, 2009.

Baert, Barbara. *Interspaces between Word, Gaze and Touch: The Bible and the Visual Medium in the Middle Ages.* Leuven: Peeters, 2011.

———. "'Noli me tangere': Six Exercises in Image Theory and Iconophilia." *Image & Narrative* 15 (2006): n.p.

Baisch, Martin. *Textkritik als Problem der Kulturwissenschaft: Tristan-Lektüren.* Berlin: de Gruyter, 2006.

Baldwin, Charles S. *Medieval Rhetoric and Poetic.* Gloucester, MA: Peter Smith, 1959.

Baker, Donald C., John L. Murphy, and Louis B. Hall, Jr., eds. *The Late Medieval Religious Plays of Bodleian MSS Digby 133 and E Museo 160.* Early English Text Society, Original Series 283. Oxford: Oxford University Press, 1982.

Barbetti, Claire. *Ekphrastic Medieval Visions: A New Discussion in Interarts Theory.* New York: Palgrave Macmillan, 2011.

———. "Inhuman Ekphrasis: The 40(plus)-Year Ekphrasis of Julian of Norwich." In *Ekphrastic Medieval Visions: A New Discussion in Interarts Theory,* 123–40. New York: Palgrave Macmillan, 2011.

Barnum, Priscilla Heath, ed. *Dives and Pauper.* Early English Text Society, Original Series 275. London: Oxford University Press, 1976.

Barr, Helen. "*Pearl*—Or 'The Jeweller's Tale.'" In *Socioliterary Practice in Late Medieval England,* 40–62. Oxford: Oxford University Press, 2001.

———. *Socioliterary Practice in Late Medieval England.* Oxford: Oxford University Press, 2001.

Barr, Helen, ed. *The Piers Plowman Tradition.* London: Dent, 1993.

Barr, Jessica. *Willing to Know God: Dreamers and Visionaries in the Later Middle Ages.* Columbus: Ohio State University Press, 2010.

Barthes, Roland. "The Reality Effect." In *The Rustle of Language,* translated by Richard Howard, 141–48. New York: Hill and Wang, 1986.

Bartsch, Shadi, and Jaś Elsner. "Introduction: Eight Ways of Looking at an Ekphrasis." *Classical Philology: Special Issue on Ekphrasis* 102.1 (2007): i–vi.

Baudri de Bourgueil. "Adelae Comitissae." In *Baudri de Bourgueil, Poèmes: Tome 2,* edited and translated by Jean-Yves Tilliette, 1–43. Paris: Belles Lettres, 2002.

Bauer, Max. *Precious Stones: A Popular Account of Their Characters, Occurrence and Applications, with an Introduction to Their Determination, for Mineralogists, Lapidaries, Jewellers, etc. with an Appendix on Pearls and Coral.* Translated by L. J. Spencer. London: Charles Griffin, 1904.

Bawcutt, Priscilla J. "Introduction—The Palice of Honour." In *The Shorter Poems of Gavin Douglas,* xv–lii. Scottish Text Society, Fifth Series 2, 2nd ed. Edinburgh: Scottish Text Society, 2003.

Bawcutt, Priscilla J., ed. *The Shorter Poems of Gavin Douglas.* Scottish Text Society, Fifth Series 2, 2nd ed. Edinburgh: Scottish Text Society, 2003.

Becker, Andrew Sprague. *The Shield of Achilles and the Poetics of Ekphrasis.* Lanham, MD: Rowman & Littlefield, 1995.

Beckwith, Sarah. *Signifying God: Social Relation and Symbolic Act in the York Corpus Christi Plays.* Chicago: University of Chicago Press, 2001.

Belting, Hans. *The Anthropology of Images: Picture, Medium, Body.* Translated by Thomas Dunlap. Princeton, NJ: Princeton University Press, 2011.

———. *Bild-Anthropologie: Entwürfe für eine Bildwissenschaft.* Munich: Fink, 2001.

Bender, John B. *Spenser and Literary Pictorialism.* Princeton, NJ: Princeton University Press, 1972.

Benjamin, Walter. *The Arcades Project.* Translated by Howard Eiland and Kevin McLaughlin. Cambridge, MA: Harvard University Press, 1999.

Benson, Larry D. "The 'Queynte' Punnings of Chaucer's Critics." In *Contradictions: From Beowulf to Chaucer,* edited by Theodore M. Andersson and Stephen A. Barney, 217–42. Aldershot: Scolar Press, 1995.

Benson, Larry D., ed. *The Riverside Chaucer.* 3rd ed. Boston: Houghton Mifflin, 1987.

Biernoff, Suzannah. *Sight and Embodiment in the Middle Ages.* Houndmills: Palgrave Macmillan, 2002.

Bleeth, Kenneth. "Joseph's Doubting of Mary and the Conclusion of the 'Merchant's Tale.'" *Chaucer Review* 21 (1986): 58–66.

Bloch, R. Howard. *A Needle in the Right Hand of God: The Norman Conquest of 1066 and the Making and Meaning of the Bayeux Tapestry.* New York: Random House, 2006.

Bode, Georg Heinrich, ed. "Tertius Vaticanus Mythographus." In *Scriptores rerum mythicarum latini tres Romae nuper reperti,* 152–256. 1834. Reprint, Hildesheim: Olms, 1968.

Bogdanos, Theodore. *Pearl: Image of the Ineffable; A Study in Medieval Poetic Symbolism.* University Park: University of Pennsylvania Press, 1983.

Borges, Jorge Luis. "The Analytical Language of John Wilkins." 1942. *Wikipedia,* s.v. "Celestial Emporium of Benevolent Knowledge's Taxonomy." http://en.wikipedia.org/wiki/Celestial_Emporium_of_Benevolent_Knowledge%27s_Taxonomy.

Bossuet, Robert, ed. *Anticlaudianus.* Paris: Vrin, 1955. Reprint translated by James J. Sheridan. *Anticlaudianus, or The Good and Perfect Man.* Toronto: Pontifical Institute of Mediaeval Studies, 1973.

Bowers, John M. "'Beautiful as Troilus': Richard II, Chaucer's Troilus, and Figures of (Un) Masculinity." In *Men and Masculinities in Chaucer's Troilus and Criseyde,* edited by Tison Pugh and Marcia Smith Marzec, 9–27. Chaucer Studies 38. Cambridge: D. S. Brewer, 2008.

———. "How Criseyde Falls in Love." In *The Expansion and Transformations of Courtly Literature,* edited by N. B. Smith and J. T. Snow, 141–55. Athens: University of Georgia Press, 1980.

———. *An Introduction to the* Gawain *Poet.* Gainesville: University Press of Florida, 2012.

———. "The Naughty Bits: Dating Chaucer's *House of Fame* and *Legend of Good Women.*" In *The Medieval Python: The Purposive and Provocative Work of Terry Jones, Essays Presented on the Occasion of His Seventieth Birthday,* edited by R. F. Yeager and Toshiyuki Takamiya, 105–17. New York: Palgrave Macmillan, 2012.

———. *The Politics of* Pearl: *Court Poetry in the Age of Richard II.* Cambridge: D. S. Brewer, 2001.

Bowers, John M., ed. The Canterbury Tales: *Fifteenth-Century Continuations and Additions.* Kalamazoo, MI: TEAMS Medieval Institute Publications, 1992.

Boyle, Marjorie O. R. *Loyola's Acts: The Rhetoric of the Self.* Berkeley: University of California Press, 1997.

Brantley, Jessica. "Vision, Image, Text." In *Middle English,* edited by Paul Strohm, 315–34. Oxford: Oxford University Press, 2007.

Bridges, Margaret. "The Picture in the Text: Ecphrasis as Self-Reflexivity in Chaucer's *Parliament of Fowles, Book of the Duchess* and *House of Fame.*" *Word and Image* 5 (1989): 151–58.

Brown Jr., Emerson. "The Merchant's Damyan and Chaucer's Kent." *Chaucer Newsletter* 13.1 (1991): 5.

Brown, Margaret, and C. Stephen Jaeger. "Pageantry and Court Aesthetic in Gottfried's *Tristan.*" In *Gottfried von Strassburg and the Medieval Tristan Legend,* edited by Adrian Stevens and Roy Wisbey, 29–44. Cambridge: D. S. Brewer, 1990.

Brown, Peter. *Chaucer and the Making of Optical Space.* Oxford: Peter Lang, 2007.

———. "Journey's End: The Prologue to *The Tale of Beryn.*" In *Chaucer and Fifteenth-Century Poetry,* edited by Julia Boffey and Janet Cowen, 143–74. King's College London Medieval Studies 5. London: King's College, Centre for Late Antique and Medieval Studies, 1991.

Brown, Shirley Ann, and Michael W. Herren. "The *Adelae Comitissae* of Baudri de Bourgeuil and the Bayeux Tapestry." *Anglo-Norman Studies* 16 (1993): 55–73.

Brownlee, Kevin. "The Image of History in Christine de Pizan's *Livre de la Mutacion de Fortune.*" In *Contexts: Style and Values in Medieval Art and Literature,* edited by Daniel Poirion and Nancy Freeman Regalado, 44–56. Yale French Studies, special issue. New Haven: Yale University Press, 1991.

Bryant, Levi, Nick Srnicek, and Graham Harman, eds. *The Speculative Turn: Continental Materialism and Realism.* Melbourne: re-press, 2011.

Buettner, Brigitte. "Toward a Historiography of the Sumptuous Arts." In *A Companion to Medieval Art: Romanesque and Gothic in Northern Europe,* edited by Conrad Rudolph, 466–87. Oxford: Wiley-Blackwell, 2006.

Butterfield, Ardis. "Chaucerian Vernaculars." *Studies in the Age of Chaucer* 31 (2009): 25–51.

———. *The Familiar Enemy: Chaucer, Language, and Nation in the Hundred Years War*. Oxford: Oxford University Press, 2009.

Bynum, Caroline Walker. *Metamorphosis and Identity*. New York: Zone Books, 2005.

Camille, Michael. "Before the Gaze: The Internal Senses and Late Medieval Practices of Seeing." In *Visuality Before and Beyond the Renaissance: Seeing as Others Saw*, edited by Robert S. Nelson, 197–223. Cambridge: Cambridge University Press, 2000.

———. *The Gothic Idol: Ideology and Image-Making in Medieval Art*. Cambridge: Cambridge University Press, 1989.

Campbell, Emma, and Robert Mills, eds. *Troubled Vision: Gender, Sexuality, and Sight in Medieval Text and Image*. New York: Palgrave Macmillan, 2004.

Campbell, Mary Baine. *Wonder and Science: Imagining Worlds in Early Modern Europe*. Ithaca, NY: Cornell University Press, 1999.

Cannon, Christopher. *The Making of Chaucer's English*. Cambridge: Cambridge University Press, 1998.

Carruthers, Mary J. *The Book of Memory: A Study of Memory in Medieval Culture*. Cambridge: Cambridge University Press, 1990.

———. *The Craft of Thought: Meditation, Rhetoric, and the Making of Images, 400–1200*. Cambridge Studies in Medieval Literature. Cambridge: Cambridge University Press, 1998.

———. "Invention, Mnemonics, and Stylistic Ornament in *Psychomachia* and *Pearl*." In *The Endless Knot: Essays on Old and Middle English in Honor of Marie Borroff*, edited by M. Teresa Tavormina and R. F. Yeager, 201–13. Cambridge: D. S. Brewer, 1995.

———. "Reading with Attitude, Remembering the Book." In *The Book and the Body*, edited by Dolores Warwick Frese and Katherine O'Brien O'Keeffe, 1–33. Notre Dame, IN: University of Notre Dame Press, 1997.

Carruthers, Mary J., and Jan M. Ziolkowski. "General Introduction." In *The Medieval Craft of Memory: An Anthology of Texts and Pictures*, edited by Mary J. Carruthers and Jan M. Ziolkowski, 1–31. Philadelphia: University of Pennsylvania Press, 2002.

Caviness, Madeline H. "Biblical Stories in Windows: Were They Bibles for the Poor?" In *The Bible in the Middle Ages: Its Influence on Literature and Art*, edited by Bernard Levy, 103–48. Binghamton, NY: Medieval & Renaissance Texts & Studies, 1992.

———. "Images of Divine Order and the Third Mode of Seeing." *Gesta* 22.2 (1983): 99–120.

Caxton, William. *Dialogues in French and English*. Edited by Henry Bradley. Early English Text Society, Extra Series 79. London: Kegan Paul, 1900.

Chaganti, Seeta. *The Medieval Poetics of the Reliquary: Enshrinement, Inscription, Performance*. New York: Palgrave Macmillan, 2008.

———. "The Space of Epistemology in Marie de France's *Yonec*." *Romance Studies* 28.2 (2010): 71–83.

Chartier, Roger. *Inscription and Erasure: Literature and Written Culture from the Eleventh to the Eighteenth Century.* Translated by Arthur Goldhammer. Philadelphia: University of Pennsylvania Press, 2007.

Cheeke, Stephen. *Writing for Art: The Aesthetics of Ekphrasis.* Manchester: Manchester University Press, 2008.

Chinca, Marc. "The Body in Some Middle High German *Mären:* Taming and Maiming." In *Framing Medieval Bodies,* edited by Sarah Kay and Miri Rubin, 187–210. Manchester: Manchester University Press, 1994.

Chrétien de Troyes. *Erec et Enide.* Edited by Mario Roques. Paris: Honoré Champion, 1970.

Christine de Pizan. *Livre de la Mutacion de Fortune.* Edited by Suzanne Solente. 4 Vols. Paris: Société des anciens textes français, 1955–61.

Clancy, M. T. *From Memory to Written Record: England 1066–1307.* 2nd ed. 1979. Reprint, Malden: Blackwell, 1993.

Clason, Christopher R. "'Good Lovin': The Language of Erotic Desire and Fulfillment in Gottfried's *Tristan.*" In *Sexuality in the Middle Ages and the Early Modern Times: New Approaches to a Fundamental Cultural-Historical and Literary-Anthropological Theme,* edited by Albrecht Classen, 257–78. Berlin: de Gruyter, 2008.

Clüver, Claus. "Quotation, Enargeia, and the Functions of Ekphrasis." In *Pictures into Words: Theoretical and Descriptive Approaches to Ekphrasis,* edited by Valerie Robillard and Els Jongeneel, 35–52. Amsterdam: VU University Press, 1998.

Cole, Andrew, and D. Vance Smith, eds. *The Legitimacy of the Middle Ages: On the Unwritten History of Theory.* Durham, NC, and London: Duke University Press, 2010.

Coleman, Janet. *Ancient and Medieval Memories: Studies in the Reconstruction of the Past.* Cambridge: Cambridge University Press, 1992.

Coletti, Theresa. *Mary Magdalene and the Drama of Saints: Theater, Gender, and Religion in Late Medieval England.* Philadelphia: University of Pennsylvania Press, 2004.

Coley, David K. "'Withyn a temple ymad of glas': Glazing, Glossing, and Patronage in Chaucer's *House of Fame.*" *Chaucer Review* 45 (2010): 59–84.

Colish, Marcia L. *The Mirror of Language: A Study in the Medieval Theory of Knowledge.* Lincoln: University of Nebraska Press, 1983.

Collette, Carolyn P. *Species, Phantasms and Images: Vision and Medieval Psychology in The Canterbury Tales.* Ann Arbor: University of Michigan Press, 2001.

Colvin, H. M., ed. *The History of the King's Works.* Vol. 1. London: Her Majesty's Stationery Office, 1963.

Constans, Léopold, ed. *Le Roman de Troie publié d'après tous les manuscrits connus.* Société des anciens textes français. 6 Vols. Paris: Firmin Didot, 1904–1912.

Conway, Martin. "Some Treasures of the Time of Charles the Bald." *Burlington Magazine for Connoisseurs* 26 (1915): 236–41.

Cooper, Helen. "Welcome to the House of Fame: 600 Years Dead; Chaucer's Deserved Reputation as 'the Father of English Poetry.'" *Times Literary Supplement* 5091, October 27, 2000: 3–4.

Cooper, J. Meadows, ed. *Meditations on the Supper of Our Lord, and the Hours of the Passion, by Cardinal John Bonaventura.* London: Trübner & Co., 1875.

Cooper, Lisa H. *Artisans and Narrative Craft in Late Medieval England.* Cambridge: Cambridge University Press, 2011.

Copeland, Rita. "Naming, Knowing, and the Object of Language in Alexander Neckam's Grammar Curriculum." *Journal of Medieval Latin* 20 (2010): 38–57.

Couliano, Ioan P. *Eros and Magic in the Renaissance.* Translated by Margaret Cook. Chicago: University of Chicago Press, 1987.

Craiger-Smith, A. *English Medieval Mural Paintings.* Oxford: Clarendon Press, 1963.

Croft, Pauline. *King James.* Houndmills: Palgrave Macmillan, 2003.

Crow, Martin, and Clair C. Olson. *Chaucer Life-Records.* Oxford: Clarendon Press, 1966.

Cunningham, Valentine. "Why Ekphrasis?" *Classical Philology: Special Issue on Ekphrasis* 102.1 (2007): 57–71.

Curry, Walter Clyde. *Chaucer and the Mediaeval Sciences.* New York: Oxford University Press, 1926.

Curtius, Ernst Robert. *European Literature and the Latin Middle Ages.* Translated by Willard R. Trask. Princeton, NJ: Princeton University Press, 1953.

Dahlberg, Charles, ed. *The Romance of the Rose.* Princeton, NJ: Princeton University Press, 1971.

Daston, Lorraine, and Katharine Park. *Wonders and the Order of Nature, 1150–1750.* New York: Zone Books, 1998.

Davidson, Clifford. "The Digby *Mary Magdalene* and the Magdalene Cult of the Middle Ages." *Annuale Mediaevale* 13 (1972): 70–87.

———. *Drama and Art: An Introduction to the Use of Evidence from the Visual Arts for the Study of Early Drama.* Kalamazoo, MI: The Medieval Institute, 1977.

Davidson, Mary Catherine. *Medievalism, Muiltilingualism, and Chaucer.* New York: Palgrave Macmillan, 2010.

Dean, James M. *The World Grown Old in Later Medieval Literature.* Cambridge, MA: Medieval Academy of America, 1997.

Debiais, Vincent. "The Poem of Baudri for Countess Adèle: A Starting Point for a Reading of Medieval Latin Ekphrasis." *Viator* 44.1 (2013): 95–106.

Denery II, Dallas G. *Seeing and Being Seen in the Later Medieval World: Optics, Theology, and Religious Life.* Cambridge: Cambridge University Press, 2005.

Derrida, Jacques. *The Truth in Painting.* Translated by Geoff Bennington and Ian McLeod. Chicago: University of Chicago Press, 1987.

———. *Writing and Difference*. Translated by Alan Bass. Chicago: University of Chicago Press, 1978.

Dicke, Gerd. "Das belauschte Stelldichein. Eine Stoffgeschichte." In *Der* Tristan *Gottfrieds von Straßburg*. Symposion Santiago de Compostela. April 5–8, 2000, edited by Christoph Huber and Victor Millet, 199–220. Tübingen: Niemeyer, 2002.

Didi-Huberman, Georges. *Fra Angelico: Dissemblance and Figuration*. Translated by Jane Marie Todd. Chicago: Chicago University Press, 1995.

Dimmick, Jeremy, James Simpson, and Nicolette Zeeman, eds. *Images, Idolatry, and Iconoclasm in Late Medieval England: Textuality and the Visual Image*. Oxford: Oxford University Press, 2002.

Dinshaw, Carolyn. "Pale Faces: Race, Religion, and Affect in Chaucer's Texts and Their Readers." *Studies in the Age of Chaucer* 23 (2001): 19–41.

Donovan, Mortimer J. "Chaucer's January and May: Counterparts in Claudian." In *Chaucerian Problems and Perspectives: Essays Presented to Paul E. Beichner,* edited by Edward Vasta and Zacharias P. Thundy, 59–69. Notre Dame, IN: University of Notre Dame Press, 1979.

Douay-Rheims Catholic Bible. April 29, 2012. http://www.drbo.org/chapter/73021.htm.

Dubois, Page. *History, Rhetorical Description and the Epic from Homer to Spenser*. Cambridge: D. S. Brewer, 1982.

Dudash, Suzan. "Christine de Pizan and the 'menu people.'" *Speculum* 78 (2003): 788–831.

Dulac, Liliane. "Le chevalier Hercule de l'*Ovide moralisé* au *Livre de la mutacion de fortune* de Christine de Pizan." *Cahiers de recherches médiévales* 9 (2002): 115–30.

Dundas, Judith. *The Spider and the Bee: The Artistry of Spenser's* Faerie Queene. Urbana: University of Illinois Press, 1985.

Eagleton, Terry. *The Ideology of the Aesthetic*. Oxford: Blackwell, 1990.

Eco, Umberto. *Art and Beauty in the Middle Ages*. Translated by Hugh Bredin. New Haven, CT: Yale University Press, 1986.

———. *The Name of the Rose*. Translated by William Weaver. Orlando: Harcourt, Brace & Co., 1983.

Edmondson, George. "*Pearl*: The Shadow of the Object, the Shape of the Law." *Studies in the Age of Chaucer* 26 (2004): 29–63.

Ebin, Lois A. *Illuminator, Makar, Vates: Visions of Poetry in the Fifteenth Century*. Lincoln: University of Nebraska Press, 1988.

Elliott, Jane. "The Currency of Feminist Theory." *PMLA* 121 (2006): 1697–703.

Elliott, Ralph W. V. *Chaucer's English*. London: Deutsch, 1974.

Elsner, Jaś. "The Genres of Ekphrasis." *Ramus* 31 (2002): 1–18.

———. "Viewing Ariadne: From Ekphrasis to Wall Painting in the Roman World." *Classical Philology* 102.1 (2007): 20–44.

Epstein, Robert. "'With many a floryn he the hewes boghte': Ekphrasis and Symbolic Violence in the 'Knight's Tale.'" *Philological Quarterly* 85 (2006): 49–68.

Evans, Joan. *Magical Jewels of the Middle Ages and the Renaissance Particularly in England.* Oxford: Clarendon Press, 1922.

Evans, Helen C., and William D. Wixom, eds. *The Glory of Byzantium: Art and Culture of the Middle Byzantine Era A.D. 843–1261.* New York: Metropolitan Museum of Art, 1997.

Fabbrini, Fabrizio. *Paolo Orosio: Uno storico.* Rome: Edizione di Storia e Letteratura, 1979.

Faral, Edmond. *Les arts poétiques du XIIe et du XIIIe siècle: recherches et documents sur la technique littéraire du moyen âge.* 1924. Reprint, Paris: Champion, 1962. Translated by Margaret F. Nims. *Poetria Nova of Geoffrey of Vinsauf.* Medieval Sources in Translation 6. Toronto: Pontifical Institute of Medieval Studies, 1967.

Firchow, Evelyn Scherabon, Richard Hotchkiss, and Rick Treece, eds. *Notker der Deutsche von St. Gallen, Die Hochzeit der Philologie und des Merkur—De nuptiis Philologiae et Mercurii von Martianus Capella. Diplomatischer Textabdruck, Konkordanzen und Wortlisten nach dem Codex Sangallensis 872.* 2 Vols. Hildesheim: Olms, 1999.

Fischer, Barbara K. *Museum Mediations: Refining Ekphrasis in Contemporary American Poetry.* New York: Routledge, 2006.

Ferré, Barbara, ed. *Martianus Capella: Les noces de Philologie et de Mercure: Livre VI: La géométrie.* Paris: Les Belles Lettres, 2007.

Ferré, Michel, ed. *Martianus Capella: Les noces de Philologie et de Mercure. Livre IV: La dialectique.* Paris: Les Belles Lettres, 2007.

Fleming, John V. "Ambages; Or, The Genealogy of Ambiguity." In *Classical Imitation and Interpretation in Chaucer's* Troilus, 45–71. Lincoln: University of Nebraska Press, 1990.

———. "Idols of the Prince." In *Classical Imitation and Interpretation in Chaucer's* Troilus, 72–154. Lincoln: University of Nebraska Press, 1990.

———. *The* Roman de la Rose: *A Study in Allegory and Iconography.* Princeton, NJ: Princeton University Press, 1969.

Foys, Martin K., ed. *The Bayeux Tapestry: Digital Edition.* Leicester: Scholarly Digital Editions, 2003.

Fradenburg, L. O. Aranye. *City, Marriage, Tournament: Arts of Rule in Late Medieval Scotland.* Madison: University of Wisconsin Press, 1991.

———. "Making, Mourning, and the Love of Idols." In *Images, Idolatry, and Iconoclasm in Late Medieval England: Textuality and the Visual Image,* edited by Jeremy Dimmick, James Simpson, and Nicolette Zeeman, 25–42. Oxford: Oxford University Press, 2002.

———. "'Voice Memorial': Loss and Reparation in Chaucer's Poetry." *Exemplaria* 2 (1990): 169–202.

Francis, James A. "Metal Maidens, Achilles' Shield, and Pandora: The Beginnings of 'Ekphrasis.'" *American Journal of Philology* 130.1 (2009): 1–23.

Frederico, Sylvia. *New Troy: Fantasies of Empire in the Late Middle Ages.* Minneapolis: University of Minnesota Press, 2003.

Freud, Sigmund. "Mourning and Melancholia." In *The Standard Edition of the Complete Psychological Works of Sigmund Freud,* translated by J. Strachey, Vol XIV, 237–58. London: Hogarth, 1957.

Friedman, John Block. "Another Look at Chaucer and the Physiognomists." *Studies in Philology* 78.2 (1981): 138–52.

Furnivall, F. J., ed. *The Digby Mysteries.* London: The New Shakspere Society, 1882.

Galloway, Andrew. "Chaucer's Former Age and the Fourteenth-Century Anthropology of Craft: The Social Logic of a Premodernist Lyric." *ELH* 63 (1996): 535–54.

Garber, Marjorie. *Shakespeare after All.* New York: Anchor Books, 2004.

Garrison, Jennifer. "Liturgy and Loss: *Pearl* and the Ritual Reform of the Aristocratic Subject." *Chaucer Review* 44.3 (2010): 294–322.

Garth, Helen. *Saint Mary Magdalene in Mediaeval Literature.* Baltimore: Johns Hopkins Press, 1950.

Gayk, Shannon. *Image, Text, and Religious Reform in Fifteenth-Century England.* Cambridge: Cambridge University Press, 2010.

———. "'To wonder upon this thing': Chaucer's Prioress's Tale." *Exemplaria* 22 (2010): 138–56.

Gilman, Ernest B. "Spenser's 'Painted Forgery.'" In *Iconoclasm and Poetry in the English Reformation: Down Went Dagon,* 61–83. Chicago: University of Chicago Press, 1986.

Glauch, Sonja. *Die Martianus-Capella-Bearbeitung Notkers des Deutschen.* Münchner Texte und Untersuchungen zur deutschen Literatur des Mittelalters 116. 2 Vols. Tübingen: Niemeyer, 2000.

Gless, Darryl G. *Interpretation and Theology in Spenser.* Cambridge: Cambridge University Press, 1994.

Gnädinger, Louise. *Hiudan und Petitcreiu: Gestalt und Figur des Hundes in der mittelalterlichen Tristandichtung.* Zurich: Atlantis, 1971.

Goldhill, Simon. "The Erotic Eye: Visual Stimulation and Cultural Conflict." In *Being Greek under Rome: Cultural Identity, the Second Sophistic, and the Development of Empire,* edited by Simon Goldhill, 154–94. Cambridge: Cambridge University Press, 2001.

———. "The Naïve and Knowing Eye: Ecphrasis and the Culture of Viewing in the Hellenistic World." In *Art and Text in Ancient Greek Culture,* edited by Simon Goldhill and Robin Osborne, 197–223. Cambridge: Cambridge University Press, 1994.

———. "Refracting Classical Vision: Changing Cultures of Vision." In *Vision in Context: Historical and Contemporary Perspectives on Sight,* edited by Teresa Brennan and Martin Jay, 15–28. New York: Routledge, 1996.

———. "What Is Ekphrasis For?" *Classical Philology: Special Issue on Ekphrasis* 102.1 (2007): 1–19.

Gombrich, E. H. *Art and Illusion: A Study in the Psychology of Pictorial Representation.* Bollingen Series XXXV.5. 2nd ed. Princeton, NJ: Princeton University Press, 1960.

Goodland, Katharine. "'Vs for to Wepe No Man May Lett': Accommodating Female Grief in the Medieval English Lazarus Plays." *Early Theatre: A Journal Associated with the Records of Early English Drama* 8.1 (2005): 69–94.

Gottfried von Strassburg. *Tristan.* 2 Vols. Stuttgart: Reclam, 1987.

———. *Tristan with the 'Tristran' of Thomas.* Translated by A. T. Hatto. London: Penguin, 2004.

Gower, John. *Confessio Amantis.* Edited by Russell A. Peck. Kalamazoo: Western Michigan University Press, 2000.

Gras, N. S. B. *The Early English Customs Systems.* Cambridge, MA: Harvard University Press, 1918.

Grogan, Jane. *Exemplary Spenser: Visual and Poetic Pedagogy in* The Faerie Queene. Farnham: Ashgate, 2009.

Guillaume de Lorris and Jean de Meun. *Le Roman de la Rose.* Edited by Armand Strubel. Paris: Librairie Générale Française, 1992.

———. *The Romance of the Rose.* Edited by Charles Dahlberg. Princeton, NJ: Princeton University Press, 1971.

Guillaumin, Jean-Baptiste, ed. *Martianus Capella: Les noces de Philologie et de Mercure: Livre IX: L'harmonie.* Paris: Les Belles Lettres, 2011.

Guillaumin, Jean-Yves, ed. *Martianus Capella: Les noces de Philologie et de Mercure: Livre VII: L'arithmétique.* Paris: Les Belles Lettres, 2003.

Gustafson, Kevin. "The Lay Gaze, *Pearl,* the Dreamer and the Vernacular Reader." *Medievalia et Humanistica* New Series 27 (2000): 57–77.

Hadley, Dawn. *Death in Medieval England: An Archaeology.* Stroud: Tempus, 2001.

Hagstrum, Jean H. *The Sister Arts: The Tradition of Literary Pictorialism and English Poetry from Dryden to Gray.* Chicago: University of Chicago Press, 1958.

Hahn, Cynthia. "*Visio Dei:* Changes in Medieval Visuality." In *Visuality Before and Beyond the Renaissance: Seeing as Others Saw,* edited by Robert S. Nelson, 169–96. Cambridge: Cambridge University Press, 2000.

Haigh, Christopher. "From Resentment to Recusancy." In *English Reformations: Religion, Politics, and Society under the Tudors,* 251–67. Oxford: Clarendon Press, 1993.

Hamilton, Albert C. *The Spenser Encyclopedia.* Toronto: Toronto University Press, 1990.

Hamilton, Marie P. "The *Pearl* Poet." In *A Manual of the Writings in Middle English, 1050–1500,* edited by J. Burke Severs. Vol. 2, 339–53. New Haven: Connecticut Academy of Arts and Sciences, 1970.

Hard, Frederick M. "Spenser's 'Clothes of Arras and of Toure.'" *Studies in Philology* 27 (1930): 162–85.

Harley, Marta Powell. "Chaucer's Use of the Proserpina Myth in the 'Knight's Tale' and the 'Merchant's Tale.'" In *Images of Persephone: Feminist Readings in Western Literature,* edited by Elizabeth T. Hayes, 20–31. Gainesville: University Press of Florida, 1994.

Harper, Elizabeth. "*Pearl* in the Context of Fourteenth-Century Gift Economies." *Chaucer Review* 44.4 (2010): 421–39.

Haskins, Susan. *Mary Magdalen: Myth and Metaphor.* New York: Harcourt Brace, 1993.

Hasler, Antony J. *Court Poetry in Late Medieval England and Scotland: Allegories of Authority.* Cambridge: Cambridge University Press, 2011.

Hathaway, Ernest J., Peter T. Ricketts, Charles A. Robson, and A. D. Wilshere, eds. *Fouke le Fitz Waryn.* Anglo-Norman Text Society 26–28. Oxford: Blackwell, 1975.

Heffernan, Carol Falvo. "Wells and Streams in Three Chaucerian Gardens." In *Papers on Literature and Language* 15 (1979): 339–57.

Heffernan, James A. W. "Ekphrasis and Rape from Chaucer to Spenser." In *Museum of Words: The Poetics of Ekphrasis from Homer to Ashbery,* 61–74. Chicago: University of Chicago Press, 1993.

———. "Ekphrasis and Representation." *New Literary History* 22.2 (1991): 297–316.

———. *Museum of Words: The Poetics of Ekphrasis from Homer to Ashbery.* Chicago: University of Chicago Press, 1993.

Heller, Sarah-Grace. "Obscure Lands and Obscured Hands: Fairy Embroidery and the Ambiguous Vocabulary of Medieval Textile Decoration." *Medieval Clothing and Textiles* 5 (2009): 15–35.

Herodotus. *The Histories.* Translated by Aubrey de Sélincourt, revised by John Marincola. London: Penguin, 1996.

Herren, Michael W. "Baudri de Bourgeuil, *Adelae Comitissae.*" In *The Bayeux Tapestry: History and Bibliography,* edited by Shirley Ann Brown, with contribution by Michael W. Herren, 176–77. Woodbridge: Boydell and Brewer, 1988.

Hewlett, Janice Koelb. *The Poetics of Description: Imagined Places in European Literature.* New York: Palgrave Macmillan, 2006.

Hilmo, Maidie. *Medieval Images, Icons, and Illustrated English Texts: From the Ruthwell Cross to the Ellesmere Chaucer.* Farnham: Ashgate, 2004.

Hoccleve, Thomas. "My Compleinte" *and Other Poems.* Edited by Roger Ellis. Exeter: University of Exeter Press, 2001.

Hollander, John. "The Poetics of Ekphrasis." *Word & Image* 4 (1988): 209–19.

Holley, Linda Tarte. *Reason and Imagination in Chaucer, the* Perle-*Poet, and the* Cloud-*Author: Seeing from the Center.* New York: Palgrave Macmillan, 2011.

Holsinger, Bruce. "Lollard Ekphrasis: Situated Aesthetics and Literary History." *Journal of Medieval and Early Modern Studies* 35 (2005): 67–90.

Hoskier, Herman Charles, ed. *De Contemptu Mundi: A Bitter Satirical Poem of 3000 Lines upon the Morals of the XIIth Century by Bernard of Morval*. London: Bernard Quaritch, 1929.

Houen, Alex. "Introduction: Affecting Words." *Textual Practice: Special Issue; Affects, Text, and Performativity* 25.2 (2011): 215–32.

Howes, Laura L. *Chaucer's Gardens and the Language of Convention*. Gainesville: University Press of Florida, 1997.

Huber, Christoph. *Gottfried von Strassburg: Tristan*. Berlin: Schmidt, 2000.

———. *Gottfried von Strassburg, Tristan und Isolde: Eine Einführung*. Munich: Artemis, 1986.

Hudson, Anne. *The Premature Reformation: Wycliffite Texts and Lollard History*. Oxford: Clarendon Press, 1988.

Hudson, Anne, ed. *Selections from English Wycliffite Writings*. Cambridge: Cambridge University Press, 1978.

Huizinga, Johan. *Autumn of the Middle Ages*. Translated by Rodney J. Payton and Ulrich Mammitzsch. Chicago: Chicago University Press, 1996.

———. *The Waning of the Middle Ages: A Study of the Forms of Life, Thought and Art in France and the Netherlands in the XIVth and XVth Centuries*. Translated by F. Hopman. London: Edward Arnold, 1924.

Hulse, Clark. *Metamorphic Verse: The Elizabethan Minor Epic*. Princeton, NJ: Princeton University Press, 1981.

Hult, David, F. *Self-Fulfilling Prophecies: Readership and Authority in the First* Roman de la Rose. Cambridge: Cambridge University Press, 1986.

Hunt, Tony. *Teaching and Learning Latin in Thirteenth-Century England*. Vol. 1. Cambridge: D. S. Brewer, 1991.

Hunter, Brooke. "*Remenants* of Things Past: Memory and the *Knight's Tale*." *Exemplaria* 23 (2011): 126–46.

Illich, Ivan. *In the Vineyard of the Text: A Commentary to Hugh's* Didascalicon. Chicago: University of Chicago Press, 1993.

Ingham, Richard. "Mixing Languages on the Manor." *Medium Aevum* 78 (2009): 80–92.

Jackson, Stanley W. *Melancholia and Depression from Hippocratic Times to Modern Times*. New Haven, CT: Yale University Press, 1986.

Jacobson, Evelyn. "The *Liste* of Tristan." *Amsterdamer Beiträge zur älteren Germanistik* 18 (1982): 115–28.

Jacobus de Voragine. *The Golden Legend*. Translated by William Granger Ryan. 2 Vols. Princeton, NJ: Princeton University Press, 1993.

Jameson, Frederick. *The Antinomies of Realism*. London and New York: Verso, 2013.

Jansen, Katherine Ludwig. *The Making of the Magdalen: Preaching and Popular Devotion in the Later Middle Ages*. Princeton, NJ: Princeton University Press, 2000.

Jefferson, Lisa. "The Language and Vocabulary of the Fourteenth- and Early Fifteenth-Century Records of the Goldsmiths' Company." In *Multilingualism in Later Medieval Britain,* edited by D. A. Trotter, 175–211. Cambridge: D. S. Brewer, 2000.

Johnston, Andrew James. "Ekphrasis in the *Knight's Tale.*" In *Rethinking the New Medievalism,* edited by R. Howard Bloch, Alison Calhoun, Jacqueline Cerquiglini-Toulet, Joachim Küpper, and Jeanette Patterson, 181–97. Baltimore: Johns Hopkins University Press, 2014.

———. *Performing the Middle Ages from* Beowulf *to* Othello. Turnhout: Brepols, 2008.

———. "Sailing the Seas of Literary History: Gower, Chaucer, and the Problem of Incest in Shakespeare's *Pericles.*" *Poetica* 41 (2009): 381–407.

Jones, Timothy S., and David A. Sprunger. "Introduction: The Marvelous Imagination." In *Marvels, Monsters, and Miracles: Studies in the Medieval and Early Modern Imaginations,* edited by Timothy S. Jones and David A. Sprunger, xi–xxv. Kalamazoo, MI: Medieval Institute Publications, 2002.

Jupé, Wolfgang. *Die List im Tristanroman Gottfrieds von Strassburg: Intellektualität und Liebe oder die Suche nach dem Wesen der individuellen Existenz.* Heidelberg: Winter, 1976.

Kaeuper, Richard W. *Chivalry and Violence in Medieval Europe.* Oxford: Oxford University Press, 1999.

Kalinke, Marianne. "Tristams saga ok Ísöndar, ch. 80: Ekphrasis as Recapitulation and Interpretation." In *Analecta Septentrionalia. Beiträge zur nordgermanischen Kultur- und Literaturgeschichte,* edited by Wilhelm Heizmann, Klaus Böldl, and Heinrich Beck, 221–37. Berlin: de Gruyter, 2009.

Kane, Sean. *The Spenser Encyclopedia.* Toronto: University of Toronto Press, 1990.

Kant, Immanuel. *The Critique of Judgement.* Edited by Nicholas Walker, translated by James Creed Meredith. Revised Edition. Oxford: Oxford University Press, 2007.

Keith, Alison M. "Imperial Building Projects and Architectural Ekphrases in Ovid's *Metamorphoses* and Statius' *Thebaid.*" *Mouseion* 7. 3rd ser. (2007): 1–26.

Kennedy, George A. *Progymnasmata: Greek Textbooks of Prose Composition and Rhetoric.* Leiden: Brill, 2003.

Klarer, Mario. *Ekphrasis: Bildbeschreibungen als Repräsentationstheorie bei Spenser, Sidney, Lyly und Shakespeare.* Tübingen: Niemeyer, 2001.

———. "Ekphrasis, or the Archeology of Historical Theories of Representation: Medieval Brain Anatomy in Wernher der Gartenaere's *Helmbrecht.*" *Word and Image* 15 (1999): 34–40.

Knuuttila, Simo. *Emotions in Ancient and Medieval Philosophy.* Oxford: Oxford University Press, 2004.

Koelb, Janice Hewlett. *The Poetics of Description: Imagined Places in European Literature.* New York: Palgrave Macmillan, 2006.

Kohanski, Tamarah, and C. David Benson, eds. *The Book of John Mandeville.* Kalamazoo, MI: Medieval Institute Publications, 2007.

Kolve, V. A. "Introduction." In *Chaucer and the Imagery of Narrative: The First Five Canterbury Tales,* 1–8. Stanford: Stanford University Press, 1984.

———. "Preface." In *Telling Images: Chaucer and the Imagery of Narrative II,* xv–xxvii. Stanford: Stanford University Press, 2009.

———. *The Play Called Corpus Christi.* Stanford: Stanford University Press, 1966.

Kratzmann, Gregory C. "*The Palice of Honour* and *The Hous of Fame.*" In *Anglo-Scottish Literary Relations 1430–1550,* 104–28. Cambridge: Cambridge University Press, 1980.

Krieger, Murray. *Ekphrasis: The Illusion of the Natural Sign.* Baltimore: Johns Hopkins University Press, 1992.

———. *Words about Words about Words: Theory, Criticism, and the Literary Text.* Baltimore: Johns Hopkins University Press, 1988.

Kruger, Stephen F. *Dreaming in the Middle Ages.* Cambridge: Cambridge University Press, 1992.

———. "Dreams and Fiction." In *Dreaming in the Middle Ages,* 123–49. Cambridge: Cambridge University Press, 1992.

Lanham, Richard A. *A Handlist of Rhetorical Terms.* 2nd ed. Berkeley: University of California Press, 1991.

Layher, William. "'Sô süeze waz der schellen klanc.' Music, Dissonance and the Sweetness of Pain in Gottfried's *Tristan.*" *Beiträge zur Geschichte der deutschen Sprache und Literatur* 133.2 (2011): 235–64.

Lecoy, Félix, ed. *Roman de la Rose.* 3 Vols. Paris: Champion, 1965–70.

Lewis, C. S. *The Allegory of Love: A Study in Medieval Tradition.* 1936. Reprint, Oxford: Oxford University Press, 1990.

Lewis, Cynthia. "Soft Touch: On the Renaissance Staging and Meaning of the 'Noli me tangere.'" *Comparative Drama* 36 (2002): 53–73.

Lieberz-Grün, Ursula. "Pluralismus im Mittelalter: Eine polemische Miszelle." *Monatshefte für deutschen Unterricht, deutsche Sprache und Literatur* 86 (1994): 3–6.

Lindley, Phillip. "Absolutism and Regal Image in Ricardian Sculpture." In *The Regal Image of Richard II and the Wilton Diptych,* edited by Dillian Gordon, Lisa Monnas, and Caroline Elam, 61–83. London: Harvey Miller, 1997.

Lloyd, Rosemary. *Shimmering in a Transformed Light: Writing the Still Life.* Ithaca, NY: Cornell University Press, 2005.

Longinus. *On the Sublime.* Translated with a commentary by James A. Arieti and John M. Crossett. New York: Edwin Mellen Press, 1985.

LoPrete, Kimberly, A. *Adela of Blois: Countess and Lord (c. 1067–1137).* Dublin: Four Courts, 2007.

Love, Nicholas. *The mirrour of the blessed lyf of Jesu Christ.* Edited by Elizabeth Salter. Salzburg: Institut für Englische Sprache und Literatur, Universität Salzburg, 1974.

Lowes, John Livingston. *Geoffrey Chaucer and the Development of His Genius*. Boston: Houghton Mifflin, 1934.

Lupton, Julia Reinhard. *Afterlives of the Saints: Hagiography, Typology, and Renaissance Literature*. Stanford: Stanford University Press, 1996.

Lutz, Cora E., ed. *Dunchad: Glossae in Martianum*. Philological Monographs XII. Lancaster, PA: American Philological Association, 1944.

———. *Johannes Scotti Annotationes in Marcianum*. The Medieval Academy of America Publications 34. Cambridge, MA: Medieval Academy of America, 1939.

———. *Remigii Autissiodorensis Commentum in Martianum Capellam. Libri I–II*. Leiden: Brill, 1962.

Lynch, Kathryn L. *The High Medieval Dream Vision: Vision, Philosophy, and Literary Form*. Stanford: Stanford University Press, 1988.

Machan, Tim William. "French, English, and the Late Medieval Linguistic Repertoire." In *Language and Culture in Medieval Britain: The French of England c. 1100–c. 1500*, edited by Jocelyn Wogan-Browne, Carolyn Collette, Maryanne Kowaleski, Linne Mooney, Ad Putter, and David Trotter, 363–72. Woodbridge: York Medieval Press, 2009.

Mâle, Émile. *The Gothic Image: Religious Art in France of the Thirteenth Century*. New York: Harper and Row, 1972.

Malo, Robyn. *Relics and Writing in Late Medieval England*. Toronto: University of Toronto Press, 2013.

Mann, Jill. *Chaucer and Medieval Estates Satire*. Cambridge: Cambridge University Press, 1973.

Mansell, Darrel. "Metaphor as Matter." *Language and Literature* 15 (1992): 109–20.

Maring, Heather. "'Never the Less': Gift-Exchange and the Medieval Dream-Vision *Pearl*." *Journal of the Midwest Modern Language Association* 38.2 (2005): 1–15.

Masciandaro, Nicola. *The Voice of the Hammer: The Meaning of Work in Middle English Literature*. Notre Dame, IN: University of Notre Dame Press, 2007.

Matthew of Vendôme. *The Art of Versification*. Translated by Aubrey E. Galyon. Ames: Iowa State University Press, 1980.

McClain, Lisa. "'They have taken away my Lord': Mary Magdalene, Christ's Missing Body, and the Mass in Reformation England." *Sixteenth Century Journal* 38 (2007): 77–96.

McNamer, Sarah. *Affective Meditation and the Invention of Medieval Compassion*. Philadelphia: University of Pennsylvania Press, 2010.

———. "Feeling." In *Oxford Twenty-First Century Approaches to Literature: Middle English*. edited by Paul Strohm, 241–57. Oxford: Oxford University Press, 2007.

McPhearson, Heather. *The Modern Portrait in Nineteenth-Century France*. Cambridge: Cambridge University Press, 2001.

Meyer-Lee, Robert. *Poets and Power from Chaucer to Wyatt*. Cambridge: Cambridge University Press, 2007.

Miller, J. Hillis. "'Reading' Part of a Paragraph in *Allegories of Reading*." In *Reading De Man Reading*, edited by Lindsay Waters and Wlad Godzich, 155–70. Minneapolis: University of Minnesota Press, 1989.

Minnis, Alastair. "Medieval Imagination and Memory." In *The Cambridge History of Literary Criticism, Volume 2: The Middle Ages*, edited by Ian Johnson and Alastair Minnis, 239–74. Cambridge: Cambridge University Press, 2005.

Mitchell, J. Allan. "The Middle English *Pearl*: Figuring the Unfigurable." *Chaucer Review* 35.1 (2000): 86–111.

Mitchell, W. J. T. *Iconology: Image, Text, Ideology*. Chicago: University of Chicago Press, 1986.

———. *Picture Theory: Essays on Verbal and Visual Representation*. Chicago: University of Chicago Press, 1994.

———. "The Violence of Public Art: Do the Right Thing." In *Picture Theory: Essays on Verbal and Visual Representation*, 371–96. Chicago: University of Chicago Press, 1994.

Moreschini, Claudio, ed. *Apulei Platonici Madaurensis opera quae supersunt. Vol. III: De philosophia libri*. Leipzig: Teubner, 1991.

Morse, Ruth. "Gavin Douglas: 'Off Eloquence the flowand balmy strand.'" In *Chaucer Traditions: Studies in Honour of Derek Brewer*, edited by Ruth Morse and Barry Windeatt, 107–21. Cambridge: Cambridge University Press, 1990.

Morse, Ruth, Helen Cooper, and Peter Holland, eds. *Medieval Shakespeare: Pasts and Presents*. Cambridge: Cambridge University Press, 2013.

Most, Glenn. *Doubting Thomas*. Cambridge, MA: Harvard University Press, 2005.

Munari, Franco, ed. *Mathei Vindocinensis Opera. Vol. III: Ars Versificatoria*. Storia e letteratura, Raccolta di studi e testi 171. Roma: Edizioni di storia e letteratura, 1988.

Muscatine, Charles. "*The Canterbury Tales*: Style of the Man and Style of the Work." In *Chaucer and Chaucerians: Critical Studies in Middle English Literature*, edited by Derek S. Brewer, 88–113. Tuscaloosa, AL: University of Alabama Press, 1966.

Nancy, Jean-Luc. *Noli me tangere: On the Raising of the Body*. Translated by Sarah Clift, Pascale Anne-Brault, and Michael Naas. New York: Fordham University Press, 2008.

Neckam, Alexander. *Commentum super Martianum*. Edited by Christopher J. McDonough. Millenio medievale 64. Testi 15. Florence: SISMEL, 2006.

Needham, Paul. *Twelve Centuries of Bookbindings 400–1600*. New York and London: Pierpoint Morgan Library and Oxford University Press, 1979.

Nichols, Stephen G. "Ekphrasis, Iconoclasm, and Desire." In *Rethinking the Romance of the Rose: Text, Image, Reception*, edited by Kevin Brownlee and Sylvia Huot, 133–66. Philadelphia: University of Pennsylvania Press, 1992.

———. "Seeing Food: An Anthropology of Ekphrasis, and Still Life in Classical and Medieval Examples." *Modern Language Notes* 106 (1991): 818–51.

Norton-Smith, John. "Chaucer's Etas Prima." *Medium Aevum* 32 (1963): 117–24.

——. "Ekphrasis as a Stylistic Element in Douglas's *Palis of Honoure.*" *Medium Aevum* 48 (1979): 240–53.

Notker der Deutsche. *Martianus Capella De nuptiis Philologiae et Mercurii.* Edited by James C. King and Petrus Wilhelmus Tax. Die Werke Notkers des Deutschen 4. Altdeutsche Textbibliothek 87. Tübingen: Niemeyer, 1979.

Olk, Claudia. "The Musicality of *The Merchant of Venice.*" In *Medieval Shakespeare,* edited by Christina Wald, 386–97. London: Routledge, 2013.

Olson, Glending. *Literature as Recreation in the Later Middle Ages.* Ithaca, NY: Cornell University Press, 1982.

——. "The Profits of Pleasure." In *The Cambridge History of Literary Criticism, Vol. II: The Middle Ages,* edited by Alastair Minnis and Ian Johnson. 2005. Reprint, Cambridge: Cambridge University Press, 2009.

O'Sullivan, Sinéad, ed. *Glossae aevi Carolini in libros I–II Martiani Capellae De nvptiis Philologiae et Mercvrii.* Corpvs Christianorum, Continuatio mediaevalis 237. Turnhout: Brepols, 2010.

Otter, Monica. "Baudri of Bourgueil, 'To Countess Adela,'" *Journal of Medieval Latin* 11 (2001): 61–142.

Ovid. *Metamorphoses.* Translated and edited by Charles Martin. New York: Norton, 2010.

——. *Metamorphoses.* http://www.thelatinlibrary.com/ovid/ovid.met1.shtml.

Owen, Corey. "The Prudence of *Pearl.*" *Chaucer Review* 45.4 (2011): 411–34.

Owst, G. R. *Literature and Pulpit in Medieval England: A Neglected Chapter in the History of English Letters and the English People.* 1961. Reprint, Whitefish, MT: Kessinger, 2003.

Palmer, James M. "Your Malady Is 'No Sodeyn Hap': Ophthalmology, Benvenutus Grassus, and January's Blindness." *Chaucer Review* 41 (2006): 197–205.

Panofsky, Erwin. *Early Netherlandish Painting: Its Origins and Character.* 2 Vols. 1953. Reprint, New York: Harper & Row, 1971.

——, ed. and trans. *Abbot Suger on the Abbey Church of St.-Denis and its Art Treasures.* 2nd ed. Princeton, NJ: Princeton University Press, 1979.

Pastoureau, Michel. "L'effervescence emblématique et les origines héraldiques du portrait au XIVe siècle." *Bulletin de la Société Nationale des Antiquaires de France* (1985): 108–15.

Patterson, Lee. *Chaucer and the Subject of History.* Madison: University of Wisconsin Press, 1991.

Pearsall, Derek, and Elizabeth Salter. *Landscapes and Seasons of the Medieval World.* Toronto: University of Toronto Press, 1973.

Perkinson, Stephen. *The Likeness of the King: A Prehistory of Portraiture in Late Medieval France.* Chicago: University of Chicago Press, 2009.

——. "Rethinking the Origins of Portraiture." *Gesta* 42.2 (2008): 135–93.

Perkins, William. *State of a Christian Man*. In *The Works of the Famous and Worthie Minister of Christ in the University of Cambridge*, I, Ll3ʳ. 3 Vols. Cambridge: Cambridge University Press, 1609.

Perler, Dominik. *Transformationen der Gefühle: Philosophische Emotionstheorien 1270–1670*. Frankfurt: Fischer, 2011.

Philipowski, Silke. "Mittelbare und unmittelbare Gegenwärtigkeit oder: Erinnern und Vergessen in der Petitcriu-Episode des *Tristan* Gottfrieds von Strassburg." *Beiträge zur Geschichte der deutschen Sprache und Literatur* 120 (1998): 29–35.

Pollitt, J. J. *Art in the Hellenistic Age*. Cambridge: Cambridge University Press, 1986.

Porter, Martin. *Windows of the Soul: The Art of Physiognomy in European Culture*. Oxford: Oxford University Press, 2005.

Preston, Claire. "Spenser and the Visual Arts." In *The Oxford Handbook of Edmund Spenser*, edited by Richard A. McCabe, 684–717. Oxford: Oxford University Press, 2010.

Prior, Sandra Pierson. *The Fayre Formez of the* Pearl *Poet*. East Lansing: Michigan State University Press, 1996.

Pugh, Tison. "Squire Jankyn's Legs and Feet: Physiognomy, Social Class, and Fantasy in the Wife of Bath's Prologue and Tale." *Medievalia et Humanistica: Studies in Medieval and Renaissance Culture* 32 (2007): 83–101.

Purdon, L. O. "Chaucer's Use of Woad in *The Former Age*." *PLL* 25 (1989): 216–19.

Putnam, Michael C. J. *Virgil's Epic Designs: Ekphrasis in the* Aeneid. New Haven: Yale University Press, 1998.

Puttenham, George. *The Arte of English Poesie* (London: Richard Field, 1589). Printed in facsimile. London: Scolar Press, 1968.

Putter, Ad. *An Introduction to the* Gawain *Poet*. London: Longman, 1996.

Radulphus De Longo Campo. *In Anticlaudianum Alani commentum*. Edited by Jan Sulowski. Wroclaw: Zaklad Narodowy im. Ossolinskich, 1972.

Ramelli, Ilaria, ed. and trans. *Marziano Capella: Le nozze di Filologia e Mercurio. Testo latino a fronte*. Milano: Bompiani, 2001.

Ratkowitsch, Christine. *Descriptio Picturae: Die literarische Funktion der Beschreibung von Kunstwerken in der lateinischen Grossdichtung des 12. Jahrhunderts*. Vienna: Österreichische Akademie der Wissenschaften, 1991.

Raynaud de Lage, Guy, ed. *Roman de Thèbes*, 2 Vols. Paris: Champion, 1966–1971.

Read, Sophie. *Eucharist and the Poetic Imagination in Early Modern England*. Cambridge: Cambridge University Press, 2013.

Recht, Roland. *Believing and Seeing: The Art of Gothic Cathedrals*. Translated by Mary Whittall. Chicago: University of Chicago Press, 2008.

Reddy, William. *The Navigation of Feeling: A Framework for the History of Emotions*. Cambridge: Cambridge University Press, 2001.

Reed, Teresa. "Mary, the Maiden, and Metonymy in *Pearl.*" *South Atlantic Review* 65.2 (2000): 134–62.

Reich, Björn. *Name und maere: Eigennamen als narrative Zentren mittelalterlicher Epik. Mit exemplarischen Einzeluntersuchungen zum* Meleranz *des Pleier,* Göttweiger Trojanerkrieg *und* Wolfdietrich D., Studien zur historischen Poetik 8. Heidelberg: Winter, 2011.

Richmond, Velma Bourgeois. *Laments for the Dead in Medieval Narrative.* Duquesne Studies Philological Series 8. Pittsburgh: Duquesne University Press, 1966.

Riddy, Felicity. "The Materials of Culture: Jewels in *Pearl.*" In *A Companion to the* Gawain-*Poet,* edited by Derek Brewer and Jonathan Gibson. Cambridge: D. S. Brewer, 1997.

Roberts, Valerie S. "Ironic Reversal of Expectations in Chaucerian and Shakespearean Gardens." In *Chaucerian Shakespeare: Adaptation and Transformation; A Collection of Essays,* edited by E. Talbot Donaldson and Judith J. Kollmann, 97–117. Detroit: Fifteenth-Century Symposium, Marygrove College, 1983.

Robertson, D. W. "The Doctrine of Charity in Mediaeval Literary Gardens." *Speculum* 26 (1951): 24–49.

———. *A Preface to Chaucer: Studies in Medieval Perspective.* Princeton, NJ: Princeton University Press, 1962.

Roper, Gregory. "*Pearl,* Penitence, and the Recovery of the Self." *Chaucer Review* 28.2 (1993): 164–86.

Rosenwein, Barbara H. "Worrying about Emotions in History." *American Historical Review* 107.3 (2002): 821–45.

Rothwell, William. "Sugar and Spice and All Things Nice: From Oriental Bazar to English Cloister in Anglo-French." *Modern Language Review* 94 (1999): 647–59.

———. "The Trilingual England of Geoffrey Chaucer." *Studies in the Age of Chaucer* 16 (1994): 45–67.

Rothwell, William, ed. *Femina* (Trinity College Cambridge, MS B.14.40). *Anglo-Norman On-Line Hub.* http://www.anglo-norman.net/texts/femina.pdf.

———. *Le Tretiz.* London: Anglo-Norman Text Society, 1990.

Russell, George, and George Kane, eds. *Piers Plowman: The C Version.* London: Athlone, 1997.

Sacks, Peter M. *The English Elegy: Studies in the Genre from Spenser to Yeats.* Baltimore: Johns Hopkins University Press, 1985.

Salda, Michael Norman. "Pages from History: The Medieval Palace of Westminster as a Source for the Dreamer's Chamber in *Book of the Duchess.*" *Chaucer Review* 27 (1992): 111–25.

Sauerländer, Willibald. "The Fate of the Face in Medieval Art." In *Set in Stone: The Face in Medieval Sculpture,* edited by Charles T. Little, 3–17. New York: Metropolitan Museum of Art, 2006.

Saunders, Corinne J. *Magic and the Supernatural in Medieval English Romance*. Cambridge: D. S. Brewer, 2010.

Schaberg, Jane. *The Resurrection of Mary Magdalen: Legends, Apocrypha and the Christian Testament*. New York: Continuum, 2002.

Schiesari, Juliana. *The Gendering of Melancholia: Feminism, Psychoanalysis, and the Symbolics of Loss in Renaissance Literature*. Ithaca, NY: Cornell University Press, 1992.

Schildgen, Brenda Deen. "Reception, Elegy, and Eco-Awareness: Trees in Statius, Boccaccio, and Chaucer." *Comparative Literature* 65 (2013): 85–100.

Schmidt, A. V. C. "Chaucer and the Golden Age." *Essays in Criticism* 26 (1976): 99–124.

Schmitt, Jean-Claude. *Ghosts in the Middle Ages: The Living and the Dead in Medieval Society*. Translated by Teresa Lavender Fagan. 1994. Reprint, Chicago: University of Chicago Press, 1998.

Scott, Grant F. "The Rhetoric of Dilation: Ekphrasis and Ideology." *Word and Image* 7 (1991): 301–10.

Shakespeare, William. *Antony and Cleopatra*. Edited by David Bevington. The New Cambridge Shakespeare. Updated Edition. Cambridge: Cambridge University Press, 2005.

———. *Macbeth*. Edited by Albert R. Braunmueller. The New Cambridge Shakespeare. Cambridge: Cambridge University Press, 1997.

———. *The Tempest*. Edited by David Lindley. The New Cambridge Shakespeare. Updated Edition. Cambridge: Cambridge University Press, 2013.

———. *The Winter's Tale*. Edited by Susan Snyder and Deborah T. Curren-Aquino. The New Cambridge Shakespeare. Cambridge: Cambridge University Press, 2007.

Shanzer, Danuta. *A Philosophical and Literary Commentary on Martianus Capella's De Nuptiis Philologiae et Mercurii Book I*. University of California Publications. Classical Studies 32. Berkeley: University of California Press, 1986.

Shields, David. *Reality Hunger: A Manifesto*. New York: Knopf, 2010.

Simmons-O'Neill, Elizabeth. "Love in Hell: The Role of Pluto and Proserpine in Chaucer's 'Merchant's Tale.'" *Modern Language Quarterly* 51 (1990): 389–407.

Simpson, James. *Reform and Cultural Revolution. The Oxford English Literary History, Vol. 2, 1350–1547*. Oxford: Oxford University Press, 2002.

Skemer, Don C. *Binding Words: Textual Amulets in the Middle Ages*. University Park: Pennsylvania State University Press, 2006.

Smith, D. Vance. *Arts of Possession: The Middle English Household Imaginary*. Minneapolis: University of Minnesota Press, 2003.

Spearing, A. C. *Medieval Dream-Poetry*. Cambridge: Cambridge University Press, 1976.

———. *The Medieval Poet as Voyeur: Looking and Listening in Medieval Love-Narratives*. Cambridge: Cambridge University Press, 1993.

Spengel, Leonardus. *Rhetores Graeci.* 3 Vols. 1854. Reprint, Frankfurt a. M.: Minerva, 1966.

Spenser, Edmund. *The Faerie Queene.* Edited by A. C. Hamilton, textual eds. Hiroshi Yamashita and Toshiuki Suzuki. London: Longman/Pearson, 2001.

Spitzer, Leo. "The 'Ode on a Grecian Urn,' or Content vs. Metagrammar." *Comparative Literature* 7 (1955): 203–25.

Stahl, William Harris, Richard Johnson, and Evan L. Burge, eds. and trans. *Martianus Capella and the Seven Liberal Arts, Vol. 1: The Quadrivium of Martianus Capella, Latin Traditions in the Mathematical Sciences, 50 BC–AD 1250.* New York: Columbia University Press, 1971.

———. *Martianus Capella and the Seven Liberal Arts, Vol. 2: The Marriage of Philology and Mercury.* New York: Columbia University Press, 1977.

Staley, Lynn, ed. *The Book of Margery Kempe.* New York: Norton, 2001.

Stanbury, Sarah. "The Body and the City in *Pearl.*" *Representations* 48 (1994): 30–47.

———. *Seeing the* Gawain-*Poet: Description and the Act of Perception.* Philadelphia: University of Pennsylvania Press, 1991.

———. "Visualizing." In *A Companion to Chaucer,* edited by Peter Brown, 459–79. Oxford: Blackwell, 2000.

———. *The Visual Object of Desire in Late Medieval England.* Philadelphia: University of Pennsylvania Press, 2008.

———. "The Vivacity of Images: St. Katherine, Knighton's Lollards, and the Breaking of Idols." In *Images, Idolatry, and Iconoclasm in Late Medieval England: Textuality and the Visual Image,* edited by Jeremy Dimmick, James Simpson, and Nicolette Zeeman, 131–50. Oxford: Oxford University Press, 2002.

Stanbury, Sarah, ed. *Pearl.* Kalamazoo, MI: TEAMS Medieval Institute Publications, 2001.

Stein, Robert M. "Multilingualism." In *Middle English,* edited by Paul Strohm, 23–37. Oxford Twenty-First Century Approaches to Literature. Oxford: Oxford University Press, 2007.

Stock, Lorraine Kochanske. "'Peynted . . . text and [visual] gloss': Primitivism, Ekphrasis, and Pictorial Intertextuality in the Dreamers' Bedrooms of *Roman de la Rose* and *Book of the Duchess.*" In *Essays on Chaucer and Chaucerians in Memory of Emerson Brown, Jr.,* edited by T. L. Burton and John F. Plummer, 97–114. Provo, UT: Chaucer Studio Press, 2005.

Stone, Charles Russell. "'And sodeynly he wax therwith astoned': Virgilian Emotion and Images of Troy in Chaucer's *Troilus.*" *Review of English Studies* 64 (2013): 574–93.

Sylvia, Karen A. "Living with Dying: Grief and Consolation in the Middle English *Pearl.*" Honors Projects Overview, Paper 45 (2007). *Digital Commons @RIC.* http://digitalcommons.ric.edu/honors_projects/45.

Teeuwen, Mariken, and Sinéad O'Sullivan, eds. *Carolingian Scholarship and Martianus Capella: The Oldest Commentary Tradition.* Digital Edition. 1st ed. (2008). *Huygens Instituut—eLaborate.* http://martianus.huygens.knaw.nl/path.

Thomas Aquinas. *Summa Theologiae, I. Sancti Thomae de Aquino Opera omnia iussu Leonis XIII P. M. edita*, Vol. 5. Rome: Comm. Leonina, 1889.

———. *Summa Theologiae*. London and New York: Blackfriars, 1963.

Thompson, N. S. "The Merchant's Tale." In *Sources and Analogues of the* Canterbury Tales, *Vol. II*, edited by Robert M. Correale and Mary Hamel, 479–534. Chaucer Studies XXXV. Cambridge: D. S. Brewer, 2005.

Tilliette, Jean-Yves. "La chambre de la comtesse Adèle: savoir scientifique et technique littéraire dans le C. CXCVI de Baudri de Bourgueil." *Romania: revue consacrée à l'étude des langues et des littératures romanes* 102.1 (1981): 145–71.

Tolkien, J. R. R. "*Beowulf:* The Monsters and the Critics." In *The Monsters and the Critics and Other Essays,* edited by Christopher Tolkien, 5–48. London: Harper Collins, 2006.

Tomkins, Silvan. "Script Theory and Nuclear Scripts." In *Shame and Its Sisters: A Silvan Tomkin Reader,* edited by Eve Kosofsky Sedgwick and Adam Frank, 179–96. Durham, NC: Duke University Press, 1995.

Townsend, David. *An Epitome of Biblical History: Glosses on Walter of Châtillon's Alexandreis 4.176–274.* Toronto: Pontifical Institute of Mediaeval Studies, 2008.

Treharne, Elaine and Greg Walker, eds. *The Oxford Handbook of Medieval Literature in English.* Oxford: Oxford University Press, 2010.

Turville-Petre, Thorlac. "Places of the Imagination: The *Gawain*-Poet." In *The Oxford Handbook of Medieval Literature in English,* edited by Elaine Treharne and Greg Walker, 594–610. Oxford: Oxford University Press, 2010.

Tuve, Rosemond. *Allegorical Imagery: Some Mediaeval Books and Their Renaissance Posterity.* Princeton, NJ: Princeton University Press, 1966.

———. "Spenser and Some Pictorial Conventions with Particular Reference to Illuminated Manuscripts." *Studies in Philology* 37 (1940): 149–76.

Van Miegroet, Hans J. "Gerard David's *Justice of Cambyses: Exemplum Iustitiae* or Political Allegory?" *Simiolus: Netherlands Quarterly for the History of Art* 18 (1988): 116–33.

Vaught, Jennifer C. Introduction to *Grief and Gender, 700–1700,* edited by Jennifer C. Vaught and Lynne Dickson Bruckner, 1–16. New York: Palgrave Macmillan, 2003.

Virgil. *Eclogues, Georgics, Aeneid 1–6.* Edited by Henry R. Fairclough, revised by G. P. Goold. Cambridge, MA: Loeb Classical Library, Harvard University Press, 1999.

Von Kutschera, Franz. *Ästhetik.* 2nd ed. 1998. Reprint, Berlin: de Gruyter, 2010.

Waddell, Helen. *The Wandering Scholars.* 7th ed. London: Fontana, 1968.

Wagner, Peter. "Ekphrasis, Iconotexts, and Intermediality—the State(s) of the Art(s)." In *Icons, Texts, Iconotexts: Essays on Ekphrasis and Intermediality,* 1–40. Berlin: de Gruyter, 1996.

Wallace, David. "Afterword." In *Images, Idolatry, and Iconoclasm in Late Medieval England: Textuality and the Visual Image,* edited by Jeremy Dimmick, James Simpson, and Nicolette Zeeman, 207–14. Oxford: Oxford University Press, 2002.

Walter, Henry. *Expositions and Notes on Sundry Portions of the Holy Scripture.* Cambridge: Cambridge University Press, 1849.

Walter, Henry, ed. *Doctrinal Treatises and Introductions to Different Portions of the Holy Scriptures by William Tyndale.* Cambridge: Cambridge University Press, 1848.

Wandel, Lee Palmer. *The Eucharist in the Reformation: Incarnation and Liturgy.* Cambridge: Cambridge University Press, 2006.

Wandhoff, Haiko. "Bilder der Liebe—Bilder des Todes: Konrad Flecks Flore-Roman und die Kunstbeschreibungen in der höfischen Epik des deutschen Mittelalters." In *Die poetische Ekphrasis von Kunstwerken: eine literarische Tradition der Grossdichtung in Antike, Mittelalter und früher Neuzeit,* edited by Christine Ratkowitsch, 55–76. Vienna: Verlag der Österreichischen Akademie der Wissenschaften, 2006.

———. *Ekphrasis. Kunstbeschreibungen und virtuelle Räume in der Literatur des Mittelalters,* Trends in Medieval Philology 3. Berlin: de Gruyter, 2003.

Warburg, Aby. "Einleitung zum Mnemosyne-Atlas (1929)." In *Die Beredsamkeit des Leibes: Zur Körpersprache in der Kunst,* edited by Ilsebill Barta Fliedl and Christoph Geissmar, 171–73. Salzburg: Residenz Verlag, 1992.

Watkins, John. "'Neither of Idle Shewes, nor of False Charmes Aghast': Transformations of Virgilian Ekphrasis in Chaucer and Spenser." *Journal of Medieval and Renaissance Studies* 23 (1993): 345–63.

Watts, Ann Chalmers. "*Pearl,* Inexpressibility, and Poems of Human Loss." *PMLA* 99.1 (1984): 26–40.

Webb, Ruth. "Ekphrasis Ancient and Modern: The Invention of a Genre." *Word and Image* 15.1 (1999): 7–18.

———. *Ekphrasis, Imagination and Persuasion in Ancient Rhetorical Theory and Practice.* Farnham: Ashgate, 2009.

———. "The Model Ekphraseis of Nikolaos the Sophist as Memory Images." In *Theatron: Rhetorische Kultur in Spätantike und Mittelalter—Rhetorical Culture in Late Antiquity and the Middle Ages,* edited by Michael Grünbart, 463–75. Berlin: de Gruyter, 2007.

———. "The *Progymnasmata* as Practice." In *Education in Greek and Roman Antiquity,* edited by Yun Lee Too, 289–316. Leiden: Brill, 2001.

Westra, Haijo Jan, ed. *The Berlin Commentary on Martianus Capella's* De Nuptiis Philologiae et Mercurii. Mittellateinische Studien und Texte XX/XXIII. 2 Vols. Leiden: Brill, 1994–1998.

———. *The Commentary on Martianus Capella's* De nuptiis Philologiae et Mercurii *attributed to Bernhardus Silvestris.* Toronto: Pontifical Institute of Mediaeval Studies, 1986.

Whitehead, Christiania. *Castles of the Mind: A Study of Medieval Architectural Allegory.* Cardiff: University of Wales Press, 2003.

Wickham, Glynne William Gladstone. *Shakespeare's Dramatic Heritage: Collected Studies in Mediaeval, Tudor and Shakespearean Drama.* London: Routledge, 1969.

Willis, James, ed. *Martianus Capella.* Leipzig: Teubner, 1983.

Wilson, Richard. *Secret Shakespeare: Studies in Theatre, Religion and Resistance.* Manchester: Manchester University Press, 2004.

———. "'To excel the Golden Age': Shakespeare's Voyage to Greece." In *Vollkommenheit: Ästhetische Perfektion in Mittelalter und Früher Neuzeit,* edited by Verena Lobsien, Claudia Olk, and Katharina Münchberg, 181–204. Berlin: de Gruyter, 2010.

Wittkower, Rudolf, and Margot Wittkower. *Born under Saturn: The Character and Conduct of Artists; A Documented History from Antiquity to the French Revolution.* New York: Random House, 1963.

Wordsworth, William. "Preface to *Lyrical Ballads* (1802)." In *Lyrical Ballads,* edited by Michael Mason, 55–77. London: Longman, 1992.

Wright, Aaron F. "Petitcreiu: A Text critical Note to the *Tristan* of Gottfried von Strassburg." *Colloquia Germanica* 25.2 (1992): 112–21.

Wright, Laura. *Sources of London English: Medieval Thames Vocabulary.* Oxford: Clarendon Press, 1996.

Wunderlich, Werner. "Ekphrasis und Narratio: Die Grabmalerei des Apelles und ihre 'Weiberlisten' in Walters von Châtillon und Ulrichs von Etzenbach Alexanderepen." In *Erzählungen in Erzählungen: Phänomene der Narration in Mittelalter und Früher Neuzeit,* edited by Harald Haferland and Michael Mecklenburg, 259–71. Munich: Fink, 1996.

Wurtele, Douglas. "Another Look at an Old 'Science': Chaucer's Pilgrims and Physiognomy." In *From Arabye to Engelond: Medieval Studies in Honour of Mahmoud Manzalaoui on His 75th Birthday,* edited by A. E. Christa Canitz and Gernot R. Wieland, 93–111. Ottawa: University of Ottawa Press, 1999.

Yeager, Robert F., and Charlotte C. Morse, eds. *Speaking Images: Essays in Honor of V. A. Kolve.* Asheville, NC: Pegasus Press, 2001.

Zeeman, Nicolette. "The Idol of the Text." In *Images, Idolatry, and Iconoclasm in Late Medieval England: Textuality and the Visual Image,* edited by Jeremy Dimmick, James Simpson, and Nicolette Zeeman, 43–62. Oxford: Oxford University Press, 2002.

———. "Imaginative Theory." In *Oxford Twenty-First Century Approaches to Literature: Middle English,* edited by Paul Strohm, 222–40. Oxford: Oxford University Press, 2007.

Ziegler, Joseph. "Text and Context: On the Rise of Physiognomic Thought in the Later Middle Ages." In *De Sion Exibit Lex Et Verbum Domini De Hierusalem: Essays on Medieval Law, Liturgy, and Literature in Honour of Amnon Linder,* edited by Yitzhak Hen, 159–82. Turnhout: Brepols, 2001.

Žižek, Slavoj. *The Sublime Object of Ideology.* London: Verso, 1989.

About the Contributors

SUZANNE CONKLIN AKBARI is professor of English and medieval studies at the University of Toronto, and was educated at Johns Hopkins and Columbia. Akbari's books are on optics and allegory (*Seeing through the Veil* 2004; paperback reissue, 2012), European views of Islam and the Orient (*Idols in the East* 2009; paperback reissue, 2012), and travel literature (*Marco Polo and the Encounter of East and West* 2008). She is most recently the coeditor of *The Ends of the Body: Identity and Community in Medieval Culture* (2013) and *A Sea of Languages: Rethinking the Arabic Role in Medieval Literary History* (2013). Akbari is currently completing *Small Change: Metaphor and Metamorphosis in Chaucer and Christine de Pizan* and the *Oxford Handbook to Chaucer*. She is volume editor for the *Norton Anthology of World Literature* (Volume B: 100–1500) and coeditor of the *Norton Anthology of Western Literature*.

VALERIE ALLEN is professor of literature at John Jay College of Criminal Justice at the City University of New York. Her interests are in the history of ideas and medieval culture in general, especially aesthetics and literature.

ANKE BERNAU is senior lecturer at the University of Manchester. She has published on a range of topics, including female virginity; medievalism; medieval origin myth; and medieval theories of memory, affect, and poetics. From August 2011–January 2013, she was the holder of a Humboldt Experienced Researcher Fellowship. She is currently working on medieval aesthetic categories, with a particular interest in curiosity.

JOHN M. BOWERS is an internationally known scholar of medieval English literature with books on Chaucer, Langland, and the *Gawain*-poet. Educated at Duke, Virginia, and Oxford, where he was a Rhodes Scholar, he taught at Caltech and

Princeton before settling at the University of Nevada, Las Vegas. His work has been supported by fellowships from the National Endowment for the Humanities and the John Simon Guggenheim Foundation, and his Great Courses series, *The Western Literary Canon in Context* (2008), was released by the Teaching Company. His latest book project is *Tolkien's Clarendon Chaucer,* based on a "lost book" discovered in an Oxford archive.

DARRYL J. GLESS taught at the University of Virginia before joining the University of North Carolina at Chapel Hill, where he was awarded the Roy C. Moose Distinguished Professorship in Renaissance Studies in 2009. He is the author of *Interpretation and Theology in Spenser* (1994; paperback reissue, October 2005), and *"Measure for Measure," the Law, and the Convent* (1979), for which he won the Explicator Award, second place. He won a University Tanner Award for Excellence in Teaching in 1983 and the Board of Governors' Award for Excellence in Teaching in 2013.

ANDREW JAMES JOHNSTON is Chair of Medieval and Early Modern English Literature at Freie Universität Berlin. He studied there and at Yale University, and received his PhD from Freie Universität in 1998. His most recent English-language monograph is *Performing the Middle Ages from Beowulf to Othello* (2008). Amongst other things, he has coedited with Ute Berns a special issue of the *European Journal of English Studies* devoted to medievalism (2011), and, together with Margitta Rouse, a volume on medieval film entitled *The Medieval Motion Picture: The Politics of Adaptation* (2014). Though his research focuses primarily on both Old and Middle English literature he has also written essays on Shakespeare, Thomas Lovell Beddoes, Bertolt Brecht, J.R.R. Tolkien, and film-maker David Fincher.

ETHAN KNAPP is an associate professor at The Ohio State University. He is the author of *The Bureaucratic Muse: Thomas Hoccleve and the Literature of Late Medieval England* (2001), and other essays on medieval literature and literary theory. He also edits the series *Interventions: New Studies in Medieval Culture,* for The Ohio State University Press.

CLAUDIA OLK is professor of English and comparative literature at the Peter Szondi-Institute for Comparative Literature at Freie Universität Berlin, and president of the German Shakespeare Association. She obtained her Habilitation at Humboldt-Universität zu Berlin and earned her doctoral degree at the University of Münster. She is the author of *Virginia Woolf and the Aesthetics of Vision* (2014) and *Reisen und Erzählen. Studien zur Entwicklung von Fiktionalität in narrativen Reisedarstellungen in der englischen Literatur des Spätmittelalters und der frühen Neuzeit* (1999). She has edited *The Charleston Bulletin Supplements* (2013) and, together with Verena Lobsien, coedited *Vollkommenheit—Ästhetische Perfektion in Spätmittelalter und früher Neuzeit* (2010) as well as *Neuplatonismus und Ästhetik* (2007).

MARGITTA ROUSE is Associate Fellow at the Collaborative Research Center Episteme in Motion at Freie Universität Berlin, after having worked as a postdoctoral fellow on medieval ekphrasis at Humboldt-Universität zu Berlin and at Freie Universität. She is the author of *The Self's Grammar: Performing Poetic Identity in Douglas Dunn's Poetry 1969–2011* (Winter 2013) and she has coedited *The Medieval Motion Picture: The Politics of Adaptation* (2014, with Andrew James Johnston). She is currently working on spaces of temporality in late medieval and early modern literature.

LARRY SCANLON is associate professor of English and medieval studies at Rutgers University, New Brunswick, where he has held a number of administrative positions, including Director of Medieval Studies and Acting Chair of the English Department. The author of *Narrative, Authority and Power: the Medieval Exemplum and the Chaucerian Tradition* (1994), as well as numerous articles on medieval literature and culture, literary theory, and American literature, he has also edited *The Cambridge Companion to Medieval Literature, 1100–1500* (2009) and coedited (with James Simpson) *John Lydgate: Poetry, Culture, and Lancastrian England* (2006). He has served as editor of three periodicals, *Studies in the Age of Chaucer, Literature Compass* (late medieval section), and *The Medieval Review*. He is currently completing a long study on homoeroticism and fourteenth-century English poetry, tentatively entitled *At Sodom's Gate: The Sin against Nature and Middle English Poetry*.

HANS JÜRGEN SCHEUER is professor of medieval and early modern German literature at Humboldt-Universität zu Berlin. His research interests cover a wide range of topics, from ancient and medieval to modern literature, art, and culture. They are focused on the history of imagination, rhetorical and topical structures of literature, exemplary forms of religious communication, the intersection of political and theological thought in the Middle Ages, predramatic theater, and the return of premodern thinking in modern works of art. He recently edited a volume on the *longue durée* of premodern models of imagination: *Archäologie der Phantasie* (2012, with Elmar Locher). His publications on modern literature include his dissertation on Goethe's mannerist poetics (*Manier und Urphänomen* 1996), a coedited volume on Kafka (*Kafkas "Betrachtung." Lektüren* 2003), and articles on Goethe, Hölderlin, Kleist, Freud, Kafka, Andres, Bloch, Celan/Szondy, Botho Strauß, and Barbara Köhler.

SARAH STANBURY is Monsignor Murray Professor of Arts and Humanities and member of the English department at the College of the Holy Cross. A recipient of fellowships from the NEH and the Guggenheim Foundation, she has published widely on gender and visual culture in late medieval England. Her books include *Seeing the Gawain Poet: Description and the Act of Perception* (1991) and *The Visual Object of Desire in Late Medieval England* (2007). She has published three collaborative essay collections, and with Virginia Raguin, created the website *Mapping Margery Kempe*.

KATHRYN STARKEY is professor of German studies at Stanford University. Her research interests include medieval German literature, history of the book, and visual culture. She is the author of *A Courtier's Mirror: Cultivating Elite Identity in Thomasin von Zerclaere's "Welscher Gast"* (2013) and *Reading the Medieval Book: Word, Image, and Performance in Wolfram von Eschenbach's "Willehalm"* (2004). Professor Starkey also coedited *Visuality and Materiality in the Story of Tristan* (2012, with Jutta Eming and Ann Marie Rasmussen) and *Visual Culture and the German Middle Ages* (2005, with Horst Wenzel). Together with Edith Wenzel, she is currently working on a translation of songs by the medieval poet Neidhart entitled *Neidhart: Selected Songs from the Riedegger Manuscript*.

Index

Adelae Comitissae (Baudri of Bourgeuil), 10, 17–35; and aesthetic sensibility, 19–28, 34–35; and Bayeux Tapestry, 10, 17, 18, 18n3, 31–32; context and summary, 17–18; dedication, 18; and ekphrasis as amuletic, 34–35; hyperbole in, 18, 26–27; and materiality, 28–35; meter, 22–23, 29, 34–35; tapestry in, 19–35

Aeneid (Virgil), 64, 71–2, 168–69n8, 169n10, 186n6, 205, 257, 261; description of Aeneas's shield, 26; description of Juno's temple, 55, 69; Douglas's translation (*Eneados*), 173, 181

Aers, David, 105, 105n16, 118

aesthetic, 111–12, 132n30; and *Adelae Comitissae* (Baudri of Bourgeuil), 19–28, 34–35; aesthetic; deflection, 13, 181–83; aesthetic narcissism, 6–7; aesthetic self-consciousness, 2–3; aesthetic self-reflexivity, 6; aesthetic turn, 23–24, 35; and ekphrasis, 1–3, 6–10, 13, 17, 19–29; incarnational aesthetic, 9; preaesthetic, 22–23, 28, 35; premodern,

224–26; and realism, 250, 254–56; and theatre, 98

Akbari, Suzanne Conklin, 13, 46, 174

Alan of Lille, 171, 194–96, 205

Alhazen, 8, 235

allegory: and aesthetic, 23; and *Anticlaudianus* (Alan of Lille), 194–96; Barthes on, 256–57; Benjamin on, 13, 212; and cognition, 174–75, 180; and *Digby Play of Mary Magdalene*, 87–88; dream allegory, 166–83; and ekphrasis, 8–9, 168, 173–83, 185, 242, 263, 265–67; and enigma, 173–76, 181; and *Faerie Queene* (Spenser), 157, 160; as form of seeing, 88; of honor, 168, 170, 173–76, 178–83; and iconography, 58; and *Livre de la Mutacion de Fortune* (Christine de Pizan), 186–88, 193; and marriage, 227, 229n8, 231, 233, 235, 236n19–20, 237; and *Palice of Honour* (Douglas), 166–83; and *Pearl*, 104–5, 113, 263, 265–67; and physiognomy, 209–10, 213, 220, 223, 226n2; and symbol, 23; and *Tristan* (Gottfried von Strassburg), 139n33, 143n40

INTERVENTIONS: NEW STUDIES IN MEDIEVAL CULTURE
Ethan Knapp, Series Editor

Interventions: New Studies in Medieval Culture publishes theoretically informed work in medieval literary and cultural studies. We are interested both in studies of medieval culture and in work on the continuing importance of medieval tropes and topics in contemporary intellectual life.